Latin American Religions

Latin American Religions

Histories and Documents in Context

Edited with introductions by
Anna L. Peterson and
Manuel A. Vásquez

NEW YORK UNIVERSITY PRESS
New York and London

NEW YORK UNIVERSITY PRESS
New York and London
www.nyupress.org

Library of Congress Cataloging-in-Publication Data
Latin American religions : histories and documents in context / edited
by Anna L. Peterson and Manuel A. Vásquez.
p. cm.
Includes bibliographical references (p.) and index.
ISBN-13: 978-0-8147-6732-0 (pb   )
ISBN-10: 0-8147-6732-X (pb   )
ISBN-13: 978-0-8147-6731-3 (cl : alk. paper)
ISBN-10: 0-8147-6731-1 (cl : alk. paper)
1. Latin America—Religion. I. Peterson, Anna Lisa, 1963– II. Vásquez,
Manuel A.
BL2540.L38   2008
200.98—dc22   2008007098

New York University Press books

Manufactured in the United States of America
c 10 9 8 7 6 5 4 3 2 1
p 10 9 8 7 6 5 4 3 2 1

For Edward Cleary, O.P., and Ralph Della Cava:
mentors, colleagues, and friends

and in memory of Richard Shaull

Contents

Acknowledgments

We are grateful to many people who helped make this book a reality. A number of important scholars of Latin American religion have inspired us and provided insights and information that have proved vital for the success of this project. We thank in particular the senior scholars who paved the way for the study of Latin American religions—who collected documents and wrote analyses on which we still rely, many of which we collect in this book. Ralph Della Cava and Edward Cleary, in particular, have provided advice and inspiration to us both for many years. We are grateful for the gracious assistance of Frederick Pike, Christian Lalive d'Epinay, Nancy Johns, Jim Wafer, David Stoll, and Virginia Garrard-Burnett, and for the pioneering work of the late Lewis Hanke and the late Bradford Burns. Jody Schwarz generously gave us access to Dr. Hanke's work. We must also thank John Burdick, Charles Perrone, Kay Read, Harold Stahmer, Philip Williams, and Robin Wright, among many colleagues who have helped our teaching and writing about religion in Latin America. Further, we would like to acknowledge colleagues in Latin America and elsewhere who suggested possible selections, gave us access to their work, and, in some cases, assisted with its translation. These colleagues include José Cláudio Souza Alves, Alejandro Frigerio, Beatriz Labate, Edward MacRae, Paulo Pinto, Lúcia Ribeiro, and Cristina Rocha.

At the University of Florida, Anne Newman coordinated the process of receiving copyright permissions, along with many other tasks. Without her skilled assistance we could never have finished this book. Richard Phillips, head of the Latin American collection, played a vital role in helping us identify and secure some rare materials. We also thank our department chair, David Hackett, for his intellectual and administrative support, and Tennison Zuniga and Sam Snyder for assisting with scanning. Derek Lewis and Natalie Broadnax also helped gather materials. We are also very grateful to our students at U.F., especially Gayle Lasater and Hilit Surowitz, who have helped us think about the issues and readings included here.

Our editor, Jennifer Hammer, has enthusiastically and effectively supported this book from its inception. It has been a great pleasure to work with her. Very special thanks are due to Hector Puig, of Hector Gallery in Gainesville, Florida, who graciously provided the images of santos on the cover.

Finally, we are most grateful to the copyright holders, including presses and authors, who gave permission for us to reproduce the documents included here. Unfortunately, in some cases we were unable to include important documents due to high copyright permission fees. We have made every possible effort to contact the copyright holder for each piece reproduced here. If we have made any errors or omissions, please write to us in care of the press so that corrections can be made in any future editions of the book.

All translations of texts originally in Spanish or Portuguese are by the authors.

1

Introducing Religion
in Latin America

This book provides an introduction to the historical development and contemporary expressions of religious life in South and Central America, Mexico, and the Spanish-speaking Caribbean. A central feature of this text is its inclusion of both primary and secondary materials. Primary materials are generally those produced by insiders or participants in the events or traditions at stake. Examples include letters, sermons, journal entries, ritual manuals, and ancient sacred texts. Secondary documents, on the other hand, include articles, books, and chapters written by scholars, journalists, and other "outsiders." Primary documents are especially valuable in this sort of book because they provide direct access to the voices of the people and events under discussion, and enable readers to act as academic investigators, experiencing and interpreting the same texts on which historians draw. Secondary documents provide readers with well-informed readings by scholarly experts. The secondary texts reprinted here adopt diverse theoretical and methodological approaches in order to provide readers with a broad perspective on Latin American religious history and also to underline the fact that there is no single correct reading of any given event or issue.

In this introductory chapter, we outline a number of core themes that emerge throughout Latin American religious history, as well as some of the important theoretical issues and methodological perspectives that have been brought to bear on the field. We also provide a short summary of key periods and events in Latin American history, as context for the more detailed discussions of religious life during these periods in the chapters to follow.

Major Periods of Latin American History

With the exceptions of the chapters on indigenous and African-based religions, we have ordered this book chronologically, according to a standard periodization of Latin American history.

During the precolonial period, the Americas were populated by numerous indigenous groups, with a great diversity of cultures, religions, and forms of livelihood. These cultures experienced significant changes in the centuries prior to the European conquest, including wars, migrations, the collapse of some civilizations, and the emergence of others.

The colonial period began in 1492, with Christopher Columbus's first voyage, and ended in the early 1800s, when most Latin American nations achieved independence from Spain and adopted republican forms of government. (Brazil followed a different path, as noted below.) During the colonial period, European governments and churches dominated religious life in the Americas. Roman Catholicism was the official ("established") religion, and divergence from orthodox beliefs or practices was often punished under the auspices of church institutions such as the Inquisition, which had been established to punish heretics in Europe. The colonial period was also marked by great religious hybridization, the mixing of European, indigenous, and often African traditions into distinctly New World forms.

The Independence period spans the nineteenth century, during which most Latin American nations experienced major religious, cultural, economic, and political changes as a result of their separation from colonial authority. This era in Latin American history is sometimes called the national period because it was dominated by the formation and consolidation of modern nation-states. With independence from Spain, most Latin American nations ended the Roman Catholic Church's privileged status as the official religion. This disestablishment led not only to greater diversity within Catholicism, since enforcement of orthodoxy was less strict, but also to greater religious diversity in general, as non-Catholic religions were able to emerge and expand. This transformation continues into the present day.

The growth of Protestantism made possible by disestablishment is one of the two themes we highlight in the twentieth century. The other is the transformation of Roman Catholicism following the Second Vatican Council (1962-1965), a watershed event at which church leaders set a new course, opening the church's windows and doors to engage modern culture. (The first Vatican Council was held in 1870 and was dominated by conservative bishops who sought to protect the church from the impact of modernity.) Vatican II was especially important for Latin America because of its emphases on the developing world, on social justice and human rights, and on the importance of rooting both pastoral work and theology firmly in local conditions and concerns. Both Catholicism and Protestantism continue to experience significant changes in the twenty-first century, joined increasingly by other movements that complicate and enrich the region's religious landscape.

Key Analytic Themes

The study of religion in Latin America encompasses a number of over-arching themes, continuities, and contrasts. Not every scholar considers the same issues important, of course; most highlight particular topics according to their theoretical and methodological approaches. The themes outlined below are the ones that we find most helpful in making sense of the various religious traditions, events, and issues described in this book. Some themes are most important in particular times or places, while others recur across historical periods and regions. By focusing on these topics, we do not pretend to capture all of Latin American religious life. Rather, we hope to point readers to some important and enduring axes along which fruitful inquiries have run and may continue to run.

Continuity and Rupture

One of the broadest themes expressed in the readings collected here is the interplay between continuity and rupture. The development of the Latin American religious field has been characterized by the interplay between the establishment and preservation of age-old traditions, on one hand, and innovation and change, on the other. One set of continuities and discontinuities occurs between older and newer forms of religious belief and practice. Keeping both continuity and rupture in mind as we study Latin American religious history helps us avoid the tendencies to underestimate or overemphasize the degree of change over time. This is important, for example, with regard to indigenous religions. Some scholars declare that native traditions ended with the conquest and that what followed represented a complete rupture with precolonial history. On the other hand, others have perceived absolute continuity in religious life, with little or no change over time despite major political, economic, and social transformations. We believe that careful scholarship reveals both continuities and ruptures in indigenous religions.

It is also fruitful to look at the continuities and breaks between religious sphere and secular society. This is a theme that anthropologist John Burdick highlights in his 1993 book *Looking for God in Brazil*. Burdick characterizes Catholicism as a "cult of continuity," which reproduces the hierarchical structures of society since its lay leadership tends to come from the most established social groups. In contrast, he describes two other traditions as cults of "affliction," or rupture, which offer a radical break with the often destructive and tension-ridden world beyond the religious community.[1] Burdick's "cults of affliction" are Protestant Pentecostalism, which emphasizes the action of the Holy Spirit, healing, and ecstatic forms of worship, and Umbanda, an Afro-Brazilian tradition. Rupture is tied, for Burdick, to physical and psychic healing, a necessary task in which cults of continuity fall short.

In his more recent work, Burdick nuances his reading of progressive Catholicism and Pentecostalism. Here he follows a number of scholars who have carefully documented the capacity of progressive Catholicism to break with the past, as we will see revealed in a number of the readings included in chapter 7. There is also clear evidence of overlaps between Umbanda and Pentecostalism, on the one hand, and the larger society, on the other. Diana Brown's work on Umbanda, for example, reveals a hierarchical authority structure that parallels the larger Brazilian society. Some studies of Pentecostalism, similarly, highlight hierarchies and ideologies that reinforce, rather than break with, outside social structures. Australian sociologist Rowan Ireland notes that all of Brazil's major religions encompass divergent streams, which in turn relate differently to secular politics and culture.[2] Similarly, we believe that the themes of continuity and rupture are helpful but should not be applied so strictly that we fail to see either the continuities present in new forms or the ruptures that can occur in even the most apparently stable traditions.

Popular and Official Religions

One of the most important themes in this book concerns the identities of and interactions among popular groups and official institutions. For a long time, religion was synonymous, at least for most scholars, with religious texts and institutions. In many ways it is much easier to study religion through its official institutions and texts—they leave records, occupy public stages, and enter into well-documented interactions with other public actors. In Latin America, the Spanish colonists kept meticulous and detailed records of many aspects of political, economic, and religious life. On the one hand, this has facilitated scholarly understanding but, on the other hand, it has left an unbalanced portrait of everyday life, since many ordinary events, experienced by ordinary people, did not attract Spanish attention.

Tensions between popular and official religiosity existed even in precolonial times. Both the Aztec and Incan empires, for example, had religious hierarchies dominated by elites, whose offices and practices were sometimes removed from the everyday lives of ordinary people. Conflicts between official and popular religiosity intensified sharply after the conquest established Roman Catholicism as the official religion and its hierarchy as the keepers of religious orthodoxy. Even though Catholicism was established as the state religion in almost every nation, religious education and clerical attention failed to reach most people. During this period "folk" or "popular" Catholicism was most people's religion, and everyday religious practices in cities, villages, and countryside were enthusiastic but highly irregular from the perspective of clerical elites. Religious activity centered on pilgrimages, local shrines, and celebrations of saints and various manifestations of the Virgin Mary, and most people had little interaction with church officials or institutions. Popular adaptations of Catholic practices and maintenance of many indigenous traditions throughout the colonial period meant that everyday religious life often departed from the official version, as some of the documents in chapter 3 reveal.

As with continuity and rupture, we should be careful not to see popular and official religions as two totally distinct realms of activity, always set against each other. As the case of Padre Cicero will show in chapter 5, institutional and popular religious symbols, ideas, and practices often cross-fertilize in a dynamic and power-laden interplay. Moreover, religious institutions and popular movements are never monolithic. Rather, they often contain different sectors, each with their particular interests and modus operandi. Thus, the "miracle at Joaseiro" in which Padre Cicero was involved could be celebrated by the local Catholic clergy and simultaneously rejected by the Vatican. Cicero, in turn, could enjoin his followers to obey and respect the Catholic hierarchy while at the same time advancing a rural popular religiosity at odds with the modernizing interests of Rome.

Despite this caveat, we cannot ignore the fact that religious elites in Latin America have consistently sought to establish their worldviews and practices as the taken-for-granted way of doing things and that these attempts have had varying degrees of success at the grass-roots level. In efforts to assess the relative successes, unintended consequences, and paradoxes of this process, the tension between official and popular religion proves very helpful. The concept and experiences of popular religion have sparked numerous debates among scholars of Latin American religion. What does it mean to be "popular"? How does popular religion relate to "official" religion? Discussions of popular religion are also related, especially in North America, to discussions of "lived" religion, meaning religious practices in everyday life, a theoretical approach discussed later in this chapter. In Latin America, studies of popular religion are often politically charged, since *"popular"* in Spanish signifies urban workers, peasants, and, more generally, poor people, the "popular classes."[3]

Popular and Lived Religion

Going beyond the traditional scholarly focus on institutional dynamics, the "popular religion" approach, which emerged at the end of the 1980s, seeks to shift the focus to the practices, beliefs, and organizations of ordinary people.[4] In particular, it highlights the ways religion is practiced and performed as individuals and local communities struggle to navigate the challenges of everyday life. Attention to popular religion demands the study not only of how religion is produced in churches, temples, or synagogues but also of how it is experienced in extra-ecclesial spaces, such as the streets, work places, homes, and neighborhoods, and in the intimate relationships among generations and among social classes, races, and genders. Therefore, the popular religion approach tends to rely heavily on qualitative research methods, particularly on ethnography.

The rise of the popular religion approach in Latin America coincided with the emergence of the "lived religion" school pioneered in the United States by religious historians, notably Robert Orsi. Orsi's influential 1985 book *The Madonna of 115th Street*, which studied the mundane religious lives of Italian immigrants, exemplifies these concerns. Subsequent work by Orsi and others has shown the power of the lived religions approach, which provides an invaluable complement to scholarship on formal institutions, such as church hierarchies, and doctrines, including holy scriptures and other authoritative texts (e.g., papal bulls). In fact, some Latin American scholars have entered into dialogues with the lived religion school as a way to study the transnational religious practices of Latin American immigrants in the United States.[5]

A focus on popular religion can offer textured portraits of vast realms of activities that often take place at the margins of the official church. This marginality is manifest partly out of necessity—since historically many Latin Americans have lived in areas without regular pastoral attention—and partly out of choice, insofar as lay people have sought control and autonomy in their religious lives. Studies of popular religion in Latin America have often focused on practices such as devotions to saints, pilgrimages, home and local shrines, domestic values, and the dynamics of transculturation among Catholicism, African-based religions, and Spiritism, a Brazilian religious tradition that seeks contact and consultation with the spirit world. However, the approach has been increasingly used to understand the vitality of Pentecostalism among poor people, as well as the emergence of new religious movements mediated by popular culture and mass communications.

The danger of this approach is that, in its effort to document local everyday religious practices, it may lose sight of the institutional, structural, and systemic processes in which these practices are embedded. The decontextualization of popular religion may in turn lead to a failure to recognize the multiple ways in which power and resistance shape and are shaped by religion.[6]

Orthodoxy, Heterodoxy, and Syncretism

Related to the tension between popular and official religion is that between orthodoxy—the authoritative version of a given religion—and heterodoxy—deviations from the norm, often the result of cultural mixing. In Latin America, popular religiosity, often existing at the margins of official institutions, has tended to diverge from orthodox doctrine and practice. Indeed, many heterodox religions have resulted from creative blending and borrowing among Christian, indigenous, and African traditions, conducted by people whose lives and home places contained all these elements. However, it is important to recognize that popular religious practices and beliefs are not always unorthodox, nor do religious officials always practice strictly orthodox forms. For instance, the case of the Virgin of Guadalupe, which we will discuss in chapter 3, blended indigenous notions of sacred space, pilgrimage, fertility, and femininity with Iberian Marian devotion. Guadalupe eventually became orthodox and incorporated into the official church. Pope John Paul II, in fact, declared her the "empress of the Americas."

The Catholicism that missionaries and conquistadores brought to Latin America was itself syncretic, drawing on pre-Christian popular traditions as well as influences from Jewish and Muslim cultures that shared the Iberian peninsula until 1492. Spanish and Portuguese Catholicism was dominated by pilgrimages, processions, and other public events, as well as by private shrines and devotions. These practices, and the beliefs that accompanied European settlers, were often open to adjustment as people's lives and societies changed. In the Americas, missionaries and native peoples encountered diverse religious customs and ideas, and often mixed these in ways that satisfied and made sense to them, individually and collectively. The results of their creative blendings were condemned and often punished by colonial authorities, but many persisted nonetheless, as revealed in the letter from a Oaxacan priest reprinted in chapter 3.

In the contemporary period, religious syncretism is recognized and often celebrated, as in the African Mass, contemporary pan-Mayan revivals, and a number of new religious movements such as those discussed in chapter 8. At the same time, scholars debate the validity of the concept of syncretism for the study of Latin American religions. Some reject the term altogether because it suggests that some religions are "pure" in contrast to others that are syncretic, or that the scholar can objectively determine degrees of purity among various religious expressions. In other words, the term "syncretism" carries an implicit connotation of essentialism, the idea that each religion has a stable core that defines its authenticity across time and space. To avoid essentialism, some scholars contend that all religions are "impure" insofar as they are historical cultural artifacts. The task, then, is not to search for the timeless nucleus of a given religion amid the transformations that take place as it interacts with other religious traditions, but to trace the multiple historical struggles that go into stabilizing a particular set of religious beliefs and practices. This quest to construct orthodoxy is perhaps most evident among Pentecostal Protestant churches, although the question of doctrinal or practical correctness is also important for many other religious groups, including conservative Roman Catholics, re-Africanizing practitioners of Candomblé (an Afro-Brazilian tradition most prominent in the city of Salvador in the state of Bahia), and indigenous revivalists.

Domination, Agency, and Resistance

Although the themes of grass-roots agency and resistance have been highly influential in contemporary studies of religious hybridity, they have a longer trajectory connected to the powerful influence of Marx in the Latin American social sciences as a counterpoint to U.S.-based approaches to the region that have tended to emphasize modernization and development. In particular, the cultural Marxism of Italian philosopher Antonio Gramsci, with its stress on the role of "organic intellectuals" in the construction of alternative worldviews that can challenge the ideas and beliefs advanced by the ruling classes, has been seminal for progressive Catholics, from Brazilian educator Paulo Freire to liberation theologians. Progressive Catholics often saw themselves as organic intellectuals, drawing symbols, narratives, and themes from popular religiosity to articulate utopian visions at odds with the repressive military regimes they confronted during the 1960s and 1970s.[7]

The role of culture and religion in domination and resistance continues to be central, now for scholars working from postcolonial and feminist standpoints. Drawing from thinkers as diverse as Michel Foucault, Jean Comaroff, James Scott, Edward Said, and Gayatri Spivak, they highlight the ways in which religion can serve as a means for marginalized people, including indigenous people, women, slaves, and peasants, to resist, albeit indirectly and precariously, the impositions of dominant elites.[8] These approaches challenge the common assumption that religion is a conservative social force that inevitably reinforces established values, institutions, and practices. They also challenge the tendency to see minority or disprivileged groups as passive victims hopelessly trapped in the fog of false consciousness. Many observers from this viewpoint highlight subtle, everyday forms of resistance such as foot dragging, pilfering, or feigning obedience, which, while not confronting the power structures head on, undermine attempts by the dominant classes to control all aspects of life. Other scholars point to the work of Russian thinker Mikhail Bakhtin, who saw in the bodily excesses of the carnival the temporary obliteration or inversion of the status quo. As we will see particularly for popular Catholicism and African-based traditions, religion is often a key dimension in "antistructural" collective events like carnivals, processions, and pilgrimages.[9] It is important, however, neither to read resistance into every religious expression nor to ignore more explicit forms of resistance. We also caution against underestimating the power of established institutional forms or the difficulties faced by those who challenge them.

Personal Conversion and Social Change

The tensions between domination and resistance in religion are sometimes linked to interactions between individual and society. Some religions operate primarily at the micro level, focusing on change at the personal and family levels while ignoring or at least deemphasizing praxis at the societal level. Other religions may stress social transformation as a precondition or a co-ingredient for individual renewal. Pentecostal Protestantism, for example, sets great store by individual changes of heart, acceptance of Jesus, and narratives of personal conversion. This conversion is driven by a belief in the imminent end of time, when all things of this world, including society, will be superseded. On the other hand, progressive Catholicism, with its notion that human beings can cooperate with God in the unfolding of his kingdom through good works, has been linked to political issues and movements for social change.

The personal and social dimensions of religion are not mutually exclusive. Pentecostalism, for example, continually interacts with larger social processes, affecting them and being affected in turn. The struggles of Pentecostals to save one person at a time are often informed by the desire for a wholesale moral and spiritual transformation of societies perceived as overly secular and depraved. And progressive Catholics often have intense personal religious experiences, which may nurture their political concerns or may appear apart from them. Responsible scholarship attends to the strong emphases present in the voices and experiences of the religious people they study, without allowing those emphases to exclude other themes, perspectives, or questions. Many students of contemporary Pentecostalism, for example, have explored its actual or potential political impact, especially with regard to gender and race relations. There has not been a comparable surge of interest in the personal religious experiences of progressive Catholics, which has resulted in a somewhat unbalanced portrait.

The most accurate picture of Latin American religions will emerge from an acknowledgment that every religion operates at multiple scales from the micro to the macro. All religions entail both intensely personal feelings and experiences, on the one hand, and larger social, cultural, and political dynamics, on the other. Further, these different levels affect each other continually. The task of the scholar is to study these complex and varied relations and their relations to each other.

Studying Religion in Latin America

Studies of Latin American religion have long been dominated by scholars trained in the disciplines of political science, anthropology, history, and sociology. Historians have done most of the significant research on the colonial and Independence periods, as well as on popular religious movements such as millenarianism, in which a charismatic leader brings followers together around the expectation of a radical transformation. (The term comes from the millennium as the thousand-year reign of Christ following the second coming, although not all movements described now as "millenarian" are Christian in orientation.) African-based and indigenous traditions have received attention especially from anthropologists, while contemporary movements, including both progressive Catholicism and Pentecostal Protestantism, have been studied especially by political scientists and sociologists. Disciplinary training is significant because it shapes the methods and theoretical perspectives of scholars, including even the kinds of questions they ask, the sources they seek out, and the way they present their material. Political scientists, for example, have tended to focus on large-scale dynamics of institutional actors or on the correlation between religious affiliation and political attitudes and participation. Anthropologists, in turn, often concentrate on particular locales, seeking richly detailed portraits of community or ritual life rather than sweeping generalizations. This is not to suggest that one approach is better than another, and there are variations and changes within every discipline. Moreover, due to processes such as globalization and transnational migration, there have been growing efforts to approach Latin American religions in an interdisciplinary and comparative fashion. However, disciplinary boundaries persist and readers should always be aware of the epistemological and methodological assumptions that a writer brings to the topic. Serious students of Latin American religion will want to read widely in works by authors of diverse disciplinary, as well as theoretical and regional, backgrounds.

The discipline of religious studies has paid significant attention to Latin America only in the past decade or two. Religious studies is itself a fairly new discipline, emerging in Europe in the late nineteenth century as a result of increasing scholarly interest in the comparative study of religion. It was tied to historical and critical approaches to sacred texts and draws on literary, historical, phenomenological, and social-scientific approaches. Religious studies is distinct from the discipline of theology, which in Western societies entails discussions of issues internal to Christianity and other Abrahamic religions, such as the nature of God.[10] In the United States, religious studies scholars have tended to concentrate on Christianity, Judaism, Islam, and Asian religions, with much less attention to Latin American and African traditions until recently. Exceptions include Davíd Carrasco and Lawrence Sullivan, historians of religion who pioneered comparative work in Latin America. The most important North American professional association for religious studies scholars and teachers, the American Academy of Religion, did not include a group dedicated to the study of religion in Latin America and the Caribbean until the early 1990s. And within the Latin American Studies Association, the main hemispheric organization of area studies scholars, papers and presentations on religion have, until recently, rarely involved people trained in religious studies. This is significant not because religious studies provides the only important disciplinary perspective for studying religion in Latin America (or elsewhere) but because it is an important complement to social-scientific and historical approaches.

Interest in Latin American religion among scholars from many disciplinary perspectives has grown in recent decades. Since the 1970s, the dramatic role of progressive Catholicism in Latin American politics and the emergence of liberation theology, an intellectual movement that emphasizes social justice and resistance to oppression, sparked intense academic and journalistic attention. A spate of studies explored progressive Catholicism, followed soon after by examinations of religious diversity, and especially of the growth of evangelical Protestantism, which emphasizes personal conversion and missionary outreach. All these topics have caught the interest of scholars from many disciplines, who have employed diverse theoretical perspectives ranging from religious insiders sympathetically exploring theological developments to social scientists quantitatively measuring religious behavior. We present the most important of these scholarly currents in this book, letting their advocates speak for themselves as much as possible, while also evaluating various approaches as part of a larger, multidisciplinary field of study.

The wide range of disciplinary, theoretical, and methodological approaches to the study of religion in Latin America has contributed to better understandings of the complexity and diversity of the topic, but at times religion has been understood, especially by scholars in historical and social-scientific fields, mostly as a dependent variable, rather than as a subject worthy of study in its own right. One of our aims in this book is to bring religion to the fore as a relatively independent variable, always shaped by its historical and social contexts but never merely a reflection of these.

Institutional Dynamics

Until the past few decades, most studies of religion in Latin America focused on official religious expressions and organizations—the activities of church officials and agencies, the interactions between the institutional church and the state, and mainstream doctrinal and theological statements.[11] This approach, sometimes summarized by its focus on "church and state," has the very significant advantage of drawing on relatively accessible sources. The Catholic Church has kept excellent records throughout Latin American history, in official archives, dioceses, cathedrals, parishes, museums, and also the agencies of individual religious orders and congregations. There is also a wealth of information about the church in many secular archives, both state and private. Furthermore, relations of alliance, accommodation, or outright conflict between secular and religious elites have played determining roles throughout the history of Latin America, especially in the Independence and post–Vatican II periods.

As we have discussed, the disadvantage of this approach is that it may suggest that religious life is exhausted by its official, publicly recognized manifestations. Thus the record erases the many religious aspects of private life, the wide range of religious activities that lack official sponsorship, and the activities of people whose lives are not well documented—including most women, peasants, indigenous people, and people of African descent, together constituting the vast majority of Latin Americans. The actions and thoughts of these people are much harder to uncover. Ethnographic methods can be very helpful for exploring the nooks and crannies of present-day religious life, but for the past, scholars depend on the existing records, few of which focused on informal aspects of religion or on the practices of ordinary people. One exception is the records of Inquisition trials, which have provided an invaluable (albeit partial) resource for students of heterodox and syncretic religious forms.

Rational Choice

The popular/lived religion model has been utilized most often by anthropologists and religious studies scholars, while church and state approaches have been adopted primarily by political scientists and historians. Another theoretical perspective that has gained increasing favor among a number of social scientists studying religion in Latin America (and elsewhere) is the "rational choice" paradigm and its associated "religious market" approach, which draw from models first developed in the field of economics and then adapted to sociology and political science.[12] This perspective begins with an assumption that Latin America has witnessed the collapse of Catholic monopoly over the religious arena and that this arena has, in fact, become a pluralistic marketplace, where religious producers compete with each other to produce the most attractive goods. Religious practitioners (like economic consumers), then, survey the available religious options in largely reasonable and self-interested ways, and choose the faith that seems most likely to fulfill their individual needs and desires, e.g., for healing, companionship, or economic advance. Scholars who advance rational choice contend that this paradigm can help account for sometimes confusing religious conversions and affiliations, and that it can demystify religious adherence, treating it like other cultural goods and markets. More specifically, the religious market approach can shed light on why certain religions are successful at particular times, while others seem to decline in terms of membership and resources. For example, R. Andrew Chesnut claims that "pneumatic" religions, those that are centered around the power of the Holy Spirit or other spirits to heal the body and rebuild the self shattered by the "pathologies" of poverty and marginality, are likely to expand their consumer base very rapidly, since the majority of Latin Americans face precarious social conditions.

While often producing elegant models of religious behavior, the economistic approach to religion has many critics. Some deride its instrumentality and tendency to explain religious choices and affiliations through simple formulas that are treated as generalizable axioms. These critics argue that religious choices and affiliations cannot be reduced to decontextualized and individualized cost-benefit analysis, as they are often shaped by embodied habits and the social location of religious believers, as well as the networks in which they are embedded. Further, rational choice approaches tend to assume that religious institutions are monolithic actors with clear sets of interests, methods, and awareness of their competitors, rather than seeing these institutions as characterized by complexity and contradiction. Finally, critics point out that in order to accommodate religious "goods" such as salvation or forgiveness, economistic models must define both benefits and costs so broadly that the model loses its analytic power, becoming simply a statement of the obvious: people believe that their religion has advantages and is good in some way.[13]

Race, Gender, and Postcolonialism

In religious studies, as in many other humanistic and social-scientific disciplines, themes of gender and race have become prominent in recent decades. This is evident in studies of Latin American religion, where, for example, gender relations have formed a central theme in many studies of Protestant conversion, as well as comparisons of the role that religion plays in private and public spheres for Catholics and Pentecostals.[14] Some of these studies have echoed themes in North American and European scholarship, e.g., of women's conversion to conservative traditions, from orthodox Judaism to Islam to charismatic Christianity, as a way to empower themselves within what are still male-centered societies. Other scholars have used the categories of race and ethnicity as organizing themes for their work, asking, for example, how religious organizations and rituals can reproduce racism and/or can express minority identity or resistance to dominant ideologies and institutions.[15]

Another scholarly approach that emphasizes the perspective of under-represented people is postcolonialism, pioneered in South Asian studies. This approach has also had a significant influence on studies of religion in both colonial and postcolonial Latin America.[16] It highlights cultural hybridity, the mutual shaping of dominant and "subaltern" social groups, and the subtle and unexpected ways in which resistance and creative adaptation are expressed. This approach has been applied fruitfully to the historical and ethnographic study of indigenous religions and their relation with the homogenizing projects of the Latin American nation-state, which has been traditionally dominated by mestizos (people of mixed indigenous and European descent) and white Creoles (people of European descent born in the New World).[17] Access to the "lived experience" of subaltern groups has been enhanced by the use of alternative sources like letters, diaries, material culture, oral and performed tradition (like *testimonio*, popular theater, dance, etc.), as well as archeology. Finally, parallel to the development of postcolonial scholarship, some indigenous scholars have begun constructing their own cosmologies, drawing on indigenous as well as Christian symbols and histories.[18]

Globalization and Transnationalism

The cluster of approaches grouped under the heading of globalization and transnationalism challenges the dominant notion in the social sciences and in the study of religion that the nation-state should be the natural unit of analysis, or the only taken-for-granted context framing the activities of individuals and communities. To challenge this "methodological nationalism," globalization and transnationalism approaches stress mobility across national boundaries, as well as the contested efforts of nation-states to control widespread historic and contemporary flows of people, ideas, goods, and capital. Globalization and transnationalism approaches also seek to embed micro-religious processes at the personal, familial, and communal levels in macro dynamics not only at the national but also at the regional, hemispheric, and transatlantic scale. Thus, works operating with this optic might focus on the impact of transnational migration, the movement back and forth between the United States and countries in Latin America, in the transformation of local and national religious fields.[19] Or they might focus on how electronic media are facilitating the global spread of Latin American religions like neo-Pentecostalism (a rapidly growing form of Pentecostal Protestantism built around a prosperity theology), Santo Daime (a new religious movement in Brazil centered around ayahuasca, a powerful psychoactive agent), or neo-shamanism (a New Age form of spirituality that borrows elements from traditional, indigenous shamanic practices). Or they might seek to understand the role of religion across multiple sites in the African diaspora, or for that matter in the Japanese, Muslim, or Jewish diaspora, in the Americas.[20] The pay-off of these works depends greatly on the skill with which they can pay careful attention to the specificities of local and national religious life, while showing how this life is shaped by and shapes multiscalar processes and relations.

This brief characterization of the various approaches to Latin American religions challenges the scholar to be attentive to the methodological choices s/he makes. It is essential to evaluate carefully the strengths and weaknesses of a particular perspective, as well as its usefulness in making sense of the religious phenomenon at hand. Often a strategic combination of perspectives will yield the best results.

Organization of the Book

The seven remaining chapters of this book are organized primarily by chronology. The two exceptions to this chronological ordering are chapter 2, which contains materials on indigenous life from pre-Columbian through contemporary societies, and chapter 4, which focuses on African-based traditions from the colonial to contemporary periods. Indigenous and African-based religions are also addressed in other chapters, as part of the religious diversity of every period of Latin American history, but we include separate chapters on both to highlight continuities and connections that might not be evident in a strictly chronological ordering.

Each chapter follows the same basic organization. It begins with an introduction by the editors that both provides a broad overview of the period and its defining issues and introduces the specific texts included in the chapter. Following the chapter introduction, each chapter contains a selection of texts, both primary and secondary. We have tried, as much as possible, to coordinate primary and secondary readings, but this has not always been possible or even desirable, due to the availability and quality of both primary and secondary texts. At the end of the book we have provided a bibliography of recommended readings for each chapter topic.

Chapter 2 addresses the cosmologies and ritual practices of indigenous religious traditions. Given the diversity of indigenous cultures in the Americas, we focus on the Mayas, Aztecs, Incas, and Yekuanas, thus covering the major regions of Mesoamerica, the Andes, and Amazonia. This chapter fleshes out similarities, interconnections, and differences among these four traditions.

In chapter 3, we explore the impact of the conquest on indigenous and Iberian cultures and religions through the testimonies of eyewitnesses, missionaries, and other protagonists of the colonial drama. The aim is to stress both the destructive and the creative power of the conquest. This ambivalence is best exemplified by the emergence of popular Catholicism, which is still the dominant religious tradition in the region. This chapter also addresses issues surrounding syncretism and church-state relations, important elements of religious and social life in the colonial period.

The following chapter focuses on the religious and cultural impact of the ten million Africans who came as slaves to the Americas, from around 1502, when the first slaves were brought to the Caribbean, until 1888, when slavery ended in Brazil. The readings discuss the historical origins of African diaspora religions, as well as contemporary expressions such as Santería, an Afro-Caribbean tradition practiced in Cuba, Puerto Rico, the Dominican Republic, and immigrant communities in the United States, and Umbanda and Candomblé, both Afro-Brazilian traditions.

With chapter 5, we move into the evolving relation between the emerging nation-states and the Catholic Church during the Independence and modern period. This relation entailed outright conflict, accommodation, or cooperation, depending on historical context. Readings also focus on grass-roots responses to the secular project of emerging national elites, especially millenarian movements.

Modernization in the shape of industrialization and urbanization also played a role in the rise of Protestantism in the region, and in chapter 6 we examine this phenomenon. In particular, we analyze the dynamics of the rapid growth of evangelical Protestantism, placing special emphasis on Pentecostalism, the major stream in Latin American Protestantism, but also attending to the ecumenical movement of mainline Protestant churches, such as the Lutherans, Presbyterians, and Methodists.

Chapter 7 tracks the major transformations that took place in the Roman Catholic Church following the Second Vatican Council (1962-1965), and especially the development of progressive popular Catholicism. Readings address the social impact of liberation theology and base Christian communities, small groups of laypeople who meet to read the Bible and often to take up social projects, as well as conflicts within the church.

Taking the rise of progressive Catholicism and the explosion of evangelical Protestantism as our points of departure, we close the volume with a discussion of the emerging trends in Latin American religious life. We underline the impact of globalization, particularly transnational migration, in the production of new religious expressions as well as the revitalization of long-standing traditions, including indigenous religions and also Latin American expressions of Buddhism and Islam. Along with these changes in existing traditions, we address the emergence of new religious movements, such as Santo Daime.

Selection of Texts

In putting together this reader, we have been keenly aware that we will not be able to include all relevant texts and perspectives. To gather all the important voices in the study of Latin American religion would require a multivolume encyclopedia. Thus, given the space constraints, our aim in making our selections has been to provide as rich an introduction as we can to an evolving field. As discussed above, we chose both primary and secondary sources in order to offer readers the opportunity not only to learn what academic specialists say but also to read some of the original historical documents themselves and to hear directly from some of the people they engage. We have also selected "classic" documents, in addition to less well-known texts that illuminate important aspects of the region's religious history and evolving diversity. Many of these newer texts have been written by young scholars who will shape the field in the years to come.

In addition, we have tried to include works by scholars based in the United States, Latin America, and Europe, in order to show different methodological and theoretical emphases. Thus we have translated some pieces from Spanish and Portuguese. Finally, although our own work has focused on Central America, Brazil, and Latinos in the United States, we have tried to include pieces dealing with as many countries as possible. Here, the selection process has been influenced not only by our expertise but also by the fact that countries like Brazil and Mexico have thriving communities of scholars studying religion. Finally, we were unable to reprint a number of important texts due to cost or copyright restrictions. Despite all these limitations, we have enjoyed putting this volume together and hope that readers will experience something of our enthusiasm for this fascinating field.

2

Indigenous Religions

The selections in this section address the cosmologies and ritual practices of indigenous religious traditions, past and present. While we discuss indigenous and African-based religions in the chronologically structured chapters throughout the book, we have, as noted in the introduction, devoted separate chapters to these cultural clusters as well in order to highlight thematic continuities and historical developments within them. Following this chapter introduction, the chapter is divided by regions, with a focus on three major cultural-geographic areas: Mesoamerica, the Andean region of western South America, and the Amazonian region in northeastern South America.

The religious history of the Americas, including what is now "Latin" America, began long before Europeans arrived. Archeological and documentary records reveal the complexity, diversity, and social significance of religious practices, ideas, and organizations in the lives of people throughout South and Meso America. Most of the existing records of precolonial cultures come from the large civilizations of these regions: the Incas in the Andes; the Mayans in southern Mexico, Guatemala, and Honduras; and the Aztecs (or Mexica) in central Mexico. The many smaller, more rural or mobile groups that lived in the precolonial Americas left fewer records, for a variety of reasons. Time and, especially, conquest destroyed many documents and artifacts from these cultures, as well as oral traditions and practices. However, we still have numerous narratives, preserved in indigenous pictographs or writings (often produced postconquest, at the behest of missionaries); a number of documentary records written by early colonizers, by missionaries, and, occasionally, by indigenous people; and material artifacts such as plaques, temples, and wall murals, among others. Especially for the larger societies, such as the Mexica, these surviving sources tell us a great deal about indigenous beliefs and practices, albeit perhaps more about special celebrations than about everyday religious life. Many gaps remain, not only about ordinary everyday life in the great societies but also about the diverse smaller cultures whose religions, like their languages, were related but not identical to those of their larger neighbors.

At the center of many indigenous cultures were convictions about the nature of the world, of humans, and of what might be beyond mundane human life; practices relating to these ideas, including sacrifices, pilgrimages, festivals, and other offerings; and institutions and sites dedicated to these ideas and practices. As some scholars argue, however, the term "religion" suggests a division between it and "secular" aspects of life that did not exist in many indigenous societies. For many native groups, "lived" or "popular" religion was the only religion, passed on in oral tradition and enacted in myriad aspects of everyday life, including food production and preparation, clothing, and building, as well as rituals of passage, celebration, and mourning. Many of these cultures were nonhierarchical, with little in the way of formal religious institutions, although the Aztecs and Incas had elaborate religious and political institutions and hierarchies. Any generalizations about "Native American" cultures or religions miss the diversity of the hundreds of groups that have populated the Americas, from precolonial times to the present.

Nonetheless, some common themes emerge in numerous traditions, especially within a region such as Mesoamerica or Amazonia. One theme that is common to many native cultures throughout the Americas is reciprocity and mutual dependence between human and divine beings. Mutuality is expressed in sacrifices as well as in rules and rituals regarding planting, harvesting, fishing, and hunting; human rites of passage; changes of seasons and of lunar and solar cycles; and other natural patterns that structured people's economic, social, and religious lives. For a number of cultures, astronomy was especially important as a way of understanding and relating to natural and sacred forces. Archeologists have found remarkable evidence that many Mesoamerican structures, in particular, were built and designed in careful orientation to constellations and lunar and solar cycles.

Mutuality characterizes human relationships not only with the sacred and the cosmos but also in more mundane and intimate interactions with nonhuman animals, plants, and landscapes. While all people in all places depend on nature, indigenous peoples in the Americas often make their relationships with the nonhuman world particularly explicit in their rituals and narratives. This is evident in the Mayan story of human creation from corn, told in the sacred text *Popol Vuh*, as well as in the intricate balance between creation and destruction negotiated in Mesoamerican rituals of sacrifice. In many native myths, from Mexico to the Amazon, non-human animals play important roles—as deities and as fellow residents of sacred and mundane space. Often, attitudes toward the natural world mark one of the sharpest distinctions between Amerindian cosmologies and those of European colonizers, who had a more instrumental view of nature, often based on culturally particular ideas of human uniqueness.[1]

Religious worldviews and practices helped indigenous peoples survive, adapt to, and often resist the European conquest and colonization that began in 1492. While earlier histories of the conquest often portrayed the natives as passive victims, recent scholars have underlined the many complex ways in which indigenous people negotiated and resisted colonization. The next chapter discusses the colonial period in more detail, but it is worth highlighting here the important role played by religious values, stories, and practices in the long and ongoing indigenous response to European colonization.

Mayan Religion

Mayan culture emerged around 500 B.C.E. in the Yucatán Peninsula and other parts of southern Mexico, including the state of Chiapas and in Guatemala and Honduras. The Mayans thrived for hundreds of years, building independent city-states with significant ceremonial centers and temples, as well as attaining cultural achievements such as elaborate calendar systems, paintings, and sculpture. The Maya have traditionally been characterized as more peaceful than their Aztec-Mexica neighbors to the north, although some scholars challenge this conclusion, citing archeological evidence—such as depictions on murals at the classic Mayan city Bonampak, in Chiapas, in southern Mexico—that the Mayas also practiced human sacrifice.

By their peak around 750 C.E., the Mayan population may have been greater than thirteen million people, including several linguistic and ethnic subgroups, the largest of which was the Quiché Maya. By 1000 C.E., however, the classic Mayan civilization, centered in the city-states, collapsed. The population appears to have declined significantly and to have abandoned cities and ceremonial centers such as Copán. The diminished population of Mayas moved to more forested areas, living in smaller groups and practicing subsistence farming. While scholars agree that Mayan civilization suffered a dramatic transformation around 1000 C.E., they debate the reasons. One factor seems to have been human overuse of the natural environment, especially over-farming and excessive dependence on a single crop, which made people's food supply especially vulnerable. Evidence also suggests natural disaster, especially severe drought, whose effects likewise would have been exacerbated in people affected by malnutrition and disease. Another factor may have been military conquest by Mexicas from northern Mexico, perhaps taking advantage of a weakened population.

While the Maya abandoned their ceremonial centers, they did not abandon their cultural practices. In other words, the collapse of Mayan cities was not the end of Mayan culture, which continues to this day in southern Mexico and Guatemala. The collapse did, however, result in the loss of cultural artifacts, including temples, altars, and texts, that would have helped contemporary scholars understand classical Mayan civilization more fully. Equal, or even greater, destruction and loss resulted from the Spanish conquest of Mesoamerica in the sixteenth century. Despite these upheavals, scholars can draw on a range of sources. Among the most important are former Mayan temples, many of which are currently undergoing excavation and study.

Few texts survive, since in Mayan areas, as in other parts of the Americas, the Spanish colonial rulers prohibited much indigenous writing and confiscated or destroyed many indigenous texts, including many important religious documents. In Mesoamerica, religious and other documents were written in hieroglyphics, familiar from writings on plaques, temples, and other stone monuments. Most written works on paper-like substances were burned, although native religious leaders were sometimes able to keep or reproduce copies. This is true of the Mayan *Book of Chilam Balam*, an important Mayan sacred text that was "copied and recopied in secret, sequestered in carefully concealed hiding places for more than a century after the conquest." In Mayan, "*chilam*" means "priest" and "*balam*" means "jaguar." Together, these terms refer to powerful prophets.[2] The book probably resulted from efforts of several hands over several generations, and included different versions with local variations. The (often post facto) prophecies in *The Book of Chilam Balam* include poignant references to the Spanish invasion and conquest. What do the sacred books say? asks one poem: "They foretell the future / katún by katún, / era by era, / foretell the Maya's suffering/ foretell the anguish, / foretell the murder, / foretell the foreigners' coming." Another poem proclaims, "Know this my priests, / know that soon / a katún shall come / that will mark / the beginning of the end / of all our ways." (A *katún* is a period of twenty years, the primary Mayan unit of time.) *The Book of Chilam Balam* incorporates both pre- and postcolonial events in Mayan history, not only reflecting the tragedies caused by the conquest but also illustrating a rich capacity to incorporate new events into established indigenous narrative forms and themes.

A similar integrating function is performed by the most important Mayan text, the Quiché book *Popol Vuh*, which was probably kept or copied by a Mayan priest, hidden, and then discovered in the Guatemalan town of Chichicastenango by a Spanish priest around 1702. The priest, Francisco Ximénez, translated the text into Spanish, but his version languished for a century and a half until it was discovered and published in Spanish and French. While Ximénez based his translation on a precolonial text, it includes postconquest additions and modifications, including a description of the Spanish conquerors as the successors of earlier Maya rulers. Like many sacred texts, the *Popol Vuh* begins with a creation story. The Mayan creator gods, called the "Bearers and Begetters," "Makers and Modelers," start by creating the earth itself, then turn to nonhuman animals, an ordering familiar to Western readers. The excerpt from *Popol Vuh* included in this chapter, however, shows that when the narrative turns to the creation of humans, it differs strikingly from the biblical account. The deities are disappointed that the animals they have created cannot speak or pray correctly. Only after many adventures does the *Popol Vuh* return to the postponed creation of humans, finally successful once the gods encounter the proper material, corn. Corn remains central to Mayan cultural life (and Mesoamerican meals) today, as do many of the ritual practices and cosmological notions expressed in the *Popol Vuh*. These themes are affirmed by contemporary Mayan "revitalization" movements, which aim to reclaim native values, practices, and social forms that have been suppressed but never entirely eliminated since the colonial era.

In addition to creation narratives, *Popol Vuh* also tells many stories of the adventures of different deities, including the denizens of the Maya underworld, Xibalba. Xibalba is less a parallel to the Christian hell than it is a testing ground and a space connecting the realm of deities to the mundane world. Central figures in these adventures are the hero twins, Hunahpu and Xbalanque. The stories of the hero twins reveal many central themes and practices of indigenous Mayan, and more generally Mesoamerican, culture, including the existence of an underworld populated by deities and the ritual importance of the ball game and human sacrifice.

The hero twins in *Popol Vuh*, like Quetzalcoatl, the "plumed serpent" who is both a deity and a human hero from the Toltec capital of Tula, are "cultural heroes who fulfill the role of transmitting the basic necessities to humanity" and who enact an accord between humans and the gods, according to which "creation is an act of the gods, and the mission of humans on earth is to conserve the basic principles of this divine creation and honor the founding gods through sacrifice."[3]

The *Popol Vuh* and other precolonial indigenous texts, rituals, and symbols remain central to Mayan culture today. Activists and scholars, including Rigoberta Menchú, Victor Montejo, and Arturo Arias, draw on long-standing traditions in efforts to celebrate, express, and revitalize Mayan social and cultural life.

Aztec Religion

While sacrifice was ritually and ideologically important to the Mayas and other Mesoamerican cultures, it is most associated with the culture popularly known as Aztecs, called by scholars "the Mexica." The Mexica originated as a small tribe that traveled from northern to central Mexico in the twelfth and thirteenth centuries C.E. and took over areas previously dominated by the Toltecs, whose culture appears to have collapsed several centuries earlier. The Toltec culture, particularly the capital city of Tollan (or Tula), ruled by the prince Quetzalcoatl, has served as a fertile source of myths and images for Mexicans from the time of the Aztec empire until the present. For example, in the centuries following the Maya collapse, the early Aztecs—one among many indigenous groups in the Valley of Mexico—established themselves in the ruins of Tula, then wandered in search of a new settlement site. Guided by an image from Toltec legend, they searched for an eagle perched on a cactus, eating a snake. The eagle appeared in 1325 at Lake Texcoco, which became the site of their new capital city, Tenochtitlán.

The Aztecs built a major empire, centered in the city of Tenochtitlán (contemporary Mexico City), which was finished around 1345. The city, as scholar Davíd Carrasco argues, constituted the symbolic and ritual center of Aztec life. Archeological excavations in Tenochtitlan's Templo Mayor and other Aztec sites have provided a rich variety of information about Aztec culture. From temples, pyramids, plaques, and other monuments, scholars have compiled a portrait of preconquest Aztec society as highly stratified, ritualized, and centralized. Hereditary nobles lived at the top of the social scale, slaves at the bottom. The Aztec state existed in tension with many neighboring societies, some of which became tribute-paying vassals, and many of which provided prisoners of war and slaves to be used in sacrificial rituals.

While human sacrifice on a large scale was probably practiced only by the Aztecs, other Mesoamerican groups also used sacrificial rites, including sacrifice of nonhuman animals and objects, as well as auto-sacrificial practices such as bloodletting. For all Mesoamerican cultures, sacrificial rituals expressed and reinforced reciprocity between humans and divinities, what historian of religion Kay Read calls a necessary "creative destruction," which helped order the processes of death and change in order to preserve the processes of birth and life.[4] For Aztec, and broader Mesoamerican, culture, human sacrifice reflected the centrality of sacrificial transformation, the need, shared by gods, humans, and other beings, to eat other entities in order not to die before their time. The Aztecs' creative destructions took various forms, including not only human sacrifice but also the less dramatic kinds of sacrifice offered by other Mesoamerican groups. Mexica cosmologies and values were rooted not only in spectacular, rare ceremonies but also in everyday practices, images, and conceptions. Temples, plaques, and other archeological sources are especially important to scholarly knowledge of Aztec life in part because most of the textual sources were destroyed by Spanish soldiers and missionaries very early in the colonial period.

Bernardino de Sahagún's *General History of the Things of New Spain*, also known as the *Florentine Codex*, is one of the most important of the remaining primary texts. Sahagún was one of the few missionaries who became fluent in the Mexica language Nahuatl—the lingua franca of the Aztec empire and then the principal indigenous language of the colony called New Spain. Sahagún compiled and transcribed indigenous stories between about 1540 and 1585. The result is an invaluable source of information on preconquest and early colonial Mexica culture. In the selection from the *Florentine Codex* reprinted below, Sahagún provides detailed information about indigenous ways of life and also about the rules for Aztec priests.

Sahagún also collected a number of Mexica stories about Quetzalcoatl, an important figure for several Mesoamerican cultures, including both Mayas and Aztecs. He was originally a Toltec figure, adopted and adapted by the Aztecs and other cultures, transforming across time and space in accord with the values and concerns of various Mesoamerican cultures. Quetzalcoatl is, according to one scholar, "the only symbol with so much staying power that it can be found permeating nearly every formative culture of Mexico."⁵ We reprint here Sahagún's account of Quetzalcoatl's departure from Tula.

Quetzalcoatl's return is also the subject of many stories. Many historians have asserted that the Aztecs believed Hernan Cortés to be the return of the hero-god and thus did not fight the fair-skinned soldier who appeared from the east in 1519. While the lack of Aztec resistance to the Spaniards is often exaggerated, it is true that 1519 was an iteration of the Aztec year "One Reed," the time in which Quetzalcoatl was expected to return from the east to Tenochtitlán. The Aztecs, like other Mesoamerican societies, counted time cyclically, so that the names of years were repeated according to a 52-year cycle, at the end of which the world would end if humans did not perform the proper rituals of renewal, called the New Fire ceremonies. In a sense, the Aztec world did end in 1519, with the arrival of the Spanish conquistadores.

Andean Religion

The Andean area stretches three thousand miles, from northern Ecuador through Peru to southern Chile. The region is mostly mountainous, dry, and subject to extremes of hot and cold. Centuries before the conquest, the Andes were settled by a variety of indigenous groups, of which the earliest was the Chavins (1500 B.C.E.–300 B.C.E.), who lived in the Marañon River basin. The Chavins influenced contemporary cultures throughout the Andes, with highly developed agriculture and metallurgy as well as textiles. Following the Chavins, the Paracas (600 B.C.E.–200 C.E.) settled in what is now Peru's Ica province. The Paracas built large underground necropolises, home to mummies preserved in rich clothing. They also practiced brain surgery (craneal trepanations). The best known of the pre-Incan cultures was the Nazca, who thrived from about 300 to 1000 C.E. in the high plateaus south of Lima. The Nazca culture is especially well known today for the distinctive pottery they left behind, and also for the famous "Nazca lines," enormous drawings in the desert of figures, such as a dog and a monkey, that can be distinguished only from the air.

By the early thirteenth century, the Incas had emerged as the dominant indigenous culture in the Andes, and indeed the largest empire in the precolonial Americas. With their political and military center in Cuzco, the Incas conquered, assimilated, and administered a large part of western South America. Like the Aztecs', Inca society was tightly organized, with a strong centralized bureaucracy and complex military, economic, and agricultural systems. Unlike the Aztecs, however, the Incas incorporated defeated groups into their empire, rather than maintaining tributary states. The Incas constructed a famously elaborate system of roads, even though they did not have the wheel, and pioneered agricultural technologies, including irrigation and terracing.

Like Inca society, Inca religious life was highly complex and organized. Their pantheon included a hierarchy of deities, most associated with natural elements, including the earth, the moon, thunder, the sea, and most important of all, Inti, the sun god. Many Andean rituals celebrated the sun, including the Inti Raymi festival, which took place at the June solstice. A number of ceremonial sites at Machu Pichu, the Inca sacred city, are constructed in alignment with the sun's solstice path. The sun's representative on earth was the Inca emperor, whose wife, the Coya, was associated with the moon. The Inca and the Coya headed the system of parallel descent, with male and female hierarchical lines, that ordered the lives of members of Inca society, including the smaller Andean groups incorporated into the imperial system.

What we know about preconquest Andean culture is even more fragmentary than what we know about Mesoamerica, in part because the Incan and pre-Incan cultures had no system of writing such as Mayan and Aztec hieroglyphics. The Incas kept records with *quipu*, knotted cords that neither Andean natives nor scholars today can decipher. Most of what historians and anthropologists today know of precolonial Andean cultures comes from archeological excavations. However, a few Andean texts exist, transcribed during the colonial period by Spaniards on the basis of indigenous oral narratives. One of the most important of these, reprinted in part below, is the *Huarochiri Manuscript*, named for the region in Peru from which it comes. The account was produced by an anonymous Quechua speaker in the seventeenth century on the orders of a Spanish priest, Francisco de Avila, who was motivated both by fascination with indigenous practices and beliefs and by a desire to document the continuing "un-Christian" practices of native converts.

Like Avila, many early Spanish missionaries were preoccupied with the incomplete and often contested nature of their evangelization and conversion efforts. What appeared to frustrated missionaries as idolatry is read in a different light by many contemporary students of colonial Latin America. The survival of indigenous cosmologies and practices and the syncretism (mixing) of native and Christian elements now appear to many scholars not as evidence of "incomplete evangelization" but rather as creative efforts to salvage and transform precolonial religion in the colonial setting. These processes reflect not simply attachment to long-standing traditions but also sometimes subtle, but still powerful, forms of resistance to colonial rule. This approach to colonial Latin America, as Elizabeth Hill Boone describes it, seeks to adopt "the perspective of the native peoples as they moved within and responded to the cultural and intellectual climate of the postconquest period." Scholars taking this approach generally pay more attention to indigenous people's cultural life and everyday activities, including religion, than to the "large-scale, formal, colonial institutions" that were the focus of traditional scholarship on the colonial period.[6]

Amazonian Religion

Brazil was colonized later than Mesoamerica and the Andes. As part of a series of papal bulls establishing (in Europe) Iberian and Catholic control of the Americas, in 1493 Pope Alexander VI granted Spain all the lands west of a line one hundred leagues (about 320 miles) west of the Cape Verde Islands and Portugal, the lands to the east. That line was moved west by the Treaty of Tordesillas in 1494, which gave Portugal Brazil when the Portuguese navigator Pedro Alvares Cabral found it in 1500. The Portuguese immediately claimed Brazil but were preoccupied with their African colonies during the early 1500s, while the Spanish were conquering and colonizing their share of South America and Mesoamerica. In addition, the natural landscape of Brazil, and especially the Atlantic and Amazonian rainforests, presented numerous obstacles to explorers. (This was also true for parts of Amazonia in Spanish colonies, including Peru, Venezuela, and Ecuador.) The landscape helped protect a number of South American indigenous groups, many of which remained relatively separate from European colonizers much longer than natives in other parts of the Americas. One of these groups is the Yekuana, a Carib-speaking people who migrated several centuries ago from the Amazonian region of Brazil into southern Venezuela, where they live now. The Yekuana have retained their cultural identity more successfully than many Carib-speaking groups, and have also maintained significant autonomy vis-à-vis European and Venezuelan national ideologies and institutions, in part because of their rugged home landscape, whose mountains, rapids, and waterfalls help keep outsiders at a distance.

Religious and cultural factors have also played an important role, however. Rather than permitting challenges to undermine the stability of their society, argues ethnographer David Guss, the Yekuana have incorporated them into the traditional narratives that order their world. As Guss explains, encounters with Westerners, migrations, and other historical events "are recontextualized within an already established mythic universe," so that the Yekuana "transform the foreign into the currency of their own culture, making it safe and familiar. Through such adaptability to new historical situations the Yekuana are able to reaffirm a cosmology that forever locates them at its center."[7] The *Watunna*, a Yekuana myth cycle collected by French anthropologist Marc de Civrieux and excerpted below, provides a fascinating portrait of a distinctive sacred history and geography.

In the *Watunna*, as in many Amazonian cultural narratives, nonhuman animals play central roles, as culture heroes, deities, and reflections of human strengths and failings. The most important nonhuman character for the Yekuana is Wanadi, a woodpecker known as the "master of humans" and son of the Sun, a creator and trickster. Wanadi first discovered the earth for the Yekuana, has appeared two additional times, and will return a fourth time to return the earth to its original state of perfection. The balance of Wanadi's (and the Yekuana's) world is threatened by Odosha, to whom Wanadi himself has given birth. The relationship between Wanadi and Odosha, however, is not one of simple opposition, but rather entails a complex mutual dependence. According to Yekuana narratives, the struggles between Wanadi and Odosha take place not only in primordial or "mythic" time but also in real historical time. They are present in the creative tensions between night and day, women and men, the jungle and the Yekuana culture. Given the ambiguous nature of the cosmos, as informed by both Wanadi and Odosha, the Yekuana do not seek to reject evil but rather to purify the raw and dangerous powers of nature through ritual practices like weaving baskets and singing the oral tradition. The Yekuana have incorporated developments such as the arrival of Europeans and the introduction of new technologies and artifacts into the epic struggle between Wanadi and Odosha.

Traditionally foragers, hunters, and small-scale farmers, Amazonian peoples such as the Yekuana have established relationships of interdependence with the landscapes and creatures among which they live. Their religious beliefs and practices reflect the rhythms of daily life and of the natural cycles on which they depend. Religious practices and worldviews also reflect key aspects of social organization, including kinship ties, gender relations, generational differences, and occupational roles. Perhaps the best known profession in Amazonian cultures is that of shaman. (In fact, among the Yekuana, Wanadi is considered the first shaman.) Shamans serve as healers, ritual specialists, community leaders, and wise men who know the group's oral traditions. Shamans mediate the complex relationship between human and nonhuman worlds, a relationship that does not entail simple opposition as much as fluid and mutually influencing perspectives and experiences.[8]

Making use of myths, chants, dances, rituals, and psychoactive substances ranging from tobacco to yucca or corn-based alcoholic drinks and to ayahuasca (*Banisteriopsis caapi*), the shamans transgress the porous boundaries of human consciousness, experiencing the multiple forces that animate the universe and traveling to the world of the spirits to accompany the dead, and secure knowledge and help for the living. The shaman can also become a predator, just like a jaguar, who may "cannibalize" the soul force of humans. The shaman's "multinaturalism," his capacity to experience alterity, to assume various (nonhuman) viewpoints within a whole in which the various parts are not only interconnected but interchangeable, yet not fully reducible to each other, is what makes him "the voice of the forest."[9]

Today Amazonian groups, like most indigenous American societies, face many dire threats, including the loss of their cultures and languages and environmental destruction and development of their homelands. Amazonian indigenous leader Davi Yanomami puts matters eloquently:

> I want to speak giving the message from Omai. Omai is the creator of the Yanomami who also has created all the shaboris that are the shamans. The shaboris are the ones that have the knowledge, and they sent two of us to deliver their message. The message is to stop destruction, to stop taking out minerals from under the ground, to stop taking out the steel with which all the metal utensils are made, and to stop building roads [through forests].
>
> We feel that a lot of riches have already been taken out of the indigenous lands, and a lot of these riches are getting old and useless, and it would be much better if the Brazilian government would give these riches to the poor in Brazil. Our work is to protect nature, the wind, the mountains, the forest, the animals, and this is what we want to teach you people.[10]

In response to these threats, a diverse array of social movements has arisen. Many of these movements, such as the movimiento pan-Mayanista,[11] draw on religious principles, symbols, and practices both to affirm indigenous identity and to act as effective advocates for indigenous rights in the national and global public spheres. Religion, however, can be as much part of the problem as a part of the solution. For example, evangelical Protestantism, particularly Pentecostalism, has often produced negative effects on indigenous communities, condemning shamanistic practices as evil and producing sharp divisions among indigenous leaders that make it more difficult to mobilize collectively.[12] Moreover, even those religions that seem receptive to indigenous beliefs and practices can be implicated in neo-colonialism. As discussed in the last chapter, the figure of the shaman as an indigenous healer or spiritual guide is very prominent in new religious movements like Santo Daime, União do Vegetal, and Vale do Amanhecer. These movements point to the commodification and expropriation of local indigenous knowledges, which are then consumed by cosmopolitan elites as part and parcel of globalization. These movements, nonetheless, also attest to the enduring wisdom of native religions in the Americas.

CHAPTER 2 DOCUMENTS

The Popol Vuh[1]

I. CREATION

a. Preamble
This is the beginning of the ancient history of the Kiché land; we are going to record the traditions of all that the Kiché nation did, and reveal what has been hidden up till now. We are bringing this forth under Christianity, for the *Popol Vuh* as our Book of the Council was called, is no longer to be seen.

b. The Earth
This is the story of how everything was in suspense, everything at rest, everything silent. All was motionless, hushed; and empty was the vastness of Heaven. Here is our first document, the first account we have. There were still no men nor animals, there were no birds, fish nor crabs, no trees, stones nor caves, no ravines, grass nor woods. Only Heaven existed; the face of Earth had not yet appeared. Only the calm sea and Heaven's expanse were spread out everywhere. Nothing made a sound, nor did anything move. There was nothing which stood erect; only the water spread out peacefully, the calm and tranquil sea. There was only motionlessness and silence in the darkness of the night. Only the Creator and Fashioner, Tepeu and Gucumatz,[2] lived in the water surrounded by radiance. They lay hidden by the green and blue feathers of great sages; in this way existed the Heart of Heaven, which means God.

Then the Word was;[3] Tepeu and Gucumatz came and spoke to each other amid the darkness, consulting and meditating. They reached an agreement; they put their words and thoughts on life and light together in an effort to decide what to do when it should dawn. They finally resolved that man should appear, and thus they arranged for life to commence and men to be created. Tepeu and Gucumatz pronounced in unison:

"May the void be filled! May this water withdraw so Earth may arise! May it dawn on Heaven and Earth!

This is how they planned the creation of Earth.

"*Earth!*" they said, and it was formed at once. Like the mist, like clouds, mountains rose from the water; through a miracle—a stroke of magic— hills and valleys were formed; at the same time cedars and pines sprang up in clusters. So Gucumatz of the green feathers was filled with joy and exclaimed:

"Welcome, Heart of Heaven, O Hurricane!"

Thus while Heaven was still in suspense, Earth was created so it could rise easily from the waters. This is how the gods accomplished their task after they had considered how to bring it to a successful conclusion.

c. The Animals

Then the wild animals, the guardians of the woods and spirits of the forest, were created: deer, birds, lions, jaguars, large serpents, harmless smaller snakes, and more deadly vipers. The Creators thought matters over again and came to this decision:

"Must there be only silence and stillness under the trees and beneath the the vines? Someone should be guarding them."

So they spoke again, and at once deer and birds were created. They assigned them their dwellings as follows:

"You, O deer, will sleep along the river flats and in ravines; you will increase and feed in the meadows and woods, and walk on four feet."

As it was said, so it was done. Then they assigned the birds their homes; they told them what to do, and each flew to its nest. When the four-footed animals and the birds had been created, the Creator and Fashioner said to them:

"*Cry! Shout! Warble! Howl!* Each of you should speak according to your kind."

Yet it was impossible for them to speak like man—they only squealed, cackled, or brayed. Their language was meaningless, for each one cried out in a different manner. When the Creator and Fashioner saw it was impossible for them to speak, they remarked to each other:

"They cannot say the names of us, their Creator and Fashioner! That is not right."

So they announced: "You will be transformed; we have changed our minds because you do not speak. You will eat and live in the ravines and woods, for you do not call upon us, and we are going to make other creatures who will be more attentive. You must accept your fate, which is to have your flesh chewed and eaten."

Thus the Forerunners made their will known to every animal on Earth; but as these did not speak a common tongue they could not do a thing about it. In this way, the animals which exist on the face of the Earth were condemned to be killed and eaten.

d. The Men of Clay and Wood

Then the Creator and Fashioner wanted to try their luck again. They made another attempt to form a man who would worship them.

"Let's try again! What shall we do to be invoked and remembered on Earth? We have already tried with our first creatures, but could not get them to praise and venerate us. Let us make obedient and respectful beings. Dawn and sunrise are approaching; let us form someone to sustain and nourish us."

Thus they spoke, and then they started making fresh creations. From Earth, from plain mud, they made man's flesh—but this fell apart, for it was soft and limp and had no strength. It could not move its head, its face fell towards one side, its neck was so stiff it could not look backward. It soaked up water and would not hold together. Then the Creator and Fashioner talked things over once more.

"Let us consult an omen, since our men cannot walk nor multiply. Let us ask for some advice on this matter."

So they knocked their handiwork apart, complaining:

"What shall we do for perfect worshipers? We must find a way so the man we fashion will sustain and feed us. He must invoke and call upon us!"

Hurricane, Tepeu, and Gucumatz went off to ask the magic pair of grandparents for help, since these were soothsayers.

"Talk matters over, grandmother and grandfather: toss lots with your corn and beans, and find out if we should make a man from wood."

In order to cast a spell the old woman and old man threw lots with corn and beans:

"Get together! Speak so we can hear you! Say whether the Creator and Fashioner should make a man from wood; and whether this man will feed and nourish us. Corn! Beans! Fate! Unite! *Get together!*"

This is how the old couple talked to the corn and beans, and then they declared:

"Your figures will turn out fine if they are made of wood, and they will speak upon the face of the Earth."[4]

"*So be it!*" answered the Forerunners.

Immediately the Creator and Fashioner made their figures out of wood. They resembled men, they spoke like men, and they peopled the face of Earth. These were the first men who existed in large numbers in the world.

e. Destruction of the Wooden Men

The wooden dolls existed and had daughters and sons; but they had no soul or understanding. They did not remember who their Creator and Fashioner were, and limped around aimlessly. At first they spoke, but their faces soon withered and their feet and hands had no consistency. They quickly forgot about the Heart of Heaven, and therefore fell into disgrace. They had no blood nor moisture nor stoutness; their cheeks were hollow, their hands and feet were shriveled, and their flesh was yellowish. They were only a sample—an attempt at making man.

Since they no longer remembered the Creator and Fashioner who had given them their being and cared for them, they were destroyed. The Heart of Heaven who is called Hurricane caused a great flood to overwhelm the wooden dolls, while a shower of pitch fell from Heaven into their eyes. It cut off their heads and gnawed their flesh; it shattered their nerves and ground their bones.

The wooden men ran around in desperation; they tried to climb up on their houses, but these collapsed and tossed them to the ground. They tried to climb the trees, and were shaken off; they wanted to crawl into the caves and were chased out of them. This was their punishment for not remembering the Heart of Heaven: the face of Earth was darkened and a black rain began to fall, that lasted day and night.

Then the animals both great and small started to eat them, and even the trees and stones struck them in the face. Their jars, dishes, and pots began to murmur and their dogs, turkeys, and grindstones rose up against them.

"On your account our faces are being worn away," said the grindstones; "day after day, at nightfall and at dawn, you make us groan—'*Holee! holee! Hukee! hukee!*'[5] That was our duty toward you; but now you are no longer men; we'll see how strong we are! We will grind you and reduce your flesh to dust!" the grindstones warned them.

The dogs in turn addressed the wooden men as follows: "Why haven't you fed us? We've just looked at you from a distance, while you were eating, and you chased us away. You always had a stick handy to beat us with; this is how you treated us when we couldn't speak to you. Why shouldn't we sink our teeth into you now?"

Thus spoke the dogs, and the wooden men, attacked by their animals and utensils, perished. They say their only descendants are the monkeys in the forest; and for this reason monkeys look like men and remind us of a race who were made from wood.

9. THE MEN OF CORN

a. Preparations

When the Creators, Tepeu and Gucumatz, were ready to make man, they remarked: "Dawn is almost at hand, so let us finish our task of making the children of light and civilized men who will sustain us. May mankind appear upon the face of the Earth!"

There was very little time left before the Sun, Moon, and Stars would rise upon our Creators and Forerunners, so the latter gathered for a meeting in the darkness of the night to discuss what material they should use for man's flesh. The wildcat, coyote, magpie, and crow showed them where to find yellow and white ears of corn such as they needed for their purpose. The Forerunners were filled with joy, for they had discovered a splendid land rich in corn, cocoa, fruit, and honey; there was delicious food in the country whose road the four animals had pointed out to them.

Grandmother Ish-Mucaneh then ground the yellow and white ears and made nine drinks from them. This food furnished the energy which gives man strength and the flesh which forms his muscles. Pure corn dough was kneaded into flesh while the arms and legs were made from the cobs.

b. The First Men

The following are the names of the first real men: the first was called Balam-Kitzeh or Sweet-Smiling Jaguar; the second, Balam-Acab or Jaguar-of-Night; the third, Mahucutah or Wrapped-in-Majesty; and the fourth, Iki-Balam or Moon-Jaguar. Those are the names of our original forefathers.

It is said they had no parents, since the Creator and Fashioner, Tepeu and Gucumatz, had created them by means of a miracle. Yet they looked like men; they spoke, conversed, saw and heard; moreover they could walk around and hold things in their hands. They were handsome: men with virile features and keen minds. As they looked around they took in everything on Earth: woods, rocks, lakes, seas, mountains, and valleys. They scanned the vault of Heaven and the face of Earth and could even notice things hidden in the distance without having to move from the spot where they were standing. Indeed, Balam-Kitzeh, Balam-Acab, Mahucutah, and Iki-Balam were remarkable men.

The Creator and Fashioner then asked them: "What do you think of your lot? Don't you see and hear? Don't you like the way you talk and walk? Look around the world; count the number of mountains and valleys you can see!"

When the men finished looking at everything there was in the world they began to thank their Creators.

"Verily we thank you for creating us! You have given us a mouth and face; we speak and hear, we think and walk. We can feel perfectly and know everything far and near. We can likewise use anything no matter how big or small it is, in Heaven or on Earth. We give thanks to you, O Creator and Fashioner, for having given us our being!"

Indeed, by the time they had examined the four corners of Heaven and the ends of the Earth they knew everything. The Creator and Fashioner, however, were not happy to hear this.

"What our creatures say is not proper: they know everything great and small," they remarked. So the Forerunners held another consultation: "What shall we do with them now? Their sight should reach only nearby objects, and they should take in only a part of the Earth. Are they not our creatures by their very nature? Let's restrain their desires a little, for what we've seen is not right. Are they going to be gods too, and equal us—their Creators—simply by knowing and seeing everything?"

This is what Hurricane, the Heart of Heaven, said to the Creator and Fashioner, Tepeu and Gucumatz. Therefore, they changed their creatures' nature. The Heart of Heaven cast a mist before their eyes which clouded them over, as when you blow upon a mirror. Their eyes were darkened and they could only see what was close at hand. Thus the wisdom of the first four men was impaired.

c. The First Tribes

Then women were made; God himself fashioned them carefully. They were really beautiful, and looked like princesses. They came up to Balam-Kitzeh, Balam-Acab, Mahucutah, and Iki-Balam while the latter lay sleeping. There they were one morning when the men awoke, and the latter rejoiced when they realized they were to be their wives.

Here are their names: Balam-Kitzeh's wife was called Caha-Paluna or Rain-from-on-High; Chomiha or Choice-Rain was Balam-Acab's wife;

Tzununiha or Shower-of-Hummingbirds belonged to Mahucutah; while Cakishaha or Rain-of-Macaws was the name of Iki-Balam's wife.

These four couples produced every tribe both great and small; they were the origin of us, the Kiche people, and of our priests and sacrificers. Balam-Kitzeh was the ancestor of the Cavecs; Balam-Acab was the founder of the Nimhaibs; Mahucutah, the grandsire of the Ahau-Kiches; while Iki-Balam and his wife had no offspring. Only three families were founded, and they never forgot their ancestors' and forefathers' names. We are only describing the chief tribes; other groups were formed among the people, but we shall not mention their names here.

Many men were born in the darkness before the sun rose; they all lived together yonder in the East, where they wandered around in great numbers. Yet not one of them maintained a god; they had no way of preserving their strength. They merely raised their faces to Heaven without knowing what they should do to express their thanks; there they roamed in large numbers, both dark men and pale men speaking different tongues which were astonishing to hear. They did not worship either wood or stone, nor did they remember the words of their Creator and Fashioner, the Heart of Heaven and the Heart of Earth.

Meanwhile, our ancestors were preparing for dawn and sunrise. These dutiful and God-fearing worshipers of the divine word raised their prayers in a single tongue. They lifted their faces to Heaven and asked for daughters and sons:

> O Thou: Look down and give ear to us! Do not leave us nor abandon us,
> O God who art in Heaven and Earth! Give us offspring so long as the Sun moves and there is light! Give us good roads! Grant the nations peace and happiness! Give us a good living and a useful existence! O Thou, Hurricane; Thou, Tepeu; Thou, Gucumatz! May dawn come and there be light!

These are their words as they prayed that dawn should come. At the same time as they were waiting for the sunrise, they watched in particular for the morning star, that great planet which precedes the Sun and lights up the vault of Heaven and the face of the Earth, and shows men where they should tread.

d. Their Gods Arrive

Those knowing men, Balam-Kitzeh, Balam-Acab, Mahucurah, and Iki-Balam, never grew tired of waiting for the Sun.

"Before it dawns, let's go and look for our symbols," they said, "and for something to burn before them."

They had heard about a city named Tula[6] yonder in the land we call Mexico today, and they went off to receive their gods there. When the latter came forth, the men were filled with joy:

"At last we've found the object of our search!" they exclaimed.

The first to come forth was Tohil; Balam-Kitzeh brought him out in a chest on his shoulders.[7] Next Balam-Acab brought forth the god called Avilish; Mahucutah, the god Hacavitz: while the god Nicahtacah was carried by Iki-Balam. Mighty indeed was the nature of these three gods, Tohil, Avilish, and Hacavitz.[8]

Our forefathers were mighty men, even though they were dressed only in wild animal skins. There in Tula the four men kept a constant fast as they waited for dawn to arrive; they took turns watching for bright Ikokih, the great star which comes up before the Sun. Great was their wisdom in the darkness of the night. Yet they did not receive their power and dominion there, but merely subdued the great and small tribes which lived around Tula.

Then all the kindred nations met—the men of Rabinal, the Cakchikels, those from Tzikinaha, and many foreigners who are now called Yaquis. It was impossible to count the men who marched in orderly formation, for all the nations taken together were very numerous. It was there that the speech of various tribes became different, and they could not understand each other easily. In Tula they were separated: some went off East and many came this way.[9]

The Florentine Codex[10]

Third Chapter, which telleth the tale of Quetzalcoatl, who was a
great wizard: where he ruled and what he did when he went away.

This Quetzalcoatl they considered as a god; he was thought a god; he was prayed to in olden times there at Tula. And there was his temple. It was very tall, very high, exceedingly high, exceedingly tall. Very many were its stair steps; verily they lay in a multitude, each one not wide but only very narrow. On each one the sole of one's foot could not lie.

It is said he just lay covered, he just lay with his face covered. And it is said he was monstrous.

His face was like something monstrous, battered, a monstrous fallen rock. There was no human creation [in it]. And his beard was very long, very lengthy. He was heavily bearded.

And the Tolteca, his vassals, were highly skilled. Nothing was difficult when they did it, when they cut the green stone and cast gold, and made still other works of the craftsman, of the feather worker. Very highly skilled were they. Indeed these [crafts] started, indeed these proceeded from Quetzalcoatl—all the crafts work, the learning.

And there stood his green stone house, and his golden house, and his seashell house, and his snail shell house, and his house of beams, his turquoise house, and his house of precious feathers.

And for his vassals, the Tolteca, nowhere was [too] distant [where] they dealt. Indeed swiftly they quickly reached where they went. And so very quickly they went that they were called *tlanquacemilhuime*.

And there was a hill called Tzatzitepetl. It is also just so named today. It is said that there the crier mounted. [For] what was required, he mounted there to cry out a proclamation. He could be heard in Anauac. Indeed everywhere was heard what he said, what laws were made. Swiftly was there going forth; they knew what Quetzalcoatl had commanded the people.

And also they were indeed rich. Of no value was food, all our sustenance. It is said that the gourds were each exceedingly huge; some were quite round. And the ears of maize were each indeed like hand grinding stones, very long. They could only be embraced in one's arms. And the palm-tree-like amaranth plants: they could climb them, they could be climbed. And also the varicolored cotton grew: chili-red, yellow, pink, brown, green, blue, verdigris color, dark brown, ripening brown, dark blue, fine yellow, coyote-colored cotton, this. All of these came forth exactly so; they did not dye them.

And there dwelt all [varieties] of birds of precious feather: the lovely cotinga, the resplendent trogon, the troupial, the roseate spoonbill. And all the various birds sang very well; indeed gladdening one they sang. And all the green stones, the gold were not costly. Very much [of this] was kept. And also cacao grew—flowery cacao. In very many places there was chocolate.

And these Tolteca were very rich; they were wealthy. Never were they poor. They lacked nothing in their homes. Never was there famine. The maize rejects they did not need; they only burned them [to heat] the sweat baths with them.

And this Quetzalcoatl also did penances. He bled the calf of his leg to stain thorns with blood. And he bathed at midnight. And he bathed there where his bathing place was, at a place called Xippacoyan

Twelfth Chapter, which telleth how Quetzalcoatl fled, took flight, when he went there to Tlapallan, and of the many things he did on the way.

And still many more portents came upon the Tolteca until Tula was destroyed. And when these were happening, Quetzalcoatl, who already was troubled, who already was saddened, was thereupon minded to go, to abandon his city of Tula.

Thereupon he made ready. It is said that he had everything burned—his house of gold, his house of seashells; and still other Tolteca craft objects which were marvelous achievements, which were costly achievements, he buried, all; he hid all there in difficult places, perhaps inside a mountain or in a canyon.

And also the cacao trees he changed into mesquites. And all the precious birds, the resplendent trogons, the lovely cotingas, the roseate spoonbills, all of them he sent away beforehand. They kept themselves before him; they went toward Anauac.

And when this was done, thereupon he departed; thereupon he followed the road.

Then he came to arrive elsewhere, at Quauhtitlan. A very thick tree stood [there], and it was very tall. He stood by it. Thereupon he called forth for his mirror. Thereupon he looked at himself; he saw himself in the mirror; he said: "Already I am an old man." Then that place he named Ueuequauhtitlan. Thereupon he stoned, he threw many stones at the tree. And as he threw the stones, the stones indeed went into it in various places, were stuck to the old tree in various places. Just the same has it continued to exist; thus is it seen. Beginning at the foot, [the stones] extend rising to its top.

And when Quetzalcoatl followed the road, they went blowing flutes for him.

Once again he came to rest elsewhere. Upon a stone he sat. He supported himself on it with his hands. Thereupon he looked toward Tula, and thereupon he wept. As one sobbing violently did he weep. Two hailstones fell as his tears; over his face did his tears spread; as they dripped they indeed pierced holes in the stone.

Which telleth of the way of life which was observed [in] the *calmecac*, where lived or were instructed the fire priests and the offering priests.

First: All the priests slept there in the *calmecac*.

Second: It was brought about that everyone slept when it was yet dark.

Third: When it was already daytime, those already a little strong then went to seek maguey thorns. As they said, they broke off the maguey thorns.

Fourth: When they were already indeed novice priests of whatever kind, they went forth when it was still dark, or at midnight. They started to go to the forest; they took the wood; they carried on their backs what they called logs which they burned at the *calmecac* all night as the priests kept watch. And if somewhere preparation of mud [for adobes], a wall, agricultural land, a canal were to be undertaken, there was going forth when it was still quite dark; there was going leaving those who were to guard and then those who went to serve the food. They went in a group. None were absent. In good order they passed the whole day.

Fifth: Soon after they ceased working they went to see to their godly obligations, the obligations to the *calmecac*, the doing of penances. When there was still a little sun, or when night had already fallen, it was said they cut maguey spines. When it was quite dark, when it was already deep night, then the priests began, as was said, the placing of the maguey spines. No more than one at a time they went. First they bathed; then they took the shell trumpets and the incense ladles, the bag [which] went full of incense, and they took up pine torches. Thereupon began the placing of the maguey spines. They went naked. Those who performed great penances went perhaps two leagues; maguey spines were placed.

Sixth: When the priests slept, no two lay [together]. All lay by themselves. None were covered together.

Seventh: The food which they ate they prepared together only for themselves, for what they ate was their own. And if anyone gave one his food, not by himself did he eat it.

Eighth: At midnight, when, as was said, night divided in half, everyone arose; they prayed. If one failed to do so because he slept, if one did not awake, then, for this, there was a gathering together. They drew blood from his ears, his breast, his thighs, the calves of his legs. Verily, because of this fear descended.

Ninth: No one at all became proud; no one at all became vain. Well ordered was living. If at times it appeared that one perhaps drank pulque, perhaps was given to women or committed a great [fault], then they went to apprehend him. No mercy was shown. He was burned, or strangled, or burned alive, or shot with arrows. If he sinned only lightly, they drew blood from his ears, his flanks, his thighs with maguey spines or with a [sharpened] bone.

Tenth: The small boys were so educated that if they did nothing of great evil, they then drew blood from their ears or switched them with nettles.

Eleventh: At midnight the principal [priests] went down to the water. They bathed themselves in the water.

Twelfth: When it was a time of fasting, indeed all observed it. Verily when midday arrived, all the small boys ate. But when it was the time of fasting they called Atamalqualo, they tasted nothing at all. Some ate at midnight; they went to eat the next midnight. Some ate at noon; the next time, next day at noon they went to eat. No chili, no salt did they eat. Not, in order to sleep, [did they] even [drink] water. They said the fast was broken if they ate, if they drank, a little bit.

Thirteenth: Most especially was there teaching of good discourse. He who spoke not well, who greeted others not well, they then drew blood from [with maguey spines].

Fourteenth: Especially was there teaching of songs which they called the gods' songs inscribed in books. And especially was there teaching of the count of days, the book of dreams, and the book of years.

Fifteenth: A strict vow of the priests was [that of] chastity, a pure life, that nowhere would they look upon a woman. A strict vow of theirs was [a life of] moderation. No one whatever lied. The priests were very devout. They were very god-fearing.

Enough of this. Here is told what the way of life of the priests was. Yet much is left [unsaid] which requireth to be said. It will be told in another place.

The Huarochiri Manuscript[11]

The tradition about the Yunca is like this. In this community of Checa lived the ones called Colli, building their settlements all over the communal territory. To relate all the Yunca settlements in the whole area would be very laborious.

So in what follows we shall choose only a few of them for our consideration, compiling all their customs, because all the Yunca shared one single way of life.

Paria Caca then established his dwelling on the heights, on the same territory where he had conquered, and began to lay down the rules for his worship.

His law was one and the same law in all the villages.

The law we speak of was this: "We are all of one birth." [This is taken to mean of one family.]

They say he gave a command to one particular person in each village: "Once every year you are to hold a paschal celebration reenacting my life."

He said, "As for their titles, the title of these people will be *huacasa* or *huacsa*." The *huacsa* will dance three times each year, bringing coca in enormous leather bags."

To first become a *huacsa*, people in fact perform a certain ritual.

It's like this: a man of the Caca Sica *ayllu* functions as officiant for these ceremonies. From early times these officiants were only one or two people, and, as for their title, it was *yanca*. [The master is called *yanca*.]

The same title is used in all the villages.

This man observes the course of the sun [That is, the shadow that the wall casts in the sun.] from a wall constructed with perfect alignment.

When the rays of the sun touch this calibrated wall, he [proclaimed] to the people, "Now we must go"; or if they don't, he'd say, "Tomorrow is the time."

Following this command, people go to Paria Caca in order to worship. In the old times they used to go to Paria Caca mountain itself.

But now they go from Checa to a mountain called Ynca Caya [The snowcap of Paria Caca is visible from this mountain.] to worship from there.

[This mountain rises over the ruined buildings of Purum Huasi and abuts on another mountain called Huallquiri.

It's on this mountain that all sorts of people, men and women alike, go to worship.]

People run a race on their way to this mountain, in accordance with the *yanca's* instructions, driving their llama bucks. The strongest ones even shoulder small llamas. They scramble upward, each thinking, "I mean to get to the summit first!" [Which is where Paria Caca can be seen from.]

The first llama to arrive at the mountain top was much loved by Paria Caca.

In the old days Paria Caca himself used to give a name to this llama buck, proclaiming, "Let its name be thus!" [different names each time, of one sort or another, such as Yauri or Yllaca] And as for the first little llama to arrive, the *yanca* would display it and praise it before all eyes, announcing, "The bearer of this llama is very fortunate. Paria Caca loves him."

This time of worship, as we know, is called the Auquisna. [Auquisna 'for our father' or 'creator']

Similarly the worship of Chaupi Namca is called the Chaycasna. [Chaycasna 'for our mother']

But we'll explain the Chaycasna later.

Nowadays the Auquisna season comes in the month of June or close to it. It either occurs close to [Corpus Christi] the great pasch or actually coincides with it.[12]

All the *huacsas,* who might be ten or even twenty, dance on this occasion. This dance is not something their ancestors appropriated.

The *huacsas* reportedly perform this dance with absolutely no interruption. If someone who stops dancing ever happens to die people comment about him, "He died because of the fault he committed."

For that reason, they make little children or any other kind of people carry on the dance. The people from Surco especially prefer to call on the Huayllas to dance in their stead.

If a Huayllas man is married to a native Surco village woman and performs these rituals, the members of that community don't take away his fields or anything else of his, even though he's an outsider. On the contrary, they respect him and help him.

What's more, when Huayllas people who live in Surco come to Sucya Cancha to trade coca, regardless of their standing they bargain, saying, "Give me a little extra, ma'am; I'm a h*uacsa.*"

Nowadays, as we know, people perform this pasch by making it coincide with any of the major Christian paschal rites, and the people from Surco still excel over all the other communities.

On account of this dance, the Catholic priests in their villages exact collections of chickens, maize, and all sorts of other things. The people hand these things over more than cheerfully.

The *huacsas* dance likewise during Chaupi Namcas paschal festival. This paschal festival sometimes comes close to Corpus Christi, and sometimes actually coincides with it. In another chapter [We'll set forth Chaupi Namca's life in a different chapter later on.] we'll record Chaupi Namca's life, where she lived, and how people worshiped her. But now let's return to Paria Caca's story and to all the things people did during the season of his paschal festival.

The story that explains these events is like this. On the eve of the day when they were to arrive at Paria Caca for worship, people whose kin, whether men or women, had died in the course of that year would wail all night long, saying, "Tomorrow we'll go and see our dead by Paria Caca's side!"

They said regarding their deceased of the year, "Tomorrow is the day when we'll deliver them there."

They offered the dead food and even fed them that night, and spread out the ingredients for their rituals. They said,

"Now I deliver them to Paria Caca forever.

They will never come back any more!"

And they worshiped with the sacrifice of a small llama, or, if they had no llamas, they'd bring coca in large skin bags.

As we know, they'd examine this llama's innards. If the signs were favorable, the *yanca* would prophesy, "Everything is well." If not, he'd say, "It's bad. You've incurred a fault. Your dead relative has angered Paria Cacao. Ask forgiveness for this transgression, lest that fault be charged to you as well."

After completing these rituals, the *yancas* carried off the heads and loins of those llamas for themselves, no matter how many thousands there might be, declaring, "This is our fee!"

The *huacsas*, who'd dance on three occasions in any given year, would finish their term on that day. In order to enter a new cycle, when the old dance round was about to come to an end, all the people came to the center in Llacsa Tambo, and the Concha were in the plaza, too, carrying a macaw-wing display or the sort of thing known as *puypu*.

They'd lay these items in the center, on the rock called Llacsa Tambo. After they deposited these things, they stayed there all night long, in the place where a cross now stands, wondering, "Will I be well this year?"

The next day they went to all the villages, including Macacho hill, Chaucalla, and Quimquilla, and remained there until five days were up. At the end of the fifth day, all the *huacsas* who'd collected coca in bags would dance. At daybreak on the same day, in Llacsa Tambo, they used to worship the demon with their llamas or other possessions.

Those who are privy to these customs do the same in all the villages. Nowadays, it's true, some have forgotten these practices. But since it's just a few years since they've had Doctor Francisco de Avila, a good counselor and teacher, it may be that in their hearts they don't really believe. If they had another priest they might return to the old ways.

Some people, although they've become Christians, have done so only out of fear. "I'm afraid the priest or somebody else might find out how bad I've been," they think. Although they say the Rosary, they still carry some pretty *illa* amulets everywhere; although they themselves might not worship these native divinities, they contract some old people to worship in their stead. Lots of people live this way. . . .

As we said earlier, the Concha, too, worship during Paria Caca's season from that other mountain called Huaycho. Their *huacsas* do just the same as the Checa's own do, that is, they dance. Likewise, the Sunni Cancha also worship in the same manner during Paria Caca's season from that mountain called [crossed out in original text].

The residents of Santa those who live in San Juan and all the ones called Chauca Ricma, during Paria Caca's season, reportedly worship from the mountain called Acu Sica, the one we descend on our way to the Apar Huayqui River.

In fact they'd never let anything stop them from performing these rituals.

Some people make this festival coincide with the great pasch, Easter; others set it close to Pentecost.

When it comes to celebrating it, the people in this village would be delighted if the priest were absent from town or went to Limac.

This is a completely true account.

Regarding all these places on mountains for worship of Paria Caca, it was only later on, when the Spaniards had emerged and came to look into it, that they were established.

But, in the old times, they say all these people used to go to Paria Caca mountain itself. All the Yunca people from Colli, Carhuayllo, Ruri Cancho, Latim, Huancho Huaylla, Pariacha, Yanac, Chichima, Mama, and all the other Yunca from that river valley;

Also the Saci who, together with the Pacha Camac come from another river valley and the Caringa and Chilca, and those people who live along the river that flows down from Huaro Cheri, namely, the Caranco and other Yunca groups who inhabit that river region, used to arrive at Mount Paria Caca itself, coming with their *ticti*, their coca, and other ritual gear.

When those who'd come to worship returned from Paria Caca, people in their villages, aware of their impending arrival, used to await them in a gathering to ask, "How is our father Paria Caca?"

"Is he still well?"

"Isn't he angry?"

Then they'd dance full of happiness until the end of the fifth day, or however many days was their custom.

Regarding this worship, it may be that the Yunca don't practice it anymore, or that not all the Yunca do. But they do perform it away from their own places. When they don't do it people speculate, saying,

"It's because of that fault of theirs that the Yunca are becoming extinct."

The Watunna[13]

SERUHE IANADI

There was Kahuña, the Sky Place. The Kahuhana lived there, just like now. They're good, wise people. And they were in the beginning too. They never died. There was no sickness, no evil, no war. The whole world was Sky. No one worked. No one looked for food. Food was always there, ready.

There were no animals, no demons, no clouds, no winds. There was just light. In the highest Sky was Wanadi, just like now. He gave his light to the people, to the Kahuhana. He lit everything down to the very bottom, down to Nono, the Earth. Because of that light, the people were always happy. They had life. They couldn't die. There was no separation between Sky and Earth. Sky had no door like it does now. There was no night, like now. Wanadi is like a sun that never sets. It was always day. The Earth was like a part of the Sky.

The Kahuhana had many houses and villages in Kahuña and they were all filled with light. No one lived on the Earth. There was no one there, nothing, just the Earth and nothing else.

Wanadi said: "I want to make people down there." He sent his messenger, a *damedede*. He was born here to make houses and good people, like in the Sky Place. That *damedede* was Wanadi's spirit. He was the Earth's first Wanadi, made by the other Wanadi who lives in Kahuña. That other Wanadi never came down to the Earth. The one that came was the other's spirit.

Later on, two more *damodede* came here. They were other forms of Wanadi's spirit.

The first Wanadi to come was called Seruhe Ianadi, the Wise. When he came, he brought knowledge, tobacco, the maraca, and the *wiriki*. He smoked and he sang and he made the old people. That was a long time before us, the people of today.

When that spirit was born, he cut his navel-cord and buried the placenta. He didn't know. Now the worms got into the placenta and they wanted to eat it. The placenta rotted. As it rotted, it gave birth to a man, a human creature, ugly and evil and all covered with hair like an animal. It was Kahu. He has different names. They call him Kahushawa and Odosha too. This man was very evil. He was jealous of Wanadi. He wanted to be master of the Earth. Because of him, we suffer now. There's hunger, sickness, and war. He's the father of all the Odoshankomo. Now, because of him, we die.

When that old Wanadi's placenta rotted, Odosha sprang out of the Earth like a spear. He said: "This Earth is mine. Now there's going to be war. I'm going to chase Wanadi out of here."

He misled those people who had just been born. He taught them to kill. There was a man fishing. He had lots of fish. Odosha told them: "If you kill him, you'll have lots of fish."

They killed him. Odosha was happy. Then the people were turned into animals as punishment. Because of Odosha, Seruhe Ianadi couldn't do anything on Earth. He went back to the Sky and left the old people as animals with Odosha. He didn't leave any of Wanadi's people on the Earth though. That was the end of the first people.

The birth of Kahu on that old Earth is a sign to us, the people of today. When a baby is born, we should never bury the placenta. The worms get it. It rots. Another Odosha will come again like in the beginning to hurt the baby, to kill it. Like what happened when Kahu fought against Wanadi for control of the Earth. When a baby is born, we put the placenta in a nest of white ants. It's safe there. The worms can't get it. Okay. Now you can bury the nest of white ants.

That was the story of the old people. That's all.

NADEIUMADI

Later on, the other Wanadi, the one that never left Kahuna, thought: "I want to know what's happening on Earth. I want good people living down there."

So he sent a second Wanadi, a *damodede* called Nadeiumadi. When he came there he thought: "The people are going to die now because Odosha is here. Because of Odosha they're sick. They're dying. But I'm here now. People are going to be born again soon. Through my power, they're going to live again. Death isn't real. It's one of Odosha's tricks. People are going to live now."

The new Wanadi wanted to give a sign, a show of his power. He did it to show us that death isn't real. He sat down. He put his elbows on his knees, his head in his hands. He just sat there in silence, thinking, dreaming, dreaming. He dreamt that a woman was born. It was his mother. She was called Kumariawa. That's the way it happened. That man was thinking and smoking. He was quietly blowing tobacco, dreaming of his mother, Kumariawa. That's the way she was born. He made his own mother. That's the way they tell it. He gave birth to her dreaming, with tobacco smoke, with the song of his maraca, singing and nothing else.

Now Kumariawa stood up and Wanadi thought: "You're going to die." So Wanadi dreamed that he killed his mother. She was born full-grown, big like a woman. She wasn't born like a baby. And right away she died, when he dreamed her death, playing the maraca and singing. It wasn't Odosha who killed her but him himself. He had a lot of power when he thought. When he thought: "Life." Then Kumanawa was born. When he thought: "Death." Then she died. Wanadi made her as a sign of his power, of his wisdom. He knew that that wasn't real. Death was a trick.

The new Wanadi had *Huehanna*. He brought it from Kahuña to make people with. He wanted new people for the Earth. He wanted lots of people. *Huehanna* was like a great ball, huge and hollow, with a thick, heavy shell as hard as stone. It was called *Huehanna*. Inside *Huehanna* you could hear noises. words, songs, laughter, screaming. It was filled with people. You couldn't see them. You could just hear them. Wanadi's unborn people were all in there talking. He brought them down to Earth from Heaven. They were happy. That's why they were singing and dancing and making so much noise before being born. Wanadi wanted *Huehanna* opened on the Earth so its people could spread over it. "They'll die," he thought, "because Odosha is here. He doesn't want them to be. He doesn't want good people. He's going to make them sick. He's going to kill them as soon as they come out. But I'll bring them back to life. They'll get born again and won't die."

Wanadi killed Kumariawa as an example. He did it to bring her back to life again. He wanted to show Odosha his power. He was the master of life, His people can't die. Now when he killed his mother, he thought: "She's dead. She'll come back again soon. She'll live again just as my people will live again. Because Odosha's going to kill them as soon as they come out of *Huehanna*. But I'll make them live again."

After he killed Kumariawa, he went hunting. When he left, he said: "I'm going." He called Kudewa and asked him to help bury the woman. It was the first burial. They buried Kumariawa in the ground. "I'm going," he told Kudewa. "I'm going hunting. I'll be back soon. Guard the grave.

Kumariawa is going to reappear in this spot. When she comes out, it will be a signal for the people to come out of *Huehanna* and live. Watch my mother's body. Don 't let Odosha near it." Now he called his nephew, Iara-karu. "Watch *Huehanna!*" he called out as he left.

Wanadi forgot his *chakara*. That's where he kept his power, his tobacco, his cigarettes. He kept the night in the *chakara* too, because at that time, they didn't know about the night. There was only light on the Earth like in the Heavens. It was all one world, Sky above and daylight here below. When Wanadi got tired, he just opened the *chakara* and stuck his head inside and slept. Hidden sleep, the night, was in there. That's the way he slept. When he got up he closed the *chakara* again and shut the night inside.

Wanadi had warned Iarakuru: "Never play with the *chakara*. It's my power! Be careful! Don't open it. If you do, the night will get out."

When Wanadi left, Kudewa kept guard over Kumariawa. Kudewa kept watching to let out a scream when it began to move, when the body began to rise again. "Call me right away. Shout and I'll come," Wanadi told him when he left.

When the ground began to move, Wanadi was far away. Kudewa saw a hand stick out, Kumariawa's arm. The earth opened. He turned into a parrot and began to shout and scream the warning. When Wanadi heard him, he came running to see what his new mother looked like. He came running to see if the *Huehanna* had burst. As he ran, night fell. All at once, EVERYTHING went dark. Suddenly, the WHOLE world went out and Wanadi was running through the night. "They opened the *chakara*," he thought. "Iarakaru did it." And that's just what happened. Iarakaru was too curious. Someone said to him: "Open it!" It was Odosha. He didn't see him. He just heard him, like in a dream. "Open it!" Odosha said. "You'll learn the secret. It was as if Iarakaru was dreaming. At first he didn't dare. And then he did it. "What's this secret hidden in Wanadi's *chakara*?" he thought. I want to see. I want to smoke and be powerful like Wanadi. I want to meet the night." So he opened the *chakara* to look inside and right away the night burst out. Sky hid itself. The light went out over the Earth.

That's the way darkness came to our world. It was Iarakaru's fault. It didn't exist before that. I didn't see it. But that's the way it's told.

When it burst, he was like a blind man. He couldn't see Sky or Earth. He was terrified. He just started running in the dark, not like a man but like a white monkey. And that's the way he stayed, as punishment. He's the grandfather of all the iarakaru (capuchin monkeys) that exist today. He was the first one. He gave them their form. As soon as they were born, the monkeys took his form. That's why they call them iarakaru. They're all children of that same Iarakaru, the one who let out the night long ago. He was Wanadi's nephew and he was punished. That's the way they tell it.

When Wanadi went hunting, Odosha thought: "That man has power. He wants to make his own people on the earth. He thinks the Earth is his. He thinks he owns everything, that his people are going to be born, that it's always going to be light. He left that woman's body in the ground and he thinks, 'She's dead but she's going to live again. The *Huehanna* will open.' He left guards to warn him when the signal comes. I don't like it. The Earth is mine, not his. I'm not going to let Kumariawa out of her corpse nor the people out of *Huehanna*."

Then Odosha hid. He spoke to Iarakaru as in a dream. He said: "Open the *chakara*!"

He was happy when it was opened. "Now it's dark. The night is mine. No one's going to live. I'm the ruler of the Earth."

He had his own people. They could see and move and do lots of things in the dark. Wanadi's people couldn't see. They couldn't do a thing, just be scared and nothing else. This really made Odosha happy.

Odosha sent a hairy dwarf named Ududi to watch the grave. Ududi told him: "She's coming out!" Odosha heard him and knew what to do. He pissed in a gourd. He gave it to Makako and sent him to the woman's grave. Makako was like a small lizard. He ran with the gourd full of urine. Kumariawa split the Earth and began to rise. The little lizard threw the gourd. Odosha's urine was like a poison, seething with fire. It covered the woman. It scorched her body. The flesh was roasted. The bones fell apart. The parrot kept on screaming and the Earth closed up. "It's done," said Makako when he went back to Odosha.

When Wanadi arrived, he found darkness, ashes, bones, cinders, the monkey gone, the parrot silent, the *chakara* opened. "I can't do anything now," he thought. "There's no flesh, no body. She won't come back to life. There's no light. The Earth isn't mine anymore. The people will all die now."

Then he went to find *Huehanna*. It was still there. Those people were inside there, screaming, shaking with fear. They hadn't been born. They hadn't died. They weren't anything yet, like in the beginning. They couldn't be born. When he burned the woman, Odosha went with Makako to open *Huehanna*, to smash it to pieces, to kill the people about to come out. They found it and started beating it with their clubs, but nothing happened. They couldn't do a thing to it. *Huehanna* was as hard as a stone with that thick shell. They couldn't break it. They just left it there.

Wanadi found *Huehanna*. When he picked it up, he heard the voices inside. It made him sad. "They'll have to wait now," he thought. "I'm going to hide them." He took them to Mount Waruma hidi. He hid *Huehanna* with all the unborn people up in that mountain.

It's waiting there, in peace, since the beginning of the world, and it will stay there till the end. When the night came, Wanadi hid *Huehanna*. The good people inside haven't been born yet. They haven't died either. They're waiting there in Waruma hidi for the end of the world, for the death of Odosha.

Odosha is the ruler of our world, but he's not eternal. He'll die when evil disappears. Then Wanadi will go back to Waruma hidi again. The light from Kahuña will shine once more. We'll see Heaven from here like in the beginning. Wanadi will come looking for *Huehanna*. The good, wise people who couldn't be born in the beginning will finally be born. He'll tell his people that their time has come. In the place called Warumaña, they're waiting. I haven't seen it. But that's what it's called.

Wanadi left the Earth in darkness. He left it to Odosha and went back to Heaven. He put Kumariawa's skull and bones in a palm basket and took them with him. He threw his mother's bones into Lake Akuena and the woman came back to life once again. She's still living there in Heaven now.

I haven't seen her. But that's what they say.

3

Colonial Encounters

Europe and European Perceptions of the New World

The colonization of Latin America began, as every school child knows, with Columbus's first voyage across the Atlantic, in 1492. Columbus's trip was sponsored by Spain's "Catholic monarchs," Ferdinand and Isabella, who funded his three subsequent voyages as well. Religion played a central role in the attitudes, expectations, and hopes of both Columbus and his royal patrons, as it did in the centuries of colonization that followed that first trip across the Atlantic. One of the voyage's primary stated goals was to convert the people of the new world to Roman Catholicism, thereby expanding the church's power and scope. No priests appear to have accompanied Columbus on his first trip, but five joined his second journey in August 1493. The evangelization and conversion of native peoples began in earnest at that point. Although the Catholic Church enjoyed a monopoly on official religious expression and institutions throughout the colonial period in Latin America, the conversion and ongoing religious life of the region's indigenous people remained ambivalent and pluralistic.

Equally conflicted and diverse was the Europe from which Columbus sailed. The same year that Columbus first landed in the Caribbean, Spain's Catholic leaders succeeded in "reconquering" Iberia for Roman Catholicism. The Reconquista expelled all Jews and Muslims from Spain and Portugal, except those who converted to Catholicism. One of the consequences of the Reconquista was that only Spanish Catholics were permitted to travel to the new colonies in the Americas, although there is evidence that some non-Catholics made the voyage quite early in the colonial period.

While the Reconquista marked a high point of sorts for both the Catholic Church and Spain's Catholic monarchs, that success was soon overshadowed by other events in Europe. Perhaps most important, in October 1517, the German monk Martin Luther nailed his ninety-five theses to the church door in Wittenberg, Germany, and thereby launched the Protestant Reformation. Building on centuries of dissatisfaction with corruption and rigidity in the Roman Catholic hierarchy, Luther's movement spread rapidly in many parts of Western and Central Europe. A host of other reformers and reform movements emerged, to challenge not only the Roman Catholic Church's religious monopoly but also many secular power structures. In response, Catholic and secular authorities persecuted religious minorities. Most famous were the trials and executions that made up the Inquisition, although there were many other localized persecutions not only by Catholics but also sometimes by Lutheran and Calvinist authorities, especially of Anabaptists, radical Protestants whose rejection of infant baptism and the pope and refusal to swear allegiance to the state or to take up arms enraged both princes and bishops. Of special import for Latin America, of course, was the Spanish Inquisition, an official set of practices and rules established by Ferdinand and Isabella in 1478 to maintain orthodoxy in Spain and, later, in Spanish colonies in the Americas.

Beyond Protestant movements in Europe, Catholic officials faced a diverse, often heterodox lived religion that did not always reinforce the hierarchy's interests. The dominant religious form in both Spain and Portugal at the dawn of the colonial period was a "folk" Catholicism that emphasized shrines, pilgrimages, and the cult of saints over official institutions, rituals, and doctrines. This was especially true in rural areas, where many people did not have regular contact with clergy but rather participated in local and seasonal festivals and other events. The often informal, lay-driven religiosity of Iberian Catholicism provided the context for the ideas and practices that conquistadores, missionaries, and ordinary immigrants carried to the Americas. The Catholicism that developed in Latin America during the colonial period thus reflected the centrality of pilgrimages, saints' images and days, and seasonal festivals in Iberian religious identity, and was often driven by lay groups such as *cofradías* and *hermandades*, which oversaw the most important rituals and events of popular religious life, including processions, songs and dances, and theatrical performances.[1]

The Conquest

The European conquest of the Americas wrought unprecedented destruction of human lives and cultures and of the natural world. The biggest killer of indigenous people was epidemic disease, including smallpox, which Europeans unknowingly imported. Native Americans, without any immunities, fell to the new diseases in huge numbers, with as much as 90 percent of the indigenous population dying within a few decades in some areas. Forced labor in mines, plantations, and other European enterprises also killed many native people, as did military conflicts.

Native responses included both explicit and subtle forms of resistance to Spanish rule, as well as various strategies of negotiation, accommodation, and escape. Some indigenous people could hide in remote or difficult-to-reach areas, such as Andeans living outside the colonial capital of Cuzco, who maintained their cultural identity and traditions on the margins of colonial society. Women, in particular, preserved indigenous practices and beliefs, often withdrawing from villages under colonial control.[2] Those who lived in the centers of empire, however, were forced to confront the conquistadores. The most famous encounter took place in 1519 between Hernan Cortés, the Spanish captain who led the conquest of Mexico, and the Aztec ruler Montezuma II, and was described in the *History of the Conquest of New Spain,* written by Bernal Díaz de Castillo, a soldier traveling with Cortés. Bernal Díaz's detailed account is an essential resource for historians studying the conquest. Of particular interest are his portrayals of both Spanish and Aztec religiosity. Bernal Díaz firmly believed that the Christian God supported the conquistadores in their exploits and makes frequent reference to divine intervention. During one difficult period, for example, he reflects that "as with God's help we had survived these perilous battles, Our Lord Jesus Christ must be preserving us for some good purpose."[3]

As strong as Díaz's belief in his own cause is his abhorrence of the Aztec "idols" and sacrifices. Like most of the European colonizers, he seems unable to understand indigenous religiosity other than as a perversion of his own faith. Early in his account, for example, he mentions an encounter with a chief and a *papa,* which he defines as "a sort of priest who serves their idols."[4] Like Cortés himself, Díaz found human sacrifice particularly repellent. Even after his imprisonment, Montezuma "never ceased his daily sacrifices of human beings," recalls Díaz. Cortés "did not dare not put a stop to this practice for fear of arousing the city and the *papas* of Huichilobos." On the advice of his captains, Cortés threatened Montezuma that if he did not stop sacrificing to his "false gods," the Spanish would remove the images of Aztec deities from the temple and replace them with images of the Virgin Mary and a cross. Montezuma's response, as Bernal Díaz recounts it, is revealing: "how can you wish to destroy our whole city? Our gods would be enraged against us, and I do not know that they would even spare your lives. I pray to you to be patient for the present, and I will summon all the *papas* and see what they reply." Cortés offered a compromise: he would not remove the Aztec images if Montezuma would provide a space for the Spaniards to erect an altar with an image of the Virgin and a cross. Then, Díaz explains, "in course of time, [Montezuma's] people would see how good and advantageous it was for their souls and for their health, prosperity, and good harvests." After consulting with his *papas*, Montezuma agreed to set up the altar—"at some distance from their accursed idols."[5]

Bernal Díaz shares the almost universal colonial assumption of European supremacy in religion, as in most other matters, and an equally uncritical rejection of indigenous worldviews and practices. These assumptions justified the destruction of "accursed idols," the burning of texts, and often violent efforts to suppress rituals and dismantle indigenous religious institutions. Active struggles against native religion were reinforced by the physical toll of disease, war, and forced labor, which killed such large numbers that survivors were often hard pressed to conduct active cultural and religious lives. Still, it is important to note that many native practices, organizations, and ideas survived, especially in areas farther from colonial centers of power.

In addition to the human costs, wholesale destruction of the natural world followed upon the European conquest. Much of the damage was done not only by the immediate effects of the conquest but, more momentously, by the importation of European attitudes toward nature. The Europe of the colonizers, as environmental writer Kirkpatrick Sale argues, "was estranged from its natural environment and had for several thousand years been engaged in depleting and destroying the lands and water it depended on, and justifying that with one or another creed or conviction."[6] When Iberian and later English and French settlers moved to the Americas, they brought with them destructive attitudes and technologies. They also brought European animals and plants that wreaked much the same havoc on New World ecosystems as European diseases did on Native American people.

The Europeans' cultural and ecological destruction of the New World sometimes stemmed from ignorance about the consequences of their actions, but it also emerged from the complex feelings of fear and awe engendered by the physical reality of the Americas. The conquistadores encountered a new world that seemed, to many, utterly distinct from the places they knew—another world (*otro mundo*), as Columbus himself put it. The evaluations and descriptions of this other world were infused with religious assumptions, fears, and hopes. The New World was a paradise to some visitors. To others, it seemed a hell, its human and nonhuman inhabitants monsters.[7]

The Catholic Church played a central role in the conquest and its negative consequences. As one study of colonial church-state relations summarizes, "The church functioned as a political and economic institution and as the social and intellectual catalyst of conquest and colonization in Hispanic America." The Roman Catholic Church was not simply a religious institution but also "an instrument of conquest, colonization, and governance of native peoples and colonists in the new world."[8] Church officials, missionaries, and other pastoral agents helped bolster the colonial project not only religiously but also politically and economically. As both the crown and the church faced challenges in Europe, Vatican officials found the Spanish monarchs Ferdinand and Isabella vital allies in the battle to maintain religious and social power. The crown, in turn, found the church an essential part of its effort to maintain Spain's international leadership in the face of challenges from other European colonial powers such as France, Holland, and Great Britain. The European discovery and conquest of the Americas provided new opportunities for political and religious authorities alike to consolidate and extend their power. Both the Vatican and the crown sought to ensure the supremacy of Roman Catholic orthodoxy in the new colonies, using a range of means, including strict rules about emigration and the establishment of the Inquisition in the New World, as well as active missionary efforts, with priests present in the Americas from 1493 on.

The relations between the Catholic monarchs and the Catholic Church were mutually reinforcing but often tense during the early colonial period. Both the crown and the Vatican faced internal and external challenges, and both looked to the newly discovered lands across the Atlantic to bolster their literal and metaphorical fortunes. The negotiations between the two powers resulted in the Royal Patronage, or Patronato Real, a series of public documents in which the pope "gave" the Americas to Spain and Portuguese monarchs. In turn, papal bulls gave the crown power over the establishment of churches, cathedrals, convents, hospitals, and dioceses in the colonies. The Patronato was, in part, a joint effort to claim the Americas for Catholic monarchs, but it also reflected a struggle between church and state. The most important statements comprising the Patronato Real were, first, Pope Alexander VI's bull of May 4, 1493, giving the Spanish crown title over the Indies and responsibility for converting the population. Alexander issued another bull on November 16, 1501, that established the crown's right to collect taxes, from which it was to provide revenues for churches and missions. On July 28, 1508, Alexander's successor, Julius II, gave the crown universal patronage over the church in the Indies.

The summary result of these proclamations was that the Spanish crown gained practical power over ecclesial appointments, while local colonial authorities handled lesser appointments—in short, effective state domination of the church—the price, popes decided, that they had to pay for a religious monopoly in the New World. While the Patronato bolstered the Catholic Church's singular position in the New World, ultimately it probably gave the crown more power over ecclesial affairs than vice-versa, insofar as it made the church structurally—as well as economically—dependent upon the Spanish rulers.

Treatment of Native Peoples

The European colonization of the New World entailed a complex, long, and uneven process of conquering, or at least containing, many of the diverse human cultures that occupied the Americas. Efforts to control native people, on the one hand, and to monitor the conquistadores' treatment of them, on the other, preoccupied the Spanish authorities for many decades, as revealed in the Spanish ordinances on "pacification" reproduced below. The pacification, domination, and control of native people were necessary in order for Spaniards to use and profit from their land. The mechanism by which the colonial authorities strove to maintain control was the *encomienda* system, in which Spanish emigrants—soldiers, nobles, sometimes even priests—were named trustees of parcels of land, along with their indigenous inhabitants. Although technically the native peoples retained ownership of the land, in practice the *encomendero* possessed both the natives and their land, and abuses were frequent.

The church played a crucial role in the pacification of native people and the expropriation and use of their land. The Spanish understood the "Christianization" of the region as a key part of their mission, which historians have summarized, not inaccurately, as the pursuit of "God, glory, and gold," not necessarily in that order. Often, Christianity served the cause of suppressing the native populations of the Americas (and, later, slaves brought from Africa). At many points in the colonial period and beyond, however, religious values, symbols, and groups were also used in political resistance.

While many missionaries participated in and justified the conquest, some sought to protect native peoples from the conquest, or at least from its excesses. The best known was Bartolomé de las Casas, a Spaniard who sailed on Columbus's third voyage (1498) and who in 1510 became the first priest ordained in the Americas. After witnessing the cruelty of Spanish soldiers and landowners in Hispaniola (Cuba), las Casas became the best-known defender of "the Indians," arguing to the monarchs and others in power that the conquest was cruelly un-Christian. In 1550, King Carlos V of Spain arranged a debate, held in Valladolid, Spain, between las Casas and the Spanish scholar Juan Ginés de Sepúlveda, who argued on behalf of forceful, even violent conquest and evangelization of natives. Las Casas contended, in contrast, that indigenous people had souls and should be converted to Christianity by peaceful means. Las Casas insisted that a live Indian, though an infidel, was preferable to a dead Indian, though a Christian—reversing the common colonial contention that conversion to Christianity was necessary even if it required force, the view supported by Sepúlveda. Las Casas summarized his arguments against Sepúlveda in the preface to his classic *In Defense of the Indians*, reproduced below. The Valladolid debates did not result in any definitive conclusion; the *encomienda* system and other abuses that las Casas attacked continued throughout the colonial era, though perhaps less intensely than in the early decades.

Las Casas was the most famous but far from the only priest to protest these abuses. Nicaragua's Bishop Antonio Valdivieso, another defender of native rights, was killed in 1550 by agents of the Spanish crown for his defense of the native people. Valdivieso is celebrated today as the first popular martyr of Latin American Christianity. A century later, the Portuguese Jesuit Antonio Vieira protested the exploitation of Native Americans in terms even more emphatic and fiery than las Casas. In a sermon delivered for Lent, 1653, in the Brazilian city of Maranhão, he began, "Christians, nobles, and people of Maranhão: Do you know what God wants of you during this Lent? That you break the chains of injustice and let free those whom you have captive and oppressed." Addressing the aversion to physical labor of many European colonists, Vieira continued, "You, your wives, your sons, all of us are able to sustain ourselves with our own labor. It is better to live from your own sweat than from the blood of others."[9]

Evangelization and Conversion

As European and indigenous cultures met, both were transformed in powerful, sometimes subtle ways. A range of syncretic cultural forms developed, including what is usually called "popular" Catholicism, in which indigenous deities, practices, and landscapes interacted with the Trinity, Mary, and countless saints as well as Catholic sacramental practices. The best known example of this syncretism is the Virgin of Guadalupe. The dark-skinned Virgin appeared to an Aztec man, Juan Diego Cuauhtlatoatzin, on the 9th of December, 1531, at Tepeyac, a hill near Mexico City dedicated to the indigenous goddess Tonantzín. The Virgin asked that a shrine be built at the place in her honor. Juan Diego took her request to Bishop Juan de Zumárraga, who refused to believe him and asked for proof of the apparition. Days later, Juan Diego returned to the site and was instructed by the Virgin to pick up roses, which miraculously appeared off season amid the rocky terrain, and take them in his rough cloak (*tilma*) to the bishop. As Juan Diego unfolded his mantle in front of the bishop, the iridescent image of the Virgin appeared impressed on the tissue. To this day, the picture on Juan Diego's *tilma* is kept at the basilica that was eventually erected in the Virgin of Guadalupe's honor.

It is hard to overstate the importance of the Marian apparition at Tepeyac. It marked the emergence of a Latin American Catholicism with its own characteristics but in communion, albeit a tense one, with European Catholicism. The fact that the Virgin did not appear to a European priest or bishop but to an indigenous person, just a few years after the obliteration of his culture and religion, had enormous consequences for the process of evangelization, providing a way for the natives to become Christian without losing their dignity and some of the richness of their culture. Guadalupe may be Mexico's paramount national symbol; "La Lupita" or "La Morenita," as she is popularly known, is the country's patroness and figures prominently throughout the country's history as a symbol of collective identity and resistance. However, she also lies at the heart of Latin American Catholicism, as is reflected by the fact that to-day, the site is the region's premier pilgrimage center. Pope John Paul II made it the centerpiece of his "new evangelization" project and, in 1999, declared her "Empress of the Americas," while canonizing Juan Diego in 2002.

The Virgin of Guadalupe simultaneously embodies *mestizaje*, the mix-ing of peoples, and cultural hybridity, the coming together of cultures to give rise to new identities and practices. This creative, power-laden tran-sculturation, which would later be enriched by the contributions of Afri-can slaves and their descendants, continues to evolve but remains strongly marked by the colonial context in which it first emerged. This interplay between continuity and rupture is evident in the ongoing appropriations and recastings of Iberian Catholic saints and the rituals associated with them.

Evangelization proceeded in an uneven, varied, and often ineffectual way in the European colonies. Many missionaries did not speak native languages or understand indigenous cultures, which meant that their efforts at religious education and conversion were superficial, at best. The huge differences between indigenous and Catholic worldviews made it difficult for native converts to understand official doctrine. For example, people raised in cultures that recognize a multiplicity of spirits or deities did not always find the complex Christian doctrine of Trinitarian monotheism easy to grasp. In many instances, superfi-cial similarities between European and indigenous images or practices complicated the task of conversion by leading missionaries, converts, or both to misunderstand the other's worldview and convictions. In the Andes, for example, Spanish missionaries were very interested in the Inkan institution of the *acllawasi* (or *acllahuasi*), houses where the *acllas*, young women consecrated as wives of the Sun, or Inti, lived to-gether under the supervision of older female authorities and dedicated themselves to religious duties. To Iberian observers, the *acllawasis* ap-peared much like Catholic convents.[10] (In fact, a number of colonial convents were built on the sites of *acllawasis*, just as cathedrals were often constructed on the sites of indigenous temples and pyramids.) Events in Europe also complicated the evangelization process. For ex-ample, as theologian Orlando Espín points out, missionary teachings often emphasized God the Father and Christ over the third member of the Trinity, at least partly out of fear of the *alumbrado* heresy in Spain, which stressed the Holy Spirit.[11]

Syncretism, Heterodoxy, and Cultural Conflicts in the Colonial Period

Throughout the colonial period, religious diversity and heterodoxy led to fears of witchcraft, devil worship, and other "non-Christian" practices. One well-documented case, mentioned in the previous chapter, concerned the "recurrent idolatry" of residents of the parish of Gonzalo de Balsalobre, a priest in Oaxaca. In a letter written in 1653 (and reprinted below), Balsalobre wrote to his bishop complaining that his parishioners continued many preconversion religious rituals despite his exhortations and in some cases punishment.

The historical context for Balsalobre's complaints, and more importantly for the practices of his parishioners, was the ongoing conflict between Spanish political and religious authorities, on the one hand, and native Oaxacans, on the other. At stake in these conflicts, as David Tavarez argues, was "the convergence of local autonomy aspirations, the honorable defense of local forms of identity, and the preservation of ancestral devotion."[12] Central to these debates over native autonomy were the proper spaces and forms in which traditional religion was practiced. Confrontations over popular religion in Oaxaca and other areas of New Spain (Mexico and Central America) escalated in the second half of the seventeenth century and included violent attacks on friars and churches and on local residents who appeared too closely allied with them.

Indigenous Americans were not the only group to cause problems for Spanish religious authorities in the colonies. New World missionaries feared, and sometimes encountered, some of the same religious irregularities that preoccupied church authorities in the Old World, including idolatry and witchcraft, as well as more mundane offenses such as bigamy and blasphemy. Accusations of heresy, the most serious offense, were relatively rare in the records of the Spanish Inquisition in the Americas. Most missionaries were more concerned with insincere or partial conversions by the so-called new Christians. This category encompassed recent converts to Catholicism, often Jews or Muslims who faced an untenable choice after the "reconquest" of Iberia and expulsion of non-Catholics in 1492. Iberian (Sephardic) Jews who converted, or appeared to convert, to Catholicism were called "new Christians," *conversos* (converts), *marranos*, or "crypto Jews" (converts to Catholicism who continued to practice Judaism).

Although non-Catholics were prohibited from settling in the Iberian colonies, people of Jewish origin traveled to the Americas beginning with

Columbus's first voyage. The early Jewish immigrants settled throughout the region, with larger and more stable communities in areas under Dutch and English control, including Suriname, Curaçao, Jamaica, and Barbados. Jewish settlements also existed in Spanish and Portuguese colonies, including Brazil, Cuba, and Mexico, although they were strongly discouraged under the watchful eye of the Inquisition. By the mid-sixteenth century, however, Jews in the Americas were connected to a self-governed "nation" (*La Nación*), an imagined transatlantic community bonded by diasporic memory and sustained by a myriad of mercantile and religious networks and flows linking Iberia, Amsterdam, North Africa, Jerusalem, and the New World. In an article partially reprinted here, Nathan Wachtel describes the dynamics of cultural hybridization that gave rise to a distinctive "marrano religiosity." Such a religiosity would later come into conflict with the processes of re-Judaization that accompanied the rise of *La Nación*. He concludes that, through this experimentation and conflict, "New Christians contributed considerably to the emergence of modernity in the Western Hemisphere, not only in the economic arena, but also in that of religious and intellectual history."

Just as ecclesial authorities had fears and worries regarding the correctness of lay people's beliefs and practices, many residents of colonial Latin American societies had concerns, and sometimes harsh criticisms, regarding the church. One frequent issue was the less than pious behavior of many priests, as the Peruvian mestizo chronicler Felipe Guaman Poma de Ayala describes below.

The abuses committed by priests contributed to scholarly and popular portrayals of indigenous people primarily as victims of Spanish brutality and ethnocentrism. Without downplaying the destructive aspects of the conquest, contemporary scholarship emphasizes the creative adaptations and often opposition to colonial rule that emerged in many indigenous communities. Religious ideas, symbols, and rituals were central to this resistance. Both the maintenance of precolonial religious forms and the creation of syncretic practices offered opportunities for critique and resistance. A number of scholars have described diverse ways in which natives and mestizos adapted preconquest rituals and practices in complex, creative, and often oppositional responses to colonization.

A fascinating example of this adaptation and subtle resistance is the first known extant script of a play in any Native American language. The play, called *Miércoles Santo* (Holy Wednesday), was translated into Nahuatl from a Spanish play, *The Beacon of Our Salvation*. The original was written by a Spanish bookseller, Ausías Izquierdo Zebrero, in the early 1580s. Izquierdo's play, which dramatized Jesus' conversation with the Virgin Mary prior to his arrest and crucifixion, was intended as part of Holy Week celebrations, which were central to popular Catholicism in colonial Iberia. The Spanish text was carried to New Spain, probably by a Franciscan missionary, and translated into Nahuatl by an unknown scholar, who made a number of changes and additions to the original. The Nahuatl text was collected by a Franciscan friar around 1591, but otherwise we have no information about its author, source, or performance history. Such anonymity was a common fate for popular texts, and especially for dramatic scripts. Although theater was a common genre in the early colonial period, very few scripts remain, which leads historian Louise Burkhart, translator of *Miércoles Santo*, to conclude that scripts must often have been passed from hand to hand, used, and then discarded. As Burkhart notes, the original play was part of Spanish domination of the indigenous people. However, "once it was adapted by its native interpreter, it was rendered culturally ambivalent. . . . Its alterations and elaborations, by revealing what the Nahua author accepted and what he saw as inadequate or inappropriate for his purposes, constitute a cultural critique of the Spanish model, and through it of Spanish culture and Christianity more generally."[13]

Miércoles Santo is an especially illuminating text because it reverses the usual order: instead of a Spanish missionary translating—and in the process revising—indigenous texts (as in the *Florentine Codex, Popol Vuh, Book of Chilam Balam,* and the *Huarochiri Manuscript*), the play is an indigenous reading of a European Christian text. Its recasting of the Christian passion story aims to accommodate old myths, especially regarding ancestors. It conflates "indigenous and Christian pasts," as Burkhart notes, an effort made as well by other indigenous redactors, including Guaman Poma, who drew analogies between Old Testament persons and the Andean culture of his time. A good example of this conflation in *Miércoles Santo* is its narrative of Christ's passage into hell to rescue "his precious ones" from non-Christian deities. Jesus' descent, Burkhart points out, echoes indigenous tales of Quetzalcoatl's journey to the underworld and transformation into the morning star.[14]

The play not only connects indigenous and Christian religious themes but also integrates the ritual forms of the two traditions. Religious plays, including those performed during Holy Week, such as *Miércoles Santo,* were often organized by *cofradías* (brotherhoods), usually led by native officials. Such public rituals were central both to Spanish popular Catholicism and to indigenous religious life before and after the conquest. Another fascinating example of a hybrid colonial ritual is the Corpus Christi festival held in the Andes and described by art historian Carolyn Dean in her book *Inka Bodies and the Body of Christ*. The Catholic festival of Corpus Christi, important in medieval Spain, celebrates the body of Christ transubstantiated in the wafer of the eucharistic host. Dean argues that native Andeans used Corpus Christi to reinterpret and resist the culture of the colonizers, incorporating precolonial practices and even forbidden indigenous *wak'as* (sacred places and things) into Corpus Christi events. The Spanish tried to crush such "idolatrous" practices but faced inevitable shortcomings in their abilities both to understand and to control their colonial subjects. One way in which they failed, Dean points out, was in misreading or ignoring the important distinctions within native society. Despite Spanish attempts to blur ethnic distinctions, "Colonial-period Andeans did not see the world as composed of *indios* in opposition to *españoles*."[15] Inka nobles (*caciques*) continued to understand themselves as such and to make use of Corpus Christi to express and reinforce their elite position vis-à-vis other Andeans as well as their role as mediators between Andean and Hispanic culture.

In Dean's reading, Corpus Christi contains diverse elements—Spanish and Andean, Christian and "pagan," assimilation and resistance—that did not absorb or erase each other. Similarly, many religious practices and events of the colonial period reflected native efforts to construct distinctive identities despite colonial efforts at domination. They were not, as Dean points out, simply shaped by the tools of the dominant culture; they used those tools themselves, in creative although inevitably limited ways.[16] The same can be said for people of African descent in the Americas, for whom religion also served as a powerful, yet ambivalent, force for cultural identity and resistance to oppression.

CHAPTER 3 DOCUMENTS

"Royal Ordinances on Pacification, 1573"[1]

. . . Discoveries are not to be called conquests. Since we wish them to be carried out peacefully and charitably, we do not want the use of the term "conquest" to offer any excuse for the employment of force or the causing of injury to the Indians.

After a town has been laid out and its buildings constructed, but not before, the government and settlers are to attempt peacefully to win all the natives of the region over to the Holy Church and obedience to our rule. In this they are to show great diligence and holy zeal and to use the best means at their disposal, including the following:

They are to gather information about the various tribes, languages, and divisions of the Indians in the province and about the lords whom they obey. They are to seek friendship with them through trade and barter, showing them great love and tenderness and giving them objects to which they will take a liking. Without displaying any greed for the possessions of the Indians, they are to establish friendship and cooperation with the lords and nobles who seem most likely to be of assistance in the pacification of the land.

Once peace and amity with the Indians have been assured, the Spaniards will try to bring them together in one spot. Then the preachers, with as much solemnity as possible, will start to teach our Holy Faith to those who wish to be instructed in it, using prudence and discretion and the gentlest methods possible. Accordingly, they are not to begin by rebuking the Indians for their vices and idolatry, nor by taking away their women and idols, so that they will not be shocked and form an aversion to Christian doctrine. Instead, it should be taught to them first, and after they have been instructed in it, they should be persuaded to give up of their own free will those things that are contrary to our Holy Catholic Faith and evangelical doctrine.

The Indians should be brought to an understanding of the position and authority which God has given us and of our zeal in serving Him by bringing to His Holy Catholic Faith all the natives of the Western Indies.

They should also learn of the fleets and armies that we have sent and still send for this purpose, as well as of the many provinces and nations that have rendered us obedience and of the many benefits which they have received and are receiving as a result, especially that we have sent ecclesiastics who could have taught them the Christian doctrine and faith by which they could be saved. Moreover, we have established justice in such a way that no one may aggravate another. We have maintained the peace so that there are no killings, or sacrifices, as was the custom in some parts. We have made it possible for the Indians to go safely by all roads and to peacefully carry on their civil pursuits. We have taught them good habits and the custom of wearing clothes and shoes. We have freed them from burdens and servitude; we have made known to them the use of bread, wine, oil, and many other foods, woollen cloth, silk, linen, horses, cows, tools, arms, and many other things from Spain; we have instructed them in crafts by which they live excellently. All these advantages will those Indians enjoy who embrace our Holy Faith and render obedience to us.

Even if the Indians are willing to receive the faith and the preachers in peace, the latter are to approach their villages with prudence and with precautions for their own safety. In this manner if the Indians should prove unruly, they will not be inclined to show disrespect to the preachers; otherwise, the guilty persons would have to be punished, causing great damage to the work of pacification and conversion. Although the preachers should keep this in mind when they visit the Indian settlements, it should be concealed from the natives so that they will not feel any anxiety. Difficulties may be avoided if the children of the caciques and nobles are brought to the Spanish settlements and are kept there as hostages under the pretext of entertaining them and teaching them to wear clothes. By means such as these is conversion to be undertaken in all the Indian communities which wish to receive the preachers in peace.

In areas where the Indians refuse to accept Christian doctrine peacefully, the following procedure may be used. An arrangement should be made with the principal lord who is a proponent of peace so that he will invite the belligerent Indians to his territory on one pretext or another. On this occasion, the preachers, together with some Spaniards and friendly Indians, should be hidden nearby. At the opportune moment they should disclose themselves and begin teaching the faith with the aid of interpreters. In order that the Indians may hear the faith with greater awe and reverence, the preachers should carry the Cross in their hands and should be wearing at least albs and stoles; the Christians are also to be told to listen to the preaching with great respect and veneration, so that by their example the non-believers will be induced to accept instruction. If it seems advisable, the preachers may attract the attention of the non-believers by using music and singers, thereby encouraging them to join in. If the Indians seem inclined to be peaceful and request the preachers to go to their territory, the latter should do so, taking the precautions previously described. They should ask for their children under the pretext of teaching them and keep them as hostages; they should also persuade them to build churches where they can teach so that they may be safer. By these and other ways are the Indians to be pacified and indoctrinated, but in no way are they to be harmed, for all we seek is their welfare and their conversion.

Once the region has been pacified and the Indian lords and subjects have tendered us their fealty, the Governor, with their consent, is to distribute the land among the settlers who are to take charge of the natives in their parcels, defending and protecting them and providing them with clerics to teach them Christian doctrine and administer the sacraments. They should also teach them to live in an orderly fashion and fulfill all the obligations of encomenderos as set forth in the clauses dealing with this subject.

The Indians who offer us obedience and are distributed among Spaniards are to be persuaded to acknowledge our sovereignty over the Indies. They are to give us tributes of local produce in moderate amounts, which are to be turned over to their Spanish encomenderos so that the latter may fulfill their obligations, reserving to us the tribute of the principal villages and the seaports, as well as an amount adequate to pay the salaries of our officials. If it appears that the pacification of the natives will be accomplished more easily by temporarily exempting them from tribute payments or by granting them other privileges, this should be done; and whatever is promised should be carried out. . . .

"Preface" to *In Defense of the Indians*[2]   BARTOLOMÉ DE LAS CASAS

. . . Therefore when Sepulveda, by word or in his published works, teaches that campaigns against the Indians are lawful, what does he do except encourage oppressors and provide an opportunity for as many crimes and lamentable evils as these [men] commit, more than anyone would find it possible to believe? In the meantime, with most certain harm to his own soul, he is the reason why countless human beings, suffering brutal massacres, perish forever, that is, men who, through the inhuman brutality of the Spaniards, breathe their last before they hear the word of God, [or] are fed by Christ's gentle doctrine, or are strengthened by the Christian sacraments. What more horrible or unjust occurrence can be imagined than this?

Therefore, if Sepulveda's opinion (that campaigns against the Indians are lawful) is approved, the most holy faith of Christ, to the reproach of the name Christian, will be hateful and detestable to all the peoples of that world to whom the word will come of the inhuman crimes that the Spaniards inflict on that unhappy race so that neither in our lifetime nor in the future will they want to accept our faith under any condition, for they see that its first heralds are not pastors but plunderers, not fathers but tyrants, and that those who profess it are ungodly, cruel, and without pity in their merciless savagery. Furthermore, since Sepulveda's book is polished, painstaking, persuasive, and carefully built up throughout with many tricky kinds of argument, it will permanently deceive these thieves, these enemies of the human race, so that they will never come to their senses nor, admitting their crimes, flee to the mercy of God, who, in his unutterable love, is perhaps calling them to penance, nor will they implore his help. Under the pretext of religion, Sepulveda excuses the criminal wickedness of these men, which carries with it all the evils to be found anywhere in the lives of mortal men. He praises with lofty language these plunderers who loot with utmost savagery, and he commends their warlike virtue.

Finally, it is intolerable that a man to whom has been entrusted the duty of writing the imperial history should publish a destructive error that is in total disagreement with the words of the gospel and the meekness and kindness of which all Christ's teaching is redolent and which the Church, imitating its master, exercises toward those who do not know Christ. For men of the future will, with good reason, decide that a man who has gone wrong so disgracefully in a matter so clear has taken no account of the truth when writing history, a fact that, no matter how learnedly and gracefully that history will have been written, will tarnish the most celebrated victories of the Emperor.

Therefore I considered the many misfortunes, the great harvest of evils so deserving of rebuke, and the severest punishment which will arise from his teaching: offense against God, ill repute and hatred for our most holy religion, irreparable damage, the loss of so many believing souls, and the loss of the right of the kings of Spain to the empire of the New World. I considered also that these opinions of his will spread through all the nations of the world the savage and firmly rooted practice of seizing what belongs to others and increasing one's property by shedding human blood (an evil reproach under which the Spanish people have labored for so long), which, Sepulveda claims, are for the power and glory of Spain. I could not contain myself. Mindful that I am a Christian, a religious, a bishop, a Spaniard, and a subiect of the King of Spain, I cannot but unsheathe the sword of my pen for the defense of the truth, the honer of God's house, and the spreading of the revered gospel of Our Lord Jesus Christ so that, according to the measure of the grace given to me, I might wipe the stain from the Christian name, take away the obstacles and stumbling blocks hindering the spread of belief in the gospel, and proclaim the truth which I have vowed in baptism, have learned in the religious life, and finally, however unworthy, have professed when consecrated bishop. For by all these titles I am bound to set myself up as a wall against the wicked for the defense of a completely innocent people, soon to be grafted onto the true house of Israel, whom the ravening wolves unceasingly pursue. I am also obliged to block the road along which so many thousands of men are lured to their eternal destruction and to defend with my life my sheep, whom I promised by a solemn oath to protect against every wolf, ecclesiastical or lay, who breaks into my sheepfold.

Finally, I want to set forth the true right of my prince, that is, the title by which he may possess the New World, and to hide *[sic]* the frightful and disgraceful crimes that my own people, the Spaniards, have inflicted in violation of justice and right during these last few years on the Indians, who have been ruined by terrible butchery, and to wash away the shame brought upon that name among all the nations.

"An Account of the Idolatries, Superstitions and Abuses in General of the Natives of the Bishopric of Oaxaca"[3]

Most Illustrious and Reverend Sir:

Moved by reverence for God Our Lord, and zealously concerned by the slight satisfaction which the natives of the kingdom give generally in things of the Faith, and to fulfill the obligations of my office, I have for some time had strong doubts regarding my parishioners and many of the natives of this bishopric. Although in public, whether forced by Ministers of the Doctrine, whether from habit, or whether to palliate the disobedience of their repeated and perfidious idolatries and superstitions that have continued from heathen times until now—with loss of many souls that have died and are dying disobedient and impenitent in that detestable crime, into which they are born, for they have inherited it from parents to children to grandchildren, by succession from one to the other (except that die in the state of innocence preserved in Baptismal grace) they perform acts suggestive of true faith and pretend to appear as true Christians.

And by the experience that I have acquired from communication with them during *twenty-two* years as Minister of the Doctrine, desiring with tireless care by all roads to set them upon that of the State of Blessedness, I have always found them inwardly very far removed from it, although outwardly they show the contrary. And living among them with this sorrow and affliction, motivated by the causes referred to, Our Lord permitted that the falsity of their simulated faith commence to show itself in a case of relapse that I prosecuted on the twenty-third of December of the past year, fifty-three, against Diego Luis, elder and teacher of these same natives and a native of a barrio under the jurisdiction of my aforementioned district, whom a little more than nineteen years ago I punished for these same transgressions.

This and other teachers who are there, and who are called in the common language "wise men" and have continually taught those errors that they held during their heathenism, for which purpose they have had books and handwritten notebooks of which they avail themselves for this doctrine; and in them [are prescribed] the customs of and the teaching about thirteen gods, with names of men and women, to whom they attribute various effects, such as the ruling of their year, which consists of two hundred and sixty days; and these are divided into thirteen months, and each month is attributed to one of these gods who governs it according to the conditions of the said year, which is also divided into four seasons, or "lightnings"; and each one of these "lightnings" consists of sixty-five days, which together make up the year.

From these [books], with sorceries, they take their different magical answers and prognostications; such as for all kinds of hunting, and for any fishing; for harvest of maize, chile, and cochineal; for any sickness and for the superstitious medicine with which cures must be effected; and in order to ward off hardship and death, that these will not come to their houses; for success in pregnancy and childbirth among their wives, and that their children will prosper; for [the interpretation of] the songs of birds and animals that to them are auguries; for dreams and their explanation, and for the outcome of one thing or another; and in order to counteract the omens which are predicted for them.

Finally, for any thing which they need they apply to one of these wise men or teachers, who, casting lots with thirteen grains of maize in honor of the aforementioned thirteen gods, teaches them to make horrendous idolatries and sacrifices to the Devil, of small dogs, of native and cocks, beheading them and sprinkling with their blood thirteen pieces of copal, or native incense, and burning it and offering it in sacrifice to the god of whom they expect the remedy for the affliction which they hope he can set right; for which purpose they make fasts of twenty-four hours, in the manner of the Jews, especially like the fast of Queen Esther, mixing these with many superstitious rites and ceremonies.

And I specify this particularly: on collecting the first ears of green maize from their fields, on the day indicated by the teacher of these rites, they sacrifice a black native hen, sprinkling with its blood thirteen pieces of copal in memory of their thirteen gods, and burning this copal, and with the rest of the blood sprinkling the patio of the house.

This they offer to the god of maize and all food, called in their language *Locucuy*, in thanksgiving for the good harvest that they have had; and on offering it they say certain words in a very low voice as when they pray. And they do the same on cutting the first chile, offering the sacrifice to the god of lightning called *Lociyo*, in the manner described above.

And on planting the nopal cactus, or on gathering the cochineal, they sacrifice a white native hen to the god whom they call *Coqueelaa*, and they say he watches over it [the cochineal]. And for the hunting of deer and wild animals [they make this sacrifice] to the god of the hunters called *Niyohua*, or in the event of not succeeding in the hunt through the intervention of this god, they make a second sacrifice a second time with penance for three days and a fast of twenty-four hours.

For the same purpose [they sacrifice] to *Nocana* [god] of their ancestors. In pregnancies and childbirths, [they sacrifice] to the goddess *Nohuichana*, and to this same [goddess] on fishing for trout; to her they burn copal and light candles at the edge of the fishing hole at the river, for success in fishing.

And [they sacrifice] to the aforementioned goddess about the alms that they bring to the church. For sicknesses and to cure them [they sacrifice] to the gods of those things, who they say are called *Lera Acuece, Lera acueca*. To the god thirteen called *Lete acquichino*, and to the god of the sorcerers whom they call *Lexee*, [they sacrifice] for dreams and auguries and their interpretations. To the god *Nonachi* [they sacrifice] for several different kinds of happenings.

[They sacrifice] to the god of hell, invoked by them with three attributes: namely, *Coqueetaa*, the great and supreme Lord; *Leta ahuila*, the god of hell, and *Coqueehila*, the lord of hell. And to another goddess from that place, who they say is his wife, commonly called *Xonaxihuilia*, they make sacrifices for the dead, and to ward off sickness and death, that these will not come to their houses. This is done in the following way:

When a person expires, they wash the body and head with cold water; and if it is a woman they comb the hair and tie it with a white cord of cotton, and they shroud her with the newest clothes that they have; they put on the body two or three pairs of skirts and *huipils*, more or less, depending upon the wealth of each one, and over this they usually put an ordinary shroud, placing inside of it a number of small stones tied in a cloth, in memory of the sacrifices that had been made in order to cure this dead person, or [in memory] of the superstitious remedies that the wise men applied to them, to no avail.

Before or after the burial, they again consult the wise men, or one of them, about this death; and the latter, casting lots with thirteen grains of maize in honor of their thirteen gods, orders them to do that penance which they have to do; and the usual thing is that, for nine days if the dead person is a male, or for eight days if it is a woman, they do not wear clean clothes, nor take anything in their hands, nor give or receive anything by hand, nor sleep with women; and they must bathe at dawn in the river; and at the end of the said penance they must fast for twenty-four hours, one, two or three days, depending upon how the cast lot indicates the fast. And [he orders them] to make ready, in the same way, little dogs, and native hens and cocks, and copal for the sacrifice that they have to make at the end of the last day of the fast, which having arrived, and the twenty-four hours having passed, the wise man comes to the house of the deceased, taking with him one or two persons most closely related to the deceased.

And [with] these hens, or cocks, or little dogs, copal and fire, he goes out of the town, and having come to a place which seems to him fitting, he digs one, two or three holes, each about a foot deep, one after the other; and breaking into pieces the aforementioned copal, he throws into each hole thirteen pieces of it in reverence to his thirteen gods; and he orders one of his assistants or ministers to behead the native hen or cock, or the dog, and to sprinkle the copal with its blood, and to pour the rest [of the blood] into the said hole; and likewise in exactly the same way for the other holes, if he has to make this sacrifice more than once; and placing on the outer edge of each hole a piece of copal without blood he orders that this copal be set on fire; and it having burned, he throws into [the hole] the dog or native cock (but if it is a large hen he orders it to be taken to the house of the deceased in order that, cooked, it be eaten in company by those who have fasted); and he makes them cover the hole with dirt, saying these words, or others like them:

"This sacrifice I offer to the devil for this deceased one; namely, to the god of hell, and to the goddess his wife, and to such and such god," if the sacrifices go on from one to two to three to four, depending upon what the cast lot showed him; [this he does] to ward off from the road sicknesses and deaths, that they will not come out of this place nor to the house of the relatives of the aforementioned deceased. And with this, the sacrifice and fast are ended, all of them returning to sup at the house of the deceased.

At other times they make sacrifice for the dead, after the penance and fast, and in the same apartment or room where the death took place, beheading there a native hen and sprinkling this place and thirteen pieces of copal with its blood and burning the copal; and with the rest of the aforementioned blood, sprinkling the said room and offering it in the manner referred to.

On this occasion they usually have some other ceremonies and superstitious rites; and since all of them end up as sacrifices to the Devil, although at times they vary the mode of making the sacrifice, in substance it is always one and is directed to one end.

They are accustomed likewise in pregnancies, childbirths and other types of confinements to promise that if all goes well they will sacrifice to such and such a god a small dog or native hen, in the manner related above, offering it to the said god; this been preceded by consulting some wise man of this jurisdiction, and the latter, casting lots, has told them that such and such a god is imposing justice upon the ill or imprisoned, and that in order to placate him they must make him that promise, aforesaid and those of his household accept and make; and they fulfill it punctually in thanksgiving for the fortunate outcome.

And the same thing happens with pregnant women and women who have just given birth; and for this they have designated places to which they go to fulfill their vows; such they have on a hill within the jurisdiction of my province, called in the common language of the natives *Quijaxila*, which is about half a league from the Pueblo of San Juan, distant from the seat [San Miguel] by another half-league, on whose summit are seen the ruins of a building which is commonly known to have been a temple of their idols in heathen times; and there they go to carry out their sacrifices.

For offering alms in the church, they have good and bad days; and these are indicated to them by some counselor who judges of that, according to his computation from the book of their doctrine. If the day is good, although it be during the week, all or many of them come together to light candles or to bring other offerings, which, it is evident by their own declarations, they do in reverence of their thirteen gods.

For example: if such a day is good for offering, and the counselor told them to perform it at the altar of the Virgin offering or lighting so many candles, they do it; and offer them in reverence of the goddess *Nohuichana;* and if at all of the altars they perform this sacrifice, it is done in reverence of all the thirteen gods; and the other offerings are made in the same respect.

They are accustomed to perform many other ceremonies and rites on burying the dead, upon getting married, on copulating with their wives, on building their houses, on sowing, and on gathering their harvests; and finally, all that they do in general is superstitious and so varied that only with difficulty can it be reduced to number and form.

Everything contained in this account is verified by a large number of witnesses, judicial confessions of many of the prisoners, and statements of others. Either induced by fear of punishment or by the repentance which they claim to feel, they have accused themselves, asking for mercy and planning to make amends.

"Marrano Religiosity in Hispanic America in the Seventeenth Century"[4] NATHAN WACHTEL

What is marrano religiosity? We can legitimately discern among New Christians throughout the Iberian world beliefs and practices that indicate the persistence of a possible crypto-Judaism. But does it suffice merely to make an unquestioning inventory of such elements? For indeed, the range of beliefs held by New Christians was not limited to the clandestine pursuit of more or less impoverished Judaizing practices. Hence, we must avoid using the reductive schemas of an apologetic history and instead restore to marrano religiosity its full measure of complexity and diversity. We must cover a broad spectrum between two poles—that of actual fervent Judaists and that of sincere Christians—with a whole series of intermediate cases and syncretic combinations.

Conversos can be distinguished from Old Christians both negatively and positively: legally, the "pure blood" statutes left them (in principle) relatively marginalized; but we know that in social terms the New Christians were united in vast networks reinforced by kinship and marriage, and that this solidarity was reinforced to varying degrees by the shared feelings of a community of memory. But what about their religious beliefs? In seeking to answer this question, we are confronted with a paradox, arising from the complex and manifold forms of religious life. On the one hand, there is a (potentially) common body of Judaizing practices, and on the other, extreme diversity among various individuals, groups, places, and periods under consideration. It is as if the very object of our study dissipates before our eyes. The essential point is in the paradox itself: what is specific about the religious domain of New Christians is precisely the tension they experienced between two religions—Judaism and Christianity— with all the resultant doubts, hesitations, vacillations, and at times skeptical detachment, as well as the "interferences," cross-fertilization, and dual sincerity.

Here a brief consideration of terminology is in order. It is no accident that the terms "marrano" and "marranism," despite their once pejorative connotations, have come to be accepted for the sake of convenience: they correspond to an objective reality, that of a certain religiosity. By religiosity, I mean not a religion as clearly defined by theological doctrine, but rather a set of concerns, practices, and beliefs grouped together in a configuration made up of various, even contradictory, elements whose diversity does not preclude a kind of unity—a generic style that makes it possible for us to identify and label it with a specific term, in this case "marrano."[5]

Marrano religiosity as it pertains to the New Christians in Hispanic America, and more particularly in New Spain, during the first half of the seventeenth century is the focus of this essay.[6] The overwhelming majority of the New Christians—Judaizing or otherwise—who came to the American continent in large numbers, particularly starting in 1580 with the Union of the Two Kingdoms, were of Portuguese origin. Many of them were the descendants of Spanish Jews who had originally fled to Portugal in 1492, sometimes making a detour through Spain again for one or two generations before ultimately pursuing their migration as far as the New World. In the American context, these *conversos* exhibited very particular characteristics: like the Amerindian societies, but in a very different milieu, they constitute a virtual laboratory for the study of problems related to acculturation processes, syncretic phenomena, and cultural *métissage*.

In the Americas—which were open to new arrivals but which retained a population that, despite the demographic catastrophe, remained predominantly indigenous—heterodox beliefs and practices could indeed escape detection and denunciation more easily than in the metropolis (all the more so because the jurisdiction of the Inquisition tribunals extended here over vast areas). Conversely, in those faraway lands to which Hebrew literature made its way only surreptitiously, and exceptionally at that, it was difficult to sustain a Jewish Orthodox tradition. Thus the New Christians who immigrated to Hispanic America had recourse to a whole range of multiple syncretic combinations, which we shall examine more closely in order to discover the specific characteristics of marrano religiosity.

The Range of Beliefs: Christian Influences

By definition, the *conversos* had received some Christian education that had inevitably left traces, even to the point of stamping their personalities with indelible mental reflexes. There are many accounts describing the shock experienced by an adolescent to whom a parent had suddenly revealed that everything the child had previously learned, and in which he ardently believed—Jesus Christ, the Virgin Mary, the Holy Trinity, the saints, and so forth—was false and that salvation was to be found not in the "law of Jesus" but in the "law of Moses." Such expressions were not confined only to the vocabulary of the Inquisitors; they were totally assimilated by the New Christians as well, whatever the nature of their faith. What was at stake was still the salvation of the soul: this peculiarly Christian concern formed the basis for a range of beliefs within which the alternatives were arrayed, along with the doubts and hesitations of those who, from the moment of revelation on, found themselves faced with a dramatic choice.[7] Often a single family would be split into sincere Catholics and fervent Judaists, the relations between them oscillating between mutual distrust and compromising solidarity. Sometimes parents would argue over their children's education, as in the example of Antonio Díaz de Cáceres and his wife Catalina de León de la Cueva (the sister of the famous Luis de Carvajal El Mozo). Their fourteen-year-old daughter, Leonor de Cáceres, reported a remarkable episode:

> One day, in the presence of the said Doña Mariana (who was quite crazy) and the said Doña Anna, Antonio Díaz fought at length with Doña Catalina because she made her [Leonor] fast during the holy days of the Lord and he ordered her [Leonor] to get dressed, saying, "Stand up, you bad woman of poor breeding, and do not ever return to this house" and so Ysabelica *china*, who is now dead, dressed her and she went with her father down to the street corner where she said to the said Antonio Díaz, "My Lord and father, where are you taking me so that I might cry in someone else's home?" and the said Antonio Díaz responded, "Be quiet, you sly vixen of poor

breeding. I am taking you to Machado's house." And as she knew not who he [Machado] was, she cried, and the said Antonio Díaz shed tears when he heard her ask where he was taking her so that she might cry in someone else's home, and he took her back to her mother's house, saying, "Go on, you poorly bred woman and thank God for what you said to me, for it is because of this that I am taking you to this bad woman," and her father, the said Antonio Díaz, left her at the door and went about his business.[8]

Let us take another example that illustrates the persistence of Christian practices in the midst of Judaizing observances, or rather, in this case, a Judaizing reinterpretation of Christian practices and beliefs. This is the case of Antonio Fernández Cardado, born in Moral in La Mancha (of parents native to Portugal). After a complicated itinerary that took him through Bordeaux and Saint Jean de Luz, he arrived in Spain in 1613. He amassed some capital by working as a peddler between Vera Cruz and Puebla, and then opened a wholesale supply company in Mexico, extending his business to Tlaxcala and the mining town of Pachuca. When he ended up in front of the Inquisition tribunal in 1634, this is how Cardado described his conversion to Judaism:

> The said Talaveras, his cousins, told this confessant that the law of Jesus Christ was not the good one and that there was only one God who was to be adored, and that the Messiah had not come, nor was Jesus Christ the Messiah, although they said that there was a Holy Ghost who had spoken through the prophets and patriarchs of the old law.[9]

Thus, at the very moment when the reconversion took place, as Jesus Christ was rejected, there remained a trace of Christian doctrine in the presence of the Holy Ghost transposed onto the Old Testament. Antonio Fernández Cardado went on to say that, as a child, in the school where he was taught by priests to read and write, he had learned a prayer that the children had recited every afternoon, and he repeated it to the Inquisitors: "We pray to you that you have mercy on us and the souls of our deceased relatives and friends, and please Lord, save them from the pain they suffer and take them to your Holy Kingdom. Amen Jesus."[10] Antonio Fernández Cardado added that he remained quite attached to this prayer and that he continued to recite it even after his conversion to the "law of Moses," although he took care to stop before he got to the "Amen Jesus" with which it ended. However, sometimes he would slip and unintentionally utter the final "Amen Jesus" without meaning to; the mechanism of a prayer learned by heart, inculcated at an early age, reproduced itself like a reflex.

Let us note further how Antonio Fernández Cardado excused himself for making these slips: his real intention, he insisted, was truly to pray as one who observes the "law of Moses" and to address the God of Israel exclusively.[11] So even in private prayer he maintained a mental reservation and drew a distinction between the words he actually uttered and the faith within his heart of hearts; in other words, there was a discrepancy or gap between the prayer as literally expressed and his inner feelings, the authentic faith that alone guaranteed salvation. Antonio Fernández Cardado's observation is similar to certain admissions concerning the Christian confession: those *conversos* on trial often related how, when they went to church for the purpose of confessing, it was because they were obliged to keep up appearances. Although they confessed to the priest, they too had mental reservations, taking care to think of the God of Israel to whom their prayers were really addressed (and to whom they had prayed beforehand in order to ask for forgiveness).

Another type of ambiguity is illustrated by a scene that was played out in the house of Simon Vaez Sevilla, one of the richest business men in New Spain during the 1630s. The occasion was a Passover celebration, in a ceremony at which Blanca Enríquez was officiating. Considered a "dogmatist" and rabbinist, she was the mother-in-law of Simon Vaez Sevilla and had been imprisoned and tortured in the dungeons of the Inquisition in Sevilla. The faithful gathered together in the back room of the house where Blanca Enríquez proceeded to distribute the unleavened bread that had been secretly prepared. They lined up before her, one behind the other; for each of them, she broke off a small piece of unleavened bread and placed it in the worshipper's mouth, according to, and as if in atonement for, the Christian model.[12]

[. . . .]

The Rejection of Image Worship

Let us return to the first half of the seventeenth century in Mexico. We have seen that Francisco Botello [Antonio Fernández Cardado's nephew] condemned Christians to hell for their idolatry. This leads us to another major theme, one of the most fundamental elements of marrano religiosity: the rejection of image worship. This refusal found expression in scorn and mockery, such as we know Blanca de Rivera and her daughter indulged in while watching Holy Week processions with statues of the saints, the Virgin, and Christ pass by their windows.[13] Did their aversion go as far as sacrilege, provoking insulting or violent gestures such as spitting upon images or subjecting them to flagellation? Such accusations frequently appear in the documents of the Inquisition, and we must consider whether they are slanderous or not. While the sincerity of certain witnesses (often household servants) is dubious in some cases where such practices are described, many indications seem to confirm that they did indeed occur (even if they were perhaps not as widespread as claimed by the denunciations).

Let us look at a few more examples. This type of insulting gesture is mentioned at the end of the preceding century, even in the entourage of Luis de Carvajal El Mozo, whose piety bordered on mystical illuminism, but who turned his back on images of the Virgin and the saints when praying in his own home:

> And so they had images of Our Lady of the Conception and of Pity and other saints in Santiago's chapel in order to keep up appearances because they revered them as idols and when they prayed, they turned their backs to them, and she saw the said Luis de Carvajal, Doña Catalina her mother, Doña Francisca her grandmother, and Doña Ysabel her aunt, spit on the images, saying, "I do not know for what reason we have these idols."[14]

In the 1630s and 1640s, Blanca de Rivera and her daughters, once again, were accused of striking a crucifix with a whip.[15] Likewise, Duarte de Leon Jaramillo and his wife Isabel Nuñez flagellated an image of Christ and dragged it across the room.[16] Regarding this last case, one account deserves to be quoted at length: firstly, because it is an extraordinarily vivid recreation of a scene from daily life portraying children in a Mexican street; and secondly, because the plethora of lifelike details suggests that the narrative could not have been purely and simply invented by Inquisitors running short of accusations. Here, then, is the record of the account by María de Luna y Vilchas, who was eighteen years old in 1648. She was about eight years old when the incident, ostensibly about sweets, took place:

> She said that she knows very well that a little more than ten years ago, the said Duarte de León and his wife, Ysabel Nuñez, and their daughters, Clara

Antonia and Ana, and their sons, Francisco, Simon and Jorge, the smallest, had all been condemned by the Inquisition with *San benitos* . . . because they lived as neighbours for years on Azequia Real Street, and it was common for this witness and her sisters, Francisca and Petronila, to be friendly with all of the sons and daughters of the said Duarte de León because as children they had all been raised together and she remembers that about ten or more years ago, Jorge came across this witness in the doorway of the store where her father, Juan de Vilches, held the right to sell ice, and he said to the witness, "Give me a piece of ice and I will tell you something," and the witness, standing in the doorway, said to him, I won't give you any ice unless you tell me." So the said Jorge said that his father, Duarte de León, flagellated a Holy Christ with a barbed wire whip at night in the chamber where he slept . . . and without asking any more questions, nor saying another thing to him, the witness gave Jorge the piece of ice that he had asked for.[17]

If we admit that such sacrilegious practices did take place, how are we to understand them? Why insult images, if one considers them to be no more than lifeless paintings on pieces of wood? The aggressive gesture, in the circumstances described, takes on a ritualistic quality that implies, paradoxically, that the images are thought to possess a certain power or at least that this black magic is expected to have some effect. In other words, the aggression is also a transgression, insofar as it betrays a form of adherence to the dominant beliefs, that is, Christian beliefs; but the adherence is inverted.[18] Confirming this is an observation that Juan Pacheco de León (a native of Livorno, where he was educated in the Jewish community) made when he was accused of participating in such sacrilegious rites at the home of Simon Vaez Sevilla. Although in his refutation he admits that he does not believe in Jesus Christ, he denies ever having committed blasphemy; his argument is based on a telling comparison between the Jews of his native land, Italy, and those of the Iberian territories where they were obliged to convert to Catholicism:

And although it is true that he did not believe in Our Lord Jesus Christ and believed the images to be merely sticks and paintings, he has never blasphemed Jesus Christ Our Lord, nor the Holy Virgin, nor any of the saints in heaven, because there in his native land they only cared about teaching the old law and observing its commandments, performing the rites and ceremonies while awaiting the Messiah, but they have nothing to do with

Jesus Christ Our Lord, seeing as the Jews who whip Christs and perform
other crimes of that sort are those who live here as Catholics, because they
are the worst, and those who go to live in those lands are the most unlaw-
ful, they are held in low esteem by other Jews.[19]

Juan Pacheco de León's remarks are of a general nature (he avoids com-
menting on the specific point of subjecting the image of Christ to flagellation in the home of Simon Vaez Sevilla), but his distinction between Jews
who could freely profess their faith in certain European countries (*allá*,
there) and those in Mexico or Spain (*acá*, here) who were obliged to conceal
it, in fact corroborates the accusation: the latter Jews were the ones guilty
of sacrilegious offences, and if they behaved thus, he says explicitly, it was
because "they live like Catholics." Marked by their Christian education, imbued with the beliefs that surrounded them, and suffering from persecution
at the hands of the Inquisition, they expressed their hatred and resentment
through such gestures. Secrecy and repression led them to assert their true
faith in this perverted manner, and when they were back in Jewish communities in Europe (or Muslim lands), they were treated with scorn.

Transgressive behavior directed at images can therefore be considered as
one form—here superstitious or magical—among many syncretic combinations that are found in such wide variety among the New Christians. . . .

"Appeal Concerning the Priests"[20]   GUAMAN POMA

The aforementioned priests, fathers, and pastors who stand for God and
his saints in the parishes of this kingdom of Peru do not act like the
blessed priests of Saint Peter and the friars of Our Lady of Mercy, Saint
Francis, Saint Dominic, and Saint Augustine, and the hermits of Saint Peter who preceded them. Rather, they give themselves over to greed for silver, clothing, and things of the world, and sins of the flesh, appetites, and
unspeakable misdeeds, of which the good reader will learn later so that
they can be punished in exemplary fashion. May they be charged by their
prelates and members of [religious] orders, and punished by the Holy Inquisition. Their acts do harm to the Spaniards and even more to the new
Christians who are the Indians and Blacks. By fathering a dozen children,
how can they set a good example for the Indians of this kingdom?

The fathers and parish priests are very angry, imperious, and arrogant,
and are so haughty that the aforementioned Indians flee from them in fear.
These priests seem to have forgotten that Our Lord Jesus Christ became

poor and humble in order to live among and bring in poor sinners, leading them to His Holy Church and from there to His kingdom in Heaven.

[. . . .]

These fathers and parish priests in this kingdom all keep mita [corvee labor] Indians busy: two Indians in the kitchen, another looking after the horses, another in the garden, another as janitor, another in the kitchen, others to bring firewood and fodder, others as shepherds, harvesters, messengers, field workers, and tenders of chickens, goats, sheep, cows, mares, and pigs. And in other things they insolently put the aforementioned hapless Indian men and women of this kingdom to work without pay. And for this reason they leave their homes.

These parish priests pasture ten mules and others belonging to their friends, which they fatten up at the expense of the Indians and single women who must take care of them. Some have many cows; also a thousand head of goats or sheep and pigs, mares or native mountain sheep, one or two hundred chickens and rabbits; and planted fields. And people are put in charge of all of these things with their corrals and buildings, keeping the poor Indians busy and without pay. And if one is lost, [the person responsible] is charged for one hundred; and they [the workers] are neither paid nor fed. With so much work, they leave.

These fathers and parish priests in this kingdom keep in their kitchens four unmarried women mita workers, cooks, and the head cook who oversees the preparation of meals, [and in addition to] the mita women and women under the priest's supervision, there are beautiful unmarried women. They also keep more than eight boys and overseers, and much equipment, all at the expense of the Indians. These males, plus the servant women, consume a bushel and a half of food daily and they are paid nothing. And these Indian women give birth to Mestizos and become wicked women, whores in this kingdom.

These fathers and parish priests of this kingdom ask for Indians to carry to market their wine, peppers, coca, and maize. Some have Indians bring mountain wine and coca down from the high plains to the hot lowlands. Being highland people, they die from fever and chills. And if the goods are damaged in transit, the Indian is forced to pay for them.

These parish priests have thread spun and woven, oppressing the widows and unmarried women, making them work without pay on the pretext that they were living in illicit unions. And in this the Indian women become notorious whores, and there is no remedy. And they do not wish to marry, staying with the priest or a Spaniard. Consequently, the Indians of this kingdom are not multiplying, only Mestizos, and there is no remedy.

These parish priests take from every pueblo things belonging to the church, hospital, or members of confraternities, saying that they must help them; and they use them up with impunity. They do so with the help of the corregidor or the visitador [administrative inspector, or inspector and judge of idolatry]; and in this way the Indians are robbed of their belongings and community.

These parish priests of this kingdom keep the offerings and alms for the Masses in honor of the departed. For a sung Mass they demand six pesos; if it is ordered, three pesos; for a spoken Mass they demand four pesos; if it is ordered, one peso. Some collect ten or twenty pesos. And they do not perform the said Mass and offering for four reales, which is supposed to be voluntary and suitably returned. Their belongings should be returned to the poor Indians, and these fathers should be punished in this kingdom. [But] there is no remedy for it.

These priests demand five pesos for the banns and candle and offering for a marriage, and four pesos for a baptism, without accepting that Your Majesty pays them a salary. [These collections] should be returned and [the act] punished.

[. . . .]

These parish priests clamor to involve themselves too much in judicial matters. Having become secular priests, they want to become assistant pastors, then titular priests, and even corregidor and recklessly order about the alcalde and principal cacique [or kuraka, native lord and governor]. As a result they enter into disputes and initiate petitions and are bad examples for the pueblo. They cause destruction for the caciques and other leading Indians, and for the corregidores and encomenderos, and there is no remedy. They treat them so imperiously and thereby destroy the Indians of this kingdom.

Father Juan Bautista Aluadan [whom Guaman Poma isolates as an offender on two other occasions as well] was pastor of the pueblo of San Cristobal de Pampa Chire. He was a most imperious, cruel father; the things he did were unspeakable. For example, he took an Indian from this pueblo named Diego Caruas who had not given him a ram and put him on a cross like that of Saint Andrew [that is, in the shape of an X]. He tied him up with leather strips, began to burn him with a tallow candle, applying fire to his anus and private parts, abusing him with many lighted candles. And he opened his buttocks with his hands, and they say he did many other unspeakable things of which God will take note, a great many harmful and evil acts. Thus he tormented the painters he summoned. He did this because the unmarried women of Don Juan Uacrau complained that Father Aluadan stripped his [Uacrau's] daughter naked and examined her anus and genitalia and put in his fingers and gave her four beatings on her bottom. Every morning he did this to all the unmarried women. [The native] governor, Don León Apouasco, tried to oppose this and entered a petition, but the aforementioned Father Aluadan responded by saying that [the governor] hid Indians during the visita [general inspection]. And so he was exiled; from this misfortune, Apouasco died.

[. . . .]

These women and their parents and relations cannot confess [to such a priest], nor is the sacrament of confession valid, nor is he worthy of a salary from them. Because how can he confess and absolve someone with whom he sins mortally, a sacrilegious sin with these Indian women?

All of this deserves great punishment; and even more than punishment, such a sin should be made known to the Inquisition. Properly punished, this will be a good example to the faithful Christians of Jesus Christ in the world and in this kingdom.

These fathers hire other priests in the vicinity, because their bad deeds are known among them, to confess these unmarried Indian women on the pretext of saying that they are helping each other. In this way they are a bad example for the Christians and show no fear of God and punish [the women's] parents. And there is no remedy for the poor Indians. And thus they die off and do not multiply.

These parish priests have Indian women in the kitchens or elsewhere who act as their married woman, and others as mistresses, and with them they have twenty children, which is a public and well-known fact. And they call these Mestizo children their nephews and nieces and say that they are the children of their brothers and relatives. In this way many sins mount up, and the Indian women learn them from one another, and thus many little Mestizo boys and girls multiply. This is a bad example to the Christians; everyone of these [priests and women] needs to be convicted and punished and exiled from the parish.

[. . . .]

The ancient [Andean] priests of metals, idols, demons, and gods, high priests of stone according to their law, [these] priests of metals acted devoutly and gave good example, as with the virgins and nuns of the temples. And so the rest submitted to their justice and law. They were Christians in everything but their idolatry.

Now the priests and ministers of the eternal, living God are [as I have described them]. From such a bad father springs a bad child, lost to the things of the true God. From a bad tree comes bad fruit, from a bad foundation comes a bad root. This badness is what God punishes most severely in Hell and in this life.

These fathers and pastors are very fierce. They punish the aforementioned fiscales and sacristans and cantors and schoolchildren. They punish very cruelly, as if they were punishing a Black slave, with such malice and harm and vehemence, and they do not stop. They [the Indians] run away and flee and are put in shackles and stocks. With this, these Indians die, and in this kingdom there is no one who takes their side. . . .

4

Religions of the African Diaspora

Origins and Development

The broad spectrum of practices, cosmologies, and institutions grouped under the term "African-based religions" emerged as a result of over three centuries of slavery in the Americas. From the late 1530s, when the first Africans were brought to Brazil to replace indigenous labor in nascent sugar plantations, to 1850, the year when the slave trade officially ended, between ten and eleven million slaves came to the New World. Of those, only 650,000 were brought to North America. By contrast, four million went to the Caribbean Islands, with Cuba and Jamaica receiving the lion's share (at more that seven hundred thousand each), while South American countries imported close to five million, 3.6 million of whom landed in Brazil. Within Brazil, the state of Bahia alone absorbed more than a million slaves.[1] Given the massive numbers, it is not surprising the slaves and their descendants had a major impact on Latin American cultures and economies. By the 1820s, slaves constituted about one-third of the population of Brazil, with another third made up by Blacks who had purchased or won their freedom (a process less onerous in Brazil than in the United States) (Postma 2003: 78). While the numbers in Cuba were not as great, slaves and free people of color made up the majority of the population by 1846 at approximately 53 percent.

Colonial masters instituted a policy of domination by division, mixing the various African groups in order to prevent the formation of solidarities based on language, place of origin, and kinship. However, the sheer numbers of slaves and the fact that they came from relatively few regions of Africa and concentrated around ports of entry and large plantations undermined this policy. While limited, contact with people from the same linguistic and ethnic groups allowed Africans in diaspora a certain latitude to reconstruct their identities. For example, in many towns and cities in Cuba, slaves and freed Blacks formed voluntary mutual aid associations called "*cabildos*," built around "*naciones*," peoples hailing from roughly the same parts of Africa.[2] The colonial government saw *cabildos* as means of social control, of allowing the slaves to express their collective energies in activities other than revolt. However, by serving as spaces of fraternization and entertainment, spaces where slaves played their music, performed their dances, and passed on their oral traditions, these clubs became crucibles for the emergence of African-based religions. *Cabildos* became prototypes of the temples and houses that are central to these religions.

Given the importance of mutual aid associations in the cultural lives of slaves and freed people of color, the Catholic Church understood that they could serve as effective vehicles for catechization. As the first reading (on the black brotherhood of Our Lady of the Rosary in Recife) shows, colonial church officials in Brazil encouraged the creation of *irmandades*, lay organizations dedicated to the promotion of saints that expressed the slaves' conditions and aspirations. The proliferation of *irmandades* was made possible by the rise of a new class, the *negros de ganho* (wage slaves), that had the financial means and relative freedom to care for the sick, support the construction and upkeep of chapels for patron saints, and purchase and administer cemeteries for association members.

As in the case of indigenous peoples, the attempts to convert slaves and regulate their religious lives had contradictory effects, especially given the clash between the Catholic Church's concern for the spiritual well-being of slaves and its support for the inhumane institution of slavery. On the one hand, the church did not want owners to abuse and exploit their slaves to such an extent that the latter would not be able to engage in their religious obligations. On the other hand, the church clearly stated that its immunity would not extend to runaway slaves. Despite this contradiction, black brotherhoods' relative autonomy allowed them to develop a rich ecclesiology, iconography, and liturgy that contributed to the formation of Brazilian traditional popular Catholicism, always in tension with the official church. As shown in chapter 5, after Independence and emancipation, the emerging national governments tried to suppress *cabildos* and *irmandades*, seeing them as potential incubators of separatist movements. At the same time, church leaders tried to bring their practices in line with institutional orthodoxy.

Slightly more than 40 percent of imported slaves came from the West Central region of Africa, which now includes Angola and Congo. This influx served as the basis for the Bakongo "nations" in the Americas, which, in turn, contributed to the emergence of *Regla Palo* (Palo Monte or Palo Mayombe) in Puerto Rico and Cuba.[3] Close to 20 percent of the slaves came from the Blight of Benin, a region that includes southeastern Ghana, Togo, Benin, and southwestern Nigeria, constituting the second significant influx. Slaves in this group brought Dahomeyan rituals and beliefs that served as the basis for Vodou in Haiti and the *Regla Arará* in Cuba. This flow also brought a variety of peoples, such as the Oyo, Egba, Ijebu, and Nagô, who in the New World came to be identified as the Yoruba, the main source for some of the most visible African-based religions, including *Regla Lukumí*, popularly knows as Santería (in Cuba, Puerto Rico, Dominican Republic, and more recently the United States), Candomblé (in Bahia and Rio de Janeiro), Xangô (Recife, Brazil), Tambor de Minas (in Sao Luíz Maranhão, Brazil), and Batuque (in Porto Alegre, Brazil).[4]

This genealogy and cartography of African-based religions in the Americas is necessarily rough, since there was quite a bit of cross-fertilization among African religions and with Catholicism and Native American religions. Moreover, the fact that a slave came from a specific port does not guarantee that she or he was from a particular ethnic group. Slavery transformed the sociopolitical landscape in Africa, contributing to the collapse and emergence of kingdoms and altering the sources and dynamics of slave flows. In his influential book *The Black Atlantic*, Paul Gilroy characterizes the exchanges between various African and diasporic populations as discontinuous and often paradoxical. Nevertheless, the issue of the "retention" of Africanisms in a matrix of change and hybridization has been central to the study of African-based religions since its early days. The terms of the debate were set by anthropologist Melville Herskovits, who sought to refute the notion that "the Negro is . . . a man without a past," since his ancestors had abandoned or forgotten their cultures and religions in response to the pressures of slavery and in their quest to enter modernity in the New World (Herskovits 1958: 2). He argued, instead, that the slaves experienced a process of differential accommodation, resulting in varying degrees of "acculturation," ranging from "aspects of Negro culture where Africanisms have been most retained" to "those where the least of the aboriginal endowment is manifest" (Herskovits 1958: 8) In effect, Herskovits placed the tension between purity and syncretism at the core of the study of African-based religions. Thus, the task of the student of religion was to identify and analyze "survivals" from Africa that persisted in the process of cultural evolution, to recover religious patterns subsisting underneath the dominant religion.

The concern for degrees of purity shaped Roger Bastide, a French sociologist and Candomblé initiate who published in 1960 his now classic

Les Religions Afro-Brésiliennes, of which we are reprinting a chapter. In it, Bastide argues that Black Islam in Brazil has all but disappeared, as the Malê have reverted back to the beliefs of their "animist" and "fetishist" ancestors because these beliefs were more compatible with Catholicism, the religion of the dominant classes.[5] Here Bastide trades with many Orientalist prejudices about Islam and Muslims—highlighting, for example, their "quiet conversational, restrained gestures, and pointed beards [which] symbolized their ethnic and religious separateness." Bastide also subscribes to a primitivism that was characteristic of the anthropology of his time: pre-Islamic African traditions are dismissed as purely instrumental, individualistic magic and superstition.

Furthermore, and more importantly, Bastide also tends to underplay the powerful legacy of Malê insurrectional experiences throughout Brazilian history. Irving (1992), for example, argues that Fulani, Hausa, and Mandigo, most of whom were very likely Muslim,[6] participated in *quilombos*, alternative, self-sufficient communities formed by fugitive slaves (maroons), which from the late 1570s resisted the plantation economy. The *quilombo dos Palmares*, under the leadership of Zumbi, has in particular attained a quasi mythical place in Brazilian culture. From 1678 to 1694, Palmares resisted militarily repeated attempts by the Portuguese to dissolve it. In the end, Zumbi was killed and his head publicly displayed in Recife. Nevertheless, his legacy of resistance was rekindled during Malê uprisings in Salvador, Rio de Janeiro, and other coastal cities during the 1830s (Reis 1993). These rebellions were put down violently and many of their Malê leaders were killed or sent back to Africa. Such a systematic repression accounts for the low visibility of African Islam in Brazil, as Bastide rightly claims. Nevertheless, all these insurrectional episodes in Brazilian history have inspired a vigorous contemporary *Movimento Negro* (Black Movement) that seeks to recover many of the traditions brought by African slaves, including those of resistance, pride, and self-sufficiency associated with the Malê (Sansone 2003).

Despite the limitations of Bastide's piece, it shows an important dimension of the African diaspora in the New World that has normally been ignored with all the attention given to Yoruban religions. It also demonstrates that, like Judaism, Islam has had a historical presence in the region, leaving a legacy now being transformed by the rise of new Muslim communities, as discussed in chapter 8. Finally, the piece also underscores the challenges faced by a strongly monotheistic religion like Islam in the context of slavery, which not only restricted certain religious practices but also encouraged cultural mixing among the various ethnic groups thrown together.

Many contemporary scholars and practitioners have challenged the assimilationist and essentialist assumptions behind Herkovits's view of syncretism. They argue that the Catholic saints can best be seen as masks that the African spirits wore in public in order to avoid censure. These African spirits lay in wait behind their Catholic cover, serving as the basis for resistance and rebellion through the colonial period and for the recent attempts to re-Africanize the traditions (De La Torre 2004: 8). Between these two positions, some scholars accept that, for example, Yemanjá is different from Our Lady of Conception. However, pointing to the non-dualistic character of African-based religions, they argue that practitioners see them as two manifestations of the same principle. Thus, "the two spiritual realities have come to be lived . . . as noncontradictory and even complementary" (Walker 1990: 112).

The issue of syncretism is especially relevant for Umbanda, a Yoruban-derived tradition that originated in Rio de Janeiro in the 1920s and is now very popular in large Brazilian cities like São Paulo, as well as in Montevideo, Uruguay, and Buenos Aires, Argentina (Brown 1994; Frigerio 2002). Umbanda has explicitly incorporated not only aspects of Catholicism and Native American religions but also elements of Spiritism, as inspired by Allan Kardec, a famous French medium active in the mid-1800s.[7] Kardecism subscribes to the notions of karma and reincarnation. After death, disincarnate spirits return to the material world in order to work up toward higher levels of wisdom until they become pure light. Spirits that have been stunted in their evolution due to negative karma might disturb the living, causing psychosomatic problems (*obsessões*). The role of the spiritist is to educate these spirits to help them attain higher levels of consciousness. A key part of the spirits' evolution involves performing charity for the living and providing moral instruction. The spirits of the dead perform their good deeds by periodically visiting the living and giving advice through the services of mediums, like Allan Kardec (Hess 1991).

Thus, in Umbanda, African divine entities share the stage with a host of other spirits, including *caboclos* (the untamed spirits of Indians, cowhands, and sailors) and *pretos velhos* (the docile but wise spirits of old slaves in the New World), and *exús* (representing the transgressive spirits of prostitutes, rogues, and other street figures that are part of everyday life for the urban poor). It is not uncommon for Umbanda centers even to pay homage to *o povo do oriente*, to Hindu and Buddhist sages that can be called up to advise the living. The chart below offers a simplified panoramic view of the multiple spiritual forces that populate Umbanda's cosmos.[8]

Umbanda's unabashed syncretism has earned it the title of the only "true Brazilian religion," an expression of Brazil's mix of races and cultures. It has also led some Candomblé leaders to denounce and abandon it as irredeemably *enbranquecida* (whitened). However, as anthropologist Jim Wafer argues in his piece here, in the shifting Brazilian religious field, this drive to purify might be impossible to sustain and ultimately contradictory. Paul Johnson (2002: 52) reports attending a "house of 'Umbandomblé,' which practices both Umbanda and Candomblé in the same *terreiro* [house], alternating formats weekly."

Worldviews, Practices, and Forms of Social Organization

In the current postmodern intellectual climate, it is perilous to claim that a given religion has a core that defines it for all places and times. The danger of essentialism is heightened in the case of African-based religions because of their great diversity and fluidity. However, a comparative study of African-based religions, particularly those of the Yoruba nation, yields some heuristic "family resemblances."

As Wafer demonstrates below, African-based religions are nondualistic since they posit that the universe is made of the same vital force, known as *Axé* in Portuguese and *Aché* in Spanish. This force animates everything from natural phenomena to humans and spirits, allowing for an integrated whole, in which the various entities exchange energies in order to maintain balance and harmony. Like many indigenous cultures, African-based religions tended to see the natural and spiritual worlds as characterized more by balance and mutual interaction than by the rigid dualisms that often marked Christian worldviews. This dynamic, tightly interrelated cosmos, thus, requires an ethos of humility, respect, and reciprocity that for humans translates into the need to offer good works—prayers, sacrifices, and special celebrations—to the spirits, particularly to the ancestors and to those spirits that are closely associated with one's personality or birthday. Practitioners also have duties toward each other that ensure the well-being of physical religious community so that it can become a propitious setting in which to interact with the spirits. Something of this ethos is revealed in the selection of the Candomblé manual included in this volume.

Most prominent among these ancestors are the *orixás* (in Portuguese) or *orichas/ochas* (in Spanish), the spirits of the great African kings, queens, and warriors, who by virtue of their great deeds have become part of a divine royal family to which all practitioners trace their origins. As the chart below shows, *orixás* have distinct personalities, histories, desires, and natural domains. Because the material and spiritual worlds are closely intertwined in African-based religions, the *orixás* are not detached, ethereal entities. Rather, they have physical appetites that need to be satisfied—hunger for certain foods and desires for certain drumming and dance patterns and for the proper recognition of their royal nature. Thus, the task of the practitioner is to learn the complex etiquette required to attain the purity necessary to interact with and respond to the *orixás*, through sacrifices and other offerings, as well as to incorporate them so that they can be in community with humans.

Ritual sacrifices are particularly powerful means of redistributing *axé* (*aché*), for the blood of the victim, which contains life itself, feeds the spirit, so that the recharged spirit can work effectively on behalf of the practitioner, opening auspicious roads, granting health and success, protecting against misfortune, and resolving everyday problems. Arguably the highest relationship that a practitioner can have with the spirits is to lend his or her body to allow the saint or *orixás/orichas* to materialize. Spirit incorporation requires a rigorous training, since practitioners cannot just receive the raw power of spirits. The initiate (*Yaô* or *iyawó*) must learn to let himself or herself go, so that the spirits can come to occupy his or her body, riding the initiate effortlessly just like an expert jockey. David Brown's summary of the initiation process in Santería reprinted here demonstrates the complexities of "making the saint," of physically and spiritually cleansing and preparing the initiate to receive his or her *orichas*, who literally land on the *iyawó*'s head, becoming the rulers of his or her path.

For African-based religions, the structure of the cosmos is not only a reflection of the dynamics of *axé/aché* but it is also a template for how practitioners organize themselves in tightly knit albeit hierarchical houses (*terreiros* in Candomblé and *ilé* in Santería) led by an initiated leader (*pai* or *mãe de santo* in Candomblé, literally a father or a mother of the saint, or a *padrino* or *madrina*, a godfather or godmother, in Santería) who sponsors and educates a group of would-be initiates (*filhos de santo* in Candomblé, literally children of the saint, or *ahijados/as* in Santería). As the titles imply, the relationship between priests and initiates is a parental

Table 4.1 *Umbanda's Cosmos*

I. ORIXAS

SANCTITIES	CATHOLIC CORRELATE	ASSOCIATION & DOMINION	COLOR	RITUAL OBJECT	FOOD
Olorum (Oludumare)	God, the Father	Androgynous Supreme Deity; Creator of the Universe	White	Invisible but Omnipresent	
Oxalá (Obatalá)	Jesus Christ	Sky God/Heaven; Pombinho: Baby Oxalá; Oxaguiã: Young Oxalá Oxalufã: Elder Oxalá	White	Shepherd Staff	Yams
Iroko (Loko/Tempo)	St. Francis, The Holy Spirit	Time, Weather, and Trees	Green	Sacred Leaves	
Xangô	St. Jerome, Moses, St. Peter	Justice/Thunder and Lightning; Dwells in Rain and Rocks	Red	Double-Headed Ax	Okra with Shrimp
Oxum	Our Lady of the Candles	Goddess of Sensuality, Love, and Fertility; Dwells in Rivers and Waterfalls; Represents Female Vanity	Yellow	Golden Mirror	Beans
Yemanjá	Our Lady of Glory, Our Lady of Conception	Salt Water; Dwells in the Sea	Blue	Silver Fan	Rice with Fish
Ogum	St. George, St. Anthony	War and Smiths; Associated with Metal	Blue or Green	Iron Sword	Black Beans with Pork
Oxosse	St. Sebastian	Hunting; Dwells in the Forest; He Has a Close Association with the Caboclos	Green	Iron Bow	Corn with Slices of Coconut
Iançã	St. Barbara	Storms and Winds	Dark Red or Brown	Fly Wisk	Bean Dumplings (*Acarajé*)

SANCTITIES	CATHOLIC CORRELATE	ASSOCIATION & DOMINION	COLOR	RITUAL OBJECT	FOOD
Omolu (Obaluayé)	St. Lazarus	Illness, Death, and Medicine; Dwells in Cemeteries; Associated with Exús	Black	Sceptre with Cowries	Popcorn
Oxumaré	St. Bartholomew	Fresh Water and the Rainbow; This Orixá Is Both Male and Female	Yellow, Green, Black	Metal Snakes	Sweet Potato

II. "INTERMEDIATE" ENTITIES

Pretos Velhos	The spirits of the old slaves (The Civilized World)				
Erês	Child spirits of the orixás (Their Catholic correlates are St. Cosmo and Damian,); associated with games, practical jokes, and the carnival				
Caboclos	Principally the spirits of the Indians, but also of cowboys and other folk heroes (The World of Nature)				

III. THE "LOWER" SPIRITS

Exús	Spirits of the Scoundrels (Zé Pilintra, Sete Facadas, and Tranca-Rua) and Prostitutes (Pomba-Gira, Corquisa, and Padilha). They are the messengers/slaves of the orixás. Normally associated with Satan, Lucifer, and Jezebel (The Underworld). Associated with life in the street (brega); collectively known as o povo da rua.				

IV. HUMANS

	They may receive the spirits with the proper training and once they have been initiated.				

V. DISINCARNATED SPIRITS

Eguns	Wandering spirits of the dead which need to be educated/enlightened (aparacás) or are here to help the living understand the spirit world and educate aparacás (babás). Babás include Buddha, Gandhi, Plato, and Socrates. Iançã rules over the realm of the eguns. Shows the influence of both the African cult of the ancestors and European Spiritism.				

one. Just as the initiate's head saint plays a key role in directing his or her fate, teaching the mysteries of the cosmos through personal devotion, so do fathers and mothers of the saint bring up their children within the tradition.

Training the initiates includes not only teaching the right way of conducting rituals or the ethos of humility, respect, and reciprocity. It also involves instructing the initiates to become diagnosticians of the varying configurations of *aché/axé*. Santería, for example, relies on two sophisticated systems of divination. When the santero is consulted about a particular matter such as sickness or misfortune, he throws the *dilogún*, a long string of sixteen interspersed cowry shells, and discerns the emerging patterns according to the position in which these shells fall.[9] For each pattern, there are verses of Lukumí poetry and lore about the *Orichas* that the santero has memorized and interprets to make sense of the situation at hand. On the basis of this interpretation, he recommends a course of action that might call for a work for the saint (*ebó*) or the preparation and ingestion of an herbal infusion. Thus, the santero is, as Gonzáles Wippler (1987: 66) puts it, "a consulting expert. His expertise is human life." He works the powers of the universe to assist his *ahijados* and those who seek his help.

Religions of the African Diaspora Today

Today, the struggles over the question of purity and syncretism in African-based religions are not only part and parcel of the racial politics of countries like Cuba and Brazil, with large black populations (Sansone 2003). Following the Cuban revolution in 1959, the successive waves of Cuban exiles have brought the Regla Lukumí to cities like Miami and New York in a second diaspora. In Miami, the presence of Regla Lukumí has generated serious tensions, particularly around the issue of animal sacrifice. These tensions came to a head in the early 1980s, when Oba Ernesto Pichardo and his Church of Lukumi Babalu Aye Inc. (CLB) sued the city of Hialeah for its ordinance against the "unnecessary" and "cruel" slaughter of animals for "any type of ritual," particularly those rituals that are "inconsistent with public morals, peace, or safety."[10] Pichardo argued that the Hialeah prohibition not only reiterated widespread prejudices about Santería but also violated the constitutional right to freedom of religion. The suit made it all the way to the Supreme Court, which in 1993 ruled in favor of Pichardo, recognizing that animal sacrifice was essential to the Santería. Noting that the practice of animal sacrifice is mentioned throughout the Hebrew scriptures and is performed in modern Islam, the justices wrote that "given the historical association between animal sacrifice and religious worship . . . petitioner's [Pichardo's] assertion that animal sacrifice is an integral part of their religion cannot be deemed bizarre or incredible." The ruling, in effect, brought Santería out of the shadows, opening the door for it to move from being a national and ethnic religion (connected with Afro-Cubans and Hispanics of African descent) to being a global religion. The documents from the Church of Lukumí included here demonstrate this move to universality, particularly in the simultaneous drive to recover African dimensions of Santería and to codify and normalize them. Particular noteworthy are the Lukumi efforts to "establish a formal setting for the religious education of adherents, clergy, and general public." While some critics have decried similar attempts to professionalize and "churchify" a tradition that owes its vitality to grassroots diversity and innovation,[11] the Church of Lukumí can be seen as yet another example of how African-based religions adapt creatively to changing social and cultural demands.

CHAPTER 4 DOCUMENTS

*"The Archbishop of Bahia Rules on Slave
Evangelization and Aspects of Their Treatment (1707)"*[1]

4. We order all persons, ecclesiastics as well as secular, to teach or have taught the Christian doctrine to their families, and especially to their slaves, who because of their ignorance are those most in need of this instruction, sending them to church so that the priest may teach them the Articles of Faith, so that they may know what to believe; the Pater Noster and Ave Maria, so that they may know how to pray; the Commandments of the law of God and of the Holy Mother Church, and the moral sins, so that they will know how to behave; the virtues, so that they may recognize good values; and the seven Sacraments, so that they may receive them with dignity, and with them the grace which they give, and the other prayers of Christian doctrine, so that they may be instructed in everything which is important to their salvation. . . .

6. And because the slaves of Brazil are those most in need of Christian Doctrine, so numerous are their nations and so diverse their languages, we should search for every means to instruct them in the faith, or for someone who may speak to them in their languages, and in ours, when they can already understand it. And there is no more profitable way than a kind of instruction accomodated [sic] to the rudeness of their understanding and the barbarity of their speech. Thus the Parish Priests are required to have topics made . . . of the brief form of the Catechism, which is to be found in Title XXXII, for distribution to the houses of the parishioners, in order that they may instruct their slaves in the mysteries of the Faith, and Christian Doctrine, in the manner of the said instruction, and so that their questions and answers will be those examined by them when they confess and take Christian communion, and this will be easier than studying from memory the Lord's Creed; and others which those of greater ability learn. . . .

50. And for greater security in regard to the Baptism of the brute and raw slaves, and those of unknown language, such as are those who come from Mina, and many also from Angola, the following will be done.[2] After they have acquired some knowledge of our language, or if there are

interpreters, the instruction of the mysteries [special catechism] will be used, which as we said is contained in the third book [Title XXXII] number 579. . . . And aside from this the raw slaves referred to above will be asked only the following questions:

> Do you want to wash your soul with holy water?
> Do you want to eat the salt of God?
> Will you cast all the sins out of your soul?
> Will you commit no more sins?
> Do you want to be a child of God?
> Will you cast the devil out of your soul?

51. And because it has happened that some of these raw slaves have died before it could be learned whether they wished to be baptized or not, the first chance that they may be asked the above questions, either through interpreters or in our own language, they possessing some understanding of it, it is very important for the salvation of their souls that this be done, because then, in the event of death, since they have already expressed their desire, even if this was long before, they may certainly be baptized *sub conditione,* or even absolutely, depending upon the assessment of their ability which has been formed up to that time.

52. We order all our subjects who are being served by infidel slaves that they labor hard to convert them to our Holy Catholic Faith, and to receive the Sacrament of Baptism, coming to a knowledge of the errors of their ways, and the state of perdition in which they walk, and that for this purpose they should be sent frequently to learned and virtuous persons, who will point out their errors to them and teach them what is required for their salvation. . . .

54. We order the Vicars and Curates to take great care to acquaint themselves with the slaves of both sexes in their parishes, and having learned that they do not know the Pater Noster, the Ave Maria, the Lord's Creed, the Commandments of the Law of God and of the Holy Mother Church, they being able to learn all this, they [the priests] should take steps against their masters so that they will teach them the Holy Doctrine or have it taught to them, and so that they will send them to church to learn it, and that as long as they do not know it they should not administer to them the Sacrament of Baptism, or, having already been baptized, any other Sacrament.

55. Since experience has revealed to us, however, that among the many slaves who exist in this Archbishopric there are many so coarse and rude

that, although their masters make every possible effort to reach them, they always seem to know less, while pitying them for their coarseness and misery, we grant permission to the Vicars and Curates to administer to them the Sacraments of Baptism, Penance, Extreme Unction, and Matrimony, it being apparent to them that, although the masters have been diligent in teaching them, the slaves are too coarse to learn. They should first catechize them in the mysteries of the Faith, in the intentions required for receiving them, and the obligations which accompany them; so that from their replies it may be understood that they consent, possess understanding, and everything else which is needed for the said Sacraments.

56. And let the Vicars and Curates know that they should not make use too lightly of this permission to administer the Sacraments to the slaves. In fact, they should not administer them at all until they are convinced that the masters have made a great effort and that, because of the slaves' great ignorance, this was not enough, and that in the future what they have been doing will most probably not be enough. Instead they should proceed with great care, first examining them, and teaching them, to see if they can derive something from it, because they should not give the masters a chance to neglect their obligation to teach their slaves, which they perform so badly that rarely is a master found who makes the effort he should, erring also in the way they teach, because they do not teach the doctrine point by point, and at leisure, as required by ignorant people, but rather all at once, and with a great deal of haste.

Concerning the Labors Which Are Prohibited on the Holy Days of Obligation, and the Penalties Which Will Be Imposed upon Those Who Perform Them

377. Because it is not good that on the few days which God reserves for his cult and veneration the faithful occupy themselves in servile labor, ungratefully denying Him this little bit of time which He took for Himself, directed toward the spiritual relief of our souls, laboring or following those whom they have under their supervision to labor, adding to sins committed these new sins, desiring as we do in fulfillment of our pastoral function to remedy (as much as it is possible for us) the abuses and negligence which exist in this matter, we order all our subjects to abstain from all work, servile and mechanical labors on Sundays and on Holy Days of Obligation; and we order the Parish Priests to exercise the greatest vigilance in this matter, warning their parishioners about this; and our Vicar

General, Visitors, District, and Parish Priests will sentence those who do not comply with the punishments later stated.

378. And because the most notable abuse which can exist in this regard is the openness with which the Lords of the Mills [*senhores de engenho*] order the milling done on Sundays and Holy Days, we order all our subjects of whatever category to abstain from all servile labor done either by themselves or by others, fully observing the precept of God's law which forbids work on such days; which is understood to be from midnight Saturday until the following midnight Sunday, and in the same way on Holy Days. And if some particular need exists, such as a burning cane field, or the cane being in such a condition that delay would probably result in its loss, or some other similar need, and therefore labor is performed: this may be allowed if a license is first requested from the Superior, who in our absence or in the absence of our Vicar General we declare to be the Parish Priest, to whom we grant the power and authority to issue the said license, if he convinces himself that the need exists. And anyone acting in a contrary fashion will be condemned by the Parish Priest to a fine of ten *tostões* [a *milréis*] on the first occasion, on the second to two *milréis*, and on the third to four *milréis*, which will be used to maintain the church; and if he should remain stubborn, our Vicar General will be informed, so that he may act as required by law, and the strongest action will be taken against any Parish Priest who does not comply with this decree.

379. No less detestable is the inhuman, brutal, and depraved abuse which many slaveholders have adopted to the great harm of God's service and the welfare of souls: making use of the miserable slaves during the entire week, without giving them anything for their sustenance, or any clothing with which to cover themselves; this need, which is based in natural law, is met by giving them Sundays and Holy Days free so that at that time they may obtain their required food and clothing. As a result, the miserable slaves do not hear Mass, nor keep the Law of God which forbids labor on those days. To banish such an evil abuse against God and mankind, we exhort and ask all our subjects, recalling the wounds of Christ our Lord and Redeemer, that from now on they grant their slaves the needed support, so that they may observe the said precepts and live like Christians. And we order the Parish Priests to very carefully observe and inform themselves whether this abuse is continuing, and when encountering guilty persons who are not complying with this provision, that they take full action against them in the manner prescribed in the previous decree in Paragraph 378.

380. The same procedure and punishment will be imposed upon the sugar cane, manioc, and tobacco planters who allow their blacks and slaves to work openly on Sundays and Holy Days, planting gardens for themselves or for others, fishing, or loading or unloading boats, or any other kind of labor service which is forbidden on those days, unless there is an urgent need, and a license is requested for this purpose (as we stated in another place). . . .

Concerning the Persons and Cases in Which
the Immunity of the Church Does Not Apply

754. Although normally the immunity of the Church is valid and defends delinquent persons who seek shelter there, nevertheless there are exceptions to this rule concerning some crimes which, because of their material gravity or for other reasons or circumstances, are excepted by law, custom, and the doctrines of the Church; and they are the following:

755. The heretic, the apostate and the schismatic do not enjoy the immunity of the Church. Nor the blasphemer, the sorcerer, the maker of false blessings, soothsayer, or witch. Nor does the public thief or highwayman who is in the habit of killing, wounding, or stealing. Nor those who during the night destroy fields or crops, or deliberately set fire to cane, manioc, or tobacco either already harvested or about to be harvested. . . .

757. Nor the slave (even if he is a Christian) who flees from his master to free himself from slavery. However, if he runs away from his master because the latter intends to treat him with relentless severity, the slave will not be taken back to him unless he first makes a sworn promise, when he can make no other, that he will not mistreat him, or he will be sold in cases when this is required by law.

"The Black Brotherhood of Our Lady of the Rosary in Recife in the Eighteenth Century"[3]

The black people, and captives, have proved themselves so devoted to the service of the Mother of God, Our Lady of the Rosary, that they themselves, although poor, resolved to establish a beautiful church, in which they alone are the founders and administrators. This temple has an outstanding and sumptuous structure; its façade is a splendid edifice of white stone, an admirable example of inspirational architecture. Our Lady of the Rosary is the comfort, the consolation of these people, because all of them have recourse after their labors to the sovereign Empress of Glory. And it is with such faith and devotion that they go in quest of her and experience her favor that they are reluctant to take leave of her presence, offering up their prayers to her. It is certainly highly inspiring and touching to witness the fervor, zeal, and expense with which they serve Our Lady. Every day of the year, if some event does not prevent it, they chant in liturgy the third part of the rosary. On Saturdays at five o'clock in the afternoon they chant a recital, and at seven at night again the third part of the rosary. On holy days they all attend the mass of their chaplain, which they enrich with their singing, their recital of the rosary, and the minor office. At three o'clock in the afternoon they chant another rosary and at night at the door of the church yet another. On the second Sunday of October they worship Our Lady with great solemnity, and to increase the fervor of their devotion, they engage in dances and other licit entertainments with which they devoutly gladden the hearts of the population.

In the five chapels of the church are the images of Our Lady of the Rosary, who is the patron of the house; and those of Our Lady of Boa Hora, and Saint Dominic, as well as those of the black saints, Estebão, Moíses, Benedito, Antonio de Catalagirona, Efigenia, and His Holiness King Balthasar. Everyone is gladdened by the solemn festivities devoted to our Lord, the chanted mass and sermon. These ceremonies are preceded by novenas, which they celebrate with great devotion and a large participation. Every Saturday and on the first Sunday of each month they go into the streets singing the rosary of Our Lady with such a pleasing combination of voices that a smooth harmony results which is both agreeable and edifying.

"Black Islam in Brazil"[4]   ROGER BASTIDE

The Mussulman religion in Brazil was the religion of certain colored slaves known as Musulmi or Malê. The name "Musulmi" is self-explanatory; the name "Malê" has been much discussed.[5] Obviously it is a corruption of Mali, the name of one of the Mohammedan kingdoms of the Niger valley, inhabited in the thirteenth century by the Malinka. The Malinka are also known as Mandinga, and, as we shall see, in Brazil the word *mandinga* came to designate black magic. Strictly speaking, however, it was the Hausa, not the Malê, who introduced Mohammedanism to Brazil. While the Hausa certainly constituted the majority of Islamized Negroes, slavery threw them together with other tribes of the same religion, including some of the Nagô, the Bornú or Adamana, the Gurushi, Guruncu or Grúnce, the Mandinga, and the Fuláh or Peul.[6] Early travelers and historians also speak of Minas as Mussulmans, but the name "Mina," which originally designated not an ethnic group but a place—the big Portuguese slave market on the coast of West Africa—was . . . applied to anyone who did not belong to the Bantu groups. Hence some Mina were Mussulmans; some were not.

With very few exceptions, all these tribes were either pure Negro or of mixed Negro and Harnite blood. They were therefore Islamized animists, not Mohammedans by origin. Their old beliefs had not entirely died out.[7] It was this Mohammedan-fetishist syncretism, not the pure Islam of Mohammed, that was introduced into Brazil.

These tribes were unusually successful in resisting Christianization and clung to their proud, intractable faith with jealous steadfastness. All travelers agree on this point. . . .

It has been stated that a mosque founded by Mohammedan Negroes existed in 1840 in the Rua Baron Saint Felix, but the only evidence I have been able to discover is the existence of a black named João Alabah who occasionally requested police permission to hold celebrations in his house. Although he regarded the Mussulmans as "brothers," his religion did not go beyond fetishism. The only Mohammedan whose address Alabah was able to furnish stated that there was no mosque in Rio, and he could name only six Negro Mussulmans, who practiced their cult in their own homes. Perhaps these contradictory statements can be reconciled by the hypothesis that the Moslem "Mina" in Rio, although numerous, were all to some degree fetishists and stayed out of sight to avoid persecution, celebrating their rites in their own homes.

The Moslems were distributed practically all over Brazil. We know specifically that they existed in São Paulo, where, according to the testimony of a slave, there was a mosque for the practice of their cult,[8] and in the states of Alagoas, Pernambuco, and Paraíba.[9] But the greatest concentration was in Bahia, where they were the life and soul of the slave revolts and where, according to Nina Rodrigues, at the end of the nineteenth century they still constituted one-third of the population of African origin and maintained a highly organized cult. . . .

The second major center of the Moslem population after Bahia was Rio. Within a few years of Nina Rodrigues's description of the last Mohammedan survivors in Bahia, João de Rio wrote an account of the religions of the [now former] Brazilian capital. He distinguished two types of

African religious survivals: the *orixá* and the *alufa* cults, i.e. the cults of the Yoruba and the Moslem sects.[10] He also noted that the Moslems observed the religious holidays of the other blacks, but this does not necessarily imply the emergence of a racial consciousness in resistance to slavery; it merely shows the depth of religious syncretism and the persistence of primitive paganism among the Islamized Negroes.[11] The Pernambucan cult illustrates this syncretism. There the *alufa* or Moslem priest would foretell the future by pouring palm oil and blood over three purple stones. One of these was known as the "Saint Barbara stone," and the others were meteorites.[12] Now Saint Barbara is the Catholic equivalent of Xangô, the thunder god, whose emblem is the thunderbolt or meteorite. Obviously the Islamic and Yoruba religions had intermixed. . . .

But if the Mohammedan faith was so proud and so resistant to Catholic proselytizing, is it not paradoxical that it should have so suddenly died out or undergone such profound adulteration? There are several explanations. First, the number of Hausa diminished considerably after the revolution of 1813, when the troublemakers were either massacred or deported to Africa.[13] Those who remained made few converts, largely because of their racial or religious snobbery, which caused them to hold aloof from the other Africans, keeping to themselves and not mixing with their brothers in misfortune,[14] going to bed early while the other Negroes preferred to stay up late to celebrate their pagan rituals.[15] By establishing Catholicism as the religion of the masters and Mohammedanism as the religion of the insurrectionary leaders, slavery tended in early times to promote Islam, especially within groups that retained their African languages. But abolition and the theoretical equality of all Brazilians before the law destroyed one of the major incentives to conversion. The *iman* Luis told Nina Rodrigues how painful it was to him to see sons of Malê embracing fetishist sects or Christianity rather than holding fast to the faith of their ancestors.[16] Just as an animal species becomes extinct when its last representatives die out, Mohammedanism in Brazil, having lost all potential for renewal or propagation, died out along with its old adherents. But before it became totally extinct, just as its death agony was beginning, such men as Mello Moraes, Manoel Querino, Etienne Brasil, Nina Rodrigues, and João de Rio were able to observe and study it. From their descriptions we shall try to reconstitute the life of the black Islamic community in colonial Brazil.

It was essentially a Puritan community. Its outward morality, sobriety, and temperance contrasted strongly with the other Africans' noisy exuberance and their liking for alcohol and for singing and shouting. The Moslems' appearance, their quiet conversational tone, restrained gestures, and pointed beards symbolized their ethnic and religious separateness.[17] Above all, the Moslem's faith set the rhythm of his life, marking its every phase from birth to death, accenting the passage of the day from sunrise to sunset.[18]

It appears that a Mussulman baby was baptized at birth.[19] By the time he was ten he had been circumcised.[20] Then his instruction would begin, for the Mohammedans attached great importance to education.[21] Since his faith required the reading of the Koran, he had to be able to read and write Arabic script. Schools were therefore established in conjunction with the Moslem places of worship, in the homes of free Africans. House searches conducted after Hausa or Mina revolts produced alphabets, reading primers, and wall posters of lessons to be learned.[22] In Rio, Arabic grammars written in French were used.[23] Free members of the community even went to Africa to study so that they might later devote themselves to teaching the slave population of Brazil.

Marriage was a sacrament marking the end of childhood and the Mussulman's entry into adult society. The *iman* presided over the ceremony. He would begin by calling upon the couple to think carefully so that they would never regret the action they were about to take. After giving them a few minutes to reflect, he would ask if they were sincerely marrying each other by free consent. If the reply was affirmative, the bride, "dressed in white, her face covered with a tulle veil," placed a silver ring on the finger of her future husband, and he, "dressed in wide Turkish-style trousers," gave his future wife a silver chain as they repeated the words "*Sadaca do Alamabi* (I give this to you in the name of God)." . . .

Now married life began. Polygamy was permitted and practiced among the Mussulmans in Brazil.[24] The women were subject to an extremely strict code of honor. "Any woman who failed in her conjugal duties was a general outcast; no one would show her any favor. Nevertheless the husband could not beat her. An unfaithful wife was allowed to leave her house only in the evening, chaperoned by someone whom her husband trusted."[25]

Married women retained some of the customs of their native country, especially the use of cosmetics. They painted their eyelids as a sign of beauty.[26] They did not, however, veil the face as they did in Africa.[27] It appears that these Malê led a quiet life, getting up and going to bed early, observing scrupulous rules of hygiene and keeping to themselves.[28]

When a Mussulman died, his body was washed, then dressed in a white shirt known as an *abada*. A cap with a white tassel called a *fila* was placed on his head; this was in fact the ritual headdress. The funeral was conducted in the Brazilian manner.[29] It was rumored that the bones of the corpse were broken and dislocated before it was placed in the coffin, but this seems not to be true; "they simply laid it on its side, not supine," in the coffin.[30] Although society prevented the Malê from conducting their funerals exactly according to their own tradition, they made up for this by holding their own festival of the dead twice a year. . . .

[R]eligious observance set the rhythm of life for the faithful and determined the fate of the souls of the dead. The principles of the Koran dominated not only the essential frameworks of existence but daily life too. The devout Mussulman's day began at four o'clock in the morning. Dressed in a tight shirt, trousers, and a tasseled skullcap, all made of the whitest cotton, and holding his *teceba,* a rosary fifty centimeters long consisting of ninety-nine big wooden beads and ending in a ball, he stood on a sheepskin and recited his prayers.[31] This was called "performing *sala."* The Portuguese word *sala* is probably a corruption of *sara,* which, as we shall see, designated the most important religious ceremonies of the Moslems. No doubt the corruption stems from an awareness of the distinction between private and public worship and represents an attempt to express this distinction linguistically. Everyone who could do so recited his prayers four more times in the course of the day. The Bahian names for these five exercises were: *açubá* (morning), *al-lá* (noon), *ay-à-sari* (afternoon), *alimangariba* (sunset), and *adisha* (night); they were preceded and concluded by sacramental phrases such as *"Bi-si-mi-lai* (In the name of God, forgiving and merciful).[32] Every prayer was preceded by an ablution, for which the Negro removed his ordinary clothes and donned a white shirt with long sleeves called an *abada.*[33] . . .

Obviously slaves could not undertake the pilgrimage to Mecca because of their status, and free Negroes could not because of the distance,[34] but they always observed the fast of Ramadan.[35] The Mussulmans also abstained from certain foods, notably salt pork.

[. . . .]

The Mussulmans were notorious among the other Negroes for their powerful magic. They had all kinds of amulets, talismans, and charms, most commonly in the form of Solomon's seals, and papers on which verses from the Koran were inscribed and which they carried in little bags hung around the neck.[36] A favorite procedure for gaining immunity to bullets—one which Nina Rodrigues saw in use during Hausa revolts—was to write certain Arabic signs on a black tablet, then rinse the tablet and drink the waters.[37] The same procedure was used to cast a spell, but in that case the water, instead of being swallowed, was sprinkled on a path that the victim would use. The signs inscribed and then washed off would then, of course, be curses.[38] How deeply this magic impressed other Africans can be seen from the survival of the names *mandinga* for an object used in black magic and *mandingueiro* for the practitioner. . . .

In Rio, as in Bahia, the Malê were regarded as masters of black magic, and many of them earned their living—and a good living—by selling spells and charms. João de Rio notes that, despite their monotheism, in preparing these spells they had recourse to *aligenum* (devils), a term which is obviously a corruption of *djinn*,[39] and that some of them had acquired great reputations in this art. *Alikali*, for instance, made *idams* to induce rain.[40]

How much of this rich tradition survives today? In 1937 the Bahia Union of Afro-Brazilian Sects still included a *candomblé* of the "Mussurumin" nation situated on the Rua da Liberdade and directed by Pedro Manuel de Espirito Santo.[41] We know little about it, but the corruption of the name "Mussulman" is in itself enough to suggest that its Mohammedanism—if any—must have been considerably modified. Some of the hymns sung at Bantu or Nagô *candomblés* include the name of Allah. . . .

In Rio the spirits that incarnate themselves during the *macumba* establish "lines." One of these lines still exists and is called "the line of Mussurumin, Massuruman, Massurumin, or Massuruhy." Since Malê magic was considered particularly effective and dangerous, this line consists entirely of evil spirits who come down to earth to wreak vengeance. They are invoked by tracing on the ground circles of gunpowder surrounding cigarettes, drinks, pins, tobacco, chickens, etc. The gunpowder is lighted, and the spirits descend during the din of the explosion. The heads of these lines are called "Alufa," "Father Alufa," or "Uncle Alufa."[42] In 1934, in Alagoas, Arthur Ramos collected a Malê hymn to Ogun:

> Little Ogun is of the Malê race. Nu-ê, nu-ê!
> Little Ogun is of the Malê race. Nu-e, ê-rê-rê-rê![43]

Olorun, the chief Nagô god, was finally merged with Allah, producing the new divinity Olorun-ulua *(uluà* being a corruption of *Allah).*[44]

[. . . .]

What happened in Brazil was the opposite of what happened on the black continent. In West Africa Islam triumphed over fetishism, steadily driving it back and gaining a firmer grip on the black continent. It even opposed the Christian missions—often victoriously. In Brazil, however, Islam died out, leaving the Gêgê-Nagô religion and Christianity in the lead. How can this sociological contrast be explained?

In the first place the Mussulmans never amounted to more than a minority of the colored population. They were also what might be called "passive" Moslems, i.e. Islamized blacks, converts, not pure Semites. Lacking all proselytizing spirit, the best they could do was to hold out as long as possible. In addition to this demographic explanation, there is also a psychological one: the Moslem's pride, his unwillingness to mix with other slaves, his desire to live in a world apart. Hence a change in his social situation produced a change in collective behavior; a proselytizing faith turned into a religion of mystical isolation.

So far as the fetishist Negroes were concerned, Islam and Christianity exchanged positions in moving from Africa to Brazil. In Africa Islam demanded less individual sacrifice than Catholicism or Protestantism. It discarded mythology in favor of dogma. It imposed certain taboos and prayers but required no strenuous moral effort. It accommodated itself to the sensuality of the Negro. In Brazil, on the other hand, Catholicism was the most appealing and the most tolerant religion. Confident that the influence of the environment would gradually change the African's heart and soul, all it asked of him was to learn by rote a few gestures and words, not to remake his personality. Hence in Brazil Islam came to represent Puritanism—especially because of its prohibition of excessive drinking, which was particularly hard on wretched slaves seeking an escape from reality in the sugar cane brandy known as *cachaça*.[45]

To the Negro the Mohammedan was not a comrade in slavery. Only in an insurrectionary situation—i.e., in exceptional circumstances—could he become a leader. The white man represented the world of liberty to which manumission gave access. But the *sine qua non* of such access was to imitate the whites. Hence the attraction of Catholicism.

All these factors combined to persuade the African to remain fetishist or to recognize only Christian leadership. This explains both Islam's lack of success in Brazil and the return of the last generation of Malê to the beliefs of their animist ancestors. Indeed, as the Malê came into contact with fetishists in Brazil, as their revolts failed and their numbers dwindled, the veneer of Mohammedanism began to disintegrate. All that remained was the old vital core, the ancient propensity for worshiping the forces of nature. The Mussulmans were absorbed by the Gêgê-Nagô cult.

This produced another curious reversal. In black Islam Mohammedanism was the official religion, and the old cults were regarded as nothing more than magic rites. In Brazil, however, Mohammedanism became, and remained, sorcery. In differing demographic and social conditions, the collision of races and cultures can produce the most surprising happenings and the most contradictory religious metamorphoses.

The Taste of Blood: Spirit Possession in Brazilian Candomblé[46] JIM WAFER

Axé is Candomblé's ultimate value term, and has two main usages. In the first usage it is a "container" and in the second a "content" or attribute. From the perspective of the first usage, it means something like "the ethos of Candomblé." For example an *exua* called Corquisa once said to me, "you were not born within the *axé.*"

The sense of the second usage is harder to convey in English. It means something like "the quintessence of the ethos of Candomblé." In this usage things "have" *axé*, though not indefinitely. The term "presence" would express something of its intangible quality, but not its dynamism. *Axé* moves around. A thing that "has" *axé* at one moment may lose it the next. From this perspective *axé* has a lot in common with fashion. Like the *exus* and the stock market, it is not entirely predictable.

It is because of the mobility of *axé* that ritual objects in Candomblé require repeated sacrifices. Blood renews the *axé* of these objects, and helps to stabilize their value. There is a close link between *axé* and blood, for which reason the term is sometimes translated as "vital force." The ethos of Candomblé—*axé* in the first sense—is like an organism defined by and sustaining itself by means of the circulation of its animating force—*axé* in the second sense—among its parts.

But this image fails to account for the role played by human motivation in the circulation of *axé*. Since *axé* is Candomblé's ultimate value term, humans are necessarily interested in the way it moves around.

The ethos in the first sense is like any ethos in that it consists partly of certain conventionalized notions about the comparative value of the various phenomena that make up its conceptual world. It is these notions which give Candomblé the "flavor" that distinguishes it from other cultures.

But these notions are to some extent relativized, or opened to contestation, by *axé* in its second sense. The value of a thing may change if *axé* is attributed to it—or not attributed to it. Thus stones, in themselves, have little intrinsic value. But if a person finds a stone that seems to have *axé*, that stone may become an *otá*, the head of a god, the central item among ritual objects that make up a "seat."

[. . . .]

The term *caboclo* (which in Candomblé is usually pronounced without the l), is said to come from the Tupi word *kari'boka*, meaning "deriving from the white." . . . Thus its primary meaning is "mestizo," "a person of part Indian and part European descent." But it may also be used to refer to any Brazilian Indian. The difference between these two uses of the term in ordinary Brazilian Portuguese has carried over into Candomblé, where there are two basic categories of *caboclo* spirits: those called *boiadeiros*, or "cowboys," "backwoodsmen" (Boiadeiro is also the proper name of one particular who wear hats of leather or straw, and sometimes also fringed leather jackets and knickerbockers) and those called "Indians," who often wear feather headdresses, and may be costumed in feathers, fur, or hide.

These are the only types of *caboclo* I myself saw at the festivals I attended. However, I have heard of others. There are, for example, various foreign *caboclos* such as the King of Hungary (who is the *caboclo* of a famous Bahian mother-of-saint called Olga of Alaketu . . .) and Italian and Japanese *caboclos*. There are also *caboclos* of the "village of the sea," such as the sailor *caboclos*.

Taís [one of Wafer's informants] once said to me *"caboclos* are infinite," in contrast with the *orixás*, of whom there is a fixed number. It seems that in spite of the nationalistic overtones of the utopian sentiments with which the *caboclos* are associated, these same sentiments are capable of creating a sense of universal brotherhood, into which non-Indians and non-Brazilians can be incorporated. Perhaps the etymological link between the *caboclo* and the blending of races makes the tradition the obvious symbolic vehicle for the incorporation into Candomblé of foreign elements.

I have called the sentiments motivating the tradition of the *caboclos* "utopian." But we could also think of them as "carnivalesque," in the sense in which this notion has been elaborated by Mikhail Bakhtin. In his work on Rabelais, Bakhtin has developed a "carnival principle," which underlies not just the carnivals of the Middle Ages and Renaissance that provided imagery for Rabelais, but any manifestation of the "nonofficial, extraecclesiastical and extrapolitical aspect of the world, of man, and of human relationships" (Bakhtin 1984:6). Carnival celebrates "temporary liberation from the prevailing truth and the established order"; it marks "the suspension of all hierarchical rank, privileges, norms, and prohibitions" (1984:10).

Structurally, at least, one could say that Candomblé as a whole has traditionally stood in a "carnivalesque" relationship to official Brazilian culture. Like the folk celebrations of the Middle Ages, the festivals of the African gods were originally the popular, "nonofficial" counterparts of the feasts of the church. In Candomblé every *orixá* corresponds to a Christian saint, and was traditionally celebrated on a date close to that of the saint's day, with dancing, drinking, and feasting. (It is worth recalling also that the colonization of Brazil began during the lifetime of Rabelais; so the possibility of a historical link between Candomblé and the European folk traditions of that era is not implausible. Cf. Williams 1979:9). However, since the early decades of this century certain leaders of Candomblé, aided by anthropologists and other sympathetic intellectuals, have struggled to make Candomblé an "official" religion, with a status on a par with that of the Catholic Church. Their strategy for doing this has entailed attempting to divest Candomblé of its carnivalesque elements, and emphasizing its orthodoxy as an African religion. The result has been the evolution of a notion of degrees of "purity" in Candomblé: religious centers that are "pure" are those that have tried to discard all that is "folkloric" and "syncretistic," and to incorporate as much as possible that is African (cf. Dantas 1982; Birman 1980:6-31; Frigerio 1983; on the prejudice against syncretism, cf. Berling 190: 4-9).

Perhaps the most extreme example is a famous *terreiro* called Ilê Axé Opô Afonjá, which in its process of re-Africanization has been largely purged of Christian iconography. (But even this *terreiro* has not been able to remove all traces of syncretism. Its ritual calendar is still tied, at least in part, to the feast days of the church [Maia 1985:99].) The mother-of-saint of this *terreiro*, Stella Azevedo, wrote a short paper called "Syncretism and Whitening" for the Third International Congress of Orisa Tradition and Culture, which I attended in New York in 1986. After stating that freed slaves, through a desire to "whiten" themselves, adopted practices that syncretized Catholicism and "traces of Africanism," she concludes with these words: "But, in the present times of total liberation, it is worth remembering that these maneuvers ought to be abandoned, with all people assuming the religion of their roots" (1986:2).

I am not unsympathetic to the political motivation behind these remarks. I recognize that the re-Africanization of Candomblé, based on the idea of throwing off white domination, has considerable symbolic significance for the Movimento Negro Unificado—a loose affiliation of Black activist groups in Brazil, concerned with political and economic justice for Blacks, and the fostering of a positive Black identity.

However, the re-Africanization movement in Candomblé has a number of consequences that in some ways undermine the aspirations that inspired it. To begin with, it promotes comparison between *terreiros* on the basis of the degree to which they are "orthodox" or "traditional." These terms are frequently encountered in the literature on Candomblé, but it is hard to know what justifies their usage. Since Candomblé, unlike the Catholic Church, has no central body responsible for the formulation of doctrine and the regulation of practice, and every initiatic lineage is, in effect, a law unto itself, there is no basis for judging any *terreiro* as more or less "orthodox" than any other. Moreover, if one uses "traditional" to mean "based on long-standing custom," there would be grounds for arguing that "syncretistic" *terreiros* are more "traditional" than the re-Africanized ones, since, as Mother Stella herself points out, syncretism historically *preceded* the re-Africanization movement (cf. Mott 1988).

REFERENCES

Azevedo, Stella (1986) "Sincretismo e branqueamento." Abstract of an unpublished paper presented at the Third International Congress of Orisa Tradition and Culture, New York, October 6-10, 1986.
Bakhtin, Mikhail (1984) *Rabelais and His World*. Bloomington: Indiana University Press.
Berling, Judith (1980) *The Syncretic Religion of Lin Chao-en*. New York: Columbia University Press.
Birman, Patrícia (1980) "Feitiço, carrego e olho grande, os males do Brasil são: Estudo de um centro umbandista numa favela do Rio de Janeiro." Master's Thesis, Postgraduate Program in Social Anthropology of the National Museum of the Federal University of Rio de Janeiro.
Dantas, Beatriz Góis (1982) "Repensado a pureza Nagô." *Religião e Sociedade*.
Frigerio, Alejandro (1983) "The Search for Africa: Proustian Nostalgia in Afro-Brazilian Studies." M.A. thesis, Dept. of Anthropology, University of California, Los Angeles.
Maia, Vasconcelos (1985) *ABC do Candomblé*. Edições GRD.

Mott, Roberto (1988) "Acotundá: raizes setecentista do sincretismo religioso Afro-Brasileiro." In Mott, *Escravidão, Homosexualidade e Demonologia*, pp. 87-117. São Paulo: Ícone.

Williams, Paul V. A. (1979) *Primitive Religion and Healing: A Study of Folk Medicine in North-East Brazil.* Cambridge: D.S. Brewer and Rowman and Littlefield, for the Folklore Society.

Guia do Pai de Santo no Candomblé[47] OGÃ GIMBEREUA

The Responsibilities of the (Female) Initiate [Yaô][48]

As for any other religion, ours depends on the pure faith of its sons and daughters so that the saints can become incorporated. Since the Orixá is an entity that is part of the mysteries of the Creator, s/he needs the physical and spiritual purity of her/his children to be able to fulfill his/her divine duty: to guide and protect their children through dreams or even messages, directing them in the path of truth and keeping them away from the path of evil. We have to consider that since the Orixá is an entity, we do not have the right to meet him/her personally. This would cause us instant death. From this we deduce the need for matter to be always in the right condition to receive the Orixá. This means that the body of the female initiate must be cleansed from the bad deeds of the past through works [*Ebós*].

[. . . .]

Ebó of Intôtum [The Foundation of the Candomblé House]

It is the main one. It ensures the life of the female initiate or any person already made in the Saint. This Ebó means feeding fortune and the earth, since from them come all that our body needs in life and death. People only remember the earth to leave in it only rotten matter. On the contrary, we need to give it everything that is good, that is tasty and healthy, just as our Orixás eat. This earth food is made in the following manner: on the land where the Candomblé is located, you dig a hole of three hands on either side by five hands in depth. In it you place all the animals that will be offered to the Orixás. For female Orixás, you separate a hen and, according to the means of the person, a four-footed female animal, leaving all male animals for the male Saints following this order. . . .

Yaô [Female Initiate]

For a Yaô, when she is in the period of initiation, just like for a child, it is necessary to have norms and restrictions to follow, which have as their goal her own good and safety, as well as the perfect success of her obligations as Orixá. It is for this reason that, since the ancestral times of our sect [*seita*], there have been norms and responsibilities that must be observed by those who become initiate in the foundations and secrets of Candomblé.

[. . . .]

It is the duty of the Yaô: to respect her Father or Mother-of-the-Saint with the same respect and the same veneration that she has for her physical parents. When asking for the Father's or Mother-of-the-Saint's blessing, the Yaô must do it on her knees, touching the ground softly three times with her forehead. The blessing should be asked in the language used in the sect and given in it as well. When talking to the [Father or Mother-of-the-Saint], she must, as long as the mouth allows it, stoop, with the greatest respect.

It is the duty of the Yaô: to respect her little mother [*Mãe-pequena*][49] and give her the same consideration that she has with her father or mother, since it is the little mother who works most intensely with the Yaô, from the day that she comes in until the day in which, with all her precepts fulfilled, she receives from her Father or Mother-of-the-Saint, the *Deká.*[50] [Yaô must also] respect the *Ogãs, Pegi-gãs, Alabês, Agibonans, Cotas, Ekedês, Akiregebós, Ocidagãs,*[51] as well as all the elders in the sect.

It is the duty of the Yaô: to exhibit the greatest respect when the Orixá of her Father or Mother-of-the-Saint is dancing, stooping down, only opening her mouth to respond to the chants of the Orixá, maintaining the same respect for the other Orixás. [She] must also respect her brothers and sisters-in-the-Saints, seeking not to create enmities among them, but trying to help each other without any self-interest.

It is the duty of the Yaô: to guard jealously the secrets revealed, as well her *dijina* [sacred name within the candomblé center] and the name of her Saint, until authorized by her Father or Mother-of-the-Saint. She must honor the days consecrated to her Orixá.

It is the duty of the Yaô: when she is secluded in the *Roncó* [the sacred inner room that serves as the initiate's retreat] to write in a book, especially chosen for this task, her dreams. If she is illiterate, she will have to tell them to a person designated by the Father or Mother-of-the-Saint.

These dreams will, stage by stage, bring the enlightenment that the Orixás give to their children, supplementing their spiritual lives.

It is the duty of the Yaô when still in the living quarters: to tell all doubts to her Father or Mother-of-the-Saint and to ask clarification regarding these matters. She must not take off the *Mocan* [a bracelet that marks religious status] from her arm. It can only be taken off by direct order from her Father or Mother-of-the-Saint. When there are public celebrations [*festas*], the Yaô must come with her *Mocan*. Or, if there are new Yaô just gathered, the bracelet will be placed by the Father or Mother-of-the-Saint or any person designated.

While in the *Roncó*, the Yaô cannot talk to unknown persons or any other person, unless through the person that is taking care of her. She cannot read newspapers, magazines, or letters, without them being examined first by her Father or Mother-of-the-Saint.

When in the *Roncó*, the Yaô must only elevate her thoughts toward God and to the Orixás, not worrying about the material life. She must try to elevate her spirit at every step to give strength to her guardian angel.

When in the *Roncó*, if the Yaô needs anything, she must clap her hands and wait to be taken care of. It is the duty of the Yaô, when secluded in the ritual room, that before eating anything, she clap her hands and ask for the blessing of her Father or Mother-of-the-Saint. When praying she must do it prostrated and with the greatest respect, because, at that moment, all the Orixás are by hers. They must feel totally satisfied. So, the act must be made with true faith and devotion.

It is the duty of the Yaô to come to all the drummings and celebrations of her Father or Mother-of-the-Saint, except in cases when it is impossible due to illness. When the physiological conditions do not allow her to go the house of the Father or Mother-of-the-Saint, the Yaô must leave behind her material and sexual life, remember that she is a religious temple, where she must take care of the Orixás and the duties of the religion [*o culto*].

All initiates have the responsibility to do the Océ [routine ritual tasks including ablutions] of her Saint. For this, she must sleep on a reed mat, take a bath de Abô and, in the early dawn, get up without talking to anyone. She can then proceed to cleanse the tools where her Orixá is seated.

It is prohibited to the Yaô to sit in a high place, to cut or stretch her hair, to use clinging or indecent clothes, swimming suits, or make-up, to accompany burials, enter cemeteries, dress in black, eat from cracked or broken vessels, or to use plates, mugs, spoons, combs, soaps, and all objects that do not belong to her.

It is expressly prohibited to the Yaô to visit other Candomblés, unless with the permission or accompanied by her Father or Mother-of-the-Saint.

It is prohibited to the Yaô to eat garlic, pepper of any kind, pumpkin, fish of sandy or soft skin, drink alcohol, to eat or to accept any piece of food from people outside the sect or even of the house. She must not drink anything from the street unless in her own mug. It is prohibited to the Yaô to go to dances, nightclubs, or use masks or indecent costumes. It is prohibited to the Yaô to take of the *Kelê* [the sacred bead collar] under any excuse. During the time that the Yaô has the *Kelê*, she cannot be in the streets at six o'clock in the afternoon, nor can she have love affairs or sexual relations.

The bead collars of our Orixás are their symbols and, as such, must be treated with the greatest respect and consideration. They can never be used in profane celebrations, nor can they be used when the body is not clean.

It is forbidden to the Yaô to enter in the *Peji* [room of the saints] during her period. The *Peji* is the sacred place [*sacrario*] of our Orixás, and thus, it deserves our highest respect. During a whole year, the Orixá of the Yaô cannot speak, just as in the day of the *Orucó* [the collective event at which the saint descends], the Orixá does not prostrate at the feet of anybody. The Yaô, during a whole year, cannot dance with immoderate gestures.

"The Consecration of Ocha: A Capsule Summary"[32]   DAVID H. BROWN

The first full day of initiation, the "Day of the Asiento," involves the"birth" of two critically related earthly manifestations of the *orichas'* spiritual power *(aché)*: a set of potent objects that will later be enshrined in the home, and the consecrated head *(orí)* of new priest. Both are "washed," "nourished," and "fortified" through the incorporation of the *orichas'* *aché*, which is drawn from elements of *la naturaleza* ("nature"), including fresh plants and the vital blood of sacrificial animals. *Asiento* refers to the Lucumí ritual technique of "seating" or "mounting" the *aché* of an *oricha* on the head *(orí)*. The *orichas'* objects consist of their consecrated material "foundations" or "supports" *(fundamentos)*—sets of color-coded rounded stones *(otán,* or *piedras)*—which are accompanied by sets *(manos,* "hands") of cowrie divination shells called *dilogún* and miniature metal or wood icons *(herramientas,* "tools"). These stones, shells, and *herramientas* are contained within metal, wood, or ceramic vessels, generally called *soperas*.

The initiate—the "child" *(omó)* of a particular *oricha*—"makes Ocha" and becomes the earthly "representative" of that *oricha*, previously determined by divination to be the "guardian angel" or "owner of the head" *(angel de la guardia, dueño de la cabeza, cabecera)*. On the Day of the Asiento, the *orichas* objects and the initiate's head and body are consecrated with herbal infusions, called *osains*, concocted principally of fresh plants *(ewe)* and cool water, and "seasoned" with various activating (hot) and cooling (sweet or balmlike) ingredients. The *oricha cabecera* is then "mounted" on the head in a series of ceremonies. The *sopera* of the guardian angel is placed over the head, which is draped with four squares of cotton cloth in white, yellow, blue, and red. With a series of invocatory songs by the soloist *oriaté* and participant chorus that "call down" the *oricha*, the initiate may become possessed or spiritually "touched." Upon completion of the mounting ceremony *(montaje del santo)*, the initiate becomes known as *iyawó*, the *oricha's* "junior wife" *(iyá-awó)*. The initiation procedure as a whole in the Lucumí ritual language is typically called the *kariocha*, literally "to put ocha on the head" (from *ka* [put], *orí* [head], and *ocha* [*oricha*]; see Cabrera [1957] 1986, 185; [1974] 1980, 128-7; Murphy 1988, 87; 1994, 92-104). The primary *oricha* "guardian angel" or *cabecera* is often referred to as one's "crown," an internalized spiritual presence that "rules" the head *(orí)* and authorizes, in turn, the priest's potential governance of a "house" of initiated "godchildren." These telescoping, hierarchical authority relations of *orichas*, individual heads and bodies, and the social body of the house are nicely encapsulated by a Lucumí divination proverb from the cowrie divination sign Eyionle: "The head rules the body and only one king governs a town" (Elizondo [1934?] n.d., 9, 39).[53] Following the "washing" and *montaje del santo* ceremonies, during which the *iyawó* has been blindfolded, the *iyawó* is permitted to "see" his or her throne, a beautiful cloth canopy that functions to symbolically evoke and instrumentally invoke ("call down"; see M. Drewal 1989) the *orichas* to take up residence with the *iyawó*. The throne becomes a kind of incubator for the *orichas'* collective *aché*. The canopied installation not only will serve as a royal seat and stage for the formal presentation of the initiate the next day, the Middle Day; it is also a spiritually protective space, a seclusion hut for a liminal initiate, and a symbolic birth site on the floor for the "newborn baby" of the house. Some *santeros* regard it as a kind of cell of "protective custody" and benign house arrest by the *orichas*. In fact, the throne's cloth and the white sheet and towel the *iyawó* uses for the week act as prophylactic and purifying *ebó* (sacrificial media). The *iyawó*'s white clothes for the week are stored in a large wicker basket (*canasta*), just as it was the Cuban custom to store the clothes of newborns in a basket. The *iyawó* lives in her "throne"–"house" for six days, in proximity to the line of *soperas* that contain the *orichas*' objects.

The *asiento* day is completed with the *matanza* (the killing), when the *orichas*' stones and shells "eat" the warm, *aché*-imbued blood of two-and four-legged animals symbolically appropriate to each deity. The *iyawó* is cleansed and fortified also by the *matanza*, as each of the animals sacrificed is touched to the cardinal points of the *iyawó*'s body. Thus identified through physical contiguity with these sacrificial animal messengers to the "other world," the *iyawó*'s death and rebirth is reenacted in objectified form; at the same time, the animals are sacrificial substitutes, which clean, and give their lives for the health, well-being, and salvation of the *iyawó*.

Following the Middle Day (often a Sunday), a special intensive divination reading called *itá* is conducted, in which the *iyawó*'s new *orichas* "speak" for the first time through their cowrie shells (*dilogún*). The *itá* identifies the spiritual coordinates (*odus*) and their associated bodies of "taboos" (*egües* or *awaws*), guiding stories (*historias*), and protective sacrifices (*ebó*) that will serve to maintain the equilibrium of the *iyawó*'s consecrated head (*orí*), indicate auxiliary *orichas* to be received in the future, determine the particular "paths" or "roads" of the *iyawó*'s *orichas* (a number of *orichas* have different avocations), and identify the *iyawó*'s second "parent" *oricha* and Lucumí sacred name. The multivocal term for the human head, *orí*, also refers to the initiate's "destiny": the *itá* inscribes the *iyawó*'s "past, present, and future"—that is, the "path" the *iyawó*'s head travels in this world, and what must be done to insure that this head's destiny is fulfilled (see Cabrera [1974] 1980, 179-224).

After five nights of sleeping and reposing beneath the throne's protective canopy, the *iyawó*'s consecrated *orí* is "presented to the sun" (often on a Thursday morning) in a brief ceremony conducted by the *padrino* or *madrina* and *oyubona*[54] to advise Olorun that this is the last day of the initiation week's intensive process of the head's incorporation of *aché* substances through baths and special "African breakfasts." This is the last time the head will be colorfully painted with the head oricha's special "signature" (*firma*). On the seventh day (often a Friday), after the sixth night under the throne, the *iyawó* emerges from seclusion and is reincorporated into the community on this "Day of the Plaza." In the morning, the *iyawó* is dressed in fine white clothes, shoes, and hat and is escorted to a "market" (*plaza*), a place of exchange, transition, and sociality. In Havana, this is typically the large market that stands at the intersection of Cuatro Caminos (Four Roads). In New York City, the market is often the Latino "La Marketa" in Spanish Harlem. Offerings at the four corners to Eleguá on a walk around the market are little *ebó* to protect the *iyawó* as he or she reenters the social world. Fruit that the newborn *iyawó* symbolically steals (but that is paid for by the accompanying *oyubona*) is carried back to the room in a wicker basket. The throne has been taken down—signaling the end of the weeklong period in which the *orichas' aché* is actively incorporated by the *iyawó*; the fruit is placed before the *iyawó*'s *orichas* in order to "refresh" them prior to a coconut divination that clears the way for their transition, along with their new owner, to the *iyawó*'s home, which will become a new "house of ocha." For three months, the *orichas* repose on a mat, and the *iyawó* takes meals and sleeps (in some houses), likewise, on a mat. The *iyawó* is subject to many social and personal restrictions, such as going out unaccompanied by a *santero* and looking in the mirror. After a special *ebó* of the three months, the *orichas* themselves take up residence in a *canastillero*, a multishelved cabinet or armoire, often within their own sacred room (*cuarto de santo, igbodú*). At this time, the *iyawó* is "presented to the table," so that meals may be taken with adults, as well as "presented to the mirror." The *orichas* have become the true "owners" and "rulers" of the house (see Cabrera [1974] 1980, 225-28; Castellanos 1977, 85-99; Gleason 1992; Gonzalez Huguet 1968; Brown 1999).

WORKS CITED

Brandon, George. 1983. "'The Dead Sell Memories': An Anthropological Study of Santería in New York City." Ph.D. diss., Rutgers University.
Brown, David. 1999. "Altared Spaces: Afro-Cuban Religions and the Urban Landscape." In *The Gods of the City: Religion and the Contemporary American Urban Landscape*, ed. Robert A. Orsi, 155-230. Bloomington: Indiana University Press.
Cabrera, Lydia. [1957] 1986. *Anagó: Vocabulario Lukumí (el Yoruba que se habla en Cuba)*. Miami: Ediciones Universal.
———. [1974] 1980. *Yemayá y Ochún*. New York: C.R. Publishers.
Castellanos, Isabel Mercedes. 1977. "The Use of Language in Afro-Cuban Religion." Ph.D. diss., Georgetown University.

Drewal, Margaret Thompson. 1989. "Dancing for Ogun in Yorubaland and Brazil." In *Africa's Ogun: Old World and New*, ed. Sandra Barnes, 199-234. African Systems of Thought series. Bloomington: University of Indiana Press.

Elizondo, Carlos [1934?] n.d. *Manual de la religión Lucumí*. Union City, NJ: n.p.

Gleason, Judith. 1992. *The King does not Lie: Initiation of a Shango Priest*. Film. Distributed by Filmakers Library, New York.

Gonzalez Huguet, Lydia. 1968. "La Casa-Templo en la Regla de Ocha." *Etnología y Folklore* 5 (January-June): 33-57.

Murphy, Joseph. 1988. *Santería: An African Religion in America*. Boston: Beacon.

————.1994. *Working the Spirit: Ceremonies of the African Diaspora*. Boston: Beacon.

"Declarations from the Church of Lukumi, Miami"[55]

Purpose Statement

CLBA is focused on three social religious principles, which we consider essential for the preservation of the Lukumi/Ayoba faith. We believe that maintaining a professional organization and good character can sustain our religious and cultural prestige. Prestige in the long run will provide a longstanding powerful institutional foundation.

CLBA aims to provide an institution to address the social and religious needs of its members and of clergy members worldwide and to preserve the Lukumi/Ayoba religious ethics and morals as prescribed in our tenets. CLBA is primarily centered on the religious education of adherents, clergy, and the general public.

The general purpose of this Church is as follows:

- To maintain, own, operate, and have a secured religious place of worship, according to the teachings of the Lukumi/Ayoba religion.
- To establish a formal setting for the religious education of adherents, clergy, and the general public, according to the Lukumi/Ayoba tenets.
- To hold sessions and ceremonies for the worship of ancestors.
- To promote and study supernatural phenomena, according to the African-based philosophy and religion known as Lukumi/Ayoba.
- To perform traditional baptism, marriage, birth rite, priesthood ordination, death rite.
- To engage in the certification of its ordained members.
- To take appropriate legal action to ensure our constitutional protection of religious freedom.

- To elect and appoint officers and agents, as its affairs shall require.
- To conduct its affairs and operations in any state or possession of the United States, or any foreign country.
- To establish affiliations and support with other corporations or legal entities.
- CLBA represents the following practices in belief that they are important for the perseverance of the Lukumi/Ayoba religion.
- Explanation of our central dogma as found in the religious teachings of Ifa.
- Inspiring confidence to provide relief and assurance through divine explanation which permits us to confront insecurities and life's challenges.
- Reinforcing customs and values to preserve our culture.
- Social Integration: It's important for a group in the society with a common belief and religion, to be unified under a centralized formal tribal order, for the perseverance of its lineal customs and traditions.
- Preserve our religious ethics and morals.

Declaration in Relation to Non-Lukumi Religions: The Relation of the Church to Non-Lukumi Religions, Promulgated by Oba Ernesto Pichardo, January 28, 1998

On Non-Lukumi African Religions

1. In preparation for the next millenium, the Church examines more closely its relationship with other religions. Mankind is being drawn closer together by global trends and nations are becoming more inter-dependent. In our task of promoting unity, the Church considers in this declaration what we have in common and what draws us to fellowship.

2. The whole human race is one community, one in their origin, for Olodumare is the one creator of all. Mankind from the various religions of the world seeks answers to unsolved questions in relation to its existence and thereafter. A universal denominator among the various peoples, is its beliefs, or recognition of a Supreme Being, and the existence of a spiritual reality that influences their physical world.

3. African religions bound by universal precepts in relation to natural law, contemplate the divine mystery and express it through human inquiry and experience. In various forms, each in their own religious manner, seeks what is true. All follow teachings that may differ in many aspects. Nonetheless, in sincere, devout, and confident manner, by their

own human effort and supreme illumination, they try to recognize, preserve and promote that which enlightens all humankind. Each religion proposes ways through teachings, rules of life, and sacred rites: a genuine certitude of spiritual, moral, and social truth. However, this certitude is at times stained by ruinous manifestation.

4. The Church of the Lukumi Babalu Aye does not reject what is true and holy in other African religions. Therefore, the Church earnestly urges the establishment of formal relations to promote good will and reason in mutual compatibility, through dialogue and collaboration with representatives of African religions.

5. Furthermore, while each religion holds to its respective tenets and rites, the Church rejects discrimination because of race, color, condition of life, or religion. Following the teachings of Ogbe 'Di, Lukumi faithful should maintain good fellowship regardless of their state in life.

On Christian Denominations

1. While it is true that Christian authorities in past eras, and those led by their precepts, committed grave destruction justified by their truth, what happened in their passion cannot be held against present and future generations. The Church wants to foster mutual understanding and respect, following the teachings of Baba Ejiogbe, where in wisdom requires the use of practical objectivity. The Church rejects being bound to past passions, without distinction that, in error, surrenders the human spirit to bondage (Ogbe Osa).

2. Christian Holy Scripture attests, Christianity cannot be reconciled with our faith. Nonetheless, the human community shares universal values. It is those values consistent with the universal dignity of the human person that foster fellowship.

3. Therefore, as the next millenium develops into more global interdependence among nations, the Church recommends movement towards an inter-denomination fellowship based on common tenets whenever possible.

On Yoruba Indigenous Religion and Brazilian Candomblé

1. Muslim and Christian "passions" of the past curtailed the originality of the Yoruba indigenous religion. This caused an alteration in its form, but not in its essential religious tenets. From the Old World experience of the Yoruba, diffusion occurred that gave birth in the New World to a new experience that survived in Brazil as Candomblé. The old and the New

World manifestations of the Yoruba religion have adapted to its past and present environments: political, social, and civic (okanran irosu).

2. The Church rejects nothing that is true in these two religious forms. Moreover, bound by their moral obligation to seek the truth, especially in matters religious, both religious forms are one and the same.

3. Thus, the Church acknowledges the bond that spiritually ties them with the Lukumi manifestation. Since the spiritual patrimony common to the three forms is so great, the Church wants to establish a "formal fraternal order" for mutual respect and theological studies.

5

Independence and Modernity

Religion, along with almost every other aspect of life, changed dramatically in Latin America as the colonial era declined, starting around the mid-eighteenth century. Conflicts increased both within the Catholic Church and between the church and governmental authorities. Moreover, Catholicism, African-based religions, and indigenous religious traditions played significant roles in a variety of popular movements, including millenarian movements whose political meaning was not always clear either to participants or to observers, as well as in explicitly political uprisings by mestizo, black, and indigenous people against the ruling classes and colonial rule. After Independence, religious diversity grew, as Protestant and non-Christian European immigrants arrived in larger numbers and new cultural and ideological streams emerged within Latin America. At the same time, popular or folk Catholicism, integrating indigenous and Iberian traditions, continued to serve as the dominant faith for most Latin Americans, despite attempts by a resurgent Vatican to bring it into line with official orthodoxy.

Europe in the Eighteenth Century

In order to make sense of events in Latin America during this period, it is important to understand developments in Europe that strongly influenced life in the colonies. Political changes were especially important. In Spain, a new royal family—the Bourbons—came into power with the coronation of Philip V in 1700. The Bourbons replaced the Hapsburgs, who had ruled since 1504 and overseen successes both domestically and internationally. The Hapsburg rulers, including Ferdinand and Isabella, had been closely linked to the Catholic Church. The Bourbons, on the other hand, were less religiously oriented and also less politically successful. During their rule, Spain's political fortunes declined (as did those of Portugal). At the same time, Britain and France became increasingly important as world powers, with expanding empires in North America and Africa.

Iberia's political troubles were related to global economic transitions. During the late colonial period, much of Europe and its colonies moved away from feudal economic models toward market economies that incorporated, and depended upon, steadily increasing international trade in raw materials, finished products, and slaves. These economic developments, in turn, fed ideological trends that challenged the legitimacy of empire by the late eighteenth century. The rise of capitalist markets was accompanied by emerging political ideologies that emphasized contractual relationships, individual rights, representative government, and the separation of church and state. These ideas and values were at the core of republican and revolutionary political projects in Europe, especially France and the United States, serving as models and inspiration for independence movements in Latin America led by Simón Bolívar and others. Given the strongly humanist and secularist tenor of republican and nationalist ideals, it is not surprising that they would have momentous consequences for Latin American religious life.

In addition to new political philosophies in Europe during the eighteenth century, new scientific perspectives and methods also emerged. New emphases on rationality and on the testing of hypotheses contributed to secular impulses that weakened the political status of the Roman Catholic Church in Europe and, later, in Latin America. The debilitating effects of secular philosophies followed on two centuries of increasing religious diversity and Catholic decline in the wake of the Protestant Reformation, which had been launched in 1517.

The Vatican responded to these threats by trying to consolidate its political power in the remaining Catholic regions and also through measures intended to strengthen the church internally. The Council of Trent (1545-1563) had launched the Catholic- or Counter-Reformation, which continued into the eighteenth century. The Catholic Reformation was especially powerful in Spain and Portugal, including efforts to crush heterodoxy through such means as the Inquisition and the Index of Prohibited Books.

Late Colonial Crises

Bourbon rule ended the established system of colonial governance in which viceroys and the Council of the Indies oversaw the colonies. Instead, the Bourbons installed intendants, who reported only to the king and were supposed to make administration more efficient and centralized. This innovation ultimately weakened colonial control by reducing the royals' knowledge of events in the Americas and also by increasing resentment among different social groups in the colonies.

In economics, the European shift away from a feudal model and towards mercantilism encouraged a shift in the colonies from haciendas to plantations. These economic changes affected social-class relations in Latin America, especially in regard to the growing political and economic power of Creoles (people of European origin, born in the Americas) and competition between them and mestizos (people of mixed indigenous and European heritage). These groups of New World origin began to take over from *Peninsulares*, people born in Europe, who had since the conquest wielded most of the economic, social, and political power in the colonies. As the colonial period waned, Creoles and mestizos became increasingly restless and ambitious, and ultimately it was these groups who led independence movements throughout the region.

The Enlightenment faith in reason and concomitant suspicion of religion struck a chord with many Latin American *independentistas* who resented the Catholic Church's close ties to the crown and the church's role in suppressing dissent. As we saw in chapter 3, these ties were forged through the Royal Patronage, which, in effect, made the church dependent on the crown for its operation in the New World. Structurally, the Catholic Church was deeply invested in the survival of the colonial order.

European economic and political events contributed to an increasingly tense situation for the Latin American church in the years leading up to the Wars of Independence. One of the most significant conflicts concerned the Society of Jesus, or Jesuits. The society had been formed by Ignatius of Loyola in 1534, with the goal of strengthening the Catholic faith in the wake of the Protestant Reformation. The society received official recognition in 1540 and played a central role in the Catholic- or Counter-Reformation that developed following the Council of Trent. Jesuits also worked as missionaries in Asia and the Americas. They founded a number of schools and also *reducciones*, mainly in Brazil and Paraguay, among the Tupís and Guaranís. The *reducciones* were compounds, often encompassing a great deal of land, on which indigenous people resided and worked. The aim was to bring dispersed native peoples together to facilitate catechization and integration into European ways. However, given the abuses committed by *encomenderos, reducciones* also offered indigenous people a measure of protection. The Jesuits ran the missions with relative independence from both ecclesial (diocesan) and political authorities. The nature of the relations between the priests and the other residents was debated. To some the missions were benevolent, even utopian, islands of relative equality, peace, and Christian brotherhood amid the conflicts and inequalities that plagued colonial society, as in the document by Cunningham Grahame reproduced here. The article by Blas Garay reveals, however, that others saw the *reducciones* as sites in which conniving and ambitious priests exploited indigenous people for their own political and economic gain.

During the mid-eighteenth century, the Jesuits were caught in struggles between the Vatican and the new European secular republics, resulting in 1773 in the suppression by Pope Clement XIV of the Society of Jesus in all Catholic countries in the region. These conflicts had transatlantic effects, providing a focal point for growing tensions between church and crown in the Americas. By the mid-eighteenth century, the *reducciones* had become central issues in the Jesuits' conflicts with both ecclesial and political authorities. *Reducciones* appeared as alternative forms of economic organization that held land and diverted labor away from the emerging plantation system. Wishing to retain its privileged status vis-à-vis the colonial government, the church was willing to sacrifice the Jesuits. Pressure on *reducciones* grew when seven of them along the Uruguay River were ordered to relocate due to a strategic land trade between Spain and Portugal (as part of the 1750 Treaty of Madrid). The natives refused to move and rose up in arms in the so-called Guaraní Wars (1754-1756), which proved very costly to this indigenous group. In the end, although the *reducciones* declined in the hands of disinterested royal caretakers, they left an important cultural legacy that included the preservation of Guaraní language. Conflicts over the Jesuits continued until, finally, the colonial authorities expelled them in 1759 from Portuguese America and in 1767 from Spanish America.

Eighteenth-century conflicts like those surrounding the Jesuits foreshadowed the church-state tensions that would emerge in the Independence period, as the church accommodated itself to the demands of the new creole elites.

The Church in Spanish America in the Independence Period

The independence movements of the early 1800s built on centuries of resentment against colonial rule among various segments of Latin American society. As we saw above, the Catholic Church was generally royalist, or at least, the bishops and upper clergy (mostly *peninsulares*) were aligned with the crown. The alliance of church leaders with royalist forces reinforced anticlericalism that was implicit in some of the Enlightenment values—rationalism, secularism, and individual liberty—and that motivated many Independence leaders. For instance, Simón Bolívar, the father of South American independence, was an avowed atheist who was excommunicated by the Catholic Church. Separation of church and state was central to his political and philosophical vision.

Not surprisingly, many church leaders resented and often resisted the anticlerical activities of the independence movement. However, there were exceptions to the general rule of church-crown alliances and republican anticlericalism. Most members of the lower clergy were creole, and like the creole elite as a whole, they were divided in their loyalties during the independence struggles. A significant number of lower clergy, however, supported independence movements, due in part to their antipathy toward the upper clergy and hierarchies, which were generally European born and allied with the crown. Most famous was the Mexican priest Miguel Hidalgo y Costilla (1753–1811). On May 5, 1810, Hidalgo called for independence from Spain, racial equality, and land reform, and urged his people to rebel against the colonial authorities in the name of the Virgin of Guadalupe. Hidalgo helped ignite a difficult and bloody war that led to Mexican independence from Spain in 1821. September 15, the anniversary of Hidalgo's call for rebellion ("the Grito de Hidalgo"), is now celebrated as Independence Day in Mexico.

After Independence, the church's moral and practical position was significantly weakened in most of Latin America. While Catholicism was still the official religion, its legal and political status greatly diminished in most of the new nations. The Spanish Inquisition was abolished, religious toleration was legalized, and Protestantism began to enter through immigrants and some missionaries. (After Independence, immigration was no longer limited to citizens of Spain and Portugal, which added to the growing ideological and religious diversity of Latin America.)

Many *independentistas* saw the church as a hindrance to modernization, progress, economic development, and political independence. They sought to weaken the church's legal position and its role in important social institutions, especially education. In many areas, anticlerical laws and sentiments encouraged the growth of more conservative factions within the church, including the ultramontane movement, which emphasized the centrality of the Vatican and the opposition between the church and secular society. Church-state conflicts were especially sharp in Mexico, where they led to violent confrontation in the 1850s and 1860s and ultimately to strong anticlerical measures in the post-Revolution constitution. The anticlericalism of many republican governments, combined with changes and weaknesses in Rome, made it difficult for Latin American churches to negotiate the new political and social terrain. Church organization at the diocesan and local levels declined, as many episcopacies remained vacant, and church organization at the lower levels also declined as many priests died or left and were not replaced.

Brazil in the Nineteenth Century: Empire and Republic

Brazil often followed a different path from Spanish America. Portugal's colonization in the Americas began later, in part because the Portuguese crown was preoccupied with its colonies and trade in Africa and Asia. Although Pedro Álvares Cabral arrived in Brazil in 1500, there was little intensive settlement until the 1550s, following the establishment of the colonial capital, Salvador, in 1549, and the arrival the same year of Jesuit missionaries. The Portuguese faced challenges from French and Dutch settlers in parts of their region, in addition to difficulties emerging from the dense forestation and challenging terrain of the Atlantic and Amazonian rainforests, with their scattered smaller native settlements, very different from the large urban centers of the precolonial Andes and Mexico. Another difference between the two Iberian powers was that the Portuguese did not divide their colonies into different territories or states, but rather maintained Brazil as a single colony from the start.

A final peculiarity of Brazil's colonial history was the fact that independence did not coincide with the establishment of a republican form of government. Instead, Brazil was an independent monarchy ruled by King Dom João VI, starting in 1808, after the Portuguese royal family fled to Brazil during the French invasion of Portugal. João declared Brazil a kingdom equal to Portugal in 1815. In 1821, João returned to Portugal, leaving his son Pedro in Brazil as regent. In 1822, Pedro declared Brazil's independence and named himself emperor. Thus Brazil was the only nation in Latin America to achieve independence from Europe without violence. Brazil became a republic in 1889.

During the transitions in the early 1820s, many priests played important political roles, and Brazil experienced less anticlericalism than Spanish America. Religious-social conflicts in Brazil during the nineteenth and early twentieth centuries focused instead on internal economic and political changes, especially those that gave rise to millenarian movements.

Popular Catholic Groups and Movements

While the official church did not fare well during the period leading to the wars of independence and their aftermath, most people in Latin America practiced the syncretic forms of religiosity that had emerged during the early colonial period. Faced with a severe shortage of priests, many people, particularly in rural areas, confronted the problem of how to conduct their religious lives. Many rural residents saw a priest only once a year, when he would come to their village, often during the feast of the patron saint, to administer the sacraments such as baptism, confession, and communion. The priest would then spend several days resacralizing the town, a practice that in Brazil came to be known as the *desobriga*, literally the collective "unburdening" of sins and "discharging" of spiritual duties.

During most of the year, lay Catholics relied on a myriad of lay specialists like *rezadoras*, who used a combination of prayer and folk medicine to heal the sick, or *beatos*, ascetics who consecrated their lives to the church and would roam the countryside preaching, advising people on moral and spiritual matters, and repairing sanctuaries and cemeteries. António Conselheiro (the counselor), the protagonist of the significant millenarian movement in Canudos, was one of these itinerant holy men.

The decline in the number of priests and bishops and in support for parishes also helped push lay people to form and strengthen their own organizations. The most significant among them were *cofradías* (or confraternities) and brotherhoods (*hermandades* or *irmandades*). As noted in chapter 3, these were groups run by laymen (and on occasion lay women) that organized religious activities such as festivals, pilgrimages, and saints' days. Brotherhoods often collected and managed funds to care for the sick or to cover the cost of funerals for members. Frequently, brotherhoods even built and maintained chapels, monasteries, and other parish property. Their relations with representatives of the official church varied. Some groups worked closely with the parish priest and diocesan officials, while others had distant or even hostile relations. Characterizing the role of *irmandades* in Minas Gerais, Brazil, Marjo de Theije writes,

> From the very beginning, Catholicism was completely in the hands of the brotherhoods. It was these sodalities who built the churches, organized the feasts, recruited the priests to say Mass, and took care of their co-members' funerals. They were very autonomous, for they financially supported the clergy. In the absence of a well-organized coordinating institution, the superior church authorities interfered only in approving the articles of association and collecting the corresponding contributions. They were only, if ever, consulted in the case of conflicts between a parish priest and a brotherhood or between the brotherhoods themselves. Both religious life and sociocultural life was focused on the feasts in honor of the patron saints of the various brotherhoods. (1990: 193-94)

Brotherhoods were often quite traditional in outlook and organized hierarchically according to class and race (and most excluded women). Nonetheless, these lay organizations provided people with opportunities to resist not only ecclesial inequities but also cultural, economic, and political injustices. They were especially important for Indians, mestizos, and Africans, who lacked opportunities for leadership and full participation in the institutional church. The "black brotherhoods," described in a reading in chapter 4, provided important organizational, moral, and economic resources for Brazilians of African descent. In many areas, *cofradías* offered indigenous people spaces to preserve traditional (precolonial) and syncretic practices (*costumbres*), which found little welcome in the institutional church and its rituals.

Given their autonomy of lay practices and organizations, it not surprising that the *cofradías* and brotherhoods were objects of concern to the institutional church. Under enormous pressure due to the collapse of royal patronage and the rise of secular republics, church officials sought to control lay practices and organizations as a way to recenter the church's position in the postcolonial context. In Brazil, there was a particularly intense process of "Romanization" toward the end of the nineteenth century and the beginning of the twentieth century. On the one hand, the Brazilian bishops strengthened their links with the Holy See and arranged for the arrival of numerous [European] religious congregations to be in charge of the schools, hospitals, parishes and missions. On the other the Bishops pushed a pastorale [sic] of modernizing Brazilian Catholicism, by fighting against popular traditional Catholicism and by adopting beliefs and practices of a model of Roman Catholicism that was common in Europe. (Oliveira 1985: 310)

More specifically, the Brazilian church hierarchy introduced popular European devotions like the Sacred Heart of Jesus and Jesus the King (Cristo Rey, whom we will encounter later on in the Cristero war), as a way to undermine the local devotions overseen by brotherhoods. *Irmandades* and other popular groups resisted this Romanization, as did a growing number of Brazilian priests who came to resent the rigidity and ethnocentrism of European orders that controlled many seminaries.

Millenarianism

In interaction with economic and sociopolitical transformations, the struggle to regulate and centralize popular devotions played an important role in grass-roots millenarian and messianic movements that developed in a number of countries, especially Brazil, in the late 1800s and early 1900s. Millenarian movements typically emerge during periods of great crisis or rapid change, when the taken-for-granted structures that orient the activities of individuals and keep them connected with each other disintegrate without new norms in place to deal with the disorder. Under these conditions, people become receptive to apocalyptic and eschatological messages that either offer a utopian vision of the future in which all current contradictions are resolved or a reimagining of the broken order. Often these movements are built around the teachings and actions of a prophetic leader (a messiah). Many millenarian leaders call for a return to or retention of traditional cultural and economic patterns, seen as crucial to maintaining the identity and autonomy of a particular social group. Because most millenarian movements oppose the present in the name of an alternative sacralized vision of history, they frequently come into conflict with established earthly powers. Some withdraw from mainstream society in relative peace, while others enter, intentionally or not, into dramatic conflicts with the government and ruling social groups. Still others negotiate with these elites to make possible the emergence of a new kind of community.

One of the earliest and most famous millenarian movements in Brazil took place in the Canudos region, in the interior of the northeastern state of Bahia, which had experienced a series of devastating droughts (*secas*).[1] From 1893 to 1897, Antônio Conselheiro presided over a village he called "Bello Monte," where thousands of poor people had come to seek refuge from the *seca* and the disarticulation of the traditional rural moral economy that, while making slaves and sharecroppers subservient to the local landowners, guaranteed them protection and survival. The emerging market economy effectively severed the old feudal bonds and made them landless salaried peasants at a time when the economy of northeast Brazil was in decline. Conselheiro, like Padre Cícero—our other example of post-Independence grass-roots Catholicism—became a surrogate saintly patriarch for these dislocated masses.

At Canudos, Conselheiro preached a stern ascetic message of conversion and regeneration, challenging the republic for undermining the moral fabric of Brazilian society by separating church and state and, more specifically, instituting civil marriage. He also denounced the taxation of the impoverished peasants who followed him. In his classic account of the movement, *Os Sertões* (translated as *Rebellion in the Backlands*), Brazilian journalist Euclides da Cunha made much of Conselheiro's sermons against the republic, portraying the *beato* as a pathological religious fanatic opposed to the values of modern, cosmopolitan Brazil.[2] Da Cunha stressed Conselheiro's avowed appeal to King Sebastian I of Portugal, who reigned from 1557 to 1578, the golden era of Portuguese imperial expansion.[3] For Da Cunha, the "Sebastianism" among Conselheiro's followers proved that Canudos was a threat to the democratic republic. Canudos was for Da Cunha "an ebb, a backward flow, in our history. What we had to face here was the unlooked-for resurrection, under arms, of an old society, a dead society, galvanized into life by a madman." This madman gathered around him "a motley crew of human failures, accustomed to living in idleness and by their wits" (Da Cunha 1944: 161, 129). Da Cunha's incendiary rhetoric helped justify the government's decision to send the army to crush the movement. After several embarrassing defeats, the military finally destroyed Bello Monte in 1897, killing as many as thirty-five thousand people (Levine 1995).

Da Cunha's modernist and secularist prejudices led him to overstate the social dimensions of Conselheiro's millenarianism. Conselheiro's sermon on the republic, reprinted here, shows him as far more concerned with salvation, personal moral transformation, and the erosion of the Catholic ideal of family than with overthrowing the "godless" republic. He attacks the republic not because he wants to build a different earthly political order but because he would like to reaffirm the eternal city of God, which, in his view, has been undermined by republican values. For Conselheiro, secular power is legitimate only if it mirrors the hierarchical cosmos intended by divine providence, a cosmos governed by God as king of kings. Clearly, the republic contradicts this vision, claiming to derive its legitimacy solely from the will of men. It is interesting to note, however, that despite his hierarchical view of the world, Conselheiro shares the republic's abhorrence of slavery.

Conselheiro's apocalyptic language may have intensified as the Canudos came under increasing military pressure, although his words bidding farewell to "birds, trees, fields . . ." (uttered as Canudos was in the last days of a protracted siege) suggest a figure more along the lines of St. Francis of Assisi than of John the Baptist. However, the fate of his city was ultimately the result of conflicting state and national political interests. Comparing Canudos and Padre Cícero's Joaseiro, historian Ralph Della Cava argues that it is simplistic to see these millenarian movements in dualistic terms, as the struggle between a waning, reactionary, and religiously informed order in the backlands and an emerging progressive secular project advanced by the coastal elites of Rio de Janeiro and São Paulo. Della Cava shows that both of these movements were embedded in larger socioeconomic and political processes, as well as dynamics within the Catholic Church, in Brazil and in Rome, that shaped differential outcomes.

Padre Cícero's movement started in Joaseiro, Ceará, in 1889, when the host that he was giving to *beata* Maria de Araújo turned into blood, which was said to be the blood of Jesus Christ. Although the "miracle at Joaseiro" repeated itself in front of various witnesses for several months, the Bishop of Ceará refused to sanction the event as legitimate. Appeals went all the way to Rome, which eventually sided with the hierarchy and its attempt to disqualify the religious practices at Joaseiro, the inhabitants of which increasingly made Padre Cícero into a latter-day messiah. The miracle at Joaseiro clearly flew in the face of the Holy See's quest to Europeanize the Brazilian church. In fact, Della Cava notes that there was a generalized feeling among Brazilian priests that the Europeans rejected the veracity of the miracle because they were sure that "Our Lord does not leave France to work miracles in Brazil" (1970: 48).

Even when he was removed from his post and forbidden to say mass, however, Padre Cícero sought to reconcile with Rome, sending advocates from among the local Catholic elites and even traveling there himself. Padre Cícero and his supporters argued that the miracle at Joaseiro and the fervor generated around it would help restore Brazilian Catholicism, an antidote against the secularizing advances of Masons, Protestants, and positivists. Certainly, today, Padre Cícero stands as a saint of the people, the quintessential paragon of the enduring vitality and relative independence of Brazilian traditional popular Catholicism. Today Joaseiro is an important regional and national center of pilgrimages (*romarias*).

Padre Cícero's capacity to negotiate with the established civil and religious powers while preserving the movement's charismatic force at the grass-roots level made it possible for his "holy city" to have an altogether different fate than that of Canudos. As a priest, Padre Cícero had the crucial support of a Brazilian clergy disgruntled with the excesses of Romanization, a support that *beato* Conselheiro never had. This support gave him enough maneuvering room to convert his city into an autonomous economic center of power, establishing relations of patronage over a growing group of pilgrims. Eventually, state and national political bosses had to reckon with his influence. Padre Cícero's ability to position himself favorably in the local and national scenes sheds light on the ways in which the Latin American Catholic Church sought to accommodate to the new post-Independence reality. As historian Ken Serbin (2006: 124) puts it, "Padre Cícero embodied the new clerical nationalism" emerging in Brazil and throughout the Americas.

Padre Cícero's creative work of mediation is evident in his testament, which we reprint here. He distances himself from Canudos and other insurrectional movements, arguing that he never "made revolutions." In fact, he portrays himself as a reluctant politician, forced to interact with fractious secular elites by his desire to protect the pilgrims and to preserve peace and order. His testament also shows the benevolent patriarch at work, highlighting his role in distributing resources for the good of the community of believers. Noteworthy also are his appeals to the importance of charity, penance, prayer, pilgrimage, Marian devotions, and obedience to the Holy Church, all values he shares with Conselheiro as part of the fabric of traditional popular Catholicism.

The Institutional Church in Transition

In the late 1800s, the institutional church crafted its response both to dramatic social changes in Europe and Latin America and to the popular religious movements that emerged in response to these changes. The first Vatican Council, held in 1870, set the stage for doctrinal and institutional tightening. The council was dominated by the arch-conservative ultra-montane movement, which aimed to recreate the social order known as Christendom, in which the institutional church anchored a conservative moral and social order. Conservatives at the council strengthened the power of the church hierarchy by declaring the doctrine of papal infal-libility and by defining the papacy's "all but complete jurisdiction over the universal church."[4] This meant that national churches and priests owed allegiance to Rome rather than to national governments. These changes were meant to reinforce the church's resistance to "anti-Christian" forces of modern culture and to centralize power in the Vatican.

This "Romanization" movement strengthened the church internally in some ways, but it also triggered an intensified anticlericalism in many parts of Latin America. This anticlericalism was institutionalized in sev-eral national constitutions. One notable example was Great Colombia's 1824 Patronage Law, reprinted here, which gave the state the right to cre-ate Catholic dioceses, among other powers over the church. The law was incorporated into Venezuela's 1911 constitution. Institutionally, and per-haps in popular sentiment as well, anticlericalism has been the strongest in Mexico, whose 1917 constitution prohibited worship outside the con-fines of churches, banned foreign religious orders, and severely restricted pastoral agents' civil and political rights. The rules were particularly se-vere in regards to education, which according to the constitution "shall be maintained entirely apart from any religious doctrine and, based on the results of scientific progress, shall strive against ignorance and its effects, servitudes, fanaticism, and prejudices." The 1917 constitution also confis-cated lands owned by the church:

> Bishoprics, rectories, seminaries, asylums, and schools belonging to re-ligious orders, convents, or any other buildings built or intended for the administration, propagation, or teaching of a religious creed shall at once become the property of the Nation by inherent right, to be used exclusively for the public services of the Federal or State Governments, within their respective jurisdictions. All places of public worship hereafter erected shall be the property of the Nation.[5]

Mexican anticlericalism can be understood in light of the support the church offered to Porfirio Diaz's dictatorship (1876-1910), a period of time when foreigners had great influence over the Mexican economy, including control over public and indigenous lands. When the revolution against the Porfiriato broke, the Archbishop of Guadalajara declared in a pastoral letter,

> As all authority is derived from God, the Christian workman should sanctify and make sublime his obedience by serving God in the person of his bosses. In this way obedience is neither humiliating nor difficult. . . . Poor, love your humble state and your work; turn your gaze towards Heaven; there is the true wealth.[6]

Church-state tensions came to a head when in 1926 a law was promulgated that required the registration of all clergy with civil authorities and imposed steep fines for the violation of articles in the 1917 constitution concerning religion. In reaction, priests throughout Mexico refused to say mass. Eventually, some twenty thousand Catholic peasants and workers took up arms against the government to the cry of "Viva Cristo Rey! Viva la Virgen de Guadalupe!" From 1926 to 1929, Cristeros, as the rebels were called, fought the Mexican army in nineteen of Mexico's thirty-one states. Only a negotiated peace accord between the bishops and a new government put an end to hostilities. No changes were made to the constitution, but the new administration pledged that it would not apply the anticlerical law in its full rigor. As in the case of Canudos and Joaseiro, neither the church nor the state was a monolith in opposition to the other. In addition, as in the Brazilian cases, land was also an issue, since the Cristeros were supported by many landowners who were affected by reforms introduced in the aftermath of the revolution. Thus a variety of social groups was involved in producing, sustaining, and resolving the conflict. One legacy of the Cristero war was the rise in the late 1930s of the synarchist movement, which tried to wed a quasi fascist nationalist stance with a Catholic agenda. Synarchism represented an attempt to reconstitute Catholic hegemony within the republican structures.[7]

Later in the twentieth century, the Argentine leader Juan Perón drew on anticlerical sentiments in his populist campaigns. While Perón saw Catholicism as a powerful bulwark against communism, he sought to fuse state and religion in a way that left no space for the church to pursue its own interests and methods in civil society. In particular, he disliked the church's attempts to form Catholic-based political parties and unions that could weaken his own efforts to control the growing Argentinean working class. While carefully noting that his criticism was not against the church in general, Perón insisted that distinctly Catholic groups of laborers, lawyers, and so forth were not necessary: "We are simply Peronists, and within this context we can be Catholic, Jewish, Buddhist, Orthodox, or what have you. It is not necessary for us to ask a Peronist which God he prays to." Perón also insisted that priests and church officials would not receive special legal privileges: "There is no law of the republic that will prevent us from taking measures against any citizen, of any profession whatsoever . . . when he is guilty of transgressing the laws of the Republic." Peronism serves as an umbrella ideology, within which Catholicism and other religions can be subsumed, although Perón remains careful to distinguish between the church as an institution and "certain churchmen" who "fail to fulfill their duties, both as Argentines and as priests."[8]

One of the groups that aroused Perón's ire in particular was Catholic Action, a church-sponsored lay group that first emerged in the late nineteenth century with the aim of organizing working-class Catholics in specifically Catholic groups, under the oversight of the church hierarchy, as a counter to unions dominated by secular ideologies such as socialism, communism, anarchism, or, in Argentina, Peronism. The movement reflected an effort by church officials to direct and contain secular ideologies and organizations, while also recognizing that it was impossible to prevent Catholics from organizing politically. Although Catholic Action originated as a conservative initiative, it evolved rapidly in the context of dramatic social changes in Europe and Latin America in the 1940s and 1950s. Eventually, it became an important influence on the progressive Catholicism that was to emerge following the Second Vatican Council, as we discuss in chapter 7.

CHAPTER 5 DOCUMENTS

"The Guarani Missions—A Vanished Arcadia"[1]
ROBERT CUNNINGHAME GRAHAM

The problem which most writers on the Jesuits have quite misunderstood is how two Jesuits were able to keep a mission of several thousand Indians in order, and to rule supreme without armed forces or any means of making their power felt or of enforcing obedience to their decrees. Undoubtedly, the dangerous position in which the Indians stood, exposed on one side to the Paulistas and on the other to the Spanish settlers, both of whom wished to take them as their slaves, placed power in the Jesuits' hands: for the Indians clearly perceived that the Jesuits alone stood between them and instant slavery. Most controversialists who have opposed the Jesuits assert that the Indians of the missions were, in reality, half slaves. Nothing is further from the truth, if one consults the contemporary records, and remembers the small number of the Jesuits. The work the Indians did was inconsiderable, and under such conditions as to deprive it of much of the toilsomeness which is incident to any kind of work. The very essence of a slave's estate is being obliged to work without remuneration for another man. Nothing was farther from the Indians than such a state of things. Their work was done for the community, and though the Jesuits, without doubt, had the full disposition of all the money earned in commerce and of the distribution of the goods, neither the money nor the goods were used for self-aggrandisement, but were laid out for the benefit of the community at large. The total population of the thirty towns is variously estimated at from one hundred and forty to one hundred and eighty thousand, and, curiously enough, it remained almost at the same figure during the whole period of the Jesuit rule. This fact has been adduced against the Jesuits, and it has been said that they could not have been good rulers, or the population must have increased; but those who say so forget that the Indians of Paraguay were never in great numbers, and that most writers on the wild tribes, as Dobrizhoffer and Azara, remark their tendency never to increase.

All this relatively large population of Indians was ruled, as has been seen, by a quite inconsiderable number of priests, who, not disposing of any European force, and being almost always on bad terms with the Spanish settlers in Paraguay on account of the firm stand they made against the enslaving of the Indians, had no means of coercion at their command. Hence the Indians must have been contented with their rule, for if they had not been so the Jesuits possessed no power to stop them from returning to their savage life. . . .

Though it has been stated by many polemical writers, such as Ibañez and Azara, and more recently by Washburne, who was American Minister in Paraguay during the war with Brazil and the Argentine Republic (1866-70), that the Jesuits had amassed great wealth in Paraguay, no proof has ever been advanced of such a charge. Certainly Cárdenas made the same statement, but it was never in his power to bring any confirmation of what he said. This power alone was in the hands of Bucareli (1767), the Viceroy of Buenos Aires, under whose auspices the expulsion of the Jesuits was carried out. By several extracts from Brabo's inventories, and by the statement of the receivers sent by Bucareli, I hope to show that there was no great wealth at any time in the mission territory, and that the income was expended in the territory itself. It may be that the expenditure on churches was excessive, and also that the money laid out on religious ceremonies was not productive; but the Jesuits, strange as it may appear, did not conduct the missions after the fashion of a business concern, but rather as the rulers of some Utopia—those foolish beings who think happiness is preferable to wealth. . . .

What was it, then, which raised the Jesuits up so many and so powerful enemies in Paraguay, when in the districts of the Moxos and the Chiquitos where their power was to the full as great, among the Indians, they never had a quarrel with the Spaniards till the day they were expelled? Many and various causes contributed to all they underwent, but most undoubtedly two reasons must have brought about their fall.

Since the time of Cárdenas, the report that the Jesuits had rich mines, which they worked on the sly, had been persistently on the increase. Although disproved a thousand times, it still remained; even today, in spite of "science" and its wonderful discoveries, there are many in Paraguay who cherish dreams of discovering Jesuit mines. Humanity loves to deceive itself, although there are plenty ready to deceive it; and if men can both forge for themselves fables and at the same time damage their neighbours in so doing, their pleasure is intense. I take it that many really believed the stories of the mines, being unable to credit that anyone would live far from the world, surrounded but by Indians, for any other reason than to enrich themselves. So that it would appear one of the reasons which induced hatred against the Jesuits was the idea that they had enormous mineral wealth, which either they did not work or else worked in secret for the benefit of their society.

The other reason was the question of slavery. Once get it well into your head that you and yours are "reasoning men" *(gente de razón),* and that all coloured people are irrational, and slavery follows as a natural sequence; for "reasoning men" have wit to make a gun, and on the gun all reason takes its stand. From the first instant of their arrival in America, the Jesuits had maintained a firm front against the enslavement of the Indians. They may have had their faults in Europe, and in the cities of America; but where they came in contact with the Indians in the wilds theirs was the one protecting hand. . . .

On many occasions, notably in the time of Cárdenas, the Jesuits openly withstood all slavery, and among concessions that Ruíz Montoya obtained from of Spain was one declaring all the Indians to be free. If more examples of the hatred that their attitude on slavery called forth were wanting, it is to be remembered that in 1640, when Montoya and Taño returned from Spain and affixed the edict of the Pope on the church doors in Piritinanga, threatening with excommunication all slave-holders, a cry of robbery went forth, and the Jesuits were banished from the town. . . .

"The Guaraní Missions—A Ruthless Exploitation of the Indians"[2] BLAS GARAY

We find two notably different periods of Jesuit history in Paraguay; first, the primitive, during which the Fathers laid the foundations of their future republic, running great risks although they were always protected by the force of arms; enduring all sorts of discomforts with no other compensation than the satisfaction of augmenting the Christian fold; seeking only spiritual goods, and never searching for advantages from which the neophytes could not obtain copious benefits. They were dedicated to the service of God and religion, unmoved by personal ambition. They were surrounded by popular affection because they respected the rights of outsiders, and because power had not yet made them arrogant. However, after a few years their behavior changed, and in direct ratio to their increased power. They who were at first unselfish and humble missionaries became the ambitious rulers of the towns who little by little shook off all the natural laws to which they should have been subject. They concerned themselves with accumulating material wealth to the detriment of their Christian and civilizing mission. They persecuted those who sought to end their abuses or tried to combat their influence. They mastered the wills of the governors and bishops, sometimes because the latter owed their positions to the Jesuits, then again, perhaps, because greed and the promise of rich profits converted them to devotees. And finally, they turned their republic into a vast collective society of production. Shielded by the great privileges they had been able to obtain, they ruined the province of Paraguay to whose worthy inhabitants they owed recognition for so many ideas. . . .

The Jesuit organization was completely dependent on the equality the Fathers maintained among the Guaraní, an equality so absolute that it annihilated their individual initiative by depriving them of every impulse for emulation, every inducement that might move them to exert some energy. For the bad received the same portion as the good, the industrious the same as the lazy, the quick as the slow, the intelligent as the dim-witted; they were fed, dressed, and treated according to their needs, not their deeds, and no one could evade the completion of his appointed task. Those who exercised a little authority were obliged to be the most assiduous and punctual of all, so the others might learn from their example.

The women did the same work as the men; they could not avoid it by virtue of their sex, even if they were pregnant or nursing mothers. They helped the men plow, weed, and sow the earth, and then to gather in and store the crop. It is said that they celebrated only the major festivals. The provincials did attempt to relieve the neophytes from such continual labor, though with little success, and when they observed the pernicious fruits the mixing of the sexes bore, they tried to avoid that, too.

The Indians' work began at dawn and lasted until sunset, with only two hours of rest which were granted at noon for lunch.

. . . Agriculture was a principal source of wealth for the towns of the Jesuits. The lands employed in this were ultimately divided into three sections: the first, the *tabambaé*, belonged to the community; another, the *abambaé*, was reserved for the family heads, who each cultivated a portion as his own; the last, called *Tupambaé*, was the property of God.

All the mission Indians worked the first portion on the first three days of the week, under the strict inspection of wardens who were charged with ensuring that they applied themselves to the task diligently. The crops belonged to the community and were kept in the Society warehouses whence they were distributed as needed by the mission.

At first private property did not exist, even in name, and all the fruits of the Indians' labor were deposited in the communal granaries. The Jesuits had convinced the Court that the Guarani were so improvident and ignorant that if the work was left to their direction they would not be able to maintain themselves. This argument did some violence to the truth, for as Azara well observes, one can hardly understand then how they managed to subsist and to multiply so prodigiously before the conquest, when they were still ignorant of the political and economic maxims of the Society; nor how other towns, founded by the Spaniards, could prosper. One also wonders how, outside Jesuit jurisdiction, the Indians could accept and protect private property, even though they had to serve the encomenderos.

After this system had endured for a great many years the Court, acceding to the insistent and authoritative requests it constantly received, told the Jesuits that it was high time the Indians learned both to govern themselves and to enjoy the advantages of owning their own property. Furthermore, they were informed that it seemed that the time for ending the communal regime had arrived. After exhausting every possible means of eluding the reform, the Fathers finally assigned, to quiet the objections and complaints, a certain plot of land to the head of each family, so that he and his family might cultivate and exploit it to their own advantage. Three days of the week were to be used for this, and the other three for the public benefit. Unfortunately the new arrangement did not produce the expected results. As every administrative notion had been lost, or was, rather, unknown to these unfortunates who had never had, nor imagined that they might have anything of their own, it could hardly be expected that, by luck, they should succeed in conforming to the exact amounts which they produced, thus avoiding misery and poverty. The missionaries knew this well; they relied on it in order to resist the innovation. "The Indians are incapable of governing themselves"; but they forgot to add that this incapacity was not native, but the result and fruit of deliberate education, of the complete isolation in which they lived, and of their removal from every occasion for learning anything inconvenient to the plans of the Fathers. The latter, on the other hand, made it difficult for the neophytes to work their own plots at the time allotted them by employing them overtime in the community service and the cultivation of the yerba maté. They also refused to pay them their just salaries, and obliged them to sell what they raised or made for themselves to the Society, at a loss. They refused them oxen for plowing, forcing them to pull the plows themselves, and hindered them in various other ways. Thus, the crops were either scanty or failed altogether. The Indians lacked what they needed for subsistence, and the community no longer assuaged their hunger. As that hunger pinched, and their scruples were scarce and accommodating, they sought from robbery what their work refused them, despoiling other unfortunates who were scarcely more comfortable or well supplied. Such evil tendencies triumphed over the most energetic and best-intentioned provisions of the provincials.

So that no one would avoid doing his share, the Jesuits found a method of handling the lazy ones, who showed no inclination to work, subjecting them to a particular regime. With this in mind the children and laggards were assigned to the *Tupambaé*, which were always on the best land in town, under the vigilance of special wardens who merited the Fathers' full trust and were charged with forcing them to fulfill the duties they were assigned, according to their ability, to the letter. The wardens denounced them for punishment, always severe and never excused, when they did not.

The crops from God's portion were also stored in the communal granaries and were to be used for the support of the old, ill, widows, chiefs, artisans, and those who were otherwise employed. This designation was only nominal and intended to impress the Indians, for actually, everything the missions produced had only one purpose; to advance the plans of the Society. Only a little was kept back to supply the needs of those who produced it by the sweat of their brows, and the continuous labor to which their catechists subjected them. Careless of their spiritual education, the Jesuits were careful only to train them as hardworking agriculturists or able artisans in those arts from which they might obtain the most profitable advantages. . . .

. . . Thus the Jesuits in Paraguay succeeded, not in converting all the souls they might have gained in a populous region, but in becoming wealthy. Authoritative estimates are that the annual return of these missions was approximately one million Spanish silver pesos, and less than one hundred thousand was spent on their maintenance. Such copious profits allowed the Fathers to allay the increasing expenses of the Order in Europe generously, almost prodigiously, with the fruit of the Indians' labor. Their goal was the defense of their power structure, the eternal object of rude and obstinate attacks, made in passion sometimes, but more often in the spirit of justice.

The Jesuit solicitors, who were sent back to the old continent every six years, always bore respectable sums of money, and besides, there were the amounts sent to Rome very frequently by means of the English and

Portuguese. In 1725, 400,000 pesos were sent in one single instance, and this is not necessarily the most splendid example of the Fathers' wealth. Such a sum does explain the success the Society always had in its negotiations, despite the fact that the rightness of its cause was frequently questionable.

This wealth, combined with the fear of being judged as enemies by a group so unscrupulous in its choice of means to an end, also explains the favour shown the Jesuits by most of the governors and bishops, who seemed their humble inferiors rather than their superiors. . . .

"Sobre a República" and "Despedida"[3] ANTÔNIO CONSELHEIRO

About the Republic

The Society of Jesus—Civil Marriage—
The Imperial Family—The Emancipation of the Slaves
Now, I have to talk to you about a matter that has shocked and shaken the faithful, a matter that only the incredulity of man could have occasioned: the republic, which is indisputably a great evil for Brazil whose star was beautiful before. Today, however, all certainty abandons us because the new government has just invented and is using [the republic] as the most effective means to exterminate religion. I marvel at the actions of those who have contributed with their votes to bring about the republic, whose idea has brutally oppressed the Church and its faithful, taking incredulity to the point of prohibiting the Society of Jesus [Jesuits]. Who then is not astonished [*se pasma*] at the sight of such a degrading process? Who would think that there are men who share such an idea? The Republic is the way tyranny cheats the faithful. One cannot qualify the behavior of those who have made it possible for the republic to have such a horrible effect!! These are men who look through a prism, when they should abundantly impugn the republic, giving thus brilliant proof to religion.

The republic wants to end religion, God's masterpiece which has existed for nineteen centuries and will remain until the end of the world, because God protects his work. [Religion] has suffered persecution, but it has always triumphed over impiety. No matter how ignorant man is, he knows that human power is impotent to end God's work. Consider then these truths that should convince those who conceived the idea of the republic: that human power is impotent to end religion. The president of the republic, however, moved by unbelief, which generates all sorts of illusions, thinks that he can govern Brazil as if he were the monarch legitimately sanctioned by God. The injustice that Catholics bitterly face. Oh! Incredulous man, how your incredulity weighs in front of God! And to make [this point] obvious, see what our Lord Jesus Christ says (Mt. 16: 16): He who believes and is baptized will be saved, however, he who does not believe will be condemned.

[. . . .]

All legitimate power emanates from God's eternal omnipotence and is subject to divine rule, both in temporal and spiritual realms, such that in obeying the pontiff, the prince, the father, those who are, in reality, ministers of God for the good, we are only obeying God. Happy is he who understands this celestial doctrine, free from the yoke of error and passions, docile to the voice of God and [his] conscience, enjoy[ing] the true freedom of God. It is evident that the republic remains [based] on a false principle, [from] which it cannot derive its legitimacy. To defend the contrary would be absurd, shocking and extremely odd, because even if [the republic] could bring good for the country, it is in itself evil [*má*], because it goes against the will of God, manifestly offending His divine law. How can one reconcile divine and human laws, taking the right from those who have it to give it to those who do not? Who does not know that the noble prince Lord Dom Pedro III has the legitimate power constituted by God to govern Brazil? Who does not know that his noble grandfather, Lord Dom Pedro II, whom we dearly miss, despite being betrayed and thrown out of his government, receiving such a heavy blow, continues to have his right [to the throne], and that, as a result, his royal family has the power to govern Brazil? To deny these truths would be the same as to say that the dawn does not open the new day. The tranquility [*o sossego*] of a people consists of doing God's will and to gain his glory it is indispensable to follow his divine will.

This truth is confirmed by what Our Lord Jesus Christ says (Mt 7: 21): Not every one who says Lord, Lord will enter the kingdom of the heavens. But he who carries the will of my father, who is in heaven, will enter this kingdom. Our Lord Jesus Christ left us an example of this truth when the angel gave him the chalice, at the bottom of which was his death. He prayed this way: my father, if possible, take this chalice away from me; may my will not be done but yours (Mt 26: 39). In the meantime, He was innocent, He did not need to suffer outrage in the highest degree. . . . It is necessary to suffer to obtain true happiness, which is the glory of God. It is necessary to nurture the faith of his Church. It is necessary, in sum, to do his divine will, fighting the devil who wants to end the faith of his Church. Religion sanctifies everything and does not destroy anything but sin.

From here we can see that civil marriage annuls marriage as it is demanded by holy mother Church of Rome, against its most explicit teachings. [The Church], always benevolent [*benigna*], always generous [*caridosa*], and wise in its teaching, [is the source] of all knowledge so that men can better serve God. . . . When God authorized with his presence the first instance of marriage in the world, it was to show the great excellence and perfection enshrined in [this state] and the obligation the partners have to live in accordance with divine precepts, coming together as a single will. . . . Because marriage, as everybody knows, is a contract of two wills linked through the love that God conveys to them, justified by the grace that Our Lord Jesus Christ has given them and authorized by a ceremony with which the holy mother Church brought them together. The effect of a true marriage is to unite two souls in a body. . . .

These truths demonstrate that marriage is purely the competence of the holy Church, because only its ministers have the power to celebrate it. Temporal powers cannot, thus, intervene in any forms in marriage . . . . which Our Lord Jesus Christ elevated to the dignity of sacrament, representing through it His [own] union with the holy Church, as [St.] Paul says. Therefore, it is prudent and just that parents not obey the law of civil marriage, avoiding an extremely serious offense in religious matters that touches directly upon the soul.

[. . . .]

Civil marriage is indisputable null, it leads to the sin of scandal [*o pecado do escândalo*]. . . . Without the legitimate and natural affection that your families should have . . . corruption is invading, [producing] the terrible effect of incredulity. It is in this crisis that your responsibilities grow as guardians of your families, as if at this moment a voice tells you: fathers, defend the morality of your families.

[. . . .]

Where is your faith? Do you not have the patience to wait for the promise that beloved Jesus made to Peter saying: you are Peter and on this rock I will build my Church and the gates of hell will not prevail over it (Mt 16: 18). I affirm to you, infused with the most intimate certainty, that the Lord Jesus is all powerful and faithful in the fulfillment of his promise. Those who say that the royal family will not govern Brazil again are mistaken. If this world were absolute, I would believe [their] opinions. But there is nothing absolute in this world, because the world is subject to the most holy Providence of God, which disperses the plan[s] of men and confounds them as He wishes, without moving from His throne. The republic will fall to the ground to confuse those who conceived this horrible idea. Republicans, accept [*convençam-se*] the fact that [your] cause will not triumph because it is the child of unbelief and every movement, every step, toward it will be punished. . . . See what happened to the inhabitants of Jerusalem, who closed their eyes and did not even recognize what was going to happen to them, moved as they were by incredulity, despite being warned by Our Lord Jesus Christ.

Looking at the city, he cried for the destruction and the misfortune of his people and said:

Ah! If only on this day you would recognize what was given to you that could bring you peace, but now all of this is hidden from your eyes (Lk 19: 42). Give to God what is God's and give to Caesar what is Caesar's. But this sublime thought [*sentimento*] does not dominate in the heart of the president of the republic, who wants to govern Brazil out of his own wish [*talante*], practicing such a clamorous injustice and thus wounding the clearest and most palpable right of the royal family, legitimately constituted to govern Brazil.

[. . . .]

I must not remain silent about the origin of the hatred that [the republic] has toward the royal family. [It was] because her majesty Dona Isabel emancipated the slaves. She was doing nothing more than fulfilling the orders from heaven, because God determined that the time had arrived to liberate that people for such a state, which was the most degrading [condition] to which a human being could be reduced. [Dona Isabel's] moral force . . . with which she proceeded to satisfy divine will shows the trust she had in God to liberate those people, and it was not sufficient reason to strike the cord of indignation that produced the hatred of those who controlled [the slaves].

[. . . .]

People will be amazed at such a beautiful event [the emancipation], because they sensed the arm that supported their work, that gave them their riches, repaying with ingratitude and callousness the work that they received from those people [the slaves]. How many died under the whip for faults they committed, some almost naked, oppressed by hunger and hard labor. And what can I say of those who did not have the patience to withstand such cruelty and in the furor or intensity of their unhappiness would kill themselves? The day finally arrived that God put a stop to so much cruelty, and moved by his compassion for his people, he ordered liberation from such a harsh slavery.

Farewell

May it please the heavens that the advice you have heard produce abundant fruit. What good fortune for you if you practice [this advice]. You may be certain that the peace of Our Lord Jesus Christ, our light and force, will remain with your spirit. He will defend you of the miseries of this world. One day you will attain the prize that the Lord has prepared— if you sincerely convert to Him—which is eternal glory.

[. . . .]

Before I say my farewell to you, I ask your forgiveness if in my advice I have offended you. Although in some occasions I proffered excessively rigid words combating the damned republic, reprimanding vices, and moving hearts to the fear and love of God, do not think that I nurtured the least desire to stain your reputation. Yes, the desire for you to be saved (which speaks louder than anything . . .) forced me to act in that manner. If, however, you feel resentful toward me, I ask your forgiveness by the love of God. The moment has arrived for me to say good-bye. What sorrow, what strong feeling this farewell causes in my soul in view of the benevolent, generous, and charitable manner with which you have treated me. . . . Good-bye people, good-bye birds, good-bye trees, good-bye fields; accept my farewell. It shows the pleasant memories I take of you, that will never extinguish from memories of this pilgrim, who anxiously aspires to your salvation and the good of the Church. May it please the heavens that such an ardent desire be reciprocated by that sincere conversion that should capture your passion [*afeto*].

The Testament of Father Cícero Romão Baptista[4]

In the name of God, Amen. I, Father Cicero Romão Baptista, finding myself ill, but not seriously, and of sound mind, and unsure about the day of my death, have resolved to dictate my testament and my last wishes to dispose of my worldy goods [*bens*], as allowed by the laws of my country.

[. . . .]

I declare that I am the legitimate son of the late Joaquim Romão Baptista and Mrs. Joaquina Vicencia Romana. I was born in the city of Crato, in this state of Ceará on the 24th of March of 1844. As a profession, I adopted the priestly ministry, in accordance with the orders that were given to me by the then bishop of Ceará, Dom Luiz Antonio dos Santos,[5] whom I dearly miss. [I] carried out [this ministry] pursuant to my vocation, with love, dedication and good will, wishing to continue this way for as long as the good Lord, through his Divine Mercy, gives me strength and the awareness of my acts.

I further declare that since my ordination, and even during the short time I was the vicar of the S. Pedro do Crato parish, I never received even a penny for the religious acts I have performed as a Catholic priest. I also declare that all the moneys that were given and continue to be given only to me I have distributed in acts of charity that are known to everybody, as well as for large and beneficial works in agriculture. The results of these works I have used in assets that I leave, in large part, to the blessed and holy Salesian Congregation, so that it can found here in Joazeiro their schools to educate children of both sexes.

From very early on, when I began to be aided by the donations of the pilgrims [*romeiros*] of Nossa Senhora das Dôres who came here, together with my own effective work developing this land, I decided to use the alms received [to buy] properties, seeking to leave a patrimony to help the Instituição Pia e de Caridade continue its work of public welfare.

[. . . .]

I am certain, not only because I know the character of the people who live here but also of the populations of the interior [*sertanejas*] that come here frequently, whom I have educated through good advice to practice good deeds and the love of God . . . [that], as proof of [their] affection and friendship toward me and in praise and honor of the Virgin Mother of God, they will continue to come to this beloved Joazeiro,[6] with the same diligence, and will help the blessed Salesian Fathers, as if they were helping me, in maintaining the good Christian works of charity. I mean the schools, the existence of which in this land, will always give the greatest peace [*tranquilidade*] to my soul in the other life.

[. . . .]

I must declare, since it is a great honor to me and one of the many effects of divine grace upon me, that following a vow that I made when I was twelve years old, inspired then by my reading of the immaculate life of Saint Francis de Sales, that I preserved my virginity and chastity up to now. I affirm that I never wronged nor hated anyone. I always forgave, by the love of God and Holy Virgin, all those who did me wrong deliberately or not.

I need to clarify a matter to which my name has, because of special circumstances, been linked. But, I must add, my action[s] [in these matters, which were] peaceful, conciliatory, and always on the side of the good, have been unjustly distorted by those who let themselves be dominated by the passions of the moment and were unable to understand [these actions]. I never wished to be a politician. But, in 1911, when Joazeiro, then a small village, was elevated to the category of city [*villa*], I responded to the insistent requests of my dearly missed friend, State Governor [*presidente do estado*] *Commendador*⁷ Antonio Pinto Nogueira Accioly. At the same time, I found myself forced to help [*collaborar*] in politics in order to prevent any other citizen, from leading this people politically, someone who neither knowing nor able to maintain the balance of order that I had kept up to that time, might compromise the progress [*boa marcha*] of this land.

Despite the sudden changes in the politics of Ceará, I always sought to maintain a discreet attitude, without letting myself be carried away by passions, always avoiding incompatibilities that would have had disastrous effects. To be able to do this . . . many times I had to open myself to the opinions of men without well-defined ideas. After the fall of the Accioly government, I withdrew from politics on moral grounds, but still kept up cordial relations with the government of Franco Rabello, who had been elected third vice-president of the state. My love for [maintaining public] order was so clear that, despite the lack of good will of the dominant political party towards me, I did not hesitate to respond to the call of the people of this land and let them present my name to return to the office of mayor of this municipality, as part of the very same government that was overly hostile to me. In 1913, my friend Dr. Floro Bartholomeu da Costa, congressman [*deputado federal*] for this state and political director for this land (of our district), informed me on his return from Rio de Janeiro that the leaders of the deposed party [that of former Governor Accioly] had decided to hold a [session of the] state assembly here [in Joazeiro], since it was impossible to hold it in Fortaleza [the capital of the state] because of the pressure exerted by the party in power to control the reactionary movement. Then, with the greatest loyalty, I pondered in a confidential letter to Colonel Franco Rabello about the possible benefits of his resigning. I proceeded that way, because with the limited knowledge I had (beyond the meeting of the Assembly), I sensed, in light of the violence of the government in power, that there would be strife. Franco

Rabello, however, did not pay attention. And not being able to avoid that acts of sheer folly [*actos de desatino*], including murders and beatings, be carried out in his name, I distanced myself from politics. At the same time, I let Dr. Floro act according to the orders he received, since it was impossible to save this hardworking population from the sad condition of becoming a victim.

At the height of the struggle, the severity of which came as to me as a surprise, there are people here who can attest to the fact that my attitude was to lament the disastrous consequences of the political errors and I never ceased to try to avoid violence. That is why I can affirm in good conscience [*sem nenhum peso de consciencia*], that I never made revolutions. I never took part in them. I never sought them. Nor did I have the least bit of direct or indirect responsibility for the events that took place. I always had cordial relations with newly elected government of Benjamin Baroso, despite the fact that he had broken from Dr. Floro Bartholomeu. It is not my fault that, due to misunderstanding or a political order, there are those who want to make me responsible. I am sure that when the facts come to light dispassionately, my name will emerge untarnished, as it always has been. I make these declarations in this document so that those who survive me will know (because before God my conscience is clean) that in this world, during all my life, as a man and a priest, I never, thanks be to God, committed a dishonesty, from whatever point of view you may want to look at it. I never told or condoned any kind of lie.

I take advantage of the opportunity to ask those who live in this land, Joazeiro, and especially the pilgrims, not to leave after my death but to continue to venerate and always love the Holy Virgin Mother of God, the only remedy to all our afflictions. . . . [I] insist, as I always advised you, that you be good and honest, hardworking and faithful, friends to each other and always obedient and respectful of the laws and authorities, both civil and those of the Holy, Apostolic, Roman Catholic Church, only in whose bosom there can be happiness and salvation. [. . .] This advice that I always gave you during my lifetime I do not tire to repeat, so that after my death it remain firmly engraved in the memory of this people, whose happiness and salvation were always the object of my greatest concern.

Ley de Patronato Eclesiástico de la Gran Colombia (1824)[8]

The Senate and Chamber of Representatives of the Republic of Colombia in Congress assembled:

Decree:

Article 1. The Republic of Colombia ought to continue in the exercise of the right of patronage which the kings of Spain had over the metropolitan churches, cathedrals, and parishes in this part of America.

Article 2. This right is a duty of the Republic of Colombia and of its government, and it demands that the Apostolic See do not change or alter it; and the Executive Power under this principle will celebrate with His Holiness a concordat which will assure for all time, and irrevocably, this prerogative of the Republic and avoid conflicts and claims for the future.

Article 3. The right of patronage and protection are exercised, first, by the Congress; second, by the Executive Power with the Senate; third, by the Executive Power alone; fourth, by the intendants; and fifth, by the governors.

The High Court of the Republic, and the Superior Courts will hear cases that arise out of this matter.

[. . . .]

Article 4. The Congress is empowered to:

1. Erect new dioceses or reorganize old ones, to designate their territorial limits, and assign funds to be employed in the building and repairing of metropolitan and episcopal churches.

2. Permit, or even summon, national or provincial councils or synods.

3. Permit or refuse the founding of new monasteries and hospitals, and to suppress those existing if deemed advisable, and to assume control of their property.

4. Draw up tariffs of parochial fees.

5. Regulate the administration of the tithes.

6. Grant or refuse the exequatur to bull and briefs.

7. Enact legislation deemed necessary for the vigorous maintenance of exterior discipline of the Church, and for the conservation and exercise of the ecclesiastical patronage.

8. Nominate those to be presented to His Holiness for the archiepiscopal and episcopal sees.

9. Enact legislation for the establishment, rule, and support of the missions for the Indians.

Article 6. The Executive is empowered to:

1. Present to the pope for his approval the actions of Congress on the erection of new dioceses and the alteration of old ones.

2. Present to the pope the nominees of Congress for the archiepiscopal and episcopal positions.

3. Present to the prelates and chapters for the prebendaries and canons, nominees selected jointly with the Senate.

4. Grant or refuse consent to the nominees of the prelates and chapters for provisors and capitular vicars.

5. Guard against the introduction of any novelty in the exterior discipline of the Church, and see that the ecclesiastics do not usurp the patronage of the State.

6. Grant the exequatur to briefs on matters of grace.
Watch over the proper supervision of the dioceses by the prelates.

7. Issue administrative decrees regulating the laws of Congress to protect religion, the public cult, and its ministers.

Article 7. The intendants are empowered to:

1. Name and present to the respective prelates the curates of the diocese included within the department.

2. Erect and fix the limits of new parishes.

3. Take care that the national patronage is observed and report on same to the Executive Power.

4. See that ecclesiastics do not usurp the civil jurisdiction.

5. Keep the Executive Power informed regarding clerics worthy of advancement.

Article 8. The governors are empowered to:

1. Name the *mayordomos de fabrica* of the cathedral and parish churches of their provinces, and to make them render an account of their management according to law.

2. Name, on the proposal of the respective municipalities, the syndics, mayordomos, and administrators of the hospitals of their provinces.

3. Permit or refuse the founding of chapels and churches, but not cathedrals, parochial churches, or monasteries.

4. Watch over the observance of the patronage.

5. Visit hospitals and remedy abuses in them; propose to the Executive Power, through the intendants, the reforms that should be introduced to improve those establishments.

6. Supervise *cofradias*.

7. Inform the intendants regarding the need of establishing new parishes.

8. Inform the intendants regarding ecclesiastics worthy of promotion.

Article 9. The High Court of Justice has jurisdiction over the following subjects:

1. Disloyalty of the archbishop and bishop to the republic, and violation on their part of the national patronage.

2. Controversies between two or more dioceses concerning their territorial limits.

3. Controversies arising out of concordats.

Article 10. The Superior Courts have jurisdiction over the following subjects:

1. Disloyalty to the republic, or usurpation of the patronage, by the other ecclesiastics.

2. Conflict over jurisdiction between civil and ecclesiastical courts.

6

Protestantism in Latin America

In 1990, anthropologist David Stoll asked, "Is Latin America Turning Protestant?" noting that the decline of liberation theology under John Paul II's papacy coincided with an "invasion of the sects," meaning the explosive growth of evangelical Protestantism.[1] In reality, Protestantism in its diverse forms has a long history in the region, a presence that gained greater visibility after the wars of independence in the early 1800s, since in most countries separation from the Spanish crown was accompanied by formal disestablishment of the Roman Catholic Church. Moreover, evangelical Protestantism, and particularly Pentecostalism, has been growing rapidly in the region since the 1950s, amid the chaotic processes of modernization, industrialization, and urbanization. In this section, we trace the evolution of Protestantism in Latin America, placing special emphasis on Pentecostalism, one of the most dynamic movements on the contemporary religious scene.

Origins and Development of Protestantism in Latin America

As we have seen, during the colonial period, the Spanish and Portuguese crowns banned non-Catholic immigrants to their American colonies. This ban was far from universally effective, as there is documentary evidence that Protestants, Jews, and Muslims resided in the Americas from early in the colonial period. Most of these non-Catholics did not practice their religions openly, however, and many lived as "new Christians," or *conversos*, for fear of the Inquisition and other penalties. In the seventeenth and eighteenth centuries, the arrival of British, Dutch, and French (Huguenot) immigrants stimulated the creation of Protestant communities, particularly among African slaves in coastal cities in the Caribbean basin. Especially noteworthy is the presence of Methodist and Moravian missionaries who brought a strong version of pietism and asceticism to places such as Belize, the Miskito coast in Nicaragua, the Virgin Islands, Jamaica, the Bahamas, and Barbados.

Historian Jean-Pierre Bastian argues that emerging creole elites in Latin America found in Protestantism a strategic ally against the conservative, royalist forces within the Catholic Church. The so-called historic Protestant denominations, such as Presbyterians, Lutherans, and Baptists, contributed to the development of a dissident public sphere by founding and supporting alternative religious presses, schools, and lodges. Within these institutions emerged "a liberal civil religion that was in effect a Protestant syncretism adapted to reflect Latin American liberal values." These values included democracy, freedom of conscience, and the affirmation of human progress. Thus, it is not surprising to find Protestants "siding with the democratic forces at the heart of the republican and antislavery struggles in Brazil (1870-1889), during the Cuban independence movements (1868-1898), and in the Mexican Revolution (1910-1920)."[2]

In the years following Independence, political leaders in some countries, including Brazil, Chile, and Argentina, encouraged the immigration of European Protestants not only as a way to encourage Enlightenment values such as individualism, order, and progress but also to "whiten" the population. For example, large numbers of German Lutherans and Baptists moved to southeastern Brazil, forming tightly knit communities that to this day preserve a great deal of their religious and cultural heritage. Immigration continued to be the main engine driving the growth of Protestantism in Latin America until a world mission conference held in Edinburgh in 1910 made the spread of the gospel key to a new global Protestant identity.[3] Delegates to the Edinburgh meeting envisioned a "world church," encompassing Latin America, Africa, and Asia as "mission fields" for North American and European churches. Edinburgh, with its watchword of "the evangelisation of the world in this generation," is considered the symbolic starting point of the contemporary ecumenical movement, and certainly marks the beginning of sustained Protestant growth in Latin America, supported initially by North American missions.[4]

The European and North American missionaries who worked in Latin American in the decades following Edinburgh came primarily from historic or mainline Protestant traditions, just as was the case during and in the aftermath of Independence. A steadily growing proportion, however, came from the nascent Pentecostal wing of Protestantism. Pentecostalism emerged from early-twentieth-century revival movements in the United

States, first in Topeka, Kansas, in 1901, and most famously, five years later, on Azusa Street in Los Angeles in 1906.[5] Pentecostals see their churches as latter-day expressions of the early Christian community, which began its missionary work in earnest fifty days after the death of Jesus, when tongues of fire descended on the heads of the Apostles, empowering them to preach in multiple languages and to perform other wondrous actions as signs of Christ's imminent second coming. Pentecostalism makes baptism in the Holy Spirit the centerpiece of its worldview. From an intense and direct personal relationship with the sacred flow the gifts of the spirit (*charismata*), the outward practices that characterize Pentecostalism, such as glossolalia (speaking in tongues), divine healing, prophecy, and the exorcism of evil spirits, as well as the eschatological view that the end of time is at hand.

The connection among immigration, missionary work, and the spread of Protestantism in Latin America is clear in the story of Gunnar Vingren, who cofounded with Daniel Berg the Assemblies of God in Brazil.[6] We excerpt here his remarkable diary, in which he recounts his trajectory from Sweden to Chicago, where he was baptized by the spirit as part of the pneumatic awakening irradiating from Azusa Street and Topeka. Through a fellow believer, God had called Vingren to go missionize in Pará, an agricultural state in northeastern Brazil, which was undergoing major social dislocation after the collapse of the rubber industry in the 1910s. From their base of operation in Belém, the capital of Pará, Vingren and Berg made frequent trips to Rio de Janeiro and São Paulo to seed churches. Eventually, the headquarters of the Assemblies of God moved to Rio de Janeiro in 1930.[7]

As the example of Vingren shows, Pentecostalism in its early day in Latin America was not necessarily an urban movement. For example, in El Salvador, Pentecostalism was introduced in the early 1900s by Canadian missionary Frederick Mebius, who started preaching in the coffee plantations around the Santa Ana Volcano in the western part of the country.[8] The case of Guatemala is similar—the first Pentecostal missions started in Livingston on the Atlantic coast and later on in the coffee-growing lands of Alta Verapaz.[9] From its rural origins, Pentecostalism moved to cities, traveling with large masses of people from the countryside in search of jobs in the expanding urban and suburban industrial parks. The boom that Stoll documents in 1990 is the culmination of the growth that began in the 1950s, when the continent was entering a dramatic phase of urbanization and industrialization.

Early Studies on Evangelical Protestantism

By the late 1960s, the first serious scholarly studies of Protestantism in Latin America emerged, attempting to understand the correlation between the rapid growth of evangelicalism and widespread economic change. We excerpt here the work of the two figures who dominated the debate at the time: Christian Lalive D'Epinay and Emilio Willems. Both scholars employ a variation of the anomie thesis, according to which Protestantism appeals primarily to people who are displaced and disoriented by urbanization and other social transformations. (This argument originated with French sociologist Emile Durkheim's analysis of the transition from simple agrarian communities to highly complex and differentiated urban societies.) Lalive D'Epinay and Willems see the growth of evangelical Protestantism as the product of the breakdown of the old Catholic rural order that was based on relations of reciprocity between landowner and peasant and between saints and believers. As rural communities are torn asunder by the mechanization of the agrarian production and by massive migration to cities, there is a generalized sense of chaos and confusion that calls for the introduction of new norms to regulate social action in the new context. In the absence of the support network that the extended family, local parish, and patron saints provide, rural immigrants are vulnerable to destructive forces like poverty, alcoholism, and crime. Evangelical Protestantism, and especially Pentecostalism, with its mixture of strict moral principles and the emphasis on individual self-improvement and salvation, offers the best normative framework for navigating the chaos of rapid social change and for dealing with the temptations of life in the city.

Where Lalive D'Epinay and Willems disagree is in the analysis of the consequences of evangelical Protestantism's solution to the problem of anomie. Although Lalive D'Epinay recognizes that Pentecostalism has "liberated the Christian message from the language of the North American [missionary] culture and from the gilded prison of Catholic clergy," he sees in the figure of the Pentecostal pastor an effort to reassert the patriarchal structures left behind in the countryside. The Pentecostal pastor becomes the new *patrón* (boss) in the city, dispensing resources to his church in a clientelistic mode and protecting believers within the confines of his highly disciplined congregation. Willems, in contrast, does not see Pentecostalism as a desperate attempt to reconstitute the rural hierarchal patron-client order in an urban setting. Rather, he builds on sociologist Max Weber's famous thesis that there is a connection between the

Protestant ethic of hard work and thrift and modern capitalist accumulation. For Willems, evangelical Protestantism's appeal to freedom of conscience and to the priesthood of all believers contributes to the emergence in Latin America of a new kind of individualism more in line with the requirements of modernity. Willems, thus, sees evangelical Protestantism as a progressive force rising out of the ashes of the old, monopolistic, and patriarchal Catholic order.

Lalive D'Epinay's and Willems's readings of the connection between the growth of evangelical Protestantism and social change represent two poles of a continuum that has framed all subsequent treatments of Latin American Protestantism. As helpful as this framework has been, evangelical Protestantism, and more specifically Pentecostalism, exhibits great variability on the ground. To begin with, Pentecostal churches vary in size and levels of bureaucratization, ranging from highly established transnational organizations with full access to global electronic media, such as the Assemblies of God or the newer Igreja Universal do Reino de Deus, to small storefront congregations of forty to fifty members, which rely on old-fashioned door-to-door evangelism.

Moreover, in the 1950s, there was a process of indigenization of Pentecostalism, as Latin Americans trained by foreign missionaries began to form their own churches. For instance, in 1956, Manoel de Mello, who had converted in the Assemblies of God, founded the Evangelical Pentecostal Church Brazil for Christ, which developed a major presence among the urban poor in São Paulo and Rio de Janeiro, particularly among those who, like de Mello himself, had migrated from the rural northeast. In many cases, these indigenous churches introduced local cultural dynamics that gave rise to national or Latin American expressions of Pentecostalism at odds with the doctrines, practices, and forms of organization instituted by foreign missionaries. A case in point is the Guatemalan Evangelical Church Prince of Peace. In 1954, José María Muñoz broke from the Assemblies of God over the American missionaries' domineering ways and founded Príncipe de Paz. Although the latter "mirrored the doctrine and practice of the Assemblies of God in every way . . . it was, by Muñoz's design, 'pure Guatemalan.' It had no foreign pastors or staff, was self-consciously patriotic, and refused to accept financial support from any source outside of Guatemala" (Garrard-Burnett 1998: 116).

By the 1974 International Congress of World Evangelization held in Lusanne, Latin American Protestantism had come of age. At Lusanne, the twenty-three hundred delegates "rejoice that a new missionary era has dawned. The dominant role of western missions is fast disappearing. God is raising up from the younger churches a great new resource for world evangelization, and is thus demonstrating that the responsibility to evangelise belongs to the whole body of Christ." It is in this context that many Latin American evangelical Protestant churches now have active ministries throughout the world, especially everywhere there are Latino immigrants. In fact, recent studies show that immigrants from Latin America are having a powerful effect on the religious field in the United States, injecting a strong dose of charismaticism, even in the Catholic Church.[10]

Finally, the Lalive D'Epinay-Willems debate tends to ignore that fact that there are important theological differences among Pentecostals that may affect the reception of the message. For example, the fastest-growing churches in the region are those that subscribe to the "gospel of health and wealth," which tends to emphasize the practices of exorcism and divine healing over glossolalia, which classical Pentecostal church have always considered the first and definite sign of justification in the Holy Spirit. We will discuss these "neo-Pentecostal" churches in the chapter on contemporary religious diversity. One-size-fits-all theories of the growth of Pentecostalism also fail to account for the fact that this religion, like any, serves different purposes and provides different goods for different people, and often yields paradoxical social and political effects.

Protestantism and Contemporary Politics

The emergence of Protestantism as a major religious and social force in Latin America has been fraught with political conflict and ambiguity. Ever since Lalive D'Epinay's work, there has been a tendency to see evangelical Protestants as politically conservative or, at best, apolitical. This view was bolstered during the 1980s, when civil wars in Central America polarized Christian churches. Intellectual sectors sympathetic to progressive Catholicism and revolutionary movements in the region saw the growth of evangelical Protestantism, and Pentecostalism in particular, as an ideological and cultural ally of repressive regimes and their U.S. benefactors. For these scholars, evangelical Protestantism was primarily the result of an imperialist missionary strategy by right-wing churches, often operating in conjunction with the CIA. As journalist Deborah Huntington put it in a 1984 article, "The most striking characteristic of Central American Protestantism is that it is the product of foreign—primarily North American—evangelical mission activity."[11] The growth of Protestantism, in this view, was the result of an "invasion of the sects." Latin American Protestants were, accordingly, theologically, structurally, and financially dependent upon conservative religious and political groups based in the United States.

The high-profile case of Efraín Ríos Montt, a born-again retired general who became the president of Guatemala at the height of the civil war, from 1982 to 1983, appears to lend support to Huntington's suspicions. A member of the California-based Church of The Word (El Verbo) and endorsed by prominent conservative evangelical Protestants such as Pat Robertson and Jerry Falwell, Ríos Montt saw the civil war as a moral crusade against godless communism and an effort to build a New Jerusalem in Guatemala. To carry out his millenial vision, he implemented a scorched-earth military strategy, particularly in heavily indigenous areas, that resulted in some of the worst human rights abuses in the region.

While the case of Ríos Montt might have been an anomaly, there was a generalized perception that Latin American evangelical Protestant groups were indifferent, or even hostile, to movements for human rights and social change in the 1970s and 1980s, precisely when many Catholics adopted more oppositional and progressive social agendas. "The passivity of evangelicals in the face of repression and popular mobilization," according to Enrique Domínguez, "made it clear that the movement offered more than just an alternative faith; it was a neutralizing agent, a bulwark against social change."[12]

Against this perception, both Protestant insiders and sympathetic observers argued that personal conversions, not political agendas, were the heart of the movement's growth. Others echoed Willems and claimed that Protestant growth in Latin America marked a long-term transition from hierarchical, corporatist, and patriarchal Hispanic values toward Anglo-Saxon values of tolerance for pluralism, entrepreneurship, voluntarism, and "peaceability." For example, sociologist of religion David Martin contended that "Protestantism creates a 'free space,' though the free space reverberates with echoes from a patriarchal past. That 'free space' is temporarily protected by an apolitical stance, setting up a boundary with a dangerous, corrupt and amoral outside world. Nevertheless, the creation of any space in the conditions obtaining in Latin America remains inherently political."[13] According to Martin, evangelical Christianity is a "new faith [that] is able to implant new disciplines, re-order priorities, counter corruption and destructive machismo, and reverse the indifferent and injurious hierarchies of the outside world.

Within the enclosed haven of faith a fraternity can be instituted under firm leadership, which provides for release, for mutuality and warmth, and for the practice of new roles."[14] Moreover, Martin observes, in contrast to liberation theology, which he sees as a movement of radical middle-class intellectuals opting for the people, Pentecostalism is truly a religion of the people.[15]

Like any social phenomenon, evangelical Christianity defies shorthand categorizations. In fact, sociologist Rowan Ireland argues that it carries both conservative and progressive elements. Writing on Pentecostalism in Brazil, he notes the existence of at least two ways of being Pentecostal. One is what he calls "church Pentecostalism," which is invested in supporting the institutional growth of congregations. To facilitate this growth, church Pentecostals are willing to work with the established political elites, resulting in the brand of bossism that Lalive D'Epinay described. Then there are "sect *crentes*," who engage in a radical critique of all human projects as unavoidably sinful. These Pentecostals are suspicious of any attempt to sacralize the status quo and, thus, they carry the subversive impetus that Willems and Martin highlight. Ireland, however, notes that even for sect *crentes*, the impulse to participate in oppositional politics is directly related to local struggles. This is because, unlike progressive Catholics who see earthly struggles for justice as signs of the unfolding reign of God, sect Pentecostals do not have a vision of "the city on the hill." Rather, they believe that human history will be overthrown by a totally different sacred reality at the end of time.

Ireland's observations about the ambivalence of Pentecostalism at the micro level are validated by studies of Pentecostal patterns of political participation. Pentecostals are far more concerned with strengthening their churches and working on the politics of the personal than in transforming society wholesale. While there is a tendency to support political parties that defend a clear pro-family moral agenda, there are also cases like Benedita Da Silva, a black leader of the left-wing Workers' Party in Brazil, who belonged to the Assemblies of God.[16]

Pentecostalism and Gender

Martin and other scholars interested in Protestantism's social impact have paid particular attention to the impact of Protestant conversion on gender roles and identities. Some observers see Protestantism, especially evangelical and Pentecostal varieties, as uniformly patriarchal, sexist, and oppressive to women. In contrast, a number of scholars have argued that Protestantism holds implicit but powerful potential to challenge traditional gender roles and to strengthen women's social positions. Scholars such as Elizabeth Brusco, working in Colombia, and John Burdick, working in Brazil, have proposed a vision of Protestantism according to which women gain control over their social identities, domestic routines, and material resources through involvement in Protestant churches. Brusco articulates this thesis most succinctly when she states that evangelical Christianity is leading to the "reformation of machismo," that is, to the taming of men's public expressions of autonomy and authority that are highly destructive to the family, where women hold a central place. By curbing drinking, gambling, and womanizing, men's conversion to evangelical Protestantism neutralizes behaviors that generate conflict at home and dissipate meager household resources. Moreover, masculinity becomes redirected: to be a real man now means to be a good father and husband, to provide financially and to guide morally. In other words, evangelical Christianity "domesticates" Latin American males, turning their attention toward activities that enhance women's well-being. It does this without changing the gender roles that make men dominant. For scholars such as Elizabeth Brusco, Pentecostalism's unique power stems precisely from this ability to improve women's lives, or at least their feelings about their lives, without threatening radical social change. Lesley Gill's article reprinted in part below makes this case on the basis of fieldwork in La Paz, Bolivia. Gill doees not celebrate uncritically the relative empowerment women find in the domestication of Latin American masculinity. She notes that women confront power asymmetries that are sacralized, said to be sanctioned by God. These asymmetries are reproduced in churches, where there is still widespread resistance to women becoming head pastors.

Progressive Protestantism

While Martin and others celebrated the implicit, even subversive political potential of Pentecostal conversion and worship, other Protestant expressions in Latin America were more explicitly engaged in the public sphere. During the same period of socioeconomic upheaval that spurred the growth of Pentecostalism, a small but influential number of Protestants embraced progressive and oppositional politics, themes of human rights, and ecumenical and international connections. Influenced by the work of theologians such as American Richard Shaull and Brazilian Rubem Alves, both of whom taught at the Presbyterian Seminary in Campinas, Brazil, some mainline Latin American Protestants began to generate pointed critiques of capitalism that would anticipate and inspire the challenges posed by a nascent Catholic liberation theology.[17] Progressive Protestants began to organize nationally and regionally, giving rise in 1961 to Church and Society in Latin America (ISAL), a movement affiliated with the World Council of Churches, which gained particular strength in the southern cone until a series of military regimes suppressed it. The movement also faced opposition from conservative North American Protestants. We reprint here an excerpt of ISAL's statement of purpose that shows the urgent desire among progressive Protestants to work with Catholics to transform society in Latin America.

Argentine Presbyterian theologian José Míguez Bonino, who was also involved with ISAL, reflects the sense of urgency that many socially engaged Protestant (and Catholic) activists felt during the 1970s and 1980s in Latin America. They responded in particular to the violation of human rights and repression of opposition activists, including many Christians, throughout the region. Writing under the rule of Argentina's repressive military junta (1976-1983), Míguez Bonino called on Christians to work for human rights and dramatic social change. "There is no socially uncommitted theology," he contended; Christians who do not commit themselves to the transformation of unjust political and economic structures are tacitly supporting injustice, which is contrary to the central message of Christianity.[18]

A decade later, ecumenical Protestants in El Salvador faced similar dilemmas. The best known was Lutheran bishop Medardo Gómez, a leader (along with Baptist and Episcopalian colleagues) in the movement for a negotiated end to the nation's civil war. Like many progressive Catholic activists, Gómez and his church were subject to attacks by government and paramilitary forces. A Salvadoran Lutheran minister, David Fernández, was killed in 1984, and in 1988 Gómez's church, Resurrection Lutheran Church, was bombed. Gómez himself was abducted by one of El Salvador's infamous death squads. When his attackers threatened to kill him, Gómez asserts, "God did not allow that to happen. God saved me and converted me into a servant, prepared to testify to his love by proclaiming God's salvation, which through life, Word, and works declares the love of God."[19] Gómez's reflections highlight typically Protestant themes of individual conversion and a personal relationship with God. However, the Lutheran bishop also shares many concerns of progressive Catholicism. One of the most important of these themes, especially in Central America, is the claim that the trials of contemporary Christian activists parallel the persecution of early Christians in the Roman Empire. As Gómez writes,

> The first Christians are our model of the gift for ministry. In fervent devotion to the Christian cause, faithful to the name of the Lord, they struggled against all kinds of oppression. With the help of the divine fire, the protective fire of the Holy Spirit, they struggled against that which sought to bind the freedom of the Word of our Lord Jesus Christ, which proclaimed the good news to the poor: the New Realm of God. The first Christian communities are a spiritual model for our communities in El Salvador.[20]

The "good news to the poor" and the vision of a new form of Christian community have played central roles in the dynamics of contemporary Catholicism in Latin America, to which we turn in the next chapter.

CHAPTER 6 DOCUMENTS

Gunnar Vingren, The Pioneer's Diary[1] IVAR VINGREN

1. CHOSEN BY GOD

I was born in Ostra Husby, Ostergotland, Sweden on the 8th of August 1879. My father was a gardener. Because they were believers [*crentes*], my parents always tried to teach me God's ways and precepts since I was a child. When I was still very little, I went to Sunday school, of which my father was the director. When I turned 11, I finished my primary education and began to help my father with his gardening and I continued doing this until I was 19.

When I was only 9 years old, I felt the calling of God in my life. I felt attracted to God in a special way and I would pray a lot. Sometimes I would gather other children and I would pray with them, this when I was 11. The following year, I deviated from the Lord and became a prodigal son. I fell deeply in sin until I was 17, when the Lord called me again. In 1896, I decided to go to the New Year's service to give myself up again to the Lord. I went with my father and did what I had decided. Hallelujah!

Around this time, I had sent a request to enter as a volunteer in the War College, but it was God who directed me not to take this path. I also was afraid of not being able to remain a believer following a military career.

At 18, I was baptized in water. This took place in a Baptist church in Wraka, Smaland, Sweden, in the month of March or April 1897. In this same year, I became my father's successor at the Sunday School. This greatly increased my need of God and of his grace. Still in that year, on the 14th of July, I read in a magazine an article about the great needs and sufferings of the native tribes abroad, which made me shed many a tear. I went up to my room and there I promised God to belong to him and to be at his disposal for the honor and glory of his name. I prayed insistently so that I could fulfill this promise.

In the month of October, we gave a party to raise some money to help a brother who was leaving as a missionary. All I had at that time where 6 krones and I gave them as an offering. When I returned home after the party, I was filled with joy and I heard a voice that said: "You too will go to the field of evangelization just like Emilio!"

[. . . .]

WITH [A] PASTOR IN THE UNITED STATES

Around June 1903, I was struck by the "United States fever." The big country of the north attracted me tremendously. At the end of the month, I traveled to the city of Gotemburg and, on the 30th, I embarked on a ship that took me to the city of Hull in England, from where I took the train to Liverpool. From this city, I continued my trip on another steamer crossing the Atlantic until I arrived in Boston, Massachusetts, USA. After that, I took the train until Kansas City, where I arrived on November 19, 1903, after 19 days of traveling. The Lord was with me and kept me from all evil all the time. Glory to God!

Despite not being able to speak English, I found the house of my uncle Carl Vingren, of which I had the address. After a week, I began to work as a stoker [*foguista*] in Greenhouse until the summer when I began to work during the day. Then I was able to work as a janitor in a big store. Later on, during the winter, I began to work again as a gardener and, in the last days of February 1904, I traveled to St. Louis, where I got hired at the Botanical Gardens. On Sundays, I attended the services of a Swedish church in the same place.

At the end of September 1904, I traveled to Chicago to begin a four-year course in the Swedish Baptist theological seminary. During the time I lived in Kansas, I belonged to a Swedish Baptist church there. They recommended that I enter their university. The Lord was with me all the time during my studies and helped me marvelously. Praised be His name! . . .

In the summer of 1909, God filled me with a great thirst to receive the baptism in the Holy Spirit and with fire. In November of the same year, I asked for permission from my church to visit a Baptist conference that was taking place at the First Swedish Baptist Church in Chicago. I went to the conference with the firm intention to seek baptism in the Holy Spirit. And, praise God, after five days of waiting, the Lord Jesus baptized me with the Holy Spirit and fire. When I received the Holy Spirit, I spoke in tongues, just as it is written that happened to the disciples on Pentecost: Act. 2. It is impossible to describe the happiness that filled my heart. I will praise him eternally because he baptized me with his Holy Spirit and with fire.

When I returned to my church in Menominee, Michigan, I began to pray that truth that Jesus baptizes with the Holy Spirit and fire. As a result, I had to leave the church. It was left divided, since half believed in this truth and the other half hardened. Those who did not believe forced me to leave my pastorship. Then I went to a church in South Bend, Indiana. Everyone there received the truth and believed. On the first week, Jesus baptized ten people with his Holy Spirit and with fire. Praised be His name forever!

In the end, almost twenty people were baptized in that summer. Glory to Jesus! In that way, Jesus transformed that Baptist church in South Bend into a Pentecostal church. I left South Bend on the 12th of October 1910.

A CALL FOR BRAZIL

One day, during the summer, God put in our hearts that we had to meet on a Saturday night, at the house of a certain brother who belonged to the church that had been baptized with the Holy Spirit. When we prayed, the Lord's Spirit came to us in a very powerful way. . . . During that period of prayer, we noticed that one of the brothers was grabbed [*arrebatado*] by the spirit in a special way, in almost like a prophetic fervor. You could say about the brother what Paul said: "Because if we go mad [*enlouquecemos*], it is for God," 1 Co 5.13.

Another brother, Adolfo Ulldin, received from the Holy Spirit one day wondrous words and hidden mysteries, which were revealed to him. Among other things, the Holy Spirit spoke through that brother that I should go to *Pará*, where the people to which I would preach about Jesus had a very low social level [*um nivel social muito simples*]. I should teach them the first rudiments of the Lord's doctrine. We also heard through the Holy Spirit that the language of that people was Portuguese. We should eat simple food, but . . . God would provide for all needs. . . . What was missing was knowing where *Pará* was located, because none of us knew that name. The following day I told that brother: "Let's go to the library here in the city, to see if there is a place on earth with that name." At the library, we found out that indeed there was a place with that name, situated in the North of Brazil. We understood that God had really spoken and, in this way, I accepted my call, that is, I was totally certain about it. Glory to Jesus!

DANIEL BERG—LOYAL COMPANION

It was in November 1909 in Chicago, when I was looking for the baptism with Holy Spirit, that I met Daniel Berg. The following year, while Berg was working in a street market in Chicago, the Holy Spirit told him to travel to South Bend, Indiana, where I was pastor, so that we could praise God together. . . . Daniel then went with me to the services and he gave testimony and praised the Lord for his wonderful salvation. One day we felt that it was God's desire that we go to brother Adolfo Ulldin, the man whom God used to call me to Brazil. We arrived to his house on a Saturday in the afternoon, just as he was arriving from work. When we entered the kitchen, the power of God came over brother Ulldin, and he became possessed by the spirit just as on the other occasion. Right then and there, Daniel Berg received his call to accompany me to Brazil.

This all happened in the summer of 1910. We understood later as we were praying that we had to leave in a few months from New York to Pará and that it would be on the 5th of November, 1910. We still did not know if there was a ship leaving for Brazil on that day, but everything was later confirmed. We left from New York exactly on that day that God had revealed to us . . . .

2. GUIDED BY THE SPIRIT

SENT BY GOD

The novelty of the missionaries who had arrived from the United States echoed rapidly in the four Protestant churches in the city [Belém, Pará]. We were taken from one church to another and everybody was interested in seeing the newly arrived. When they asked us to sing in English, we sang the hymn: "Jesus Christ is made to me, all I need."[2] Then, the power of God fell on us and we sang the hymn in a duet. Everybody marveled and found it so beautiful that many years after they still talked about that hymn. Yes, it was because the Holy Spirit was with the hymn. There were three Protestants [*crentes*] that were interested in us, and to them we testified about the baptism with the Holy Spirit. Two of them were later baptized.

After being in Pará for a month . . . [a] brother member of the Presbyterian church invited us to accompany him on a trip to his parents' house, in a district where they worked with rubber, situated three days from Belém. In truth, we arrived to a romantic world, where there were enormous jungles with huge orchids and cipó [a vine] all around. We had to travel all the time on the river; there was no open place where we could walk. Even the houses were built on stilts at the muddy edge of the river. We also saw several wild animals in the forest.

[. . . .]

We participated in some small prayers and sang in Portuguese as best we could. The trip lasted a month and a half and we then returned to Belém. Upon our arrival we heard that there was a revolution and we thanked God that he protected us from being in the midst of the struggle. Now we started with efforts to study the language, and during this time we participated in the Baptist church's services. Because we did not have any money to pay for our classes, Daniel had to find work in a smelting plant. There he worked during the day while I learned the language. Then I would teach him at night what I learned during the day. In that way, with effort, we learned Portuguese.

[. . . .]

The work of God continued and the word was confirmed everyday by miracles and wonders. A brother was cured from a very serious sickness in his leg. A sister was cured from an incurable illness in her lips. Another who had headaches for ten years was cured. A paralyzed man who was on his deathbed and could not talk was cured and later came to our services. . . . A man who had been sick for many months, with fever, and had his body all swollen, was also cured and baptized with the Holy Spirit. He even received the gift of prophecy. A sister was healed on the same night of two illnesses. It was glorious to accompany those new converts to the waters of baptism. It was marvelous to see how the Holy Spirit fell on those believers and how they spoke in tongues, prophecized and sang in the Holy Spirit. With much courage they later testified in the name of Jesus and praised his name. . . .

3. THE SECRET OF THE VICTORY

On March 22, 1911, I made a first trip to a place called Soure. At the services many people gave themselves to the Lord and on the 1st of November, Jesus baptized a sister with the Holy Spirit. I was told that this sister spoke in tongues, in Latin as well as in Arabic, and from Arabic she translated to Portuguese, which was her native language. On that day three people converted to Jesus.

On that same day, Catholics had prepared an act of witchcraft [*um feitico*] against us and they wrote on a lamppost: "This Vingren is a Protestant Pope." On the following day, the Catholic priest publicly tore up a copy of the New Testament.

On the fifth of November, seven people were baptized in water, and on the 12th, seven new brothers were baptized. All of this happened in Soure. . . . .

BAREFOOT AND HUNGRY

After some time, there came a great persecution against evangelicals [*crentes*], more precisely in Guatipura. They were wounded and left to bleed until they were taken to prison. The authorities said: "Look at the type of religion they have!" The Sheriff knew that it was against the country's constitution to chase after evangelicals and to arrest them, since the law gives full freedom of religion. But he wanted to test them, to see if they would get annoyed with this injustice.

When they arrived to the jail, the evangelicals began to pray and to praise God. And the people gathered around them to hear them. There and then Jesus baptized one of these *crentes* with the Holy Spirit. The Sheriff had said: "Let us see if Jesus comes and gives you bread!" Then, one of the soldiers went and got them bread. After suffering all of this, the authorities let the evangelicals return to their homes, saying "You have a religion that we don't have!"

The work continued to expand more and more in that region [crisscrossed by] the Bragança railroad, so that many new churches were constituted, but always under persecution. It was also following that railroad—a distance of 400 kilometers—that Daniel Berg traveled on foot, carrying his suitcases full of Bible packages [*porções bíblicas*]. Many times, his feet were so wounded and full of blisters that he had to walk barefoot. Suffering hunger and needs of all kind, he walked from door to door, evangelizing the people and distributing New Testaments and Bible packages. . . .

4. THE FLOW [O DERRAMAMENTO] OF THE SPIRIT IN BRAZIL

[The editor of the diary writes:] For the year 1914, the diary contains, for unknown reasons, only notes for two months. However, it has a very interesting statistic about the number of people who were baptized in the waters and with the Holy Spirit during the years between 1911 and 1914. Here is the list.

Year	Baptized in Water	Baptized with the Holy Spirit
1911	13	4
1912	41	15
1913	140	121
1914	190	136

Thus, there were 384 persons baptized in water and 276 received the promise of the Holy Spirit during those first four years of the pioneering work in the church in Belém, Pará.

"The Pentecostal 'Conquest' of Chile: Rudiments of a Better Understanding"[3] CHRISTIAN LALIVE D'EPINAY

Origins

The Pentecostal movement in Chile still retains characteristics determined by its unique genesis. At the beginning of this century a missionary pastor, W. C. Hoover, reacted against the rationalizing liberalism of the Methodist leaders. Impressed by the revivalist vision of a church of "sanctification" in Chicago in 1895, he led his church in Valparaiso on a spiritual search centered around the Holy Spirit. His congregation responded well to biblical study, meditation on the writings of Wesley, spiritual exercises (such as prayer meetings), and the community grew. In 1907 Hoover happened to read a pamphlet describing the birth of a Pentecostal community in India distinguished by a "clear and definitive baptism by the Holy Spirit, in addition to the justification and sanctification which until then we had thought comprised the sum of Christian experience" (Hoover 1931: 14). The Valparaiso community added to its revival of Wesley the distinctive feature of the experience of the fire of Pentecost. The extraordinary and the miraculous became the daily bread of the group of believers. They experienced

> . . .laughter, tears, shouts, songs, strange tongues, visions, ecstasies in which the person fell to the ground and felt himself physically transported to Heaven, to Paradise, and spoke with the Lord, with the angels or with the devil. Those who experienced these sensations derived great pleasure from them and were generally changed by them and filled with praise, with the spirit of prayer, and with love (Hoover 1931: 33).

The "rain of the spirit" had fallen. But at the same time, the previously silent opposition of the Methodist hierarchy came out into the open, with all the more vehemence since the spiritual adventure of the Valparaiso group had been repeated in Santiago, thereby revolutionizing the life of the two principal Methodist churches in Chile. Hoover's followers were denounced and his doctrines were declared "anti-Methodist, contrary to the Scriptures and *irrational*" (Hoover 1931: 62, italics mine).

The Methodist church never completely recovered from the schism. The majority of the members of the three churches of Valparaiso and Santiago resigned and created the Pentecostal Methodist Church and asked Hoover to assume its leadership. This new church grew rapidly until about 1920 because of attrition from Methodist congregations and from some other denominations from Santiago as far as Concepción and Temuco.

Pentecostalism in Chile never constituted a sect, if by this word one designates a movement which is ebullient, disorganized, and anarchical. On the contrary, from the very moment of schism it reflected a Methodist character in its organization. What are usually called the "charismatic manifestations" were regulated by institutional forms. The freedom of the spirit was strictly organized. The most appropriate sociological concept would be that of an "established sect" (see Yinger 1957). This point is important for the study of the later evolution of the Pentecostal movement. If one takes the concept of "sect" as a point of departure, as the majority of observers do, one concludes that the movement evolved towards institutionalization. But if one recognizes the original state as an "established sect," the so-called evolution appears more ambiguous and complex.

The traditional organization of Methodism had to be adapted to the new situation. The dissidents found themselves separated from the mother church and from the Missionary Society, that is to say, from their former source of income and leadership. The only foreigner—and the only pastor with a background in theology—who joined the rebels was Mr. Hoover. It was necessary, therefore, to create a ministry. Those who had held the highest positions in the Methodist organization and who were also the natural leaders of the dissidents undertook the responsibilities of the ministry. This was a real revolution and an important key to the future expansion of the movement: *the administrative functions were no longer the exclusive province of foreign missionaries or of a national elite educated in theological seminaries.*

Pentecostalism breaks the barrier of theological education which separated the layman from the pastor. Each convert participates from the beginning in the missionary work of the community and knows that, God willing, he can one day be pastor. Within the rigidly stratified Chilean society, in which access to positions of privilege depends so completely on birth or fortune, the Pentecostal movement creates micro-societies with their own strict hierarchies but which are absolutely egalitarian and classless. A humble employee of the town hall of Lora, in the coal mining district, made the following observations: "If a working-class person wants to get on in the world, he has two ways to do it, the unions or the Pente-costal Church." To the "marginal" masses of Chilean society the Pentecos-tal movement offers "religious status" (Pope 1942: 137).

The elimination of a body of pastors with an abstract theological train-ing favors a rapprochement between the community and its leader. The latter is no longer imposed on the congregation by a hierarchical deci-sion; he is the natural leader of the group. He belongs to the same social class and has similar problems of existence and subsistence; he thinks as his flock thinks. Much has been said and written about the advantages of education and the necessity for theological education. Without wishing to deny these advantages, one ought to take into consideration the fact that the years spent in high school and college create thought processes and needs which are different from those of the urban or rural working-class member of a community. There exists between the traditional Protestant pastor (or the Catholic priest) and his congregation a cultural and social distance—frequently an abyss—with no possibility of dialogue.

The Pentecostal pastor does not face this problem. He is the expression of the united will of his community. He represents his congregation in the deepest sense. This system constitutes a powerful stimulus to the active participation of each member of the community, and since access to more important positions depends upon such participation, it should be an ob-ject of study in all churches with missionary ambitions. . . .

The clergy-lay separation was one of the causes of the schism of 1909-1910. In simple terms this schism derived from the opposition between a middle-class ecclesiastical hierarchy dominated by foreign elements and the com-munity of believers. The religious mentality of the former was rational while that of the latter was mythical. If the substratum of Pentecostal expansion is to be sought in the rootlessness of the Chilean populace, one must also see in it the search for a path to knowledge of God and to a culturally familiar expression of faith. In short, the Chilean Pentecostal movement *disalienated* God, for it liberated the Christian message from the language of the North American culture (missionary Protestantism) and from the gilded prison of Catholic clergy whose deficiencies in the first decades of this century are today admitted by everyone. . . .

Two factors permitted the Chilean movement to remain free of the dogmatic characteristics of international Pentecostalism: the heritage of Methodism and the absence of theologians. The problem of the baptism of infants, for example, prevented absorption of the Pentecostal Methodist Church by the Assemblies of God in the years immediately prior to 1930.

The absence of doctrinal complexity gives their doctrine of the Holy Spirit a flexibility that seems to be nearer to the spirit of the Bible. No branch of Chilean Pentecostalism interprets "glossolalia" (the gift of tongues) as exclusive proof of baptism by the Holy Spirit, though this experience is necessary—according to international Pentecostalism—before appointment to the position of pastor. A limited investigation has revealed that half the Chilean Pentecostal pastors have *never* spoken in tongues. The degree of possession is related to the intensity of the testimony, as this recent interview with a believer attests:

A church in which people dance, in which they speak with tongues and prophesy is a church in which the Spirit is present and enters into people's hearts . . . and it is a church in which the brethren preach in the streets more frequently and are more active in all fields. It is a growing church.

The interesting thing is that the ritual of possession by the Spirit is important, even essential, since it proves the presence of the Spirit, not so much in a certain individual but in the community. But these charismas are not defined completely by an established doctrine. The norm applied is a different one: if the Spirit is present, then the community can proselytize and grow, as explained in the gospel. This is thus a rediscovery of some of the basic themes present in the Acts of the Apostles: Pentecost permits man to be a witness. This rediscovery was made spontaneously, in response to a profound need, as Hoover's testimony proves:

When the Spirit had ceased to fall in all his power, those who had been baptized, men, women and children, felt compelled to rush into the street and to shout about their experience, to visit their friends and neighbors, to travel to other places, with the one objective of calling their fellow men to repentance and letting them know by their testimony that such a sublime experience is within the reach of everyone today as it was in the time of the Apostles. (1931: 43)

The creation of active communities without religious stratification, the emergence of a group of pastors, the translation of the gospel into Latin American terms, and the serious consideration of the Holy Spirit as the power of God—all these factors should be thoughtfully considered by professional missionary officials.

Expansion

If early expansion was due mostly to attrition provoked by the schismatics in the ranks of foreign Protestants, recruitment from the thirties onwards—i.e., from the point at which numerical growth achieved the rate it still maintains—was directed towards the Chilean populace whose Catholicism was more cultural than religious. The success was extraordinary—"a tide," we are told by a priest. The hundred dissidents of 1909 have today become more than half a million.[4]

The history of twentieth-century Chile is that of a *society in transition*. Its traditional "señorial"[5] structure has been unavoidably dissolving but the country's leaders have not been able to impose the structure to which they aspire: that of an industrialized, urban nation. The population grows, and the rural areas, where agricultural techniques, lacking radical reform, are patently incapable of increasing productivity, expel the mouths it cannot feed toward the city. In most cases the city is the capital, Santiago, where almost a third of the Chilean population lives. But it is important to note—and here lies the danger of applying European or North American theories too quickly to the Third World—urbanization is not, in this case, an index of industrialization. "Urbanization" in Chile implies rather a tentacle-like development of government and private services which, without adding one dollar to the wealth of the nation, create consumer desires. The growth of the services sector is not due to the expansion of the industrial sector. On the contrary, the former precedes and strangles the latter. Within this framework of "permanent economic crisis" migration does not take place from the farm to the factory but rather from the country shack to the city slum (Pinto 1958). The dislocation of the social infrastructure has far-reaching effects on men's consciousness. The emigrant may actually lose the relative security which his integration into the extended family of the "hacienda" afforded him; and those who remain on the "latifundios" also begin to lose confidence in the ideological myths which assure stability. According to Jorge Medina, these myths can be summed up in three beliefs: ". . . the belief in the very real value of personal relationships; the belief in miraculous protection in a time of crisis; and the belief in the unknown, and therefore unlimited, power of the landowner" (1964: 39).

The changes in the infrastructure unavoidably lead to the end of this paternalistic form of social organization, which is both oppressive and protective. The old beliefs die but without the emergence of any new ideologies or forms of organization which would help people acquire psychological equilibrium. In this long process of chaotic and painful transition there arises the marginal man, the man with no status, the man who cannot participate culturally, economically, or politically in the life or the institutions of the nation. "The best observers . . . in present-day Latin America insist on this phenomenon and agree on one single word, 'desarraigo' (rootlessness), to characterize the psycho-social state of large agglomerations, either urban or rural" (Ibid).

One can understand, therefore, the rise of popular protest in twentieth-century Chile and the efforts of the populace to organize themselves and to question the values of a society that presently alienates them. At the beginning of this century the first great strikes broke out, accompanied by police repression whose victims numbered in the thousands. In the thirties, precisely at the moment when Pentecostalism reached a definite high point in its history, the two great popular parties, the Communist and the Socialist, were organized. It was a time of political protest by organized labor but also of religious protest expressed through Pentecostalism. (It has been said that the unions and the Pentecostal Church were the only two institutional channels for progress open to the popular masses.)

Protestantism offers the alienated man status, integration into a fraternal community, and human dignity in the form of a system of rights and duties. He must preach in the streets, describe his own conversion during testimonial ceremonies, and participate financially in the work of the community. All these things prove that the humblest "brother" is important to the community. This participation in the collective effort gives substance and meaning to individual existence. To the man oppressed by a universe whose permanent dimensions are hunger, sickness, and death, Pentecostalism preaches a God who saves or, in concrete terms, "heals."

It is remarkable to what extent Pentecostalism again takes up the three beliefs which constitute the ideological basis of the "hacienda," giving them new force and meaning. The religious community is constructed on a foundation of fraternal relationships between people. If one asks the people in a poor neighborhood the reason for the success of the "canutos" (Protestant pastors), the most frequent reply is their comradeship. The tarnished image of the "hacendado," whose tyranny is no longer balanced by his protective function, is replaced by that of the pastor, intermediary to salvation. His source of power is familiar to everyone—God, perceived as present, active, and powerful. In the chaos of transition, the Pentecostal community has become established as a *substitute* society, retaining the protective elements of traditional society but eliminating what the individual considered oppressive.

[. . . .]

Eschatology and politics. . . . I suggested before that in Chile, Socialism and Pentecostalism constitute two ideologies of protest which evolved in the same period of history, which were fed by the same feeling of rebellion, and which compete in the same recruiting area, that of the popular masses. The preceding description indicates, however, how diametrically opposed they are.

[In the last ten years a new source of power has been asserting itself, the Christian Democrats. They have complicated the issue by trying to integrate religious sentiment, the necessity for a socio-economic revolution, and respect for a very liberal kind of liberty. Their success, since they came to power in 1964, does not mean that they have eliminated these difficulties which might well lead to their eventual downfall.]

Pentecostalism condemns the "world" and stands at a distance from it in order to proclaim an immanent but transcendent Kingdom of God. This is basically an apolitical position. Marxist, atheistic Socialism works towards the realization of an immanent kingdom on earth. The marriage of radical dualism and an eschatology that limits itself to waiting for a Kingdom above and beyond this world unavoidably leads Pentecostalism, as happens in the case of any other apolitical position, to constitute itself as an ideology of order rather than of movement, of conservation rather than of transformation.

[It is obvious that this aspect of theology has psychological roots. When a pastor cries out: "We are leaving the world; we shall never return to it," he is *also* expressing his fear of a brutal world in which man is oppressed by the dark forces of evil, hunger, sickness, and death.]

In a country whose predominant problem is the quest for progress this is not without importance. I would personally be tempted to say that it is a source of anxiety. And I would deplore the fact that Pentecostalism has not been able to draw upon the Christian tradition, always suppressed but continually reborn, which imbued the Anabaptists, men like Thomas Munzer, the so-called revolutionary Sects in seventeenth-century England, and many other groups of dissidents who fought so that the Kingdom might come.

[. . . .]

REFERENCES

Hoover, W. C. (1931) *Historia del Avivamiento Pentecostal en Chile*. Santiago, Chile: [no publisher provided].

Medina, J. (1964) *Consideraciones Sociológicas Sobre el Desarrollo Económico*. Buenos Aires, Argentina: Solar/Hachette.

Pinto, A . (1958) *Chile, un Caso de Desarrollo Frustrado*. Santiago, Chile: Santiago University Press.

Pope, L. (1942) *Millhands and Preachers*. New Haven, CT: Yale University Press.

Yinger, J. Milton (1957) *Religion, Society and the Individual: An Introduction to the Sociology of Religion*. New York: The Macmillan Co.

Followers of the New Faith: Cultural Change and the Rise of Protestantism in Brazil and Chile[6] EMILIO WILLEMS

Leading Hypotheses

. . . Critics of the Protestant movement in Latin America have often affirmed its incompatibility with the historical and cultural traditions of the Southern Hemisphere. Protestants themselves have frequently contrasted their own way of life to that of the surrounding non-Protestant world. In fact, many of our Protestant informants tried to convey the impression that theirs was a way of life that had no roots in the society of which they were a part. Unconvinced by the apparent incompatibilities between native traditions and Protestant values, and encouraged by the fact that cases of religious dissent stressing social reform had been recorded by historians, we began to probe for compatibilities, *on the assumption that Protestant dissent had its antecedents, if not its roots, in structural peculiarities of the traditional society, even in some of its customary ways of coping with the supernatural.* Attempts to verify this hypothesis will be made in the first part of this volume.

In the course of our field work it became abundantly clear that Protestantism, particularly its sectarian varieties, were thriving in those areas of either country where exposure to cultural change had been long and intensive. Statistical data on the distribution of Protestants confirmed that industrialized modern metropolitan areas and, to a lesser extent, rural frontiers had indeed the largest Protestant populations. A new hypothesis thus came to be formulated: *Heavy concentrations of Protestants* are correlated with changes strongly affecting the traditional structure of the society; conversely, Protestantism may be expected to be relatively weak in areas that have had little or no exposure to such changes.

Thus a seemingly contradictory possibility began to take shape: Protestantism "causing" cultural change and "being caused" by cultural change. To solve this apparent paradox it was assumed that historically Protestantism emerged as a by-product of changes affecting the social structure and values of nineteenth-century Brazil and Chile (foreign immigration and progressive secularization of the culture, for example). Once established, Protestantism began to act in a very limited way as a factor contributing to sociocultural change. Then industrialization, urbanization, internal migration, and the opening of rural frontiers not only generated conditions increasingly favorable to the growth of Protestant denominationalism but also gradually reinforced its active role in the process of sociocultural transformation, mainly because the changes intended by Protestantism proper received impulse, direction, and additional meaning from the general changes modifying the traditional social order. In other words, the value orientation described earlier as the "Protestant ethic" was assumed to be particularly rewarding under the conditions prevailing in the emerging industrial order. The verification of these hypotheses will be attempted in the second part of this volume.

While our concern has so far been with major Protestant concentrations, field experience and a careful scrutiny of census data suggested that in some regions of Brazil at least Protestantism had been moderately successful in traditional rural settings. It was hypothesized that absence of the feudal elements characterizing the traditional social order was sufficient to allow the development of Protestant dissent and that such permissive conditions prevailed in rural areas where medium-sized agricultural holdings were relatively numerous. A separate chapter deals with these hypotheses.

Upon probing the history of the Protestant movement in Brazil and Chile, one cannot help being impressed by the number of schisms and the proliferation of churches and sects. Most of them seem to push in one of two directions: away from foreign-controlled church bodies and toward "national" church organizations, or away from the historical church and toward sectarian dissent as reflected in the Pentecostal movement. It was hypothesized that the dynamics of Protestantism, particularly internal competition, conflict, secession, and sectarianism in general, were attempts, deliberate or not, to seek out those versions of Protestantism which proved to be most congenial to the particular needs, desires, or aspirations of the recipient societies. The third part of the book will concern itself with this hypothesis.

Returning to the hypothesis that Protestantism "causes" culture change, a somewhat more precise formulation seems to be in order. The basic assumption is that the acceptance and practice of a Protestant code of behavior tend to redefine the social relationship Protestants establish or maintain with one another and with non-Protestants and that, since these redefinitions are primarily concerned with reciprocal responsibilities, the changes they produce tend to affect family structure and the socialization of the child, economic behavior, political behavior, the class structure, and the structure of voluntary associations. The relevance of such newly adopted organizational patterns and modes of behavior is perceived in terms of both the decaying structure of the traditional, feudal, patriarchical society and the emerging industrial and urban order. In other words, the assumption is that Protestantism rewards ethical discipline by providing what the traditional society denies and the emerging industrial society promises.

The scope of these hypotheses seems broad enough to support the claim that our inquiry attempts to understand Protestantism within the context of Latin American culture and in terms of that culture. The decision to choose Brazil and Chile is based primarily on the fact that both countries have relatively large and old-established Protestant churches. Furthermore, if there were significant differences in the reaction to Protestantism they would probably show up in a comparison between the response of Portuguese America and that of a Spanish American country.

[. . . .]

Conclusions

The introduction of proselytic Protestantism in Brazil and Chile was dealt with as a deliberate attempt at cultural transfer and diffusion. The new faith was seen in terms of its compatibility or incompatibility with traditional Latin American values. Of the three major components of American Protestantism—religion as an emotional experience mediated by revivalism, the social organization of the churches, and the Protestant ethic—the first appears to be mostly in accord with existing patterns, as the phenomenal growth of the Pentecostal sects suggests.

The particular pattern of social organization found in Protestant churches seems at first blush irreconcilable with the traditional social structure of the two countries. As a matter of historical record, however, neither country has ever been fully able to absorb or to control sizable segments of the population that remained in a state of covert or overt rebellion. Furthermore, at least in Brazil, those segments proved to be capable of expressing their hostility in spontaneous organization as well as in religious dissent.

It has also been overlooked frequently that in both countries there is a rural middle class that could, if it chose to do so, defy traditional values and engage in organized religious dissent. In fact, religious dissent in the form of unorthodox and deviant interpretations of religious doctrine at the folk level has been extremely common and may be attributed to the weakness of the Roman Catholic church as an agency of social control and source of moral authority. Even the Protestant ethic with its emphasis on hard work, thrift, sobriety, and chastity, does not seem to be entirely at variance with existing patterns or historical precedent.

The fact that an increasing number of Brazilians and Chileans adhered to the new faith can only be understood if Latin American culture is seen as a process of continuing change. Protestantism made its first appearance in the wake of widespread secularization that dealt mortal blows to the religious and political hermetism of the colonial period. Protestant progress was slow during the first fifty or sixty years of missionary endeavor, mainly because the rate of culture change was too low and its effects too restricted to make conversion a meaningful mass experience. It could be proved however that Protestantism attracted more followers as the process of culture change gained momentum and the traditional agrarian structure of Brazil and Chile entered a phase of increasing deterioration. In other words, our hypothesis of an historical concomitance between the expansion of Protestantism and the emergence of an industrialized and urbanized society was borne out by the facts.

Further corroboration of a functional relationship between these two phenomena was seen in the ecological distribution of the Protestant population of both countries. It was found that the largest Protestant populations were concentrated in the most urbanized and industrialized areas of Brazil and Chile. On the other hand, relatively small numbers of Protestants are located in areas where the traditional agrarian structure has been preserved to some extent.

Ecological data on São Paulo also indicated, however, that dissemination of Protestantism is not exclusively associated with industrialization and urbanization. There are at least two further conditions favoring receptivity to the new faith. Rural areas that for some reason were bypassed by the hacienda system, and where an independent peasantry was allowed to develop, turned out to be moderately receptive to Protestant proselytism. Secondly, agricultural frontier areas with uprooted, highly heterogeneous populations were found to be highly responsive to Protestant missionary endeavor.

Additional evidence of a functional relationship between the dissemination of Protestantism and sociocultural change is to be seen in the fact that the new faith won most of its followers among the social classes whose formation and chances of social ascent were directly affected by structural changes imposed by the emerging industrial order.

Our data further indicate that the areas of highest Protestant concentration have also received the largest numbers of rural-urban migrants who have been more exposed to the impact of culture change than any other single group.

Only under exceptional conditions can major institutions be transferred from one culture to another without undergoing at least minor changes in the process. A number of organizational and doctrinal schisms took place in Chile and Brazil which satisfied the nationalistic aspiration of the members to rid themselves of the tutelage of foreign mission boards and to pursue the cognitive and emotional objectives of their doctrine more in accord with the cultural heritage of their own society.

To judge by membership size and proselytic zeal, Pentecostalism has proved more adaptable to the aspirations and needs of the masses than any other form of Protestantism. But the adaptability of Pentecostalism can be understood only if the functions it performs with regard to its practitioners are clarified. The organizational pattern of the Pentecostal sects seems to express a protest against the Catholic church and its ally, the ruling class. It does so by pointedly stressing egalitarianism within the sect and by opposing the Catholic principle of an ecclesiastical hierarchy and a highly specialized priesthood with the principles of the primacy of the laity, the priesthood of all believers and a self-made charismatic leadership sanctioned by the Holy Spirit. Pentecostalism thus turns out to be a symbolic subversion of the traditional social order.

Adherence to Pentecostal sects also seems to be a solution to various personality problems manifest in the practice of "vices." By substituting disreputable "vices" for conventional forms of behavior, the convert cleanses himself of social stigma and becomes respectable in the eyes of the in-group and the society at large.

In the changing society of Brazil and Chile, folk Catholicism no longer serves the functions it did in the traditional rural society, mainly because folk Catholicism is a peasant religion adapted to the problems of a peasant culture. The Catholic pantheon is predominantly local; the cult of saintly helpers is centered around local shrines and concerned with rural problems. Migration to cities and rural frontiers tends to alienate people from their local pantheons, and the problems they have to face in their new environment call for different solutions. But there is apparently no solution of continuity between folk Catholicism and Pentecostalism with its heavy emphasis upon the Holy Spirit, miracles, and other mystical experiences. Pentecostalism also continues the ancient tradition of messianism in a new and more exciting way by promising the coming of the deity here and now to the individual believer.

The appeal of Pentecostalism is strengthened by the gifts or powers of the Spirit that make essentially powerless people feel strong beyond natural limits. Seizure by the Spirit also provides a temporary escape from the hopeless squalor of life to the thrills of intense emotional experiences.

The social function of the Pentecostal sect derives from its tightly woven structure in which the *crente* finds opportunity to rebuild his personal community and to find a measure of psychological and economic security.

Some of these functions are also performed by the historical churches, but to a widely varying degree. A comparative study of the three major churches suggests that their attractiveness in terms of membership is, to a considerable extent, a function of their structure. Apparently preference is given to the egalitarian denominations in which the layman is in control of church affairs and the individual congregation enjoys complete autonomy. On the whole, Protestantization may be regarded as a selective process in which functional adaptability to the needs and aspirations of the people is rewarded with the highest membership figures and the most intensive proselytic drive.

The analysis of Protestantism as a factor of sociocultural change requires a distinction between inherent changes and contingent changes. Inherent are all those modifications which are fundamentally inseparable from the emergence of proselytic Protestantism as a social institution. They are found in the organization of churches, sects, and their individual congregations. As emphasized throughout our inquiry, they consist mainly of the primacy of the laity, local autonomy, freedom of disquisition, egalitarianism, and the absence of ecclesiastical hierarchies.

Since congregation and family appear to be tightly interwoven, changes in the traditional family structure are equally inherent in or concomitant with the institutionalization of proselytic Protestantism. An autonomous congregational structure is obviously incompatible with the primacy of family and kinship prevalent in the traditional social order. Thus the Protestant family had to accept a subordinate position within the congregation. Furthermore, the web of social relationships within the immediate family had to conform to the basic norms of the Protestant ethic, a requirement which resulted in the deletion of male sex prerogatives and thus led to more egalitarian relationships between male and female members. If the cultural process comprises major changes, as it does in the emergent industrial order of Chile and Brazil, the Protestant ethic finds opportunity to provide meaning and additional impulse to changes originated by secular forces.

The practice of the Protestant virtues is conveniently rewarded by an emerging industrial civilization that promises a higher level of living to the thrifty, sober, industrious, and well educated. It makes sense to renounce expensive "vices" in order to afford better housing, better clothes, at least some contrivances of modern technology, and a better education for the children, especially if such effort is sanctioned by religious convictions and encouraged by group expectations. The economic significance of Protestant asceticism lies in the fact that it frees part of one's income for the acquisition of things that symbolize a higher level of living.

In a broader sense, being a Protestant often means having opportunities not easily available to non-Protestants. As a rule, non-Protestants assume Protestants to be dependable, honest, and efficient beyond the limit normally expected in Brazilian and Chilean society. Protestants thus become preferred business partners, employees, and servants.

There is actually an acute awareness of and belief in economic advancement among Protestants, particularly among members of the historical churches. But this belief is somewhat commensurate with actual economic achievements as observed in four different communities.

The historical Protestant churches, especially the Presbyterians and Methodists, doubtlessly played a pioneer role in the field of economic and technical development. This role however can no longer be sustained, mainly because a variety of specialized domestic and international institutions have in recent years initiated development activities on a scale that cannot be matched by church agencies, except perhaps on the level of the local community.

Economic advancement has proved equivalent to upward social mobility, and in this sense Protestantism has contributed to loosening up the once tight class structure of Brazil and Chile. If industrialism and the opening of agricultural frontiers created chances for status achievements, Protestantism provided additional sanctions and indeed showed the way by which such objectives could be attained.

Social ascent of individual Protestants also meant ascent of the church as a whole. But the historical churches have not become class-bound institutions. The study of a number of congregations shows that their class composition varies with the social composition of the parishioners rather than with the relative position which each church occupies in the social pyramid.

The historical Protestant churches have also become way-stations to further social ascent. The high aspirational level of these churches often turns out to be self-defeating because a considerable percentage of their more successful members detach themselves from the institution if such a step promises further ascent in an increasingly secularized society.

Although the historical churches have by no means become middle-class institutions, the Pentecostal sects enjoy a number of obvious advantages in their competitive effort to attract the lower classes. The churches assume a rather accommodating attitude toward class cleavages, while the sects have proved attractive to the masses, especially in Chile, by maintaining a value system apparently consistent with the way of life of the lower class.

The former attitude of abstention from political participation character-istic of all Protestant denominations has changed as the political process has undergone a gradual democratization. Except in the Pentecostal sects, participation is now deemed not only possible but even desirable, if only to protect the constitutional guarantees of religious freedom. In Brazil, this change bears a more aggressive character than in Chile, where Protestants still seem to feel that they are defending themselves against a powerful alliance between conservative parties and the Catholic church. In Brazil, thirty-four different legislative bodies have one or more Protestant mem-bers, while in Chile only now the Protestants are preparing themselves for a more active participation in politics. In both countries, Protestantism has contributed to a strengthening of democratic principles.

Strong emphasis on literacy and social progress determined the pio-neer role of the historical church in the field of popular education. Espe-cially in Brazil, the literacy rate of the Protestant population turned out to be significantly higher than that of non-Protestants. Around the turn of the century the Protestant school was beginning to be accepted by the society at large as a model of modern education deemed more desirable by the middle and upper classes than the obsolete educational system of

Latin America. On the whole, the Protestant schools failed to live up to the role of proselytizing agencies assigned to them by their missionary founders. But as secular institutions of learning they succeeded in instilling respect and admiration for Protestant values, particularly among their middle- and upper-class alumni. By opening their doors to Protestants and non-Protestants alike they became significant channels of social mobility, although a general modernization and expansion of the state-operated educational systems and the gradual tightening of legal controls over private school systems have made pioneering rather a thing of the past.

REFERENCES

Sweet, William Warren. *The American Churches.* New York and Nashville: Abingdon-Cokesbury Press 1947.
Weber, Max. *Wirtschaftsgeschichte.* Muchen and Leipzig: Verlag von Dunker & Humbolt, 1924.

"Like a Veil to Cover Them": Women and the Pentecostal Movement in La Paz"[7] LESLEY GILL

Women and Pentecostalism

Organized religion represents perhaps the most common way that women in La Paz develop new relationships within socially prescribed boundaries, because they encounter more difficulties than men in finding emotional support and economic security once they move outside their kin networks. Household responsibilities lengthen their workdays; discrimination in the job market lowers their earnings; and the conditions under which most lower-class women work inhibit the formation of group solidarity. Domestic servants, for example, labor in isolation from their peers, and street vendors are forced to compete with one another in a milieu increasingly saturated with people desperately trying to earn a living. In addition, strong moral precepts regarding appropriate female behavior hamper the emergence of extra domestic activities centered around women and directed by them.

A number of chauvinistic stereotypes about the "perfect woman" that prevail in the dominant Spanish-Creole culture and are imposed upon rural immigrants and the urban lower class also reinforce greater female religiosity. According to these views, which are the counterpart to ma-chismo, women are semi divine, morally superior to and spiritually stron-ger than men. They are also intellectually inferior to and personally more fragile than men, but their spiritual strength provides them with an almost infinite capacity for humility, suffering, and self-denial (Stevens 1973:94). This spirituality can be strengthened by proper church guidance and reli-gious devotion (Lavrin 1981:44).

The Pentecostal *culto* [service] offers women an institutional base for developing important and enduring social relationships, and it provides the rituals to validate these emerging bonds, which help to create a shared sense of community. The *culto* occurs five times a week and is an ongo-ing process of conversion whereby believers purge themselves of Satan's diabolical influence through collective song, prayer, and music. The hu-man body, according to Pentecostals, is occupied either by Satan or by the Holy Spirit, and in order to evict Satan, one must be cleansed of sin. This requires the observance of a number of puritanical practices, which in-clude abstaining from alcohol, tobacco, sexual intercourse for nonrepro-ductive purposes, dancing, and the cinema, and also entails attendance of as many *culto*s as possible.

Participation in the *culto* is crucial to an individual's salvation, because the cleansing and healing powers of God can be mobilized most effectively by the active involvement of all believers. Indeed, attendance is so impor-tant that the pastor often asks church members to pray for those who are absent. But more than simple attendance is required. Congregants must also take part in the singing, shouting, hand clapping, praying, and testi-fying that characterize a typical *culto*.

A *culto* begins with praying and singing to the beat of musical instruments. The pastor, standing behind a pulpit with a lighted sign that reads "Jesus Heals and Saves," leads the congregation. Periodic shouts of "Hallelujah" and "Glory to God" punctuate the ceremony as congregants extend their hands toward heaven. The level of intensity gradually builds, culminating with the pastor's sermon, which, if successful, transforms the gathering. People start to writhe on the floor, speak in tongues, and even lose consciousness, all signs that the Holy Spirit is waging a successful battle with Satan for control of the individual. Individuals will then begin to testify about discovering God for the first time and the subsequent changes in their lives.

Women in this setting are not merely passive recipients of a religious message. They actively participate in the experience by singing and direct-ing hymns, receiving the Holy Spirit, testifying, and even preaching on rare occasions. Such behavior contrasts with that characteristic of the traditional Catholic liturgy, which is much less participatory and in which the sermon may be given in a language that Aymara speakers do not fully understand. Women are also involved in a range of other church activities that include proselytizing on the streets, visiting needy church members in their homes, attending family services, and traveling to church meetings in other cities and foreign countries.

In the course of these activities, women meet other women like themselves with whom they share the intensity of the Pentecostal experience, and their dealings with men are governed by rigid puritanical rules that curtail abusive male behavior—such as drunkenness and the overt expression of sexuality—which is often tolerated in other contexts. This enables them to construct new social networks that are emotionally supportive and economically useful. These ties extend well beyond the church into the individuals' daily lives. Believers provide one another with information about living arrangements, jobs, medical assistance, and business opportunities in the city, and they are readily available for assistance and support in times of crisis. To varying degrees, these ties replace ties with kin left behind in the countryside or social and marital relationships in the city that are no longer viable because of divorce, abandonment, or the death of a spouse, and they enable women to develop greater self-confidence and personal integrity.

The Pentecostal church, then, and particularly the collective setting of the *culto*, offers women the possibility of establishing new social relationships and reaffirming them on a regular basis. But the church also requires them to adopt a new set of beliefs about the world and their relation to it. These beliefs provide them with the means to validate their membership in a new community and to reinterpret past experiences in light of a changing social identity. This process begins in the *culto*, and it continues with individual possession by the Holy Spirit and the subsequent explanation of religious conversion in oral testimonies. We now turn to an analysis of this phenomenon.

Pentecostal conversion, personal history, and salvation
Although Pentecostal religious conversion demands continuous participation in the *culto*, it is also an individual experience that begins with the baptism of the Holy Spirit. This is an extremely emotional event in which a believer discovers "the truth" and the road to eternal salvation by directly encountering the power of Christ and establishing a personal

relationship with him. The experience infuses converts with a new and stronger sense of God, who, they believe, actually exists. If they submit to his will and acknowledge their sins, he will lift them up to heaven when he returns to Earth on judgment Day, and they will be saved.

Believers describe their conversion experiences in highly emotional accounts that sharply distinguish the pre- from the post conversion characteristics of the individual's life. They tell of the desperation and despair that once plagued their lives and the peace and happiness that they encountered after a surprise meeting with God changed them forever. These stories are based on actual experiences, but the meaning of the past is reinterpreted by individuals in light of the new ideology and their present social reality. The story of Rosa, a 50-year-old street vendor and mother of four, illustrates how personal biography is reworked in light of religious conversion and changing social relationships.

ROSA

Rosa has been a member of the IPU [Iglesia Pentecostal Unida] for three years and supports herself and her two youngest children by selling underwear on a La Paz street. She was born in a rural community near La Paz and migrated to the city with her parents at the age of eight. She attended elementary school in the city and, soon after becoming pregnant at the age of 21, married a bricklayer, who was also a rural immigrant.

The marriage eventually deteriorated. Rosa grew extremely frustrated because her husband spent little time at home and was often without work. She frequently lacked money for the family's domestic needs, and his constant drinking squeezed the household budget even tighter. Sometimes he would come home drunk and beat her, and he stayed away from home for days at a time. The situation eventually grew intolerable, and the couple split up: Rosa remained with the children in the family's rented room, and her husband took up residence with another woman.

The break-up of her marriage initiated an emotional as well as an economic crisis for Rosa. She could no longer count on any financial assistance from her husband and was forced to support herself and her children on the meager returns from street vending. In addition, Rosa's social life underwent a dramatic change, because she was no longer able to participate in social events in the same way as in the past. These changes eventually moved her to seek refuge in the Pentecostal church. Rosa explains the circumstances that led up to her religious conversion as follows:

My husband and I had always gone to fiestas and social gatherings of various sorts. I never drank, because I had to take care of him and make sure that he didn't fall down and hurt himself when he got drunk. I still received fiesta invitations after he left and decided to go to one or two because I liked all the food and dancing. I also wanted to see how much I could drink, since I'd never been drunk in my life.

At one fiesta I was feeling a little tipsy after several rounds of drinks. But then the band started playing really lively music, and I wanted to dance. A man I didn't know asked me to dance. His wife was sitting nearby, and I asked her if she minded. She said to go ahead, so we did, but then he didn't want to stop. We continued with one dance after another. I was a little drunk, but I realized that his wife was going to get angry if we kept it up, so I went and sat down. I didn't want to start a big scandal right there in the middle of the party, and I finally just went home.

On the way home I started to think: "I don't like this. I wasn't born to make people gossip, and there is no man who can accompany me to these fiestas. It's not a good idea to go alone." I felt lonely. All the other women were with their husbands, and I realized that there was nobody who would take me home if I drank too much or watch out for me as I had done for my husband. I could end up sleeping on the street. It was then that I decided to go to the church. People don't drink and dance there. They just pray to God, and I decided that that would be a better life.

Rosa finally settled on the IPU, after initially experimenting with another Pentecostal sect. She heard the pastor preach in a city plaza, and, at the urging of her son, decided to attend the *cultos* on a regular basis. She received the Holy Spirit six months after attending her first *culto* and this, according to Rosa, was an experience that profoundly changed her. As she explains:

When you surrender to God with all your heart, you cry and cry, recognizing the errors that you have committed and all the things that happened before knowing him. Knowing God changes everyone. You attain a peace in your home even if there isn't work or money. If there is just one cup of tea, everyone drinks it together. There aren't all these problems that people have who ignore the word of God. If you love God, then you also love your family. How can the person who loves God offend his wife? It's impossible.

If my husband had known God, I would not have lost him. But I was also ignorant. The enemy [that is, the devil] had grabbed me and would not let go of me. If I had understood the word of God, I would have married a spiritual man who feared God. Then I would have been able to live well and my marriage would not have been so difficult.

We can see from this story how Rosa's participation in the Pentecostal church and her encounter with God reshaped her understanding of preconversion life. During our interview, for example, Rosa told me that she had joined the Pentecostal church in large part because drinking and dancing were prohibited. Alcohol consumption in various forms was, indeed, a problem for Rosa: first, she had had to endure her husband's abusive behavior and the strain on the family budget caused by his excessive drinking; and second, following her husband's departure, she had suffered from ostracism in social situations where drinking and dancing were problematic for a single woman. But she had nevertheless participated in the festive drinking and dancing, because they were enjoyable activities and one way of belonging to the group.

It was only after her conversion to Pentecostalism that Rosa had come to view dancing and the consumption of alcohol as sinful behavior, inspired by the devil. Falling under the influence of the devil, whom Rosa described as the "enemy," and the absence of God in her life and the lives of others accounted for past difficulties. These understandings reflected her current interpretation of past events and constituted an important new analysis of her life in light of Pentecostal doctrine. Her account was a postconversion interpretation of the events that had led up to and constituted her religious transformation, and it represented a complex interaction of personal history and belief. . . .

Conclusion

The dramatic growth of Pentecostalism in La Paz over the past two and a half decades has been linked to profound changes in the social and economic fabric of life in the city. Female migrants from the countryside and lower-class urban dwellers, in particular, bear the brunt of a prolonged economic crisis as well as of class, racial, and gender discrimination. A disproportionate number seek refuge in the Pentecostal church, one of a growing number of fundamentalist Christian organizations struggling to gain a foothold among the poor. The converts establish new social relationships and validate emergent identities, often after experiencing severe emotional crises, and religious ideology is an important part of this process.

Through the experience of conversion, women address much of their gender- and class-based suffering by using religious ideology to recast the meaning of past events and revalidate their present social identities and relationships. This reflects a complex interaction of personal biography and belief that is an integral part of the process of change. They are also able to redefine their relationships with men because of the way in which Pentecostalism alters male behavior to suit their economic and emotional needs.

By creating new ties to one another, Pentecostal men and women overcome some of the mutual alienation that many experience every day as members of the lower class. These ties and the male resources that are channelled back to the domestic unit strengthen urban neighborhoods and help to create a new sense of community out of seeming disorder and chaos. In the process, these men and women are promoting values and practices that challenge aspects of the dominant society, even though neither women nor men have yet questioned the premises of Pentecostal ideology that obscure the common class concerns uniting them with other members of the urban working class and that reinforce women's structural inferiority to men.

REFERENCES

Lavrin, Asuncion. 1981. "Women and Religion in Spanish America." In *Women and Religion in America*. Vol. 2. Eds. R. Reuther and R. Keller. New York: Harper & Row. 42–51.
Stevens, Evelyn P. 1973. "Marianismo: The Other Face of Machismo in Latin America." In *Female and Male in Latin America*. Ed. Ann Pescatello. Pittsburgh, PA: University of Pittsburgh Press. 89–101.

On the Life of Churches and the Ecumenical Movement in Latin America[8] IGLESIA Y SOCIEDAD EN AMÉRICA LATINA (ISAL)

(e) . . . [T]hose communities that find themselves obedient [to God] discover reconciliation among themselves. Nothing separates them. They are expressions of the one body of Christ.

. . . [T]his unity looks to the future, i.e., in function of a communal commitment to God's struggle for a transformed world. The illusions of unity through tradition and verbal agreement are destroyed. And the divisions founded in our past conflicts and intellectual traditions also fall to the earth.

Naturally and necessarily, a unity born without effort or negotiation takes shape, simply out of participation in the struggles of God in the world.

It is within this perspective that we must frame the extraordinary renewal taking place in the Roman Catholic Church. It is evident that we cannot be romantic and think that this is a uniform and deep renewal in the entire church. But this should not diminish in any way the promise that these first fruits have offered and the hope that they have created in us. Not even a dry valley of bones can resist the reviving wind of the Spirit of God (Ezek. 37). From a profoundly Protestant perspective we have to rejoice at the fact that the Spirit which is not our sole possession "gives life to the dead and calls things that are not, as if they were" (Rom. 4:17).

For the same reason, we consider that the skepticism and hesitation that dominate in some Protestant circles, in the face of the Catholic church's renewal, are deeply contrary to our theological and biblical tradition. Such an attitude seems to us to contain, in the first place, a negation of the Protestant affirmation of the freedom of the Spirit of God to act and create where it wills. This lack of faith contains a presumption that the Spirit has become our monopoly. On the other hand, this doubt implies a negation of the very faith in resurrection. The hope of resurrection is based on the faith that the Spirit "gives life to the dead and calls things that are not, as if they were" (Rom. 4:17). If we do not believe that the Spirit is renewing the Catholic church, in spite of innumerable proofs, then we cannot have faith in the resurrection of the dead. If the spirit is not powerful enough to revive the ashes of an institution that was dying, then it is not strong enough to bring back to life those who have died.

(f) We suggested earlier that reconciliation with God means participation in his struggles—or in other words, non-reconciliation with all the cultural, social, economic, political, and ecclesiastical forces, the "powers of this world," that are committed to the preservation of sins transformed into institutions. What does this mean: sins transformed into institutions? God is love. Sin is anything that contradicts love, or in the words of Saint Augustine, love of oneself. This means the desire to dominate, to control, to use the other. The desire for power and dominion is transformed into institutions that serve and perpetuate this desire. Reconciliation with Christ is, accordingly, conflict with the forces of the anti-Christ, with the powers that want to abort the future and the hope that the Spirit has created. As Augustine understood very well, human history is a conflict between two political realities: the city of God, dominated by love of God, and the city of man, moved by love of self and by determination to destroy the common good for the goal of preserving private privileges.

(g) This theological and biblical perspective determines a definite vision of the missionary task. Mission means cooperating with God in what He is doing. He cannot do anything more, anything less, and anything different than that to which he is committed. And what God is doing today is a continuation of the same purposes revealed in the Bible: exalting the humble, feeding the hungry (Lev. 1:51-53), announcing the good news of the coming of the Kingdom to the poor, proclaiming freedom to the captives, giving sight to the blind, liberating those who are oppressed by injustice and announcing the good year of the Lord (Lev. 4:18-19). The good year of the lord refers to the jubilee year, now transformed into an institution of universal messianic history: the year in which all doubts will be pardoned, slaves will be liberated, lands returned to their rightful owners, in which all structures of domination will be taken apart and a totally new future will be put before men. Mission, thus, means participating in the process by which God makes all things new.

(h) Participation in the mission of the Messiah means that the community will also participate in his fate. "If they have persecuted me, they will also persecute you" (Jn. 15:20). Persecution comes precisely from the powers that are most established and recognized. Jesus was crucified by the religious and political powers, who spoke in the name of God and of order. Persecution is inevitable. And this is true because the words "God" and "order" (law) frequently hide men of disguised sins. These men place on themselves the mantle of religion and the veil of law in order to justify their desire for power and domination. And when this happens, we cannot have illusions: the Messiah and his followers will be sent to the cross.

* * *

Where should we go and what should we do?

Look toward the Bible and there we find the image of the community of the Spirit: love, commitment to the transformation of the world, directed toward the future, reconciled with all men who walk in the same direction, ready to take risks of obedience and of conflict with the powers of the anti-Christ. And look toward ourselves, whom we suppose to be the church of God in the Latin American continent, where God is suffering and dying with all those who suffer and die. Then we discover who we really are. And from this discovery should emerge the decision about what to do.

IV. IN SEARCH OF A CLEAR CONSCIENCE

We believe that it is of fundamental importance that all of us, as members of the Church of Christ, have a clear understanding of the Latin American situation—because God is operating there—and of the relations between the churches and this situation. This demands a realistic and objective study of the things, as they are, and a willingness to reformulate the church's missionary strategy, in response to the conclusions of this study.

(a) One of the most important challenges, which demands a response from Protestantism, are the *institutionalized forms of sin*, which are expressions of the powers of the anti-Christ, in its actions of aborting the new man and the new world. The churches need to have a clear vision of what are *the forms that these powers take, and where and how they operate.* The following sectors deserve our attention:

(1) economic structures; (2) structures of political power; (3) educational structures, including the communication media; (4) ideological structures; and (5) religious and theological structures.

(b) Another priority sector is the form in which the Latin American churches have participated in the struggle against the institutionalized forms of sin. This issue can be studied at three levels:

1) *Historical.* Investigate the development of Protestant thought in the last century, through an examination of its historical documents specifically in relation to our problem. This task is indispensable for faithfulness to our tradition.

2) *Ecclesiastical.* This perspective takes us to an examination of the ways in which Protestantism has reacted to the institutionalized forms of sin and how it has organized itself to combat them.

3) *Critical.* An analysis of that which, in the Protestant churches, is not in the service of the transformative purposes of God, and of the ways in which disobedience to this purpose has emerged in the churches. In other words: to what degree have the Protestant churches abandoned their prophetic and biblical character and taken on a priestly character? Are the present structures sufficiently open and flexible to permit the people of God to express themselves? How have the internal politics of the churches functioned—as an expression of the power of love, or of the love of power? As an instrument of service or as a weapon of dominion and control? In what ways has ecclesiastical language (sermons, theology, magazines, liturgy, theological education) been an instrument of love and truth (which are never separate!), contributing to the creation of free men, responsibly

dedicated to the transformation of our world? How has the church functioned in repressive ways?

(c) Investigation of the concrete possibilities for cooperation with our Catholic brothers and sisters. We believe that our Protestant tradition has a positive contribution to offer to the evangelical renewal that we are witnessing within the Catholic church. And equally, we must investigate the possible contributions that the Catholic renewal may offer to us.

(d) Finally, as a result of serious, obedient, and humble reflection, there lies before us a large field, infinite possibilities for renewal, in which the evangelical churches, like their Lord, will be able to experience the resurrection that only takes place after death. It is necessary to die in order to live. This truth applies not only to persons but also to the institutions and structures of our world. This is the reason for which there is no path to a new man and a new world which does not first require the death of the old man and old structures. The church is the institution that should have the courage to die daily, in order to be resurrected, beginning to live anew, together with its Lord.

7

Postconciliar Roman Catholicism

Changes in the Institutional Church

In the late nineteenth century, major social changes, including urbanization and industrialization, prompted Catholic leaders to revise some of the conservative positions advocated by the ultramontane faction that had dominated the church at Vatican I. The encyclical *Rerum Novarum*, issued in 1891 by Pope Leo XIII, reflected the Vatican's revised estimation of the church's appropriate (and possible) role in an increasingly secular, materialistic, and diverse world. In the decades following World War II, the church underwent an even more dramatic transformation. Ecclesial leaders and theologians began to reconsider the position of the church in modern societies, its judgments on political and social issues, and even some aspects of its internal organization. This rethinking was evident in two important encyclicals written by Pope John XIII, *Mater et Magistra* (1961) and *Pacem in Terris* (1963), which foreshadowed some of the social and internal concerns central to global and especially Latin American Catholic thinking. On the level of practice, pastoral agents and church officials concerned about the quality and level of lay participation in church activities developed a number of programs designed to increase parishioners' religious knowledge and involvement.

Among the most important of these programs was Catholic Action, which began as a set of informal programs, starting in Europe and later spreading to the Americas, that aimed to increase lay participation and to address "this-worldly" events from a Catholic perspective, while reducing the influence of secular ideologies on working-class Catholics. Catholic Action became an official church program, with branches specifically for industrial workers and youth as well, in 1930. One of the early leaders of the movement, Belgian priest Joseph Cardijn, developed an innovative pastoral method, "see, judge, act," as a tool for lay Catholics to reflect on, evaluate, and act upon in the secular world. Cardijn's dialectical pedagogy was a very important influence on liberation theology and other dimensions of progressive Catholicism in Latin America.

Catholic Action was a conservative, or at best reformist, movement, presenting the church as the "third way," a moderate alternative to both communism and capitalism. Certainly its early advocates did not anticipate their influence upon later progressive, even radical, Catholic streams such as liberation theology. Catholic Action gave rise to groups such as the Catholic student movements and a host of Catholic peasant federations, many of which radicalized in the late 1960s and 1970s.[1] Responding to the Second Vatican Council's call for Catholics to read the "signs of the times," to immerse themselves in the world, these groups encountered a Latin America scarred by widening social inequalities and political upheaval.

An early supporter of reform efforts was Manuel Larraín, who served as bishop of Talca, Chile, during the 1950s. In the document reprinted here, Larraín reflects on the changing social role of the Chilean, and more broadly Latin American, Catholic Church in the postwar period. Pioneers such as Larraín helped lay the foundations for many of the pastoral, organizational, and ideological innovations that emerged in the wake of the Second Vatican Council (1962-1965). At the council, bishops from throughout the world gathered to discuss, debate, and transform the church's position on a host of inter- and extra-ecclesial issues, ranging from Catholic schools and seminaries, liturgy and the sacraments, and the roles of pastoral agents and laypeople to the church's attitudes and responsibilities toward political and social affairs. In a host of ways, the council brought the church fully into the modern era, as reflected in the Italian term *"aggiornamento"* (updating, or bringing up to the day).

Several aspects of the council were especially important for Latin American Catholicism. First, the council included Latin American and other Third World bishops on a much greater scale than had previous ecclesial events; it marked the church's transition from a European to a global church, with particular attention to the areas of greatest Catholic population growth, especially Latin America. Second, the council affirmed proactive social and political responsibilities for the church, most notably in its final document, *Gaudium et Spes* (Pastoral Constitution on the Church in the Modern World). That document declares that the church has a responsibility to act in the world on behalf of the poor and weak;

that the right "to have a share of earthly goods sufficient for oneself and one's family"² takes precedence over the right of the wealthy to accumulate private property; and that poor individuals and poor nations have the right to political equality. Third, the bishops gathered at the council urged national and regional ecclesial bodies to meet and discuss among themselves and to adapt Vatican II's recommendations to their own particular situations.

In response, the Latin American Bishops' Conference (CELAM) met in 1968 in Medellín, Colombia, to examine their region's reality "in the light of the Council." The Latin American bishops proposed to follow the contextual methodology of Catholic Action, whose pastoral model of "see, judge, act" began with analysis of reality and later moved to evaluation and response. The Medellín meeting proved a watershed for the Latin American church, opening a new era in both ecclesial structure and the church's social role. At Medellín, the bishops acknowledged that in the past the church sometimes supported unjust social structures and affirmed Catholics' present responsibility to work for social and economic justice. They condemned poverty as a kind of "institutionalized violence," a sin embedded in political and economic structures. They concluded that in Latin America, only a transformation of these structures could achieve the social justice demanded by the Bible. Building on and expanding their discussions of social justice, the bishops at Medellín also addressed the problem of violence in Latin America in their *Document on Peace*, several sections of which are reprinted below.

The conference participants included not only bishops but also pastoral agents, including priests, nuns, and lay workers, who provided a grass-roots perspective to complement the vision of church officials. Their discussions and concluding documents encouraged pastoral innovations, and especially *comunidades eclesiales de base* (base or grass-roots Christian communities, or CEBs), which the bishops called "the first and fundamental ecclesiastical nucleus."³ In the Medellín *Document on Justice*, reprinted below, the bishops emphasized the centrality of CEBs to postconciliar pastoral work.

The Medellín meeting prompted diocesan officials to support CEBs and other structural innovations, encouraged priests, nuns, and seminarians to undertake pastoral work in poor neighborhoods and villages, and strengthened emerging theological discussions about the church's roles in, and judgments about, social and political life. Scholars and other observers cite the Medellín meeting as the crucial event sparking theological, pastoral, and organizational change in Latin American Catholicism. Its consequences spread beyond the church, as a number of church leaders, pastoral agents, and laypeople became involved in projects aimed at putting their religious values into practice. Catholic social programs usually started with local projects, such as soup kitchens, child-care centers, literacy campaigns, or neighborhood improvement efforts. In some cases, church-based activists addressed larger-scale issues such as human rights, land reform, and democratic governance. While these efforts often served as powerful catalysts for social change, they also led at times to conflict and even violence, as discussed below.

CELAM next met in Puebla, Mexico, in 1979. At Puebla, progressive church leaders confronted conservatives who hoped to roll back many of the pastoral programs inspired by Medellín. Ultimately, the two factions stalemated, and while the Puebla conference was not as momentous as Medellín, it did reaffirm the church's responsibility to the oppressed and its commitment to grass-roots pastoral projects such as CEBs. The Puebla meeting was also notable for the emergence of the term "preferential option for the poor,"[4] which has become a central concept for Roman Catholic social thought globally.

The Medellín and Puebla meetings transformed Latin American Catholicism by sparking the emergence of a cluster of organizational, practical, devotional, and theological forms that together can be termed "progressive Catholicism." However, these innovations spread throughout the region unevenly. In some countries, most notably Brazil, bishops and clerical leaders provided strong support for new theologies, practices, and organizational forms. In other areas, episcopal support was lukewarm or nonexistent, which meant either that progressive innovations faltered, as in Colombia and Argentina, or that hostility developed between church authorities and advocates of progressive reforms, as in Nicaragua. Variation existed not just between but within countries, as in Mexico, where bishops in the dioceses of Cuernavaca and Chiapas were especially active, and El Salvador, where reforms were largely limited to the Archdiocese of San Salvador.[5] Cultural and historical factors also shaped the emergence of new Catholic forms. In areas with large indigenous populations, such as the Andes, Guatemala, and southern Mexico, pastoral agents and laypeople often drew on native practices, just as church activists in parts of Brazil integrated African-based traditions.

Liberation Theology

The best known aspect of progressive Catholicism was undoubtedly the theology of liberation. This intellectual movement reconsidered central theological themes, including social ethics, church structure, and the nature of Christ, in light of an explicit commitment to social justice and the well-being of the people termed at Puebla "the least well off." One of the earliest published articles to pursue liberation theology explicitly was written by Peruvian priest Gustavo Gutiérrez, now cited as the father (or grandfather) of Latin American liberation theology. The article introduces many of the themes that preoccupied liberation theologians for decades to come: the origins and nature of social inequalities, the use of biblical and early church sources to interpret and judge social problems, and the adequacy of traditional theological and pastoral methods to address these problems. In his seminal article, reprinted in part here, Gutiérrez examines the significance of liberation itself as a theological and social theme. In his many subsequent writings, Gutiérrez has developed his theological vision more fully, and has also incorporated new themes, most significantly indigenous perspectives. He has also explored the significance of historical precursors to liberation theology, particularly the work of Bartolomé de las Casas.[6]

Perhaps the thorniest issue that liberation theologians have addressed is the structure of the church itself. A number of thinkers have tackled this topic, including Gutiérrez, the Salvadoran Jesuit Jon Sobrino, and, most famously, the Brazilian Franciscan Leonardo Boff. Largely as a result of his 1981 book *Church: Charism and Power,* Boff became the best known liberation theologian to be disciplined by the Vatican. In this and other works, Boff echoed major themes of liberation theology, including a defense of human rights and a call for the church to side with the poor and oppressed rather than the powerful members of Latin American societies. He also wrote extensively about church structure (ecclesiology), arguing for democratization of the church's hierarchical organization, greater lay participation and leadership (including leadership by women), and an expansion of the priesthood to women. He saw his hopes for this new form of church embodied in the *comunidades eclesiales de base,* the most significant of the pastoral and organizational innovations developed by progressive Catholics in Latin America.

Boff's work on ecclesiology earned him the attention of the Vatican's Sacred Congregation for the Doctrine of the Faith, then headed by

Cardinal Josef Ratzinger (now Pope Benedict XVI). Liberationist analysis of the church in history, according to Ratzinger,

> would see her [the church] "only" as a reality interior to history, herself subject to those laws which are supposed to govern the development of history in its immanence. The Church, the gift of God and mystery of faith, is emptied of any specific reality by this reductionism. At the same time, it is disputed that the participation of Christians who belong to opposing classes at the same Eucharistic Table still makes any sense.[7]

In contrast, Ratzinger defended the universality and eternal truth of the hierarchical structure of the church. After an investigation led by Ratzinger, the Vatican disciplined Boff by "silencing" him for a year in 1985. During this time the priest was prohibited from publishing or speaking publicly about his work. In 1992, Boff was again subject to investigation by the Vatican, this time primarily due to his participation in the Earth Summit in Rio de Janeiro. At that time, Boff told Rome, "The first time, I accepted punishment out of humility. Now it is humiliation. That is a sin, and I won't do it." Boff left the priesthood that year and became a member of the Franciscan lay clergy. He continues to teach theology at the state university in Rio de Janeiro and has become a leader in the development of ecological theology in Latin America.

Comunidades Eclesiales de Base

The origins of CEBs are varied and somewhat unclear. Some Catholic action projects in the 1950s used methods that were later to characterize base communities, including group discussions of the Bible and church documents. By the early 1960s, new lay-focused, locally based groups had emerged in a number of places. Among the most influential projects was one in the San Miguelito neighborhood in Panama City, where Leo Mahon, a North American priest, began working in 1963. Mahon developed a series of courses called "the family of God," which included such topics as "the Christian ideal," "sin," "the prodigal son," "sex and marriage," and "the community." The "family of God" embodied Mahon's goal of a new kind of Christian community, composed of lay people who met regularly to discuss everyday issues in the light of faith. Mahon's experiment in Panama City drew attention and visitors, including founders of some of the first CEBs in Nicaragua and El Salvador. Similar pastoral projects in the early 1960s, especially in Brazil, provided further inspiration as well as practical guidelines for the development of CEBs. Base communities received their biggest impetus from the Medellín meeting, which both endorsed the communities as a model for lay participation and encouraged pastoral agents to devote their energies to building up the CEBs.

This pastoral attention was crucial, since CEBs usually begin at the initiative of priests or nuns, ideally with moral and material support from superiors in their diocese or religious order. The pastoral workers most often start by visiting and getting to know local residents. After this acquaintance period, members (usually from twelve to thirty per community) undertake a series of courses (*cursillos*) that usually last several months. In rural areas, where many parishes lack permanent priests, *cursillos* are often offered not by local pastoral agents but by centers serving regions as large as an entire diocese. Laypeople trained in these courses then return to their own villages, to serve as catechists or as lay preachers (known in some areas as "delegates of the word of God," *delegados de la palabra*) to help form communities. In the courses, members relate the Bible to current events or local concerns, thus developing a critical understanding of their faith and their social reality. After the *cursillos*, leaders and participants often come together in a retreat, or *encuentro*, where participants reflect upon the *cursillos*, solidify their bonds with each other, and reaffirm their commitment to energetic involvement in church programs.

The defining activity of CEBs is *reflexión*, or group Bible study and discussion. Drawing from the "see, judge, act" methodology of Catholic Action developed in Europe in the 1950s and on the pedagogy of Brazilian educator Paulo Freire,[8] *reflexión* stressed a critical approach toward the established order, grounded in biblical stories that speak to CEB members' own experiences as an oppressed group. The origins and defining activities of CEBs are covered in the first two readings here by Frei Betto, the pen name of Carlos Alberto Libânio Cristo, a Dominican priest from Belo Horizonte, Brazil. The selections we reprint here are from his booklet "What Is the Base Christian Community?"—a resource for pastoral agents to use in thinking about the character and social functions of CEBs. Betto has been associated with liberationist Catholic organizations, both in Brazil and internationally. He was targeted as a radical by the Brazilian military regime in the late 1960s and spent several years as a political prisoner.

CEB members in different times and places emphasized different issues and different parts of the Bible, and their conclusions varied. Some, for example, read Exodus as a paradigm for all people struggling to free themselves from unjust rulers, or interpret the Gospels as the story of a poor man who fought for the poor and suffered the same type of persecution as people who denounce injustice today. This is evident in discussions that took place in the mid-1970s among members of a CEB that was started by the Nicaraguan priest and poet Ernesto Cardenal in Solentiname, an archipelago in Lake Nicaragua. The religious and political concerns of community members are evident in Cardenal's transcriptions of their weekly biblical reflections, reprinted here.

The Church and Politics

As pastoral methods varied, so did the political involvement of CEBs and other grass-roots Catholic projects. Many CEB members remained relatively apolitical and focused on local and pastoral issues. However, especially in Central America, many CEB members expanded their social commitment beyond spiritual and family concerns to larger-scale tasks such as community-building projects, literacy classes, and the formation of cooperatives or savings and loans organizations. Later, some members moved to more clearly political issues, starting with cost-of-living and neighborhood problems and sometimes arriving at conflicts over the nation's economic structure and political system or sympathy with revolutionary political groups.

CEBs contributed to political mobilization in at least three ways. First, democratization in the local religious community called into question "institutional structures and existing systems of authority,"[9] often leading to demands for greater democracy and accountability in larger religious and political institutions. The fact that efforts to democratize the church itself often failed, due to opposition from the hierarchy, probably encouraged Catholic activists to turn their attention to secular politics. Second, CEBs often helped people develop leadership and organizing skills that later provided the foundation for political organizing, especially in rural areas. Participation in CEBs taught many people to speak in public, to reach consensus, to act as a group, to share responsibilities, and to practice democratic methods of organization and decision making—skills that proved invaluable in the formation of peasant and neighborhood associations. Third, base communities strengthened collective identity by bringing together people who might have hesitated to gather for explicitly political purposes. Based on biblical calls to unity and on a postconciliar view of the church as the "people of God," CEBs encouraged group cohesion on a familial and local level, sometimes providing a foundation for more political forms of solidarity later on.

It is important to note that grass-roots religious groups such as CEBs, even at their most "politicized," remain religious in origin and religious at their core, as political scientist Daniel Levine has argued.[10] Even in highly polarized settings such as El Salvador and Nicaragua during the 1980s, religious language, values, and rituals were central to the identities and activities of progressive Catholic activists—they almost never became the secular, partisan groups caricatured by opponents within and outside the church. Frei Betto makes a similar point, insisting that CEBs must retain their religious identity and values, even when acting politically.

This said, the specifics of this political action varied widely. In Brazil, progressive activists generally received strong material and moral support from bishops. The Brazilian bishops conference (CNBB) has established offices and programs for women, indigenous people, landless peasants, youth, urban workers, and other disprivileged social groups. Bishops and priests have strongly supported CEBs and other lay-oriented pastoral projects, and they have also spoken out against social injustices, ranging from human rights violations committed by the ruling military junta (1964-1985) to present-day struggles over land and environmental sustainability. The Catholic hierarchy in Brazil, as throughout Latin America, has become more conservative in the past couple of decades, largely as a result of changes initiated by Pope John Paul II (1978-2006). John Paul replaced progressive bishops with more conservative ones in a number of dioceses throughout the region, disciplined some of the best-known liberationist theologians and pastoral agents, and reduced material and moral support for CEBs and similar pastoral programs. Despite recent setbacks, however, progressive Catholicism remains a significant social force in Brazil, credited as a crucial constituency of the ruling Workers Party and of the country's powerful landless movement (MST).

On the other end of the spectrum from Brazil, progressive Catholicism has probably developed least in Colombia, where the bishops have consistently constrained progressive pastoral projects. As Daniel Levine argues, however, even in the absence of institutional support, as in Colombia, CEBs offered a communitarian, participatory group very different from prevailing hierarchical models of organization that prevailed, politically and religiously, in much of Latin America. Ironically, Colombia's very conservative church nurtured one of Latin America's most famous militant Catholic activists, the guerrilla priest Camilo Torres. Torres's conflicts with the Colombian hierarchy eventually led to his laicization (removal from the priesthood) in June 1965. Like many young Latin American Catholics living amid the political debates and conflicts of the 1960s, Torres believed that true faith required a commitment to radical social change. "The Christian community cannot worship in an authentic way unless it has first effectively put into practice the precept of love for fellow man," he wrote in his statement to the press following his laicization. He continued:

> My analyses of Colombian society made me realize that revolution is necessary to feed the hungry, give drink to the thirsty, clothe the naked, and procure a life of well-being for the needy majority of our people. I believe that the revolutionary struggle is appropriate for the Christian and the priest. Only by revolution, by changing the concrete conditions of our country, can we enable men to practice love for each other.[11]

Torres joined the National Liberation Army in October 1965 and was killed in February 1966, during his first military action. Torres was an exceptional figure in the generally conservative Colombian church, and he was also an exception as a priest who chose to participate directly in armed struggle. Catholic militants were much more numerous in Brazil, Chile, and especially Central America. Although most Catholic activists, both clergy and lay, participated nonviolently, a number of lay activists did join armed groups, especially in Nicaragua and El Salvador. Many members of the community in Solentiname, for example, eventually joined the Sandinista Front for National Liberation (FSLN), the guerrilla organization that fought and, in 1979, defeated the dictator Anastasio Somoza. A number of Nicaraguan priests actively supported the FSLN, and a number became members of the post-1979 revolutionary government, including Ernesto Cardenal, who became minister of culture, and his brother Fernando, a Jesuit, who became minister of education.[12]

Progressive Catholics in Nicaragua received little support from the official church. The Nicaraguan bishops were cautiously critical of the Somoza regime and supportive of the moderate opposition during the 1970s, but after the Sandinista victory in July 1979, the church rapidly became divided. The bishops sided with moderate anti-Somoza activists who distanced themselves from the revolutionary agenda of the FSLN, while lay activists embraced the Sandinista popular organizations, especially after the anti-Somoza coalition fell apart following the FSLN victory. Episcopal hostility pushed activists into closer alliances with the Sandinista Front, which only polarized the situation more, to the point that many Catholic activists in Nicaragua during the 1980s had virtually no contact with the official church. Many Nicaraguans resented the official church for its failure to condemn the U.S.-funded counterrevolutionaries (*contras*), who disrupted agriculture and daily life and killed thousands of civilians in rural areas. Resentment against the Vatican also followed Pope John Paul II's public scolding of Ernesto Cardenal during his 1983 visit to Nicaragua.

Similar tensions existed in El Salvador. During the 1970s, when increasingly radical peasant and worker groups came under attack by military and paramilitary rightists, the Salvadoran bishops were extremely conservative. The only exceptions were Arturo Rivera y Damas and Oscar Romero, who became archbishop of San Salvador in February 1977. "Converted" in part by the assassination of his friend, Jesuit priest Rutilio Grande, in March 1977, Romero became increasingly outspoken in his criticisms of the Salvadoran government's brutal repression of the opposition, including many Catholic activists. With Rivera y Damas as his lone institutional ally, Romero struggled to lead the church through social chaos and extreme violence. His fourth and final pastoral letter, excerpted below, reflects his concerns with both social justice and Christian fidelity.

Romero's assassination on March 24, 1980, disillusioned many Salvadoran Catholics, who despaired both of the hope of peaceful change in their country and of the church's ability to work effectively on behalf of the poor. Many Catholic activists moved away from the institutional church and towards closer alliances with the political opposition, following a pattern that also occurred in Nicaragua (though not in Brazil or Chile, where antidictatorship activists received support from the bishops). During the 1970s and 1980s, Romero's fate was shared by nineteen priests in El Salvador and over forty nuns and priests in Central America. Between 1968 and 1982, Latin American governments and armies imprisoned, exiled, or killed close to a thousand priests, nuns, and bishops, in addition to countless laypeople.[13] Very few pastoral agents followed Camilo Torres in taking up arms. Violence committed against progressive Catholics was far greater than the violence committed by them.

The Future of Progressive Catholicism?

Progressive Catholicism, especially in places with dramatic political situations like Nicaragua, received a tremendous amount of attention in the postconciliar period. Many scholars, journalists, and Catholic leaders celebrated developments such as liberation theology, CEBs, and religiously based social movements as inspirational signs of a deep Christian commitment to human rights. For others, the same events and programs indicated serious problems within the church. By the 1990s, many scholars from both camps were declaring that progressive Catholicism was in decline, perhaps even dead, overtaken by external events, including the growth of Protestant Pentecostalism and the fall of the Berlin Wall, or by internal church developments such as Pope John Paul's transformation of the Latin American episcopacy and the growth of more conservative lay movements such as the Catholic Charismatic Renewal. We believe that the historical verdict remains open. Many progressive initiatives remain in force today, despite decreased institutional and moral support from church hierarchies in most countries. Perhaps even more significantly, the ethos and goals of progressive Catholicism have permeated social movements and political parties, including the MST (Movimento sem Terra, or Landless Movement) and Workers' Party in Brazil, indigenous movements in Guatemala, Venezuela, and Bolivia, and former guerrillas now working through the electoral system in Nicaragua and El Salvador. In many countries and dioceses, the influence of progressive Catholicism extended far beyond its formal institutional and organizational borders, affecting the values and worldviews even of people who never participated in CEBs or other church programs. Liberation theology became, as Roger Lancaster wrote of Nicaragua, the dominant ideology for many social movements throughout Latin America.[14] And as many liberation theologians themselves assert, as long as poverty and injustice are prevalent, there will be a place both for progressive religious critiques of oppression and for visions of liberation.

CHAPTER 7 DOCUMENTS

"Latin America Looks to Catholic Action
for a Program of Social Reform"[1] MANUEL LARRAÍN

In general terms we may describe the social physiognomy of Latin America as follows:

An aristocratic class which goes back to colonial times and which maintains up to the present the psychology of a ruling class. A plutocracy—which does not always coincide with the aristocracy—generally descended from European or Middle Eastern tradesmen who immigrated after the beginning of the republican era (second half of the nineteenth century to the present). The total absence through the nineteenth century and the beginning of the twentieth of a strong middle class comparable to the European *bourgeoisie*. The populace, the product of the intermingling of races, in a debased intellectual and economic situation. Great development of large land holdings and as a consequence a peasant class which has not come of age socially speaking. Add to this another social factor of decisive importance, common to all of Latin America: the weakness of the family as an institution. Without any attempt at statistical exactness, we can cite the high proportion of illegitimately born as a social fact common to all the Latin American nations. Various causes, also common, have brought about this situation; historically, the conquerors did not marry with the Indian women, so that the first fusion of the European with the indigenous races came about under the stigma of illegitimacy; ethnically, the tradition of polygamy among the greater part of the Indian tribes of America; socially, the fact that the European immigrant of the nineteenth century came generally without his family, and hence did not bring with him a strong family tradition (unlike the immigrants of the eighteenth century, who came with their families, whence a solid family tradition which still maintains itself); materially, an irregular way of life due to the lack of an economic basis sufficient to support settled family existence.

Finally, we must not forget the Indian problem of most Latin American nations, in many of which the Indian is only externally assimilated to western civilization. This, then, in broad outline, is the social situation of these countries. . . .

The Latin American republics came into being during a period which was especially difficult for the Church in Europe. It was the time of the triumphs of the liberal ideas of the encyclopaedists in the French Revolution. These ideas fired the men of the independence movement. Then came the most thriving period of Masonry in Europe with its anticlerical and naturalistic concepts. Next, after the mid-nineteenth century, came the rise of socialism.

All these ideas were allowed to operate powerfully on Latin America. All the American nations can tell the story of struggles, diverse in detail but identical in their basis.

What resistance did these ideas encounter from Catholic opinion? The twenty years following the achievement of independence, when the Church was almost without hierarchy, produced a great deal of confusion in the internal life of the Church in Latin America. The crisis of the seminaries brought about a decrease of the number of priests, which during the nineteenth century came to an extremely low ebb. Hence the advance of these ideas did not meet with sufficient resistance. Three areas reflect this situation: the fields of intellectual, social and political activity. I will speak only of the first two.

Latin America is a continent on the verge of profound social reforms. The terrible social inequality already described, the great proletarian and subproletarian masses which live under inhuman conditions, the continued toleration of large land holdings united to a feudal regimen in rural areas, the lack of any sense of social responsibility among many of the Catholics who enjoy a comfortable economic condition, these are factors which bring to us the urgency of taking a definite stand in this question of social reform. As His Excellency the Archbishop of Manaus said at Manizales: "Social reform will come about, whether through our efforts or in spite of them. But in the latter case, it will be anti-Catholic."

This view of the matter implies a problem: in the new world which is rapidly coming into being, does Latin America have a decisive role to play? What will that role be? Will it be an atheistic, anticlerical, materialistic role? Or will it be a Christian role, constructive and charged with hopes? . . .

The social problem has assumed an extreme seriousness in Latin America for three reasons: (a) because of the enormous social differences, greater than those which exist on any other continent, (b) because of the subhuman situation of large groups within Latin American society (the peasants, Indians, and subproletarian masses), (c) because of the rapid technological evolution of the continent, which is progressing not by easy stages, but dizzying leaps and bounds. . . .

This situation is aggravated by the lack of strong traditions of family life, social cohesion, and respect for labor. The Church does not have sufficient influence in the field of organized labor. The great syndical movements do not reflect a decisive Catholic influence.

Social disquiet is becoming more and more acute.

The power of syndicalism is becoming almost omnipotent.

Neither in national nor international affairs is there the least sign of a plan for concerted action. Latin America, due to the inequitable distribution of its arable lands, due to the abuses which have arisen from this cause, and due to the material and social condition in which the peasant exists, is ripe for agricultural reform at a very near date, although this may vary from nation to nation (for example, Mexico and Bolivia). The nature and inspiration of this reform depends upon Catholic international action. . . .

The Church in the Present-Day Transformation of Latin America in the Light of the Council: Medellín Conclusions[2]

CONFERENCE OF LATIN AMERICAN BISHOPS (CELAM)

Justice

Section 3. The Latin American Church has a message for all men on this continent who "hunger and thirst after justice." The very God who creates men in his image and likeness, creates the "earth and all that is in it for the use of all men and all nations, in such a way that created goods can reach all in a more just manner,"[3] and gives them power to transform and perfect the world in solidarity. . . .

Section 20. It is necessary that small basic communities be developed in order to establish a balance with minority groups, which are the groups in power. This is only possible through vitalization of these very communities by means of the natural innate elements in their environment. The Church—the People of God—will lend its support to the down-trodden of every social class so that they might come to know their rights and how to make use of them. To this end the Church will utilize its moral strength and will seek to collaborate with competent professionals and institutions. . . .

Peace

. . . Section 15. Violence constitutes one of the gravest problems in Latin America. A decision on which the future of the countries of the continent will depend should not be left to the impulses of emotion and passion. We would be failing in our pastoral duty if we were not to remind the conscience, caught in this dramatic dilemma, of the criteria derived from the Christian doctrine of evangelical love.

No one should be surprised if we forcefully re-affirm our faith in the productiveness of peace. This is our Christian ideal. "Violence is neither Christian nor evangelical."[4] The Christian man is peaceful and not ashamed of it. He is not simply a pacifist, for he can fight,[5] but he prefers peace to war. He knows that "violent changes in structures would be fallacious, ineffectual in themselves and not conforming to the dignity of man, which demands that the necessary changes take place from within, that is to say, through a fitting awakening of conscience, adequate preparation and effective participation of all, which the ignorance and often inhuman conditions of life make it impossible to assure at this time."[6]

Section 16. As the Christian believes in the productiveness of peace in order to achieve justice, he also believes that justice is a prerequisite for peace. He recognizes that in many instances Latin America finds itself faced with a situation of injustice that can be called, institutionalized violence, when, because of a structural deficiency of industry and agriculture, of national and international economy, of cultural and political life, "whole towns lack necessities, live in such dependence as hinders all initiative and responsibility as well as every possibility for cultural promotion and participation in social and political life,"[7] thus violating fundamental rights. This situation demands all-embracing, courageous, urgent and profoundly renovating transformations. We should not be surprised, therefore, that the "temptation to violence" is surfacing in Latin America. One should not abuse the patience of a people that for years has borne a situation that would not be acceptable to any one with any degree of awareness of human rights.

Facing a situation which works so seriously against the dignity of man and against peace, we address ourselves, as pastors, to all the members of the Christian community, asking them to assume their responsibility, in the promotion of peace in Latin America.

Section 17. We would like to direct our call in the first place, to those who have a greater share of wealth, culture and power. We know that there are leaders in Latin America who are sensitive to the needs of the people and try to remedy them. They recognize that the privileged many times join together, and with all the means at their disposal pressure those who govern, thus obstructing necessary changes. In some instances, this pressure takes on drastic proportions which result in the destruction of life and property.

Therefore, we urge them not to take advantage of the pacifist position of the Church in order to oppose, either actively or passively, the profound transformations that are so necessary. If they jealously retain their privileges, and defend them through violence, they are responsible to history for provoking "explosive revolutions of despair."[8] The peaceful future of the countries of Latin America depends to a large extent on their attitude.

Section 18. Also responsible for injustice are those who remain passive for fear of the sacrifice and personal risk implied by any courageous and effective action. Justice, and therefore peace, conquer by means of a dynamic action of awakening (*concientización*) and organization of the popular sectors, which are capable of pressing public officials who are often impotent in their social projects without popular support.

Section 19. We address ourselves finally, to those who, in the face of injustice and illegitimate resistance to change, put their hopes in violence. With Paul VI we realize that their attitude "frequently finds its ultimate motivation in noble impulses of justice and solidarity."[9] Let us not speak here of empty words which do not imply personal responsibility and which isolate from the fruitful non-violent actions that are immediately possible.

If it is true that revolutionary insurrection can be legitimate in the case of evident and prolonged "tyranny that seriously works against the fundamental rights of man, and which damages the common good of the country,"[10] whether it proceeds from one person or from clearly unjust structures, it is also certain that violence or "armed revolution" generally "generates new injustices, introduces new imbalances and causes new disasters; one cannot combat a real evil at the price of a greater evil."[11]

If we consider then, the totality of the circumstances of our countries, and if we take into account the Christian preference for peace, the enormous difficulty of a civil war, the logic of violence, the atrocities it engenders, the risk of provoking foreign intervention, illegitimate as it may be, the difficulty of building a regime of justice and freedom while participating in a process of violence, we earnestly desire that the dynamism of the awakened and organized community be put to the service of justice and peace.

"Notes for a Theology of Liberation"[12] GUSTAVO GUTIÉRREZ

Development or Liberation?

Today's world is going through a profound sociocultural transformation. Modern man has also become fully aware of the economic basis for that transformation. In the poor countries, where the immense majority of the world's population lives, the struggle for social change is being made with great urgency and is starting to become violent.

The term 'development' does not seem to express well the yearning of contemporary men for more human living conditions. A basic problem is: the notion of development is not univocal; a considerable number of definitions are given. Instead of looking at them one by one, let us see the perspectives they start from.

First, development can be taken in a purely economic sense, as synonymous with *economic growth*. In that case, a country's development will be measured, e.g., by comparing its GNP or its per capita income with those of some country assumed to have achieved a high level of development. This yardstick can be improved on and made more sophisticated, but the basic presumption will be that development is primarily an increase of wealth. Those who speak this way, explicitly at least, are few today.[13] Such a yardstick is used further to contrast with other, more integral norms. One may still ask, however, if all the norms do not retain something of the capitalist concept of development.

The inadequacies of the purely economic yardstick have popularized another, more important and frequent today, which looks on development as a *global social process*, with economic, social, political, and cultural aspects. This strategy of development, keeping in view all these aspects, permits a people to make global progress and also avoid certain dangerous pitfalls.

Seeing development as a global social process involves, of necessity, ethical values, and that implies ultimately a concept of what man is. A detailed explication of such a *humanist perspective* in development takes time and extends, without contradicting it, the point of view just presented. Fr. L. J. Lebret strove constantly in that direction. For him, developmental economics is "the discipline covering the passage from a less human to a more human phase." The same notion is contained in that other definition of development: "having more in order to be more."[14] This humanistic view places the notion of development in a broader context: a historical vision, in which humanity takes charge of its own destiny. But that involves a change of perspective, which we prefer to call "liberation." That is what we shall try to explain in the following paragraphs.

In recent decades the term "development" has been used to express the aspirations of the poor nations. Of late, however, the term has seemed weak. In fact, today the term conveys a pejorative connotation, especially in Latin America.

There has been much discussion recently of development, of aid to the poor countries; there has even been an effort to weave a mystique around those words. Attempts to produce development in the 1950's aroused hopes. But because they did not hit the roots of the evil, they failed, and have led to deception, confusion, and frustration,

One of the most important causes of this situation is the fact that development, in its strictly economic, modernizing sense, was advanced by international agencies backed by the groups that control the world economy, The changes proposed avoided sedulously, therefore, attacking the powerful international economic interests and these of their natural allies: the national oligarchies. What is more, in many cases the alleged changes were only new and concealed ways to increase the power of the mighty economic groups. Here is where conflict enters the picture. Development should attack the causes of our plight, and among the central ones is the economic, social, political, and cultural dependence of some peoples on others. The word "liberation," therefore, is more accurate and conveys better the human side of the problem. Once we call the poor countries oppressed and dominated, the word "liberation" is appropriate. But there is also another, much more global and profound view of humanity's historical advance. Man begins to see himself as a creative subject: he seizes more and more the reins of own destiny, directing it toward a society where he will be free of every kind of slavery.[15] Looking on history as the process of *man's emancipation* places the question of development in a broader context, a deeper and even a more radical one. This approach expresses better the aspiration of the poor peoples, who consider themselves primarily as oppressed. Thus the term "development" seems rather antiseptic, inaccurately applying to a tragic, tense reality. What is at stake, then, is a dynamic and historical concept of man as looking toward his future, doing things today to shape his tomorrow.[16]

This topic and this language are beginning to appear in certain sections of the magisterium. One isolated text of *The Development of Peoples,* e.g., speaks of "building a world where every man, regardless of race, re-ligion, or nationality, can live a fully human life, free of the servitude that comes from other men and from the incompletely mastered world about him." The notion is more forcibly expressed in the *Message of Fifteen Bishops of the Third World*, published in reply to *The Development of Peoples*. The topic of liberation comes up frequently, almost as the leitmotif of the document, in another text of greater importance because of its doctrinal authority: in the Medellín Guidelines.

Liberation, therefore, seems to express better both the hopes of op-pressed peoples and the fulness of a view in which man is seen not as a passive element, but as agent of history. More profoundly, to see history as a process of man's liberation places the issue of desired social changes in a dynamic context. It also permits us to understand better the age we live in. Finally, the term "development" clouds up somewhat the theological issues latent in the process. To speak of liberation, on the other hand, is to hint at the biblical sources that illuminate man's presence and actions in history: the liberation from sin by Christ our Redeemer and the bringing of new life.

In resume, then, there are three levels of meaning to the term "libera-tion": the political liberation of oppressed peoples and social classes; man's liberation in the course of history; and liberation from sin as a condition of a life of communion of all men with the Lord.

What Is the Base Ecclesial Community?[17] FREI BETTO

1. WHAT ARE THE BASE ECCLESIAL COMMUNITIES?

Characteristics
The base ecclesial communities (*comunidades eclesiais de base*, CEBS) are small groups organized around the parish (urban) or chapel (rural), on the initiative of lay people, priests or bishops. The first ones emerged around 1960, in Nísia Floresta, Archdiocese of Natal, according to some research-ers, or in Volta Redonda, according to others. Of a religious nature and pas-toral character, the CEBs can have ten, twenty, or fifty members. In parishes on the [urban] periphery, the communities may be distributed in small groups or they may form a single group to which is given the name of base ecclesial community. This is the case in rural areas, where a hundred or two hundred people meet in the chapel on Sundays to celebrate mass.

They are *communities* because they bring together people who have the same faith, belong to the same church, and live in the same region. Motivated by faith, these people live in a comm-union (*comum-união*) around their problems of subsistence, housing, struggle for better living conditions, and their liberating hopes and desires. They are *ecclesial* because they congregate around the church, as basic nuclei of communities of faith. They are of the *base* because they are made up of people who work with their own hands (popular classes): homemakers, workers, underemployed people, retirees, youth, and people employed in the service sector, in the urban peripheries; in the rural areas, they are agricultural wage laborers, tenant farmers, small landowners, renters, peons, and their families. According to unofficial estimates, the communities in our country encompass around two million believing, oppressed people.

One Brazilian diocese, for example, has 6800 communities listed in the census. One neighborhood on the periphery of São Paulo has 129 CEBs. It is clear that these numbers are relative. What is important is that they represent a new type of pastoral organization. For a long time, the only kind of pastoral organization was the parish. One cannot step on a piece of Brazilian soil without being within a parish. With the territory divided into parishes, the vicar provided sacramental attention to believers. However, our modern society does not take the parish as simply a geographic axis. It is necessary to have true parish communities, that is, that the faithful really know each other, which is only possible through a parish organized into small base communities.

Pastoral Agents

The animators of the CEBs are called *pastoral agents*: priests, nuns or lay people, trained by their own communities. Lay pastoral agents are a new vocation or a new charism in the life of the church. Many leave their families and professions in order to live exclusively from the pastoral work, when the diocese has the ability to take them on. They live in poor neighborhoods, earn a little more than the minimum wage, and take on work with the poor as the most important commitment in their lives. They do not coordinate the communities, they merely advise, taking care that the poor themselves are the agents of their own history.

Because of this, the pastoral agent must live in close connection with the people, sharing their lives so that she or he can understand their words better in the ecclesial sphere. Without doing this, the agent will risk of having the colonialist attitude of those who want to teach the poor community without first learning with them and remaking his or her elitist, academic, populist, or vanguardist categories and values.

Members of the CEBs

The members of the CEBs are generally people who earn less than three or four times the monthly minimum wage. They live in hovels (*casebres*) on the urban periphery or built-in areas taken through land invasions (*favelas*). In rural areas, they live in small towns or at the edge of cities that provide agricultural wage laborers. They are semi-literate: they can write their names and decipher letters, but they do not always understand their meanings. They know how to read without understanding much of what is written.

In the rural areas, mainly, the communities maintain their popular culture. In a celebration in Paraíba, the symbolism of the eucharistic host was realized by sharing couscous, without being replaced by it. In Linhares, north of Espírito Santo, the communities marked the cacao harvest with a celebration in which they cooked and shared the product. In the prelature of São Félix do Araguaia, the liturgical symbols are the working tools of the fishers and farmers: net, gourds, pitchfork, and so forth. The number of liturgical songs written by members of the communities is always growing larger and more frequent. The lay people are the ones who prepare the novenas and the masses, the festivals of the saints and the schedule of celebrations, always assisted by their pastoral agent.

Two related factors mark the members of the rural and urban communities: the expropriation of land and the exploitation of their labor. As oppressed migrants, the community members previously sought in religion a sedative for their sufferings, but now they find a space for critical discernment in the face of the dominant ideology and the organizational capacity of the poor to resist oppression.

2. METHOD AND PEDAGOGY OF THE BASE ECCLESIAL COMMUNITIES

Method

The base ecclesial communities employ the see-judge-act method. Meeting in a shanty, in the modest house of a worker or in the parish hall, the participants say their prayers and sing their hymns and, following that, they discuss their problems and difficulties. In general, these are domestic problems (a sick daughter, a neighbor who has lost his land, or a work project to fix a shanty destroyed by rain) and professional ones (the need to work overtime in the factory, the organization of a rural union, or unemployment). The way in which these questions are discussed varies greatly. In some communities, the monitor or coordinator simply asks the participants how their week was at home, in the neighborhood, or at work. The account reveals the problems and difficulties; one or two are seen as most important. This part is called *seeing*.

The meeting continues with a focus on the main questions. It passes to the part called *judging*. How would Jesus act in this situation? How should we act? This second part of the method is always tied to the Gospel. Someone suggests a passage of the New Testament which, in his or her view, illuminates the theme under discussion. Everyone listens in silence and, after that, makes his or her commentaries.

The relationship between Jesus' action and our action leads to the third part: *to act*, or to make a concrete plan for addressing the problem. This may combine a workday to help to harvest the beans of a worker who's at danger of losing his production, or a petition in the neighborhood to demand water or sewers for the houses or to buy food wholesale in order to avoid the high retail prices.

This system is not mechanical. Often a community may spend months focused on a single problem: the struggle against expulsion of squatters (*posseiros*). Every meeting is a moment to strengthen the resistence of the *posseiros* and to plan the next steps of the struggle.

The method does not function in a linear way, as if every moment was separated from the next in a stagnant sequence that would provoke a sequence of meetings, a kind of eternal return of see-judge-act. The method functions, in practice, as a dialectical method. *Seeing* brings with it elements of judging and demands for acting. Every moment is interrelated with the others. The ability to act in the next meeting is not a re-beginning of everything from the start, but rather a continuation of action, retaken with critical awareness of its weaknesses and errors and of its pastoral implications (theological, biblical and political, in a broad sense).

As groups with a religious nature, the communities have a pastoral character, which is political in an Aristotelian sense. Because they adopt a method which begins with reality, they suppress the faith-life dualism that is found in Christian groups that begin with doctrine and reduce "being Christian" to the intellectual and moral domain of revealed truth that is explained by the church magisterium. . . .

Biblical Circles

Many communities use, as a subsidiary methodology, the biblical circles created by Father Carlos Mesters. They use booklets, written in a popular language—a language that is visual and not conceptual, concrete and not abstract, like the parables in the Gospels—where the facts of life are compared with those of the Bible. The circles help show that holy scripture is not a book of histories in the past or a box of divine oracles: it is the history of a people, read by the people themselves, in the light of faith in the God of liberation. Thus the Bible shows us to reread our history in the light of the Father's design, shows the path of the poor. The community becomes aware that it also "is writing" its Bible.

Beginning with this consciousness, the redeeming presence of God in the struggle of the communities is made clear. Without losing the transcendent dimension, the faith of the group makes transparent the reality in which it lives: they come to understand the relative character of the status quo, the historical dimension of life, and to seek the true roots of social ills. The biblical texts help the communities move from consciousness of their geographical situation to consciousness of their historical situation. And it reveals the Father of Jesus Christ as the God decidedly committed to the history of human liberation.

3. BASE ECCLESIAL COMMUNITIES AND POLITICAL ACTION

Political maturation should be accompanied by theology, in a form which permits reflection about reality, in the light of faith, to be consolidated into categories which are adequate for the cultural universe in which they exist, and to be expressed in language familiar to the participants confronted by pastoral work. Christian life cannot sustain itself without experiencing the content of faith, unless it confuses the position of the pharisees with evangelical discipleship. Nonetheless, a certain modesty in relation to the life of prayer has sometimes impeded Christian activists, not only in the deepening of their experience of God, but also in the appropriation of the symbolic capital of the faith, which now serves the ideology of the dominant classes.

Pastoral practice is tied to political practice and possesses strong political connotations, but is not exhausted in political work. At the same time, if pastoral practice is restricted to a precarious political rationality, it is understandable if Christian activists are tempted to abandon the pastoral. In such a case, upon discovering the scientific nature of political reasoning, militant Christians would not be justified, at least theoretically, in continuing in both politics and the church. Only those who through their own lives discover the profundity of pastoral practice will be able to recognize the autonomy and importance of politics, and make it part of their own theoretical stance, while at the same time maintaining its connection to the ecclesial realm. In this connection between the pastoral and the political, activists still discover in the ecclesial sphere the freedom necessary to judge, in the light of the gospel, their political practice, sharpening their criteria of discernment and avoiding the sacralization of political activity.

The Gospel in Solentiname   ERNESTO CARDENAL

Riches (Luke 12:13-21)[18]

> Then he gave them this example:
> There was a rich man,
> and his lands gave a great harvest.
> And he thought:
> "I know what I'm going to do:
> I am going to tear down my barns
> and build other bigger ones,
> and in them I will keep all my harvests and all my goods
> and I will say to myself:
> "My friend, you have many things stored up for many years;
> rest, eat, drink, and be merry."
> But God said to him:
> "Fool, this very night you will die,
> and all you have stored up, who will get it?"
> That's what happens to the man that piles up riches for himself,
> but who is poor in the eyes of God.[19]

FELIX: "That rich man, when he dies he's not saved, because he was poor in love; he wasn't rich in God's view. And others enjoy the riches."

I [ERNESTO CARDENAL]: "Jesus gives the example of a rich man who died when he had the most riches and other people enjoyed his riches. And then he says *that's* what happens to all those who pile up for themselves. But that was an example."

OLIVIA: "The rich man is dead now, because he's selfish, and he's not enjoying his riches."

FELIPE: "The guy that has riches doesn't have love, so he's poor in the eyes of God, because God is love among brothers and sisters."

TOMAS: "That rich guy was selfish because all he thought about was making his barns bigger to store up more just for himself. That's what all the rich always do."

LAUREANO: "No doubt about it; those who store up riches when there's so many people to share with are already damned; they're damned for storing things up."

ALEJANDRO: "What the man in the parable did is what rich people do now: Keep the money in the bank and take it easy. They eat and drink and have fun like that man. They live in an endless fiesta. And they go on accumulating more, they go on exploiting and living happily off the work of the others. Like that man in the Gospel: because that man by himself couldn't have gathered all those harvests that wouldn't fit into his barns, he did it with the labor of others."

REBECA: "The bad part about wealth is that it makes them poor in God's eyes, poor in love."

OLIVIA: "And they're very unfortunate in the eyes of God, because the richer a man is, the more he has exploited. And then he owes all that money, that sweat that he's stolen from the worker. Some are poorer than others in the eyes of God, and the richest are the poorest in God's eyes. The richest one is the one who's devoted himself to screwing others, so he's the worst for the poor people, so he's the poorest in God's eyes. The ones that are the most miserable (those that are most lacking in love) are the ones that have the most riches. But Jesus speaks of the one that 'piles up riches for himself.' He's not against big harvests. He's against piling them up just for yourself. Like that man did: to keep them and rest and enjoy himself the rest of his life. Neither of the two sons-of-bitches had a right to that inheritance; all of it was the people's money. Just as it was everybody's wealth that man wanted to store in his barns. Who says he could enjoy all by himself that great harvest, if he didn't harvest it all by himself. And even less inherit it."

The Coming of the Kingdom of God (Luke 17:20-37)[20]

> The Pharisees asked Jesus when the kingdom of God would come,
> and he answered them: "The coming of the Kingdom of God
> is not a thing that can be seen.
> They are not going to say 'Here it is' or 'There it is,'
> Because the kingdom of God is already among you."[21]

OLIVIA: "I don't see how they could think for so long that the kingdom of heaven was in heaven when Jesus has clearly said that it was in the midst of human kind."

REBECA: "I think the kingdom is among us already, because the kingdom is love. When we have love, there's the kingdom."

MARIÍTA: "I think you can't see the kingdom, because it's love. Love is in people's hearts, but it's not a visible thing that we can say here it is or there it is. But I think you can look at it: when you see the changes. The whole world is changing. And so like that you can see the kingdom of God."

LAUREANO: "The kingdom of God is inside you, but you do have to make it come true. You can have love but you have to make that love come true with the others: only then do you make the kingdom of God come true."

ALEJANDRO: "No matter how far a country has advanced in making love come true, it will never reach perfection. Then you can never say: there it is. You can always do something more."

FELIPE: "And besides we have the capitalist propaganda that always confuses you, and we can't know for sure if the kingdom of God is in a particular place or it isn't."

OLIVIA: "I'd say that you can see it: it really isn't the way people have always believed, that when Christ comes we're going to see him coming in glory in the clouds: it's going to be when we see the kingdom of love. In a country where there's justice, where there's respect for human rights and there's food and schools for everybody, there's the kingdom of love: and you can see it and notice it in a little community where we love each other and we all respect each other; it's already the kingdom of love, the kingdom of God."

"Fourth Pastoral Letter: The Church's Mission amid the National Crisis" (August 1979)[22]   OSCAR ROMERO

Unmasking the Idolatries of Our Society

Adhering to the demands of the same prophetic denunciation and conversion, the church reminds us that making any created thing into an absolute is an offense against the one Absolute and Creator, because it erects and serves an idol, which it attempts to put in the place of God himself.

As well as offending God, every absolutization disorients, and ultimately destroys, human beings. It is the vocation of human beings to raise themselves to the dignity of the children of God and to participate in God's divine life. This transcendence of human beings is not an escape from problems here on earth, still less is it an opium that distracts them from their obligations in history. On the contrary, by virtue of this transcendent destiny people have the capacity to always remain critical vis-à-vis the events of history. It gives them a powerful inspiration to reach out to ever higher goals. Social forces should harken to the saving voice of Christ and of true Christians, cease their questioning, and open themselves to the values of the one and only Absolute. When a human value is turned into an absolute and endowed, whether in theory or in practice, with a divine character, human beings are deprived of their highest calling and inspiration. The spirit of the people is pushed in the direction of a real idolatry, which will only deform and repress it.

Among the evils that afflict El Salvador, I find that there are three idolatries, or absolutes, that the church ought to unmask in the name of the one God and Lord.

The Absolutization of Wealth and Private Property

The absolutization of wealth holds out to persons the ideal of "having more" and to that extent reduces interest in "being more," whereas the latter should be the ideal for true progress, both for the people as such and for every individual. The absolute desire of "having more" encourages the selfishness that destroys communal bonds among the children of God. It does so because the idolatry of riches prevents the majority from sharing the goods that the Creator has made for all, and in the all-possessing minority it produces an exaggerated pleasure in these goods.

As for the absolutization of private property, John Paul II, speaking at Puebla, gave voice to the contrary opinion of the traditional and of the modern teaching of the church. For "this voice of the Church, echoing the voice of human conscience, . . . deserves and needs to be heard in our own day as well, when the growing affluence of a few . . . parallels the growing poverty of the masses. . . . The Church's teaching [is] that there is a *social mortgage* on all private property. . . . This Christian, evangelical principle will lead to a more just and equitable distribution of goods.[23]

Absolutizing wealth and private property brings about the absolutizing of political, social, and economic power, without which it is impossible for the rich to preserve their privileges, even at the cost of their own human dignity. In our country this idolatry is at the root of structural and repressive violence. In the final analysis, it is the cause of a great part of our economic, social, and political underdevelopment. This is the capitalism condemned by the church at Puebla, following the teaching of recent popes and of Medellin. Whoever reads these documents would say that they are describing a situation in our country that only selfishness, ignorance, or servility could defend.

The Absolutization of National Security

I have already drawn attention in the first part of this letter to the doctrine or ideology of national security as the ideological foundation for repression. Puebla frequently denounced this new form of idolatry, which has already been installed in many Latin American countries. In this country it has its own particular way of working, but substantially it is identical with that described at Puebla: "In many instances the ideologies of National Security have helped to intensify the totalitarian or authoritarian character of governments based on the use of force, leading to the abuse of power and the violation of human rights. In some instances they presume to justify their positions with a subjective profession of Christian faith."[24]

By virtue of this ideology, the individual is placed at the total service of the state. His or her political participation is suppressed, and this leads to an unequal participation in the results of development. Peoples are put into the hands of military elites, and are subjected to policies that oppress and repress all who oppose them, in the name of what is alleged to be total war. The armed forces are put in charge of social and economic structures under the pretext of the interests of national security. Everyone not at one with the state is declared a national enemy, and the requirements of national security are used to justify "assassinations, disappearances, arbitrary imprisonment, acts of terrorism, kidnappings, acts of torture . . . [all] indicate a complete lack of respect for the dignity of the human person."[25]

The interests and advantages of the few thus turned into an absolute. This absolutization becomes a mystique—as if the national security regime, which attempts to give itself a good public image by "a subjective profession of Christian faith,"[26] were the only, or the best, "defender of the Christian civilization of the West.[27] This perverts the noble function of the armed forces. Instead of serving true national interests, they become the guardians of the interests of the oligarchy, thus furthering their own ideological and economic corruption. Something similar is happening to the security forces. They, instead of caring for civil order, have turned themselves basically into an organization for repressing political dissidents. And finally, the high command unconstitutionally changes the political procedures that ought to decide democratically the country's course.

The judgment merited by the ideology of national security has, for Christians, been clearly expressed at Puebla: it is "not compatible with the Christian vision of the human being as responsible for carrying out a temporal project, and to its vision of the State as the administrator of the common good."[28]

The omnipotence of these national security regimes, the total disrespect they display towards individuals and their rights, the total lack of ethical consideration shown in the means that are used to achieve their ends, turn national security into an idol, which, like the god Molech, demands the daily sacrifice of many victims in its name.

The legitimate security that the state ought to seek for its members is cruelly perverted, for in the name of national security the insecurity of the individual becomes institutionalized.[29]

The Absolutization of Organizations
There is a third absolute, typical of the present situation in this country. I am speaking of the absolutization of an organization. This is a trap into which many members of popular organizations fall. They make their own organization the supreme value, and subordinate everything else to it.

This organizational absolutization differs from the other two just mentioned. They are fundamentally evil, as has been indicated. The absolutization of an organization, on the other hand, has a good side to it because it arises from among the people, as it puts to use its right of forming organizations for the purpose, at least in theory, of attaining the good of that same people. But in practice they become so fanatical that the interests of the people are no longer their chief concern, but the interests of the group or organization. Here are some of the evils that flow from this new idolatry:

- Their activities become too political, as if the political dimension were the only, or even the main, element in the lives of campesinos, workers, teachers, students, and other members who go to make them up.
- They try to subordinate the specific mission of trade union, social, and religious organizations to their own political objectives. They try to manipulate the church, its worship, its magisterium, its teaching mission, and so on, so that they serve the political and strategic aims of a political organization.
- The leaders of an organization, by making an absolute out of the political problem of achieving power, can in practice lose interest in other real problems, and can misunderstand the ideological criteria that underlie them, despite the fact that these are the very problems and criteria that concern the majority the people—for example, some of their more immediate socioeconomic needs, or the Christian principles of the members of the organizations. Another example would be the choice of a strategy that could needlessly offend religious sensitivities (taking over churches, for example).
- They can become so highly sectarian that their partisanship gets in the way of establishing dialogue or alliances with another type of organization also fighting for justice.
- The most serious kind of this fanaticism is that which changes what might be a force for the good of the people into an obstacle in the way of achieving that same good, and into an obstacle to profound change.

I put forward a more detailed account of the evangelical service the church could offer to popular organizations in my third pastoral letter. They included defense of the right to organize, support for what was just in their demands, support of Christians who joined them, and denunciation of their possible mistakes and injustices, such as the mistake of turning them into absolutes, as I have just been saying. And above all, the church turns its entire effort for the liberation of the people toward the sole absolute, that definitive liberation toward which all strivings for justice ought to converge: the liberation in Christ, which sets sin aside and, while promoting liberation on earth, does not lose sight of the people's final vocation to the one and only Absolute.

An organization runs the risk of turning itself into an absolute and of becoming an idol when atheistic ideologies, or the limited interests of the group, cause it to lose sight of those wide, transcendent perspectives, and lose hold of the ideal of the country's common good.

Violence

I have spent a good time already, in the third part of my third pastoral letter, on the judgment of the church on violence. Here I am going to presuppose that summary of the church's traditional moral teaching on violence. I only want to dig a little deeper, to bring those ideas up to date, given the escalation of the violence that casts a shadow over so many families in our homeland. Would that this reflection might persuade Salvadorans to lay unjust attitudes aside, and to get them, with sincere change of heart, to wash clean so many hands and consciences stained by social injustice and human blood! Inspired by the gospel, the church feels itself driven to seek peace before all else. But the peace that the church urges is the work of justice (*opus justitiae pax*). Therefore its judgments on the violence that disturbs the peace cannot ignore the demands of justice. There are many different judgments, just as there are many different forms of violence. The church cannot state, in a simplistic fashion, that it condemns every kind of violence.

Structural Violence

The church condemns "structural" or "institutionalized violence," "the result of an unjust situation in which the majority of men, women, and children in our country find themselves deprived of the necessities of life."[30] The church condemns this violence not only because it is unjust in itself, and the objective expression of personal and collective sin, but also because it is the cause of other innumerable cruelties and more obvious acts of violence.

More and more Salvadorans are learning the point that the deepest root of the serious evils that afflict us, including the renewed outbreak of violence, is this "structural violence." It takes concrete form in the unjust distribution of wealth and of property—especially insofar as it includes land ownership—and, more generally, in that amalgam of economic and political structures by which the few grow increasingly rich and powerful, while the remainder grow increasingly poor and weak.[31]

Arbitrary Violence of the State

The church likewise condemns the arbitrary and repressive violence of the state. We in El Salvador well know, as did Puebla, how any dissent against the present form of capitalism and against the political institutions that support it is repressed with ever increasing violence and ever greater injustice—inspired by the theory of national security. We also know how the majority of the campesinos, the laborers, slum dwellers, and others who have organized themselves to defend their rights and to promote legitimate structural changes are simply declared to be "terrorists" or "subversives." They are therefore arrested, tortured, murdered, or they simply disappear and all without reference to the law or to any judicial institution that might protect them or give them the chance to defend themselves and prove their innocence. Faced with this prejudicial and unjust situation, many have decided that they had no alternative but to defend themselves with violence. And recently they have encountered, in response, the arbitrary violence of the state. Public authority certainly has the right to punish social disorder. But in order to do so there must be the intervention of a court of justice that gives the accused the chance to defend themselves and can declare the guilty worthy of punishment. Any other kind of sanction—arbitrary and repressive—is an abuse of authority.

Violence of the Extreme Right
The church equally condemns the violence favored by right-wing gangs of terrorists. They go absolutely unpunished, which makes one suspect official connivance. They have cast their shadow over the country's teachers, over the popular organizations, over political parties, and even over the church itself. Their intention, which they clearly cannot sustain indefinitely, is to try to uphold the unjust social order to which I referred above. Therefore they, more than anyone else, are involved in the injustice of the system.

Terrorist Violence
The church also condemns the violence perpetrated by politico-military groups or individuals when they intentionally victimize innocent persons, or when the damage they do is disproportionate, in the short or medium term, to the positive effect they wish to achieve.

Insurrectional Violence
On the other hand, Pope Paul VI's encyclical Populorum Progressio, quoted at the Medellin assembly, takes up again the classic teaching of Catholic theology, according to which insurrection is legitimate "in the very exceptional circumstances of an evident, prolonged tyranny that

seriously works against fundamental human rights and seriously damages the common good of the country, whether it proceeds from one person or from clearly unjust structures."[32] In addition, our own national constitution recognizes the right of just insurrection.

Violence of Legitimate Defense

In the same class as legitimate insurrectional violence, we can place the violence of legitimate defense. This occurs "when a person or a group repels by force an unjust aggression that they have suffered" (Third Pastoral Letter).

These are the dangerous, violent forces that are aroused when changes in the structures of oppressive violence are delayed, and when it is believed that the structures can be kept in being through repressive violence.

Conditions for Legitimate Violence

We must not forget the necessary conditions, which I recalled, in line with the church's theology, in my third pastoral letter already quoted. For the violence of insurrection or of defense to be legitimate, it is required: 1) that the violence of legitimate defense not be greater than the unjust aggression (for example, if it is enough to defend oneself with one's fists, then it is not permitted to shoot an aggressor); 2) that one resort to a form of violence, in proportion to the need, only after every other possible peaceful means has been tried; 3) that the violence used in defense not bring in retaliation an even greater evil than that being resisted. In practice it is very difficult to take account of all these theoretical measures for the justification of violence. History has taught us how cruel and painful is the price of blood, and how difficult it is to repair social and economic damage caused by war. This is an opportune moment to recall that celebrated phrase of Pope Pius XII on war: "Nothing is lost by peace, everything may be lost in war." The most reasonable and effective thing for a government to do, therefore, is to use its moral and coercive force not to defend the structural violence of an unjust order, but to guarantee a truly democratic state, one that defends the fundamental rights of all its citizens, based on a just economic order. Only in this way will it be possible to make those instances distant and unreal in which recourse to force, by groups or by individuals, can be justified by the existence of a tyrannical regime and an unjust social order.

The Christian Is Peaceful, but Not Passive

In this atmosphere of violence and of change in the country, how much to the point, and how valuable, have those guidelines become that Medellin expressed: "The Christian is peaceful and not ashamed of it. He is not simply a pacifist for he can fight, but he prefers peace to war. He knows that violent changes in structures would be fallacious, ineffectual in themselves, and not conforming to the dignity of men."[33]

The Apostolate of Companionship

By the apostolate of "companionship" or "following" I understand the personal evangelization of those individual Christians, or groups of Christians, who have made the concrete political option that, they believe in good conscience, represents the historical commitment of their faith. In this sense there are many options, charisms, and callings facing a Christian conscience, and a pastor has to respect, scrutinize, and guide consciences by the light of the Spirit.

In my third pastoral letter I spoke of the proliferation of popular political organizations as a new phenomenon to which the church must respond. We are now confronted, as a logical result of this proliferation, with the particular choices made by Christians and groups of Christians. It is not only that evangelization has a dimension that touches on politics; politicization is reaching out to our Christian communities, which often become standard-bearers for political groups.

I am not speaking of a politicized apostolate but rather of an apostolate that has to guide, in accordance with the gospel, the consciences of Christians within a politicized environment. Political life, like an human activity, needs pastoral guidance. Our situation is made the more difficult when many Christians, in an environment as politicized as the one in this country, choose their political options before finding their identity as Christians.

It is here, in order to respond to the challenge of the entirety of this complex situation, that the church requires a special kind of apostolate, one that I can call an apostolate of "following" or "companionship," one that breaks out of the already well-known molds of the mass apostolate and of the apostolate of small groups. About this Puebla says:

Speaking in general, and without distinguishing between the roles that may be proper to its various members, the Church feels it has a duty and a right to be present in this area of reality. For Christianity is supposed to evangelize the whole of human life, including the political dimension. So the Church criticizes those who would restrict the scope of faith to personal or family life; who would exclude the professional, economic, social, and political orders as if sin, love, prayer, and pardon had no relevance in them. The fact is that the need for the Church's presence in the political arena flows from the very core of the Christian faith. That is to say, it flows from the Lordship of Christ over the whole of life. Christ sets the seal on the definitive brotherhood of humanity, wherein every human being is of equal worth: "All are one in Christ Jesus."[34]

There are several requirements for this apostolate—so urgently needed in our circumstances of political and social crisis—that are essential if it is to be effective. Some of them are:

- A great spirit of prayer and discernment before taking action.
- A great clarity and firmness about the criteria and the values of the gospel and a search for greater knowledge about more uncertain issues, such as the relationship between faith and politics, commitment in faith, commitment in history, Christianity and ideology, violence, and so on.
- A great respect for the diversity of choices and charisms that the one Spirit can give rise to so that human history itself becomes the history of salvation. A great mental and spiritual purity is needed if we are to rid ourselves of personal prejudices against individuals or institutions. I am not talking about pressuring persons to join political organizations, or about pressuring them to leave organizations or to abandon the choices they have made. Rather we want to help them evaluate and question their choices, from the perspective of gospel values. This evaluation and questioning can be about their own personal behavior, about the criteria of the group, about the consequences of their actions, about the very complexity of politics. For politics is much wider and more complicated than can be encompassed by one's personal or a group's options.
- A great spirit of commitment and sacrifice. I realize that this kind of apostolate will entail risks, criticisms, and false accusations. But I believe it is necessary because the times require it.
- A deep sense of hierarchical order and of teamwork. Although encouraging priests in this kind of apostolate, and pledging them

my support and understanding, I beg them, for the honor of our church and the good of the people, never to take it up lightly, or for personal reasons, or by pure chance, letting themselves be dragged into it by the force of events, generously perhaps, but at times ingenuously or imprudently. They should rather associate themselves with an overall plan, in communion with their bishop, so that they can be part of the response of the church and as representatives of the church.

8

Contemporary Religious
Diversity and Change

We close with a discussion of some important current trends
in Latin American religious life. We focus on transformations within
Christianity and other world religions,[1] as well as on new religious movements and the ways in which religion shapes and is shaped by globalization and immigration. Although many of these trends have roots far in
the past, some scholars of contemporary Latin America portray them as
a recent development after centuries of Roman Catholic monopoly. As
the previous chapters have made clear, however, Latin America has always been religiously diverse, from the hundreds of indigenous cultures
that existed prior to the conquest throughout the struggles over orthodoxy and religious hybridity during the colonial period and continuing
to the distinctive religious movements of the post-Independence years.
Thus it would be inaccurate to describe religious diversity as a uniquely
contemporary theme. Still, it is true that today the scope and intensity
of religious diversity have greatly increased due in large part to advances
in electronic media and to transnational immigration, both of which encourage the dissemination and mixing of local and national cultures on
hemispheric and global scales.

"Globalization" has been occurring in different forms for most of
recorded history. People travel and probably have always traveled, for
a host of reasons, including trade, missionary work, forced immigration and exile, military conquest and colonization, and the thrill of
exploration and discovery. As they travel, they often take their religious ideas and practices with them. In addition, as Susanne Rudolph
and James Piscatori have noted, religious institutions themselves have
been among the "oldest transnationals," expanding from their home
bases in order to seek converts or to reach pilgrimage sites, among

other reasons.[2] Today, however, the speed and relative ease with which people, images, ideas, capital, and goods flow within, to, and from the Americas have contributed to a dramatic transformation of the region's religious field. This transformation includes the rise of "pneumatic" or spirit-centered expressions of Christianity like neo-Pentecostalism and charismatic Catholicism, as well as alternative Christian actors, such as Mormons, Seventh-Day Adventists, and Jehovah's Witnesses. Further, religions such as Islam and Buddhism have now a significant presence in the hemisphere, while the so-called New Age religions have experienced rapid growth. We turn to each of these transformative processes to illustrate the changing diversity of religion in Latin America. Several readings in this chapter focus on Brazil, which, due to its size, geography, and history, is probably the most religiously diverse country in Latin America.

Transformations within Christianity

Amid the novelty and diversity within the contemporary religious situation in Latin America, it is important to recall that Christianity remains the dominant tradition by a large majority. That said, the shapes taken by Christianity vary so widely that it is difficult to make generalizations. The traditional popular Catholicism practiced in a small town in Oaxaca, Mexico, for example, may bear very little resemblance to the neo-Pentecostalism of a thriving mega-church in Caracas or Rio de Janeiro. With these caveats in mind, we can point to some continuing and emerging trends that help make sense of contemporary Christianity in Latin America.

Roman Catholicism

The majority of Catholics in most parts of Latin America continue to engage in traditional pastoral and devotional forms, including pilgrimages, prayers, and festivals dedicated to popular saints and especially the Virgin Mary.[3] Especially in areas with large indigenous populations, such as the Andes, Guatemala, and the southern Mexican states of Oaxaca and Chiapas, popular religious beliefs and practices incorporate precolonial elements into an eclectic Catholicism, sometimes including liberationist values alongside very traditional notions. As earlier efforts at Romanization made clear, top-down initiatives and reforms have changed the way religion is lived at the grass-roots level but never succeeded in eliminating popular religious values and practices entirely.

Many folk religious practices, especially those focused on the saints, were criticized by church leaders in the wake of Vatican II. Both liberationists and conservatives sought to reduce the prominence of the saints and Mary as objects of devotion, or at least to "purify" devotional practices, purging them of what they saw as their superstitious elements, while making the faith more Christ centered. These reforms have not eliminated popular devotional practices, but they have generated a number of new pastoral programs within the church. Among the most important of these is the Catholic Charismatic Renewal (CCR), a lay-oriented movement that emerged in 1967 among university students in the United States intent on revitalizing their faith in the midst of an increasingly secular environment. The movement lost some of its impetus in the United States toward the end of the 1970s, but it has grown in Latin America since its introduction in the early 1970s by Holy Cross, Maryknoll, and Jesuit missionaries.[4] The CCR received a boost in the wake of CELAM's 1992 meeting in Santo Domingo. At the meeting, the bishops, encouraged by Pope John Paul II, launched a broad campaign called the New Evangelization (*nueva evangelización*). According to its architects, the New Evangelization represents a "call to conversion" for all Catholics, especially "baptized men and women whose Christianity is devoid of vitality."[5]

Some observers believe that the CCR competes with CEBs and other progressive Catholic programs, which were also designed to increase lay participation. Unlike the CEBs, which often sought to democratize church leadership and decision-making processes, the CCR does not challenge the authority of the clergy or the institutional character of the church. Nor does it seek to transform social and political structures. Like traditional popular Catholicism, the CCR is more concerned with personal salvation and spiritual and moral renewal.[6]

The CCR shares with Pentecostalism an emphasis on an intimate and intense relation with God through the works of the Holy Spirit. Catholic Charismatics are often ambivalent about the cult of the saints, but they unequivocally reaffirm clerical authority and the centrality of the Virgin Mary. This reaffirmation allows them to enjoy the ecstatic dimensions of spirit-filled Christianity within the safe and centralizing structures of the universal church. While this dynamic balance between antistructure and structure is creative, it also poses challenges to local parishes, which often have to reconcile the modus operandi of a global lay movement like the CCR and the traditional ways of being Catholic.

The New Evangelization and the CCR are conservative in many respects. However, these programs are not simple throwbacks to the preconciliar church, in which the priest conducted mass as a private matter between himself and God (speaking in Latin, with his back to the congregation). Charismatic Christianity is itself a modern hybrid phenomenon, combining the more participatory, informal, and biblically oriented emphases of postconciliar Catholic reforms with the savvy use of mass media and a renewed emphasis on centralized authority and obedience to the hierarchy. It reflects an effort by church leaders to strengthen institutional interests while updating pastoral and liturgical approaches. Using a rational-choice approach to religion, R. Andrew Chesnut argues that the Charismatic Renewal is a creative response by religious producers, in this case the Catholic clergy, to create and disseminate an attractive religious good within a pluralistic "religious economy." Since the Catholic Church can no longer rely on its religious monopoly, it must now sell its products to a costumer base that has greater access to a myriad of options. One of the most cost-effective ways to innovate and craft attractive products is to imitate its most successful competitors, namely, Pentecostals. More specifically, the CCR adopts a "virgophilic" pneumocentrism, which makes all the gifts of the Holy Spirit accessible, particularly divine healing, a practice of enormous significance to many Latin Americans with no access to medical care. At the same time, by maintaining the central place the Virgin Mary occupies in Catholicism, the CCR guarantees continuity within change for those not ready to abandon the religion of their parents or the dominant national religion.

Catholicism in Latin America today faces not only pastoral challenges but also a host of cultural, economic, and political events that affect both religious institutions and the lives of believers. Racism and cultural diversity are among the issues that the Catholic Church has addressed in recent years, as evidenced in John Paul's messages to indigenous and African peoples at CELAM's 1992 conference in Santo Domingo, reproduced below. John Paul speaks more openly than past popes about the contributions that indigenous and African people have made to Latin American Catholicism and about the wrongs they have suffered at the hands of some Catholic officials in the past. Ironically, perhaps, Catholic leaders today sometimes criticize evangelical Protestant missionaries for insensitivity to indigenous cultural traditions—evidence, perhaps, that the

Roman Church has learned from its often tragic relations with the native peoples of the Americas.

Another important element of the Catholic dialogue with contemporary Latin American societies has been the church's increasing attention to environmental problems. Catholic intellectuals and activists, including liberation theologians such as Leonardo Boff, have been at the forefront of religious discussions of issues such as deforestation in Latin America. Environmental concerns have been incorporated into a broader Catholic humanist position, which contends that God created all of nature in order to serve human dignity and the common good, not individual profit. This assertion of the social purpose of created goods suggests a strong connection between environmental and social problems. For example, a pastoral letter issued in December 2000 by the Apostolic Vicariate of Petén, Guatemala, titled *El grito de la selva en el año jubilar: Entre la agonía y esperanza* (The Cry of the Forest in the Jubilee Year: Between Agony and Hope) asserts, "It is not possible to speak of ecology without taking justice into account. It is not possible to defend the conservation of the forest apart from the advancement and life of the poor."[7] Excessive consumption by some harms both poor people and the natural world; the solution will entail both more restraint in human use of natural resources and a better distribution of the goods they make possible.

Another contemporary issue to which the Catholic Church has responded is immigration, in particular from Latin America to the United States. In 2000, the U.S. Catholic Bishops' Conference published a pastoral letter on immigration entitled "Welcoming the Stranger among Us," with the overarching theme of "unity in diversity." The bishops asserted both their solidarity with immigrants and the pastoral demand to integrate diverse groups: "We reject the anti-immigrant stance that has become popular in different parts of our country, and the nativism, ethnocentricity, and racism that continue to reassert themselves in our communities. We are challenged to get beyond ethnic communities living side by side within our own parishes without any connection to each other."[8]

Three years after publishing "Welcoming the Stranger," the U.S. bishops joined with the Mexican bishops' conference to write a historic joint pastoral letter on immigration, entitled "Strangers No Longer." In it, the bishops insist upon long-standing Catholic social principles, including the inviolable dignity of all human beings: "Regardless of their legal status, migrants, like all persons, possess inherent human dignity that should be respected. Often they are subject to punitive laws and harsh treatment from enforcement officers from both receiving and transit countries. Government policies that respect the basic human rights of the undocumented are necessary."[9] The letter also advocates not only social services and humane treatment of all immigrants but also legalization of undocumented migrants.

As the shifts between the two pastoral letters suggest, the Catholic Church has grown more assertive as immigration has become a more controversial issue in U.S. politics. Cardinal Roger Mahony of Los Angeles made headlines when he directed parishes in his diocese, the largest in the United States, to defy a new mandate to check people's immigration status before providing social services. In a December 30, 2005, letter to President George W. Bush, Mahony wrote, "Our golden rule has always been to serve people in need—not to verify beforehand their immigration status. . . . Speaking for the Catholic Archdiocese of Los Angeles, such restrictions are impossible to comply with."[10] While he was attacked harshly by opponents of unauthorized immigration, Mahony's sympathy for immigrants makes good sense in light of the long-standing Catholic emphasis on the well-being of the "least well off" in a given society. Some observers have pointed out, further, that the fastest-growing sector of U.S. Catholics is Hispanic, which may enter into church leaders' attitudes about immigration as well. This is not a new phenomenon, since immigrant groups, including Italians, Irish, and Germans, have long constituted a significant proportion of U.S. Catholics.

Presently, almost 70 percent of U.S. Latinos are Catholic, and, perhaps more significantly, around a third of all U.S. Catholics are Latino. A May 2007 study by the Pew Forum "projects that the Latino share will continue climbing for decades. This demographic reality, combined with the distinctive characteristics of Latino Catholicism, ensures that Latinos will bring about important changes in the nation's largest religious institution." The study also found that a much larger proportion of Latino Catholics are charismatic, in contrast to an eighth of non-Hispanic Catholics.[11] Both the sheer number of Latinos in the U.S. church and the kind of religiosity they practice have an enormous impact on virtually every aspect of Catholic life.

Scholarship on postconciliar Catholicism, especially in Latin America, often focuses on change and conflict. It is important to note, however, that continuity can be as strong as innovation. Even movements as apparently radical as liberation theology rest on the foundational principles of Catholic social thought. These principles remain at the forefront of the church's response to contemporary social issues, including immigration and environmental problems. Similarly, current pastoral programs, including the Charismatic Renewal, may appear to depart significantly from progressive initiatives of the 1970s and 1980s, but they have much in common, both in their social principles and in their organizational form. Without downplaying the important and often dramatic innovations that followed Vatican II and the Medellín conference, it is important to place these events in the context of Catholicism's larger history, in Latin America and beyond.

Evangelical Protestantism and Pentecostalism

Protestantism, like Catholicism, has undergone many changes in Latin American in the past decade or two. As we saw in chapter 6, evangelical and Pentecostal Protestantism experienced years of rapid growth between the 1950s and 1980s, leading to heady expectations and to the possibility, as David Stoll posed it, that Latin America was "turning Protestant." Some observers predicted that at least one Latin American country—probably Guatemala—would be majority Protestant by the year 2000, or thereabouts.[12] However, Protestant growth turned out to be more complex than some of the early accounts acknowledged. First, as Stoll himself pointed out, Protestant churches turned out to have back doors as well as front doors, and not every convert remained a permanent member of the congregation.[13] This point was fleshed out by studies showing that by the mid-1990s many new members were increasingly coming from other Protestant churches, and not just from the pool of "nominal Catholics" that had provided the main source of Protestant converts in earlier years. Moreover, with the push for a new evangelization in the 1990s, the Catholic Church began to invest more resources in retaining parishioners.

This is not to suggest that Protestant growth has ended. In Brazil, for example, the census shows that the Protestant population doubled from 1990 to 2000, going from thirteen to twenty-six million. By 2000, Protestants represented 15.4 percent of the country's total population (up from 9 percent in 1990). Figures such as these attest to the fact that Protestantism will continue to be a significant religious, cultural, and political force in Latin America, as Catholic hegemony gradually declines.

Not only the numbers but also the character of Latin American Protestantism underwent revision during this period. The proportion of Protestants from mainline churches such as the Methodists, Lutherans, and

Presbyterians continued to decline, while Pentecostalism established itself as the dominant stream, constituting between 70 and 80 percent of the Protestant population, depending on the country. In the last two decades, a particular variety, "neo-Pentecostalism," has become dominant. Neo-Pentecostalism builds on the original Pentecostal Protestantism that emerged in the early twentieth century, adding distinctive practices, organizational forms, and ideologies. Neo-Pentecostal groups, such as the Universal Church of the Kingdom of God (UCKG), which is the focus of anthropologist Eric Kramer's piece reprinted below, share the traditional Pentecostal emphasis on the Holy Spirit, but they stress divine healing and exorcism rather than glossolalia as the key signs of justification in the Spirit. This stress is based on a "health and wealth gospel" or a "prosperity theology" that holds that the world is a stage for a spiritual warfare between God and the devil, who seeks to capture and harm souls. Neo-Pentecostal churches seek to liberate Christians from spiritual bondage via dramatic group exorcisms. The demons exorcized are often the spirits of Umbanda and Candomblé, reflecting the hybrid character of Brazilian neo-Pentecostalism.

While the reasons for the growing appeal of neo-Pentecostalism are many, socioeconomic transformations from the mid-1980s on have undoubtedly played a key role. Following almost two decades of military dictatorships, many Latin American countries not only moved to civilian democratic rule but also implemented wide-ranging changes in their economies. Chief among these changes have been the downsizing of the welfare state, the elimination of trade barriers, and the creation of incentives for foreign investment. These reforms have generally resulted in a widening of income disparities and a worsening of life conditions for poor and working-class people. With the safety net of the welfare state weakened, many poor people have turned to churches as self-help networks. Neo-Pentecostal churches that offer the hope of success, together with the visible fruits of spiritual and physical healing, are particularly compelling in this context. Thus, it is not surprising that churches such as the UCKG have poorer congregants even than most Pentecostal churches.[14] Its appeal to a large social group has helped the UCKG grow from its modest beginnings in Rio de Janeiro in 1977 into a truly transnational enterprise, with churches throughout Latin America, the United States, Europe, Japan, and South Africa.

Because the Protestant field in Latin America is so complex and fluid, it is hard to predict its future configuration. As the UCKG indicates, however, there is a tendency towards globalization, as countries like Brazil energize a new postcolonial Christianity. In globalizing Latin American Protestantism, mass media and immigration will probably play a crucial role. Finally, as the religious market becomes saturated and evangelical churches begin to draw faithful not just from Catholicism but from each other, some Pentecostal leaders have radicalized their claims in order to distinguish themselves from other groups. One dramatic example is the newly established Miami-based International Ministry Growing in Grace, which has sent missionaries and established branches throughout Latin America. Its founder and head pastor, Puerto Rican Jose Luis De Jesus Miranda, claims to be simultaneously "Jesus-man" and the Anti-Christ. This claim is possible because the IMGC holds that the end of time is already here and that De Jesus Miranda is here to form the government of God. All other Christian churches are dismissed as false.

Alternative Christianities

The International Ministry Growing in Grace brings us to other alternative forms of Christianity that have a longer trajectory in Latin America and are now experiencing substantial growth. Such is the case with Jehovah's Witnesses, Seventh-Day Adventists, and the Mormons, or Church of Latter-Day Saints (LDS), all of which emerged in the nineteenth century in the United States. Catholics in Latin American tend to lump these new Christian groups together with evangelical Protestants under the umbrella terms *"evangélicos"* in Spanish and *"crentes"* in Portuguese. Often, Catholic pastoral agents use the more derogatory term *"sectas"* (*"seitas"* in Portuguese) to characterize Pentecostals and other aggressively proselytizing forms of Christianity.

One of the most successful new Christian movements in Latin America is the Church of Latter-Day Saints (Mormons).[15] According to church-provided figures, Mormon numbers in Latin America have grown from seven hundred thousand in 1980 to 4.5 million in 2004. Presently, Latin America accounts for about 37 percent of church membership, with that number expected to grow to 50 percent by 2020.[16] While these figures may be inflated, they show the increasing prominence in Latin America of an organization that is basically run by Americans. Part of the church's success comes from its intense mission program. All young Mormon men spend two years as missionaries, either in the United States or abroad. Young Mormon missionaries, usually wearing white shirts and ties and carrying briefcases, are a familiar sight in many Latin American cities and even small towns, and the church has found resources and converts to build large temples in a number of Latin American cities. The largest Mormon populations in the world, after the United States, can be found in Mexico, Brazil, and Chile, and the largest Mormon temple outside the United States is in Mexico City, while the largest one outside North America is in Guayaquil, Ecuador.[17]

Doctrinally, the LDS contains elements that may explain its wide appeal in Latin America. Its emphasis on the extended family dovetails with Latin American culture. Particularly, the care for the ancestors (as manifested in their baptism) resonates with indigenous traditions. However, the appeal to indigenous populations goes beyond the focus on family across generations to the Mormon narratives that map sacred history onto the Americas, placing Jesus Christ on the continent and making indigenous people a lost Israelite tribe. Finally, the figure of the young, clean, almost always white Mormon missionary may signify for urban middle classes in Latin America individualistic self-reliance and progress that do not sacrifice community or tradition.

While the Mormons have experienced tremendous success, they also face obstacles and failures. The history of missionaries Gary and Gordon Shepherd, reproduced below, reveals both the guiding religious principles and the mundane frustrations and triumphs faced by many missionaries, especially those from smaller or nontraditional religious groups.

Beyond Christianity: Other "World" Religions

The religious arena in Latin America today encompasses far more than Christianity in its various manifestations. World religions such as Buddhism have gained new prominence, particularly among the urban middle classes as part of what Brazilian anthropologist Cristina Rocha calls the quest for "a cosmopolitan modernity." Other world religions, such as Islam, have become more visible in the wake of September 11, 2001.

Buddhism in Brazil is present in many forms, from the *Soto Zen* to Pure Land and the so-called Japanese new religious movements, such as *Soka Gakkai, Seicho-no-ie,* and Perfect Liberty Kyodan. Here we focus on Zen Buddhism, which has received the most in-depth scholarly attention. Zen made its way to Brazil in the early 1900s, as Japanese immigrants began to arrive in large numbers to Brazil, fleeing economic upheavals during the Meiji government (1868-1912) and unable to travel to the United States because of growing anti-Asian sentiments.[18] Anxious to relieve labor shortages generated by the coffee boom (1850-1930) and to whiten its postindependence population, the Brazilian government contracted with Japan for a large number of laborers. Japanese immigrants tended to settle in the southern states of São Paulo and Paraná, where they formed *colônias* (communities) along the railroad lines that connected coffee plantations. Eventually, many immigrants moved to major cities like São Paulo and Curitiba or to other rural settlements to escape the harsh conditions on the coffee plantations. While many of the Japanese immigrants converted to Catholicism, others maintained their Shinto and Buddhist traditions. Although the Japanese government forbade Buddhist and Shinto priests from traveling with the immigrants, as a way to promote assimilation and avoid the anti-Japanese backlash taking place in the United States, the first temples and shrines were erected as early as the 1920s.

Today, Zen has gained popularity among non-Japanese Brazilians, particularly among the urban, college-educated middle and upper classes, who associate images of success, progress, intelligence, and self-improvement with Japan and the Japanese. This positive Orientalism has facilitated the recovery among Japanese-Brazilians of their ancestral culture, with many "converting" back from Catholicism to Buddhism. Although only a small percentage of Brazilians are Buddhists, Cristina Rocha argues in the article excerpted in this chapter that Buddhism has become a key ingredient, along with Spiritism and Theosophy,[19] of the alternative spiritualities of a growing percentage of Brazilians who lack an institutional religious affiliation.[20] Within the fluid space of alternative spiritualities, Zen has interacted with new Japanese religious movements, such as *Seicho-no-ie*, which are themselves hybrids of Shinto, Buddhism, and Christianity.[21] Moreover, because Japanese Brazilians "allowed a Brazilian Catholic lexicon to be superimposed on their Japanese cultural grammar . . . [in order] to maintain their identity in the new country," there has been a high degree of cross-fertilization between Catholicism and Buddhism. This process of multidirectional "creolization of Buddhism" has increasingly blurred the lines between "ethnics" and "converts," between what is authentically "Japanese" and what is authentically "Brazilian."

The issue of multiple religious and cultural identities is raised in anthropologist Paulo Pinto's article, excepted below, on the various ways of being Muslim in Brazil. Chapter 4 explored the deep historical roots of Islam in the country, going back to the Malês in the colonial period. Here Pinto deals with Muslim communities that have emerged as a result of the migration from the Middle East, particularly from Lebanon, Syria, and Palestine, that took place beginning in the 1880s, during the rubber boom in the Amazon region. Syrians and Lebanese, in particular, quickly became very successful entrepreneurs in the regional urban centers of Belém and Manaus.[22] Following the end of the rubber boom, they migrated to São Paulo, Rio de Janeiro, and Curitiba. There they became very successful in the areas of retail and textile production.

According to the 2000 census, there are 18,592 self-declared Muslims in Brazil. Although a small community, the Muslim population represents an instructive case study of the pressures faced by local religious groups in Latin America in the context of globalization. Especially since 9-11, being a Muslim in Brazil involves a complex negotiation of not only the pluralistic national religious field but also the images, narratives, and practices that circulate across the global Ummah (the community of believers) and the non-Muslim media. Whether a Muslim community in Brazil constitutes itself as a "religio-ethnic enclave" or as a transnational sectarian Shi'ite or Sunni group or as a part of a pan-Islamic diasporic community will depend on factors such as the nationality of the members, the training received by the community's imam, the financial and ideational resources available, and the context of reception in the larger society.

Regrettably, lack of space makes it impossible to include readings or to engage in a more extended treatment of other world religions, such as Judaism and Hinduism, which have also contributed to the vitality and diversity of the contemporary religious field in Latin America. Hinduism, for example, has a strong presence in the Caribbean, particularly in Trinidad and Tobago, Suriname, and Guyana, as a result of the importation of more than half a million indentured servants from India after the abolition of slavery (from the late 1830s to 1917). Today, Indo-Caribbean identities in these islands are being redefined through contact with transnational organizations such the Rashtriya Swayamsevak Sangh (RSS), which seek to construct a pure Hinduism with support from the diaspora.[23] In terms of Judaism, there are large Jewish communities in Argentina (at 230,000 members, it is the third-largest Jewish community in the Americas, behind the United States and Canada), Brazil, Mexico, Chile, Uruguay, and Cuba, which have created numerous synagogues, schools, and mutual-aid associations. In Buenos Aires, for instance, there are fifty conservative synagogues, five orthodox, and one reform.[24]

Alternative Spiritualities

Our discussion of Buddhism, Japanese religious movements, Islam, and Hinduism leads us to the category of alternative spiritualities, which have gained popularity among urban, well-educated upper-middle classes in Latin America. As Robert Carpenter explains,

> Alternative spiritualities encompass a diversified constellation of teachings and practices that address metaphysical, therapeutic, psychological, and/ or ecological concerns. In addition, they include various divinatory techniques, such as different astrological, Tarot, and cabalistic systems, the I Ching, and Scandinavian runes. Specifically in Brazil, the category also includes a loose-knit array of expressions, both imported and local in origin, derived from Hinduism, Buddhism, Islam, Japanese New Religions, as well as Theosophy and other occult, metaphysical, and Oriental traditions.[25]

To make sense of the category of alternative spiritualities, Brazilian anthropologist Luiz Eduardo Soares suggests that all these religious expressions reflect a paradoxical joining of "a vague and pervasive 'hedonist narcissism'" with a cosmopolitan "mystico-ecological" holism that seeks to connect humans with nature and to establish harmony in the cosmos. This characterization of alternative spiritualities reinforces some current theories of globalization. Rapid advances in communication and transportation technologies have brought the world together, leading to a sense of growing interconnectedness. Simultaneously, these changes destabilized local traditions and identities, producing a widespread need to affirm selfhood.

The same changes in the 1980s and 1990s that worsened life conditions for many of the poor people who joined neo-Pentecostal churches also affected Latin American urban elites, albeit in different ways. The end of military dictatorships and the establishment of civilian governments generated great expectations among the urban middle classes. Many thought that the region was finally on a path to peaceful development. However, the disorderly transitions to democracy and economic chaos that ensued dashed these hopes. Instead of joining the First World, urban middle classes now face a reality that, while no longer defined by open civil wars, is dominated by everyday violence, as exemplified by chronic high levels of crime and corruption. The cosmopolitan "mystico-ecological holism" of alternative spiritualities responds to unfulfilled expectations of well-being, stability, security, and real connection with the cultures of advanced Western democracies. On the one hand, alternative spiritualities allow Latin American urban elites to break with the Western modernity that has betrayed them by appealing to Eastern traditions or a return to nature. Both of these appeals are meant to offer a simpler, more intense, authentic, and harmonious life that stands in contrast with the consumerism, rational instrumentalism, and acquisitiveness of modern existence. On the other hand, the break from shallow materialism is made possible precisely by tapping into hypermodernity, by using the latest communication and transportation technologies to find bits and pieces of Eastern and native religions that can be fused and fashioned into alternative spiritualities.

Perhaps nothing illustrates modernity's hopes and shortcomings better than the city of Brasilia, founded in 1960 as a utopian modernist dream, symbolizing Brazil as the country of the future, of a new age (*a nova era*). Designed according to architectural modernism's penchant for symmetry and order—the core of the city is arranged in the shape of an airplane— and located on the highlands in central Brazil, near what many consider the heart of the planet (in the city of Alto Paraiso), Brasilia has attracted a multiplicity of "mystico-esoteric" groups such as Vale do Amanhecer (Valley of the Dawn), Cidade Eclética (Eclectic City), Cidade da Fraternidade (City of Fraternity), and Cavaleiros de Maitreya (The Knights of Maitreya). Today, the city suffers from many of the same socioeconomic problems that plague other large urban centers in the region.[26]

This tension between Western hypermodernity and Eastern or Native American "premodernity" (as imagined by global media) is also central to the emergence of ayahuasca religions, which make use of a sacred ayahuasca drink, such as Santo Daime, described by Scottish-Brazilian anthropologist Edward MacRae in the excerpt below. Santo Daime represents a creative reworking of indigenous shamanic practices and beliefs. Shamanic rituals often involve the use of psychoactive agents that aid the shaman in traveling across time and space to communicate with the ancestral spirits, often for the purpose of healing. For generations, ayahuasca, a drink made of the mixture of the *Banisteriopsis caapi* plant, commonly known as cipo or mariri, and the leaf *Psychotria viridis* (aka chacrona), has been part of sacred shamanic rituals among indigenous people of the Western Amazon region, which includes parts of Peru, Ecuador, Bolivia, and Brazil.[27] There, this brew has been consumed to facilitate contact with ancestors, to give courage, and to alter perceptions and encourage visions.[28]

Indigenous and mestizo knowledge of ayahuasca was transmitted to outsiders via rubber tappers who used the drink to help them deal with the harsh conditions in which they worked. One of these rubber tappers was Raimundo Ireneu Serra, a Brazilian of African descent who founded Santo Daime in 1930. Mestre Ireneu, as he is known to followers, understood the shamanic rituals, beliefs, and visions connected to ayahuasca through the lenses of his folk Catholicism. The name "Daime" comes from Mestre Ireneu's invocations ("dai-me luz," give me light, "Dai-me forca," give me strength) to the saint to give him revelations. The invocations involve chanting and dancing until the devotee attains *mirações* (astral visions), as in indigenous shamanic rituals. Ireneu also added elements of Kardecism and African-based religions to his teaching, making Santo Daime "a form of naturalized Catholicism/Spiritism/Umbanda."[29]

Ireneu's community, Alto Santo, suffered a series of "dissensions" that led to the foundation of other ayahuasca religions such as Barquinha (translated literally "little boat") in 1945 and União do Vegetal (Union of the Vegetable) in the 1960s. However, one of his followers, Sebastião Mota de Mello, better known as Padrinho Sebastião, continued the line developed by Mestre Ireneu, funding a new community, Colônia 5000, near Rio Branco, also in the Amazon region. MacRae's piece focuses on the main rituals of this current of ayahuasca religion.

As successive Brazilian military regimes (1964-1978) pushed aggressively to open the Amazonian frontier, ayahuasca religion moved to the large cities of southeastern Brazil. Many urban, affluent young Brazilians involved in the counterculture movement of the 1960s and 1970s and seeking to escape the repressive climate under the military regimes flocked to *ayahuasqueiro* utopian *colônias* that were emerging in Rio de Janeiro and Minas Gerais. Today, ayahuasca is used by ten thousand Brazilians, a small number that belies the influence of this religion, since its cosmopolitan adherents have taken the movement to Europe, Japan, and the United States.[30] The transnational flows pose a difficult challenge to Daimistas, since, as MacRae shows, preparation of the sacred brew requires conditions that may not be replicable outside of Brazil.

The romantic primitivism of neo-shamanism, the longing to return to nature, and the thirst for primal experiences that transcend modernity's broken promises of order and progress bring us back to indigenous religions, with which we started our account of the complex and diverse Latin American religious field. As Buddhism, alternative spiritualities, and even neo-Pentecostalism show, cross-fertilization and the simultaneous desire to impose orthodoxy continue to be the hallmark of Latin American religions. What has changed today is that global media and transnational migration allow for more widespread and intense disembedding of religious symbols, beliefs, and practices from their original local or native sources and for ever more creative recombinations of these religious fragments into new religions.[31]

CHAPTER 8 DOCUMENTS

"Descarrego"[1] ERIC W. KRAMER

At the major temple of the Universal Church in Rio de Janeiro on any Tuesday morning, hundreds of people gather for the 11:30 a.m. healing service. Tuesdays, likely the most popular day in the calendar of Universal Church services, have long been devoted to curing rituals such as prayer chains and the resolution of health problems. Now, three times a day in the 10,000-seat Temple to the Glory of New Israel, bishops administer the *sessão de descarrego* (see Braga, 2001). By its name alone the service frames healing interventions in terms of spiritual warfare. *Descarrego*, literally a "discharge" or "unloading," signals a world of spiritual affliction and intervention connected with Brazil's mediumic religions.[2] The bishop and the three assistants who administer the service dress in white uniforms, a sartorial wink at "white line" Umbanda and Kardecist mediums, as well as biomedical health care providers.

Congruent with the name change for Tuesday's service, the church has modified the terms for spiritual affliction. Pastors who used to talk about evil spirits as the cause of demon possession and related afflictions now speak of *encostos*. As does *descarrego*, this term points to a particular shared religious lexicon. Brazilians understand an *encosto* as a spirit, perhaps that of a deceased relative, that interferes with the life of the person whom it haunts (Maggie, 2001: 143). One advantage of this cultural reference from a marketing standpoint is that it distinguishes Universal Church discourse from "evangelical" speech in general.[3] In its typical fashion, the church modifies the discursive and symbolic features of other religious discourses as means of establishing meaningful forms of "passage" between them and Pentecostalism (Birman, 1996). In this new voicing, the sense of *encosto* changes as its field of reference is extended to include all manner of spirits from Afro-Brazilian religions.

Structurally, *descarrego* resembles other services of the Universal Church. It opens with hymns, and then the pastor in charge offers a biblical reading that has a direct connection to the campaign of the week before moving on to the strong prayer or ritual action that the particular service offers. Interspersed throughout the service are more hymns, calls for tithes, offerings, and sacrifices, distributions of consecrated items, and announcements of upcoming events such as the campaign finale on Sunday (typically, the occasion when people deliver and ritually offer the "sacrifice" they have pledged weeks in advance). The vast majority of the people attending any service do not "manifest" spirits when the pastor invokes them "in the name of Jesus." In fact, the pastor presents the danger of demonic possession as largely invisible, inferred from symptoms of poverty, illness, domestic problems, and so on. The ritual work of freeing the congregation from evil influence occupies the first half of the service, leaving the remaining time for the treatment of the few individuals who actively manifest spirits.

At the session I attended in July 2002, Bishop Romualdo spent the first 30 minutes on a biblical topic linked to the current week's campaign: the story of Elijah and his showdown with the prophets of Baal on Mt. Carmel to determine the true God of Israel. Pacing the floor in front of the stage, he argued that people would only change their lives and situation by faith in the "God of Elijah." Behind him, on the stage beside the massive wooden lectern, was a replica of the sacrificial pyre that Yahweh lit in response to Elijah's prayers. As in other services, the sermon featured a simplified reading of biblical narrative with occasional brief skits for comic relief. In one example, the bishop commanded his assistants to act like the Baal worshipers who called out in vain before their false God— the exact behavior of most Brazilians, he asserted.

[. . . .]

Next came a hymn that established a highly emotional searching tone for the *sacudimento,* or "shaking up," of the evil forces to be expelled. At the bishop's request, we opened our hearts and closed our eyes, "making the hymn our prayer." Pausing after each short imperative phrase, he prayed as one desperately seeking for a response. Standing with our eyes closed, we followed his instructions and repeated his phrases:

> If you want to be saved from this situation, Say this: God of Elijah, Save me now. Say: I can't take it anymore. I fear I have been a victim of the worst. But I'm here. Say: Who would have guessed that one day I could be inside this church that once even I spoke badly of but today I'm here. . . . If someone did Sorcery, Witchcraft, against me, oh, my God, Deliver me now, Free me now. If there is evil in my life, Let that evil go away. . . .

The prayer, rephrased, went on to target different categories of people with specific problems: married women, married men, business people, and those with relationship difficulties.

In the second phase of the ritual, the bishop shifted his address to the forces of evil hidden in the congregation. He prefaced this by quoting Jesus ("in my name, they will expel demons") and explaining what he was doing for newcomers. His tone of voice then changed to a more commanding register as he started ordering and "allowing" the *encostos* to appear: "You can come out, *encosto*. You can come out. The *encosto* who's in that man, who's in the marriage of that woman. The *encosto* who doesn't let that man be happy. You can come out."

Gradually, he began to name the *encostos*, identifying each with the specific affliction it caused and its social origin:

> That's right, come out. . . . . The spirit of darkness whose name is Pombagira. With the name of Maria Padilha and who is in the marriage of that woman[. . . .] The spell [*trabalho*] that was done to separate the couple. A lover performed sorcery with a piece of that man's underwear. The lover put his name in the cemetery[. . . .] You can come out, Pombagira.

The bishop's amplified discourse rose in volume and intensity above the clamor of individual voices naming afflictions and calling on God to reprehend their sources. He continued along these lines, naming more afflictions as, one by one, more people in the congregation manifested spirits. Workers took any sign of individual physical disturbance in the congregation to be a demon manifesting itself and rushed to attend to that person. (Visible possessions that required public interrogation and exorcism were limited to 4 women among the 900 or so people in attendance.)

Taking a break from calling on spirits to manifest themselves, the bishop returned to the collective prayer. Invoking God, we repeated a series of first person commands ordering evil to go out of our lives, bodies, souls, homes, paths, and minds. Then he asked us to place our consecrated hands on our neighbors' shoulders. In the name of Jesus we demanded that all evil leave us and that any *encosto* make its presence known. He then returned to summoning the spirits a bit longer and eventually handed over the microphone to his assistant. This exorcist called out in greater detail the names of spirits and the occult magic of possession. . . .

Alternation between appellation of demons and the repetition of collective prayer continued in a spiraling crescendo. We repeated once more a first person prayer that asked God to consecrate our hands. Placing our hands on our heads, three times we commanded all *encostos* acting in our lives to get out "in the name of Jesus," throwing our hands into the air with a shout of "Sai!" (Out!). The collective exorcism ended, and our attention shifted to the resistant cases of individual possession. We sang a celebratory hymn that spoke about the power of Jesus' name to drive away sickness and *encostos*. On each refrain we swept our hands back over our heads in a gesture of expulsion. Once more the music ended and the bishop took advantage of the moment of calm to return to some earlier themes. As if he were presenting a case study, he announced the presence of four possessed women before the congregation: "We're going to ask these encostos what they're doing to these women's lives. I repeat: maybe you've never manifested anything like they have, but that doesn't mean to say that you don't have the same thing they have in their lives." He reiterated the symptoms of spiritual problems that *encostos* caused, whether they manifested themselves or not. The only solution, he said, was to give oneself totally to God and to make one's faith evident as sacrifice:

> Blessed is he who believes. To believe is to surrender, and this belief can't just stay in theory. You have to do much more than simply believe in God. . . . That's where sacrifice enters, because sacrifice distinguishes the faith of the person. . . . Sacrifice indicates the quality of faith that the person has. Amen, people? So, if you want to change your situation, you have to be prepared to do what? To sacrifice.

The bishop now turned to interrogate the *encosto*. When asked its name, the rebellious spirit replied, "Lucifer." Bishop Romualdo began ordering the *encosto* to stand up, kneel, and throw back its head. Grabbing hold of the possessed woman's hair, he forced the spirit to turn around to show the congregation its "claws," the visible sign of an incorporation. (The names, the posture, and the clawlike hands of the possessing spirits clearly identify them with Afro-Brazilian religions, Umbanda in particular.) He then demanded to know what the spirit was doing to her. The *encosto* replied and said she had cancer. As yet another proof of his power over the spirit, the bishop now told us that, on his command, the woman would return to her normal state. A few more questions to the *encosto* revealed that the spirit had put a cancer in her uterus and that it was preventing her from having a relationship with a divorced man. The bishop ordered the spirit to return to its original state. The woman came out of the trance with no memory of her possession. Romualdo noted her physical transformation and asked her a series of questions to check her knowledge against what the *encosto* had said. Her testimony confirmed tangentially the things that the spirit had confessed under interrogation: that she had lower abdominal pain and that the ex-wife of her boyfriend was causing problems. Upon this, the bishop looked up and rhetorically addressed the congregation: "Pretty clear, isn't it?" He then told the woman what the *encosto* had said and counseled her to see a doctor, to follow the medical recommendations and do all the tests, but also to put her faith in God.

Next, he forced the spirit to return and again asked its name and what it was doing. Having finally identified the spirit as Exú Caveira, he then invited us to assist him in the final push to exorcise the *exú*. After a lengthy struggle, repeatedly ordering the spirit to expel the illness, the pastor called on us to extend our hands. Once more the auditorium filled with the sound of hundreds of people shouting, "Burn!" "Burn!" "Burn!" and then "Out!" On that triumph, we applauded and thanked Jesus. After a few announcements and reminders, the service came to a close.

REFERENCES

Birman, Patricia. 1996. "Cultos de Possessão e Pentecostalismo no Brasil: passagens." *Religião e Sociedade* 17 (1-2): 90-109.
Braga, Elcio. 2001. "Entre o terreiro e o altar." *O Dia*, August 6.
Maggie, Yvonne. 2001. *Guerra de Orixá: Um estudo de ritual e conflito*. Rio de Janeiro: Jorge Zahar.

Mormon Passage: A Missionary Chronicle[4]

GARY AND GORDON SHEPHERD

Language Training Mission Regulations

1. *SPEAKING YOUR MISSION LANGUAGE.* During the three months you are in the Language Training Mission you will be expected to make English inoperative and to practice your mission language at all times.

2. *DEPORTMENT.* You are under mission regulations and your deportment in every aspect should be that of a missionary who has been set apart. You should avoid assiduously all pranks, practical jokes, loud laughter, and improper manners.

3. *CLOTHING.* As Elders and Lady Missionaries, you should dress in accordance with the position you now hold. When leaving quarters, Elders should always wear a coat, tie, and suit. Lady Missionaries need not wear heels but they should always wear hose.

4. *COMPANIONS.* You must *always* stay with your companion. Pray with your companion and learn to love him or her and to work as a team.

5. *CORRESPONDENCE.* Write to parents once a week. Write to girlfriends (or boyfriends) only occasionally.

6. *TELEPHONE CALLS.* Calls to or from relatives should be limited to emergency cases only.

7. *TRAVEL.* Do not ask permission to leave Provo unless it is an emergency case involving members of your immediate family. Missionaries must have permission from the President of the Language Training Mission to operate a motor vehicle.

8. *VISITORS AT THE LANGUAGE TRAINING MISSION.* Members of your family and your friends should realize that you are on a mission and should not visit you. You should not accept invitations to dinner with parents or friends.

9. *GIRLFRIENDS OR BOYFRIENDS.* In no case should they come to your quarters or should you go to theirs. Do not plan to meet with them on campus, at church, downtown, or any other place. You should avoid excessive letter writing or any communication which would tend to distract you from your primary objective.

10. *RECORDS AND REPORTS.* Keep a daily record of the way in which you spend your time. Hand the report to the supervising elder of your district each Saturday morning. Keep an accurate account daily of the money you spend and report it at the end of each month to the mission

president. On the reverse side of the weekly report write a brief letter to the president telling him about your accomplishments, problems, or anything that is in your heart.

11. *EXERCISES.* Unless you are ill or have an excuse from your doctor you should report for exercises in the gym three times a week.

Letter from Gordon

Gar:

I've just been made supervising elder of the Chiapas District and will reign from the city of Tuxtla Gutierrez. My domain will stretch from Tapachula, bordering Guatemala, to Arriaga, along the Pacific Coast. Whatever ego-expanding satisfaction might have been derived from my new calling, however, was virtually annulled by the closing of Villa Flores. That was a shock. Elder Heber was called to Veracruz to become a new senior companion but no one was sent to Villa Flores to take our places, as I had hoped would happen. I suppose the mission home was becoming impatient (although we did have a couple of baptisms), but the real problem is that nearly half of our missionaries are ending their missions and departing for home this week. There's just a simple shortage of troops at the present time—not enough to staff every little town like Villa Flores, I'm afraid. My hope is that Villa Flores can be reopened as soon as an adequate number of replacement missionaries arrives from the LTM. I talked to President Hatch by phone and he pointed out that I could make trips from time to time, but it's a five-hour journey from Tuxtla to Villa Flores by bus. Realistically, I could never maintain investigators and a new branch of the church there under such conditions.

Fact of the matter is, though, I'm in Villa Flores right now with my new companion. We just arrived after a kidney-pounding journey by bus over the mountains from Tuxtla. We'll hold Sunday services tomorrow and stick around Monday to splash two more good people who were set to be baptized when Heber and I were pulled out. That will make four Mormons in town and a lot of big, deflated hopes.

In the meantime, I've got to get myself squared away to assume my new *cargo* [load] as supervising elder. Among other things, my junior companion, Timothy Granger, is the current problem child in the mission, and I'm supposed to pacify him or he might

get sent home. Actually, I have a strange liking for him—he reminds me a little bit of Dave Lingwall. Physically, he's right along
the same lines: stocky, muscular, and even looks like Dave, with
rubio [sandy] hair. He lacks Dave's mental capacity and sense of
humor, however, and his manners and impulsive actions are about
ten times as coarse and unpredictable. I knew Elder Granger four
months ago in Veracruz. My most vivid recollection of Granger
is of him and his companion coming close to getting into a fist-
fight at a movie theater. Elder Treanor, his most recent companion,
told me of several brawls and near brawls he had with Granger
in Tuxtla. Treanor is six feet, three inches tall, played football his
freshman year at BYU, and is big enough to sit on him. I'm not. I
suspect we'll get along though.

Also, the branch in Tuxtla is apparently in chaos—badly weakened by quarrels and bickering among the members, inept leadership, scandals (including several cases of adultery), etc. The branch
president is desperate for our help to keep things alive, further cur-
tailing my thoughts of working in Villa Flores over the weekends.
To give you an idea, President Hatch just wrote me, saying: "I realize you're short-handed there, but there is one more very necessary
part of your assignment to bring to your attention. Branch President
Esponda needs your help. Please support him in every way possible.
This does not mean to work just with members, although you will
need to do a lot of this until we are able to send some additional
help. May the Lord be with you in carrying out all your many responsibilities." Unfortunately, few of the Tuxtla members seem too
anxious to lend *their* help, and I'll probably end up teaching priesthood, Sunday school and mutual classes. The Lord's been blessing
me with problems and I hope I'm worthy to stand. I won't complain
too much, though, because if we can help get the branch back on its
feet, missionary success should also improve through better support
from members. [In 1988 Tuxtla Gutiérrez became the headquarters
city for a newly designated LDS mission in Chiapas. By 1994 a stake
center and nine wards were functioning in the Tuxtla area, with approximately six thousand members.]

A week later: I didn't get this off in the mail last week while in
Villa Flores, so I thought I'd add a few more lines. Tonight we visited a woman and her teenaged son who was partially blinded with
steel fragments in his eye from an industrial accident at his job last

week. We gave the young man a blessing and were then taken next door to a neighbor's home where we were introduced to a macabre and depressing scene. The neighbors' infant child died yesterday and had not yet been buried. Her body was lying on the kitchen table, illuminated by candles in the darkness, with small wads of cotton stuffed in her ears and nostrils, supposedly to prevent evil spirits from possessing her. We were asked to give the weeping parents a blessing, which I did, promising them that the child's sinless spirit already had returned to her Father in Heaven and not to "limbo," as the Catholics teach. The Tuxtla Branch continues to teeter back and forth on the brink of disaster. Sunday school services yesterday were about the worst I've ever attended. Sacrament meeting was vastly improved, however, with a fairly good turnout and a more congenial spirit. I was one of the *predicadores* [speakers], and actually gave one of the best talks of my mission. Sometimes I fail pretty miserably to say much of value, while other times I truly seem to speak with the power of my convictions. *Sobre todo* [above all] there's Elder Granger, a rare specimen. With a gritting of teeth, there have been no major explosions between us so far. This boy, however, has had more than his share of problems and will undoubtedly continue to have them unless he somehow learns to manage his temper, which is like a time bomb ticking away. For example, yesterday in a tracting visit he boiled over when the guy whose home we were in kept interrupting him to say he didn't want to hear anymore. Granger sputtered for a minute and then slammed his fist down on the table, abruptly stood up, knocked his chair over and stormed out the door. I was left behind to apologize to the speechless man. In addition, Granger appears to have declared war on the bees of Tuxtla, especially a variety of red wasps that are everywhere this time of year. The wasps are attracted to water and, whenever we pass the fountains in the central park, Elder Granger springs into action, smacking wasps out of the air with my "La Historia Mormona" book or the flannel board. Instead of studying at lunch time when we're home, he spends almost the entire noon hour attacking wasps in our backyard with a fly swatter. The most constructive thing I can say about this odd behavior is that it appears to be a way for Elder Granger to channel hostility and let off steam.

Speaking of unpredictable behavior, what's Chuck's newest theory? Do you really think he's departed from the church for good, or was his letter to you this summer just another intellectual tantrum? By the way, I got a recent letter from Elder Rencher, my former senior companion in Minatitlan, who has returned home and is now teaching Spanish at the Language Training Mission in Provo while attending school at BYU. It's a seducing thought. I think we could get in the LTM program. Another thing: I never thought I'd ever learn Spanish but surprised myself. With one language comfortably digested, it might not be such a bad idea to try for another. I suppose you would be inclined to the guttural tongue [German, which Gary had taken for a year in high school]. How about French?

All those padded reports you've received about me make me cringe a little because I know, in truth, that I regularly fall short in meeting my responsibilities. Keep frequent communication coming so I'll know what to do to keep my suspenders hitched up and on the right track. Keep yourself on full-throttle and we'll be side by side all the way.

Your brother, Gord

Diary Entries

December 31

I'm twenty-two years old today. We celebrated the occasion by working straight through until evening—mostly beating on doors tracting, interspersed with getting stood up on scheduled visits. These are difficult days for us to catch people at home. As soon as the holiday fogs settle down we'll be able to weed out our prospects. We started a second lesson with the Veda lady but only got as far as her declaration that she would never stop worshipping the Virgin. This one damnable doctrine binds more people in ignorance and has cost me more investigators than any other single factor during my time in Mexico. We came home about 7:00 P.M., my companion bought me a little birthday cake, I bought some ice cream, and we reflected a bit on our past, present, and future lives while eating. Greeted the New Year sound asleep in bed.

January 1, 1966

New Year's day found me directing the weekly supervisors' meeting this morning. We didn't deal with any special problems, just routine matters. Prospects for success in all the city districts this month look fair so far. Elder Judd and I flipped to see who would be traveling next week to make our supervising visits, and it looks like I'll go while Elder Judd stays at home to tend our own investigators.

January 2

A good day—almost fourteen hours' worth of effective work. About fifteen investigators showed up for Sunday school. We had the Quintero family bring the Romeros, which worked very well. But an irreverent fourth lesson with the Romeros after their return from church showed that most of them are still way off course. The Word of Wisdom is one of their problems. Checked upon an *evangelica* family (the Bautistas) whom we had previously tracted out, and before we knew it we were sitting at their table eating a dinner of chicken, tossed salad and flan. Most of the children weren't home but a teenaged girl was (quite cute, I might add) and she unleashed a steady stream of chatter and amusing comments. When we left she accompanied us down the narrow stairs and grabbed Elder Judd's hand so he wouldn't stumble. He turned pink but didn't take his hand away. On to a quick second lesson with the Reyes. The husband is becoming more animated all the time and the pigpen they live in had even seen some efforts to tidy up. We finally found the Redorta family home, minus the papa. His absence, however, was filled in by several visiting relatives, including a liquored-up uncle who kept interrupting the lesson with noisy exclamations until finally Elder Judd had to take him into another room while I finished the first half of the *plática*. Aside from that, however, the rest of the family accepted everything quite well.

January 4

Turns out my first "orienting" visit was right back to my just recently departed Churubusco District. I worked with Elder Doug Peterson, who replaced me as senior companion to Elder Silva, and we put in a lot of tracting. In fact, we didn't give any lessons during my two-day stay. Those that Peterson had scheduled all fell through, so there was nothing else to do but knock on doors. What happened to all the promising investigators I left to Peterson just three weeks ago?

"Ritual, Ethnicity, and Religious Identity in the Muslim Communities in Brazil"[5]   PAULO GABRIEL HILU DA ROCHA PINTO

. . . Brazil has a large Muslim community, close to one million strong, which was formed since the 19th century by diverse migration waves from the Middle East (Syria, Lebanon, Palestine) and by the conversion of non-Arab Brazilians. This community is mostly urban, with large concentrations in Rio de Janeiro, São Paulo, and Foz de Iguaçu. There are important sociological differences among communities in each of these sites. For example, the Muslim community in Rio de Janeiro has not received a significant influx of recent immigrants, a fact that makes the process of the creation and reformulation of Muslim identities more dependent on local and national cultural dynamics. In contrast, in the other two Muslim communities the production of Islamic identities is strongly influenced by transnational Islamic movements and by the constant contact with Islam as practiced in the Middle East. Muslims in these three communities tend to work primarily in commercial activities. There are, however, increasing numbers in qualified professions such as medicine, law, and engineering.

The majority of Muslims in Brazil are Arab immigrants and their descendants. Nevertheless, there is a growing number of non-Arab Brazilians that convert to Islam through personal relations, that is, through work relations, marriage, or friendship. Muslim organizations based in mosques or Sufi orders have also begun to undertake missionary work. . . . I will analyze here the construction of Muslim identities in Brazil in communities in Rio de Janeiro, Curitiba, and São Paulo, as a way to understand the processes that take place in each of these sites.[6]

Islam between Textual Universalism and Ethnic Distinction: The Islamic Mutual-Aid Society [Sociedade Beneficente] of Rio de Janeiro

Rio de Janeiro's Muslim community has its religious center in the Islamic Mutual-Aid Society (SBMRJ), which has a prayer hall (*musala*) in a commercial building in Lapa [a bohemian neighborhood] that serves as a mosque. This is the only mosque currently operating in Rio de Janeiro, for the mosque built in the "international Islamic" style in the city, which was constructed in the 1980s in Jacarepaguá, is closed due to fights between the leadership of the community and the builder of the mosque.[7] There is also the 'Alawi Club in the neighborhood of Tijuca, which serves as a space of sociability and for the celebration of 'Alawi rituals.[8]

I made my contact [with the SBMRJ] through the Imam (prayer leader), Abdu, who was born in Sudan, grew up in Brazil, and was educated in the religion during the period that he worked in Libya. . . . I began to attend regularly the Friday prayers, when the weekly sermon (*khutbah*) is given, as well as other community activities such as courses in Arabic and Muslim doctrine. I also attended the community meals (*iftar*) that mark the breaking of fasting during the sacred month of Ramadan. . . .

The Muslim community in Rio is rather small in comparison to those in São Paulo, Mato Grosso or Paraná. The SBMRJ has about 5,000 formally affiliated members. However, despite the small size, the community in Rio is particularly interesting because it is one of the few in Brazil in which members are not predominantly of Arabic origin. Instead, it is a multicultural and multi-ethnic group that brings together Arabs and their descendents, Africans (many whom are foreign students, in addition to immigrants from that continent), and Brazilians who have converted from other religious traditions. These Brazilians are, in fact, the majority in the community, while Arabs and their descendants make up about 40% of the membership.[9] In socio-economic terms, the great majority of the members are small merchants, generally from the Saara area in the center of Rio, or are employed in commerce, with a smaller number of university students and professionals (lawyers, veterinarians, etc.).

The multi-ethnic character of the Rio community leads to a complex process of construction of Muslim identities in interaction with Arabic linguistic and cultural traditions and with the Brazilian social and cultural reality. The Arabic language is valued as a key ingredient [*elemento constitutivo*], but not as an element that determines Muslim identity. There is concern with teaching the language to community members who are not of Arab origin (and even to those who do have this origin but have not mastered the classic Arabic of religious texts), in order to give them direct access to the sacred books, especially the Koran. Nonetheless, the lingua franca for religious activities, sermons, courses, etc. is Portuguese, with the exception of ritual formulas such as "bismallah al-rahman al-rahim" ("in the name of God the compassionate and the merciful") or "salam aleikum rhamatu-llah wa barakatu-hu" ("may the peace, mercy, and grace of God be with you"). This shows the efforts of the SBMRJ's leadership in constructing a religious and linguistic milieu that is, to some extent, integrated to local culture. Even the verses of the Koran cited in Arabic during the Friday sermon are immediately followed by a Portuguese translation.

. . . Nevertheless, the symbolic value of the Arabic language and Arab identity makes them markers of religious distinction within the community. During the moments of socialization that follow the religious rituals, it is common to see Arabic speakers use that language in their interactions, marking an ethnic boundary that separates them from the rest of the community. Those who have Arab origins but do not speak the language are constantly the target of subtle teasing and jokes that reinforce the value of Arabic as a cultural diacritic constitutive of the ethnic boundary. Beyond that, it is also a significant fact that all the positions of power and status within the community are occupied by Arabic speakers, clearly setting up an ethnic hierarchy.[10] The Imam also defines himself as Arab, notwithstanding the emphasis that he placed on his African origin after 2006, in order create a greater connection with the African immigrants and black Brazilian converts that compose the community at the SBMRJ.

Abdu legitimates his position as Imam, partially, through his Arab origin that, in principle, guarantees his linguistic mastery of Islam's textual tradition. This despite the fact that he does not have the necessary religious formation to be credentialized as *shaykh* or *'alim* [religious scholar], since his studies in Libya were at a more general level. It is also noteworthy that he has gradually emphasized the link between his Arabic cultural identity and the performance in his personal life and in his self-understanding of moral values that are construed as essentially Muslim. He has rearticulated his life and self through his marriage with a Moroccan woman who wears the veil (*hijab*), after his separation from his first wife, a non-Muslim Brazilian.

[. . . .]

Despite the relation between hierarchy and Arabic ethnicity in the religious division of labor within the SBMRJ, the leadership's public discourse promotes the dissemination of Islam and the incorporation of the converts into the community, a fact that is demonstrated by the centrality of educational activities, such as courses about Islam or "Muslim culture." Courses tend to focus on the challenges that Brazilian society and culture pose for Muslims, particularly for the recently converted or for recent immigrants. These courses touch upon subjects like the use of the veil, the prohibition against drinking alcohol or eating pork, and the interaction with friends and family members who are not Muslim. These themes are mixed with others of global scope, such as the image of Islam and Muslims in the media, which is generally considered as holding hostile and misinformed views on these topics (Montenegro 2002), the conflicts in the Middle East, and the terrorist attacks of September 11. . . .

Muslim identities in the SBMRJ are not only constituted in contrast to the beliefs and practices of non-Muslims. They are also produced by the contrast among the different Islamic traditions that are represented among members of the community, according to their diverse origins. . . . Since the dominant tradition in SBMRJ is Salafiyya, a [Sunni] reformist movement that emerged in the 19th Century, which preaches a return to the "original Islam" that is codified in the Koran and Hadith (the collection of traditions, sayings and actions of the Prophet), differences [in the ritual practices and doctrine within the community] tend to be perceived as *bid'a* (condemnable innovations), that is, as deviations from "true" Islam that must be corrected.

Thus, the SBMRJ's religious leaders are very critical of other Muslim traditions such as Sufism, the cult of the saints, or Shi'ism, seeking to avoid that members of the community fall into those deviations. In that sense, one can say that the multiethnic character of the community in Rio de Janeiro has generated an awareness of doctrinal and ritual differences among various Islamic traditions, leading to a search for the "true" Islam within the framework of a religious reform centered around the textual tradition. Thus, the disciplinary practices (Asad 1993: 130-135) developed by the SBMRJ's religious authorities (sermons, courses, normative texts, etc.) have produced a process of "objectification" (Eickelman & Piscatori 1996: 48) of Islamic tradition, generating a "purified" religious system of cultural and social practices that serves as a conscious normative point of reference in the life of the faithful.

That "objectified" Islam facilitates the integration of converts, relegating cultural difference to the background and bringing everyone under the same religious discipline.

[. . . .]

Ethnicity Overcoming Sectarianism: The Muslim Community in Curitiba

. . . The Muslim community in Curitiba has about 3,000 families (15,000 people) affiliated with the mosque of Imam Ali Ibn Abu Talib. [This mosque] was constructed in 1977 in an "oriental" style, or put in a better way, in an "international Islamic" style, with minarets, horseshoe arches, and a dome. The Muslim society, which is at the same time a social club and a mutual-aid institution, is composed almost exclusively by Syrian, Lebanese, Palestinian, and Egyptian immigrants and their descendants. Its leader is a Shi'i *shaykh* (a *shaykh* Mahdi), who was educated in Lebanon and was, prior to coming to Curitiba, the Imam of the Muslim community in Santiago, Chile, which was, according to him, "made up almost completely of Lebanese and Palestinians."

. . . In the Curitiba community, my conversations and interviews were almost always conducted in Arabic or in a mixture of Arabic and Portuguese. . . . [This] community has been functioning since the decade of the 1950s, with the creation of a Muslim society. *Shaykh* Mahdi stressed in an interview that "the community in Curitiba was very smart to create first a club and then worry about building a mosque, since the club allows for the integration of families, and particularly, keeps the youth together and interested in Islam. If young Muslims do not do things together and feel that Islam is just about praying at the mosque or following the rules of the religion, they will eventually lose interest in becoming good Muslims." . . .

Despite the fact that the community in Curitiba has a strong Arab character, it shows an important sectarian division since half of the members are Sunnis and half Shi'is. Since the 1970s, when the civil war in Lebanon and the Israeli invasion of South Lebanon intensified the migration flows, the presence of Shi'is in the community has grown. The mosque was built in 1977 as a Sunni mosque and it remained so until 1986, when the government of Iran, in its policy of disputing with Saudi Arabia the finance and control of international Islam, offered significant donations to the mosque. Following that, Iran eventually came to have the right to choose the *shaykh*, who became Shi'i. The presence of Iran is immediately felt in the beautiful *mihrab* (the niche that marks the direction of Mecca) of mosaic tiles in Persian style, with the inscription in Arabic and Portuguese: "Gift from the Islamic Republic of Iran, 1996."

According to *shaykh* Mahdi, the fervor to promote a revolutionary and militant Shi'ism supported by Iran alienated many Sunnis in the community and the Iran-Iraq war exacerbated the tensions between the two groups to the point that the community was on the verge of fragmenting or dissolving. In the words of the *shaykh* Mahdi: "it was a difficult time. To give you an idea, the Islamic school that was created at the same time as the Muslim society had to close because it was impossible to reach consensus on the content of its religious curriculum." The *shaykh* added that the situation only began to change with his predecessor, who toned down the politico-religious militancy of his discourse.

He also withdrew from the mosque all political or sectarian symbols, such as portraits of Ayatollah Khomeini or images of the holy figures of Shi'ism. Thus, a supra-sectarian Muslim identity began to be constructed through the emphasis on doctrinal and ritual elements shared by Sunnis and Shi'is.

At present, although ritual differences among Sunnis and Shi'is are evident in the collective prayers, these differences are understood and integrated as variations within a spectrum of legitimate practices. In the mosque, clay tablets (generally made of sacred soil from Karbala, Iraq) are accessible in a box [for those who wish their] head[s] to touch a natural material during prayer. Sunnis do not have this obligation. One of the consequences of such an effort at integration is the tendency to minimize the ritual and doctrinal boundaries or abandon the mechanisms of exclusion used by sectarian groups to mark their identity. As such, the rule of ritual purity demanded by the Shi'i tradition according to which a Shi'i cannot pray behind a non-Shi'i (standing between the faithful and Mecca), is not followed in the mosque in Curitiba. Shi'is and Sunnis freely mix among the rows during prayer. By the same token, the *adhan* (the call to prayer) does not include the piece only used by Shi'i, which elevate 'Ali (cousin and successor of Mohammed) to the level of the Prophet.

At the doctrinal level, overcoming sectarian differences entails a certain degree of objectification of Islam. The common denominator is deliberately found in the Koran. However, in contrast to the community in Rio de Janeiro, the process of "objectification" [in Curitiba] is not based on a conscious and integrated religious system that encompasses daily practices, but on an interpretive consensus anchored on shared doctrinal understandings and ritual practices. This strategy allowed for the incorporation of values and practices from the Arab culture in the religious worldview [of the community in Curitiba]. There is then an "ethnification" of Islam as a "religion of Arabs in Brazil," an inward-looking religious universe, resistant to the incorporation of new members and to integration into the larger society. Indeed, the *shaykh* confirmed that the community does not have any missionary or *tabliq* strategy, or one to integrate the few converts. These converts, who are generally university students who came into contact with Islam through their studies, confront a serious and powerful linguistic barrier in the community, since rituals, sermons, and a large part of the conversation, take place in Arabic, accompanied on a few occasions by translation to Portuguese. . . .

The relation that the Curitiba community has with Brazilian society follows the dynamic of an "ethno-religious enclave," similar to those, for example, in the Jewish and Armenian communities in Brazil. [But] this does not thwart a deep integration into the local social and cultural universe in other realms of life (work, friendships, etc.).

[. . . .]

Conclusion

My analysis of these Muslim communities shows how Islam in Brazil is characterized by a plurality of identities, practices and forms of organization. The connection between Muslim identity and Arab ethnicity is very strong in most Muslim communities in Brazil, with the clear exception of the one in Rio de Janeiro. While the growing number of non-Arab Brazilian converts encourages less ethnic and more universalistic interpretations and practices of Islam, the Arabic language and some Arab cultural diacritics remain as signs of religious distinction even among the converts. The appropriation, interpretation and practice of various Islamic traditions in the Muslim communities in Brazil is informed by the local social and cultural context of each one of them, as well as by the multiple connections that they establish with globalized and transnational Islamic discourses and practices.

WORKS CITED

Asad, Talal. 1993. *Genealogies of Religion: Discipline and Reasons of Power in Islam and Christianity*. Baltimore: Johns Hopkins University Press.

Chagas, Gisele Fonseca. Identidade, Conhecimento e Poder na Comunidade Muçulmana do Rio de Janeiro. Master's Thesis, Graduate Program in Anthropology, Universidade Federal Fluminense: Niterói, 2006.

Eickelman, Dale and James Piscatori. *Muslim Politics*. Princeton: Princeton University Press.

Montenegro, Sílvia. 2002. "Discursos e Contradiscursos: o Olhar da Mídia sobre o Islã no Brasil." *Mana* 8/1.

"Zen Buddhism in Brazil: Japanese or Brazilian?"[11]

CRISTINA MOREIRA DA ROCHA

Zen Buddhism in Brazil

. . . Currently, there are twenty-three Zen Buddhist centers and temples, three Zen Buddhist monasteries, thirty-four Tibetan centers, seven Theravaada centers, thirty-seven *Nishi Hongwanji* (*Joodo Shinshuu*) temples and twenty-two associations (where there is no resident monk), twenty-six *Higashi Hongwanji* (*Joodo Shinshuu*) temples and associations, two *Joodoshu* temples, four *Nichireshuu* temples (with 5,000 families of adherents) twelve *Honmon Butsuryu Shu* (a branch of *Nichiren*) temples, and four Shingon temples (with 850 families of adherents) in Brazil.[12] Tibetan Buddhism, which was the latest to arrive (1988), is undergoing a boom similar to that which is taking place in the West. In fact, Buddhism in general is becoming better known and is attracting media attention in Brazil. In June of 1998, important Brazilian magazines published three articles on the expansion of Buddhism and meditation in Brazil and its famous adherents (television stars, politicians, etc).[13] *Elle* magazine featured the American Lama Tsering Everest, as well as the Tibetan Chagdud Rimpoche, who moved from the US to Brazil in the mid-1990s. Lama Tsering noted that "[i]t is the right moment for Buddhism in Brazil . . . the involvement of Brazilians with Buddhism is karmic." The Tibetan Lama Chagdud Tulku Rimpoche is building two monasteries: one in Três Coroas in the state of Rio Grande do Sul that is intended to house 400 people during retreats, and another one in Brumadinho, in the state of Minas Gerais. The *Elle* magazine article estimated the number of Buddhist practitioners at around 500,000, distributed among the Tibetan, *Nichiren*, *Sooka Gakkai* (150,000 adherents), *Joodo Shinshuu*, *Joodo Shu*, *Shingon*, *Theravaada*, and Zen schools.[14] . . .

Although the number of Buddhists is only 0.2 percent, one has to be aware that for most Brazilians, Buddhism is more a "philosophy," a "way of life" than a religion. Zen Buddhism is often viewed as a meditation technique that helps to relieve stress. *Busshinji* abbess Koen supports this view on Zen Buddhism in an interview for the *O Estado de São Paulo* newspaper: "It's not necessary to be a Buddhist to practice this kind of meditation. The temple offers several lectures for those who wish to learn this activity, even if they have no intention of becoming Buddhist."[15] In the same report, one practitioner notes that "Zen Buddhism was a way to awaken my sensibility without denying my Catholic religion." As a result, being Buddhist does not exclude professing other religions. Many Brazilians continue being Roman Catholic while adopting Buddhism. If asked which religion they profess, it is most likely that they will state that they are Catholic (because they were baptized) or have no religious ties (if they do not profess any religion) even though they might have adopted Buddhism as a way of life.[16] The abbot of Morro da Vargem monastery, Daiju (Christiano Bitti), reinforces this point in an interview for *Isto É* magazine: "If a Roman Catholic considers his/her religion as a study of himself/herself, so he/she is also a Buddhist. Roman Catholic priests, who were initiated in Buddhism, told me that afterwards they understood the Bible better. Buddhism has neither the intention to dispute adherents nor to convert them. People loosen up because we are not disputing anything. We just want to strengthen the faith of the Brazilian people."[17] . . .

It is important to place the study of Zen Buddhism in Brazil within an analysis of the transplantation of Buddhism to the West. Although Zen in Brazil has its own history and developments, it is deeply related to the history and developments of Western Buddhism. In order to establish this relationship and further analyze Zen in Brazil, I shall use the analytical categories coined by Martin Baumann, a German scholar who works with the transplantation of Buddhism to Europe. Baumann identifies five processive modes for transplanting a religion to a new sociocultural context. . . .[18]

The first processive mode, that of contact, comprises strategies of adaptation such as the translation of scriptures. Translation is one of the main concerns of monks, nuns, and practitioners in all Zen centers, temples, and monasteries where Brazilians of non-Japanese descent are involved. Not only are *suutras* translated, but also recitations that are used in retreats before meals and manual labor (*samu*). Though translated, these recitations are chanted using a Japanese rhythm, that is, stressing each syllable as those speaking the Japanese language do. In addition, Brazilian Zen centers produce written materials in Portuguese that discuss the meaning of ordination, provide explanations and drawings on how to sit *zazen* and *do kinhin* (walking meditation), and transcribe lectures by the *rooshi* or monk in charge of the group. Furthermore, new means of communication such as websites are used to spread the word.[19] Produced by most Zen temples, centers, and monasteries, these websites include schedules of activities; articles about the history of affiliated temples, monasteries, and Zen Centers; translated *suutras*; and pictures of temples and monasteries.

The contact mode can lead to the second processive mode of transplantation: confrontation and conflict. Confrontation happens when "protagonists of the imported religious tradition are concerned with presenting the peculiarities which contrast with existing traditions."[20] The Japanese Ministry of Foreign Affairs avoided this when it prohibited Japanese monks from going to Brazil to proselytize before World War II. As shown earlier in this paper, there were already enough cultural conflicts between Brazilians and Japanese; the Japanese Government could not afford a religious one. Conflict actually arose when the Japanese community and Brazilians of non-Japanese descent started sharing the same religious space in *Busshinji*. As we mentioned above, the Japanese community and Brazilians of non-Japanese descent do not accept the other group's practices as "true" Buddhism.

"Ambiguity and adaptation" is the third processive mode of transplantation. Baumann explains that there are unavoidable misunderstandings and misinterpretations that happen when transplanting a religion into a new sociocultural context. "For members of the host culture it is only possible to interpret and understand symbols, rituals or ideas of the imported religious tradition on the basis of their own conceptions. The bearers of the foreign religion share similar problems of understanding with regard to the new culture and society. As a consequence of contact unavoidable ambiguities arise."[21] Because of the prevailing Roman Catholic environment, much of the terminology used in speaking of Buddhism in Brazil is Roman Catholic in origin. For instance, rituals such as funerals are called "missas" (masses); the abbot is called "bispo" (bishop); and there are mentions of "paraíso" (heaven), "inferno" (hell), and "rezar" (to pray).

Furthermore, there are also intentional ambiguities that are part of a strategy to make the foreign religion less exotic to the host culture, and by doing so, reduce conflicts. This involves emphasizing similarities and links with concepts of the host culture. Such ambiguous delineation can be observed at *Busshinji*, where Brazilian holidays are commemorated with the Japanese counterpart. For instance, Children's Day (October 12) in Brazil is commemorated on this date, but with a festival for Jizo, the *bodhisattva* who looks after children in Japan. In addition, the Brazilian "Day of the Dead" (November 2) is commemorated on this date, but with references to Obon, the Japanese festival for the deceased ancestors.

In the same context, *Sootoo Zen* in Japan began to emphasize the ecological connotation of Buddhism as a strategy for displaying a modern Buddhism that is in tune with current world issues. This is done through "Caminho Zen" (*Zen Way*), a Japanese magazine written in Portuguese especially for Brazilian followers. Indeed, one of the reasons given by many

Brazilians of non-Japanese origin practitioners to justify their migration to Buddhism is the religion's connection with ecology.[22]

In a lecture given in a *sesshin* (retreat) in Porto Alegre, Moriyama Rooshi connected Buddhism with Greek philosophy. Through this approach, the *rooshi* compared the term "Apathia" (lack of feeling), created by the Greek philosopher Zenon, to the idea of "Atarakushi" (to quiet the *kokoro*/spirit). By doing this, Moriyama brought Zen meditation closer to the Brazilian/Western context. He finished his lecture by saying that he is studying other "Buddhisms," because "in a globalized world people have access to an increasing number of religions, and the true religion is the one it is closer to the follower (February 14, 1998)." Tokuda also makes use of intentional ambiguities in his frequent quotations from the Bible and comparisons of Jesus to Buddha.[23] Similarly, he compares the ecstatic state mentioned by the Christian mystics, Saint John of the Cross and Meister Eckhart, to the experience of enlightenment in Zen. Tokuda says there is no difference between West and East concerning this state of ecstasy. He even refers to the image of God, affirming the Christian experience of union with God as similar to *satori*:

> As Saint John of the Cross said: the night of senses, the night of spirit, the night of soul. Through this internal voyage, we start to leave the exterior world and begin to work with our inner world, diving into our subconscious, into our unconscious. When we get to the bottom of this darkness, there is a union with God, with Love. To this experience, Zen gives the name enlightenment, *satori*.[24]

Baumann adds that a foreign religion may borrow features of the host culture, for example, organizational structures. All of the temples and monasteries in Brazil comply with Brazilian law and are registered legally as non-profit organizations. In addition, they are managed as a Brazilian organization would be: the temple in São Paulo and the Zen centers all over Brazil have a democratically elected president and a board of directors.

The fourth mode, "recoupment or re-orientation," is a critique of the ambiguities that have arisen. The foreign religion tries to reduce the ambiguities in order to regain the identity of the religious tradition. One of the examples that Baumann uses is the ordination of Tibetan lay people. When Tibetan Buddhism arrived in Germany, the Buddhist refuge ceremony was given immediately to people attending ceremonies. However, a decade later, initiations are only offered after a thorough preparation.

Such is the case of Brazilian Zen Buddhism. Until the 1980s, traditional Japanese monks gave ordination to Japanese descendants without any process or preparation. Likewise, in the 1990s, Moriyama Rooshi gave lay ordination to Brazilians of non-Japanese origin when requested. However, after arriving from Japan, abbess Koen started to carry out rituals more formally and strictly, establishing a two-year preparation course prior to lay ordination.

The last of the strategies of transplantation, "innovative self-development," deals with the creation of new forms and innovative interpretations of the religion in the host culture. This generates a tension with the tradition from which the religion developed. Many innovations took place in the United States and Germany. Feminism determined a new status for women in Buddhism. Another example is the democratic organization of Zen centers instead of strict hierarchy. In Brazil, the tension between Japanese Buddhism and Brazilian Buddhism marks the innovations that are occurring. Such innovations are mainly being imported from the Western discourse on Zen.

. . . Brazilian Zen took part in this process of Zen Buddhism "glocalization" (a process that Roland Robertson terminologically specified as the blending of the local and the global).[25] The interviews that I conducted with Brazilian practitioners of non-Japanese origin showed that their interest in Zen Buddhism is a result of the United States' influence, through the media,[26] books on Zen,[27] movies,[28] and travels. In fact, all of the people interviewed noted that their first contact with Zen was through books.[29] The United States is a strong source of ideas and material on Zen for various reasons. For example, English is more accessible to Brazilians than Japanese. In fact, most of the books on Zen now available in Portuguese were originally written in English. Moreover, due to the fact that these practitioners come from the intellectual upper-middle class and the vast majority are degreed liberal professionals, many of them can read the books in English before they are translated. Some buy books about Zen via the Internet from Amazon (www.amazon.com) and/or subscribe to American Buddhist magazines such as *Tricycle*. Some practitioners even choose to travel to Zen centers abroad.

The urban Brazilian upper-middle class seeks Zen Buddhism because it appeals intellectually to them as a philosophy of life. Their main concerns are, among others, relieving stress and acquiring inner peace, turning this symbolic field into a miscellany of religion and leisure. In order to have inner peace, practitioners feel that they have to search for their "inner self." Very frequently, the people that I interviewed said that they sought Zen meditation as a way to learn about themselves. Zen meditation worked either in place of psychotherapy or in conjunction with it.[30]

The French anthropologist, Louis Dumont, argues that in the contemporary world, religious practice is a private choice.[31] In a process of *bricolage*, the practitioner chooses characteristics from different practices to condense them into a spiritual quest. Thus, each practitioner constructs his or her religion as a unique praxis that is different from all the others, mixing various traditions in order to build a new contemporary spirituality. There are several groups of practices associated with Zen Buddhism in Brazil that are recurrent in the interviews: practices of healing (yoga, *Shiatsu, Do In, Tai Chi Chuan*, acupuncture); practices of self-understanding (many kinds of psychotherapy, astrology); martial arts (*Ai Ki Do*, karate); eating habits (vegetarianism, macrobiotics); and other religions [such as] Spiritism[32] [and] African religions. . . .

The Western construct of Zen, which was appropriated, hybridized and indigenized in Brazil, is still a new phenomenon that needs to be further studied.

"The Rituals of Santo Daime"[33]   EDWARD MACRAE

Santo Daime Rituals Performed by the Followers of Padrinho Sebastião[34]

As happens in many spiritualist centers and among the vegetalistas, the daimista rituals are called "works" and often presuppose an intense and tiring psychic activity, even though those taking part may be in an apparently relaxed and restful position such as happens during the sessions of concentration.

It is believed that taking ayahuasca leads to a perception of the "spiritual" or "astral" world and to the possibility of carrying out a series of activities in this realm. Accordingly there are different types of rituals for different purposes, and their form is invariably attributed to Mestre Irineu who is supposed to have learned about them from the Queen of the Forest, or the Virgin of the Conception, source of all daimista knowledge.

[. . . .]

The Hymnaries

Hymnaries are considered commemorative festivities for certain religious holidays, birthdays of the leaders or simply the celebration of communion and fraternity. There is a calendar of "official hymnaries," which is supposed to be observed by all the Santo Daime churches. On such occasions, those taking part wear special clothes, called *farda branca* (white uniform), predominantly white in color and of sober cut, decorated with many colored ribbons. On their heads the women wear tinsel crowns. On other occasions, simpler "hymnaries" may be held and the plainer *farda azalea* (blue uniform) is worn, consisting of white shirts or blouses and navy blue trousers or skirts.

There are different hymnaries which are sung according to the occasion. There are the, so called, "official hymnaries" which are those "received" by some of the main *padrinhos* such as Mestre Irineu, Padrinho Sebastião or Padrinho Alfredo or some of Mestre Irineu's closest followers and which are sung on some of the most important holidays. But there are also hymns "received" by other followers of the doctrine and which may be sung on other, less formal occasions. During the "hymnary" the participants stand around a central table usually in the form of a six-pointed star, on which there is a double-armed *Cross of Caravaca* and a rosary and other symbols of the doctrine. The men and women line up according to height on opposite sides of the room. According to the shape of the table, and the number of participants, they may form four or six groups: men, young men, boys, women, young women and girls.

Many play *maracas* or rattles, accompanying the singing and marking the rhythm of the dancing. The steps are simple and vary according to the rhythm of the hymn. The singing is often accompanied by musicians playing seated around the table. This orchestra is normally composed of guitars, flutes and percussion instruments, but any other instrument may be added. The ritual begins at a predetermined time, generally at sunset. To mark its beginning, the catholic rosary may be said or, on less formal occasions, simply three Lord's Prayers and three Hail Mary's. At the end of the ceremony these prayers are repeated alongside other Catholic, Esoteric or specifically daimista ones.[35]

After the opening prayers the Daime is then served; a small cup is handed to the adults, and a smaller amount to the children. This happens several times during the work, at approximately two-hourly intervals.

Depending on the occasion and on the hymnary being sung, the ritual may last between six or twelve hours. During this period, the participants must keep to their place in the line, refraining from talking or from any other kind of behavior that might hinder other people in their efforts to concentrate.

Halfway through the ritual there is usually an intermission lasting for about one hour, the only time allowed for conversation. Sometimes, still under the influence of the beverage, people may opt to remain silent and in a state of introspection.

During the intermission the participants are given permission to leave the room and may eat something light or drink a little water. Smoking is also permitted, but at a distance, so that the tobacco smoke does not reach the place where the ceremony is being held.

At the end of the ritual, a few Catholic prayers are recited again and the leader pronounces a last invocation to God the Father, The Virgin Queen Mother, Our Lord Jesus Christ, the Patriarch Saint Joseph and to all the spiritual beings of the celestial court. At the end of the session, and every time they take the brew, those taking part in the session cross themselves, thus emphasizing their commitment to Christian principles during their astral work. . . . .

During the ritual, some of the participants, moved by their visions or going through difficulties in their process of introspection, may show signs of unrest, and, maybe, even loss of control over their movements. Others go through physiological reactions to their ingestion of ayahuasca, feeling nausea and occasionally vomiting or suffering from diarrhea.

To deal with such cases, to maintain order in the room and enforce the ritual norms, some of the more experienced daimistas are nominated "guardians." It is their duty to determine where the participants must place themselves in the lines and to make sure everyone keeps to his place. They must also oversee the flow of the dancing, resolving any kind of disruption, helping those going through difficulties, controlling the entrance and the exit, etc.

The danced hymnaries are supposed to be occasions of happiness and brotherly feelings. They are therefore open to all who wish to take part, regardless of whether they wear the uniform or not, the only requirement being the compliance to the rules demanding an abstinence of sex and alcohol during the three preceding days and during the following three. Any other restriction should be simply due to practical questions such as the need to avoid over crowding or a disproportional number of newcomers in comparison to the number of more experienced daimistas in uniform.

Concentration

Other rituals are usually closed to those who do not wear the uniform. Such is the case of the "concentration works," performed by uniformed daimistas on the 15th and 30th of every month. Lasting for between two to four hours, this ritual which aims to promote spiritual development is largely performed in silence, while those taking part remain seated keeping their backs straight. Initially, they must try to focus their minds in one direction leading to a gradual quieting of the stream of thought. Once this has been accomplished, they enter into a state of meditation and identification with the "Internal and Higher Self," and with the "Divine Power," transcending all ideas, names and forms. This ceremony, which may also include reading from the Gospels and from the sacred scriptures of other great religions or instructions and sermons by the commander of the works, usually ends with all those present standing and singing Mestre Irineu's last eleven hymns which are considered to be a summary of his doctrine.

Latecomers are not usually allowed in during these sessions and the Daime is only served at given moments. The point of these rules is to avoid any disturbance of the atmosphere of tranquillity and complete silence, essential for meditation

[. . . .]

The Healing Works

As discussed above, ayahuasca is frequently used by shamans and vegetalistas to fight physical and spiritual illness. It is through healing episodes attributed to their shamanic abilities that ayahuasquero masters become respected and influential in their communities. So healing is probably the field in which variations in ritual occur most often, since the gift of healing is considered an individual attribute. Therefore, those who distinguish themselves as healers, tend to develop their own way of doing things, adopting the practices that best fit their specific powers and personal idiosyncrasies. In the case of the Peruvian *mestizo* vegetalistas, for example, in spite of their common ideas about the nature of illnesses and about the principles of healing, each shaman has his own songs, allied spirits and specific methods of healing.

Among the daimistas, Mestre Irineu was known, above all, as a powerful healer, as was Padrinho Sebastião and a few others of their followers. The daimista healers' repertoire of religious conceptions is much more restricted than that of the *mestizo* healers, familiar with elements of many Indian, European and African cultures, borrowing and adapting them in the way they find most suitable. But, even feeling a need to remain faithful to their doctrine, the followers of Padrinho Sebastião consider their center to be free and eclectic, allowing for other influences in their work and this also gives them a certain degree of flexibility in their rituals.

So, alongside the traditional ceremonies taught by Mestre Irineu, the followers of his doctrine resort to a wide range of other healing techniques. . . .[36] Some writers make a distinction between different methods used by daimista healers, calling one type "direct therapeutic techniques" (making use of medicinal plants, poultices, massages, etc.) and the "indirect" ones (using dreams, visions, "astral work," etc.). But, the basic instrument is the Daime and its main allies: the spirits of the water, of the forest and of the astral plane; certain collections of hymns, the feeling of brotherhood (in the dancing, in the help offered during healing works, etc.); other allies are the medicinal plants and different types of diets—"by the mouth," "in the bed" and "from the surroundings."[37]

The techniques employed by healers, during the works may be classified as follows:[38]

Mirações (Visions): when the healer receives detailed information, from divine beings, to be transmitted to the patients.

Autoscopy: journeying inside the patient's body with the help of a spiritual guide, who diagnoses its physical and mental condition.

Co-autoscopy: when more than one participant journey inside someone's body, a room or an open place. They feel they are having visions in common.

Ecstatic Flight: A journey through different places in the world with a specific mission.

Possession: Identical phenomenon to the mediumistic incorporation in Afro-Brazilian cults.

Among the most recent techniques, incorporated to the daimista healing repertoire, is the use of crystals to reestablish the "balance of energy" of those undergoing difficulties during the works. In São Paulo, for instance, the godmother of Flôr das Águas church had already developed a healing technique using different types of crystals, even before affiliating herself to the doctrine. Under her guidance, this practice acquired considerable importance, among daimistas in São Paulo.

The *Feitio* or the Preparation of the Daime

The making of the brew involves a complex ritual procedure which is frequently considered to be the most important of the daimista ceremonies since all the other rituals depend on the brew produced on these occasions. The manufacture of the beverage follows detailed ritual prescriptions and must be correctly executed, in order to assure the efficacy of the sacrament. Since the brew is considered to be a divine being, akin to the consecrated host in the Roman Catholic Church, the *feitio* is an act of magic and consecration, demanding that those taking part undergo a rigorous physical and spiritual preparation.

The process is extremely laborious and physically demanding. Those who go into the forest, in search of the ingredients commonly undergo all kinds of privations and discomforts and those who are directly involved in the manufacture must carry out tasks involving great physical effort such as hammering the vine to reduce it to fiber, chopping wood and cleaning the oven. But this ritual is also considered to be a moment allowing great spiritual purification and interior development, demanding silence and great concentration. It is, also, the only ritual during which the Daime supply is freely available for all to take as much as they wish.

During this ritual, the exhaustion and the effect of the brew bring the participants face to face with their weakness and personal difficulties and more than ever those taking part are led to understand the importance of the basic spiritual qualities emphasized by the doctrine: firmness, purity of heart, humility, discipline, harmony, love, justice and truth. The work is carried out in a "feitio" house, specially built for the purpose, where a Caravaca cross and an image of the Virgin are always present. Other daimista symbols are also to be seen such as the sun, the moon and stars.

In the same way as in other rites, the *feitio* has a commander directing the works, generally the local *padrinho*. In certain cases, he might be another highly experienced specialist, called in from other churches.

As in other rituals, men and women are kept separate and engaged in activities considered appropriate to their gender. The usual recommendations of abstinence from sex and alcoholic beverages apply and no food may be consumed in the *feitio* house. Men are given the heavy work, like collecting, transporting, cleaning and hammering the liana, besides preparing the brew, which involves handling big cauldrons with boiling liquid and keeping the fire. When the church has its own plantation, the women gather the *Psychotria viridis* leaves and clean them one by one. Otherwise they are gathered by the men in the forest, and brought to the village to be cleaned by the women.

The search and harvesting of the liana and the leaves is probably the most difficult part of the *feitio*, requiring great experience and knowledge of the forest. Nowadays this stage tends to be reserved for specialized groups of *mateiros*, or woodsmen, who have a great knowledge of the forest. Some churches now have their own plantations, which makes the work much easier and all can join in and help. Maybe because daimistas tend to prepare large quantities of the brew at a time (somewhere between one hundred and five hundred liters), their harvesting methods are much simpler than those used by the vegetalistas studied by Luna and Dobkin de Rios.[39] In place of the ceremonious procedures of the Peruvians, daimistas simply pull the liana from the trees, cutting it into pieces 20 centimeters long on the spot and then packing them into bags that may come to weigh up to fifty kilos.

The next stage happens in the *feitio* house, where men clean the pieces of liana, peeling off the skin and removing dirt and imperfect bits. During this work participants must remain in concentration and strive for their own inner cleansing. Next comes the "beating," the ceremonial pounding of the liana, usually set to begin at 2:00 A.M. and carried out by groups of twelve, who alternate in two hours shifts. The liana or *jagube* pieces are placed on tree stumps fixed to the ground and beaten with hard wooden hammers. Hymns are sung to help keep the rhythm of the pounding.

The next step involves the cooking of the brew. This is generally done using three sixty-litre cauldrons placed over a big furnace with three openings, one for each pan and using wood for fuel. In the cauldrons the liana fibers and the leaves are placed in alternating layers, up to the brim. It is estimated that for every bag of *jagube* half a bag of leaves must be used. The important balance between the "power" and "light" of the brew depends on the right dosing of the ingredients.

The cauldrons are then filled with crystalline water and left on the fire for several hours until the liquid has been boiled down to a third of its original volume. This is the most delicate stage of the procedure. . . . Once this point is reached the cauldrons are taken off the fire and the liquid, now called *cozimento*, is strained and set aside. The cauldrons are once again filled with liana and leaves, and the *cozimento* is then poured back in. Once again, the sixty litres are boiled down to twenty, and the, so called, "First Degree Daime" is obtained. Boiling the same liana and leaves with fresh "cozimento," one gets the "Second Degree Daime" and, repeating the procedure, "Third Degree Daime."

Once ready, the brew is cooled and aired by continuous transferring from the cauldron to bowls and jars and then back again to the cauldron. The Daime is then poured into big bottles which have been previously carefully cleaned and dried and which are filled to the brim so as to ensure that no air remains, to avoid fermentation. They are closed with wooden or cork stoppers and the quality of the brew is insured for many years. . . .

Notes

CHAPTER 1

1. John Burdick, *Looking for God in Brazil: Progressive Catholicism in Urban Brazil's Religious Arena* (Berkeley: University of California Press, 1993).

2. Rowan Ireland, *Kingdoms Come: Religion and Politics in Brazil* (Pittsburgh: University of Pittsburgh Press, 1991).

3. For discussions of the term "popular" see Daniel H. Levine, ed., *Religion and Political Conflict in Latin America* (Chapel Hill: University of North Carolina Press, 1986) and David Lehmann, *Struggle for the Spirit: Religious Transformation and Populist Culture in Brazil and Latin America* (London: Polity, 1996).

4. Two examples of this approach are John Burdick, *Looking for God in Brazil*, and Daniel Levine, *Popular Voices in Latin American Catholicism* (Princeton, NJ: Princeton University Press, 1992).

5. See the University of Florida project, "Latin American Immigrants in the New South: the Politics of Encounter," available at http://www.latam.ufl.edu/ NewFordProjectSite/ index.shtml. Last visited October 24, 2007.

6. See Manuel A. Vásquez, *The Brazilian Popular Church and the Crisis of Modernity* (Cambridge: Cambridge University Press, 1998). Ralph Della Cava's *Miracle at Joaseiro* (New York: Columbia University Press, 1970) was ahead of its time not only in its nuanced treatment of popular religion but also in its careful contextualization of a local event.

7. For an influential synthesis of the influence of Marx, Gramsci, and Weber in the study of Latin American religion, see Otto Maduro, *Religion and Social Conflicts* (Maryknoll, NY: Orbis Books, 1982). See also Roger Lancaster, *Thanks to God and the Revolution: Popular Culture and Class Consciousness in the New Nicaragua* (New York: Columbia University Press, 1989). Among other significant points of encounter between Marxism and religion are the Christians for Socialism movement and Frei Betto's conversation with Fidel Castro. See *Fidel and Religion: Fidel Castro Talks on Revolution and Religion with Frei Betto* (New York: Simon and Schuster, 1987).

8. See Jean Comaroff, *Body of Power, Spirit of Resistance: The Culture and History of a South African People* (Chicago: University of Chicago Press, 1985), Reynaldo Ileto, *Pasyon and Revolution: Popular Movements in the Philippines*

(Manila: Ateneo de Manila University Press, 1997), James Scott, *Weapons of the Weak: Everyday Forms of Peasant Resistance* (New Haven, CT: Yale University Press, 1987). David Stoll uses this idea of the weapons of the weak to explain the dynamics of evangelical Protestant growth in Guatemala during the civil war.

9. Mikhail Bakhtin, *Rabelais and His World* (Bloomington, IN: Indiana University Press, 1984). For an application to Latin America, see David Guss, *The Festive State: Race, Ethnicity, and Nationalism as Cultural Performance* (Berkeley: University of California Press, 2000).

10. The distinction between a secular study of religion in the spirit of the social sciences and cultural studies and the insider's perspective on theology is only recently gaining currency in Latin America. Because of its attempt to reflect on the reality in which it finds itself, Latin American theology has been in close dialogue with the social sciences and humanities. For example, theologians such as Gustavo Gutiérrez, Leonardo Boff, and Juan Luis Segundo drew heavily from sociology, anthropology, and economics to build their context-sensitive theologies.

11. For paradigmatic examples of this approach, see Thomas Bruneau, *The Church in Brazil: The Politics of Religion* (Austin: University of Texas Press, 1982), Daniel H. Levine, *Religion and Politics in Latin America: The Catholic Church in Venezuela and Colombia* (Princeton, NJ: Princeton University Press, 1981), and Brian Smith, *The Church and Politics in Chile: Challenges to Modern Catholicism* (Princeton, NJ: Princeton University Press, 1981).

12. See R. Andrew Chesnut, *Competitive Spirits: Latin America's New Religious Economy* (New York: Oxford University Press, 2003), and Anthony Gill, *Render unto Caesar: The Catholic Church and the State in Latin America* (Chicago: University of Chicago Press, 1998). Both of these books are influenced by the work of U.S. sociologists of religion Peter Berger and Rodney Stark.

13. For a critique of the rational choice approach, see David Smilde, *Reason to Believe: Cultural Agency in Latin American Evangelicalism* (Berkeley: University of California Press, 2007). See also the debate in "Discussion: Rational Choice Theory," available at http://lanic.utexas.edu/project/rla/papers. Last visited October 24, 2007.

14. See Elizabeth Brusco, *The Reformation of Machismo: Evangelical Conversion and Gender in Colombia* (Austin: University of Texas Press, 1995); Lesley Gill, "'Like a Veil to Cover Them': Women and the Pentecostal Movement in La Paz," *American Ethnologist* 17, no. 4 (1990): 708-21; Cecilia Loreto Mariz and Maria das Dores Machado, "Pentecostalism and Women in Brazil," and Carol Ann Drogus, "Private Power or Public Power: Pentecostalism, Base Communities, and Gender," both in *Power, Politics, and Pentecostals in Latin America*, eds. Edward Cleary and Hannah Stewart-Gambino (Boulder, CO: Westview Press, 1998).

15. See John Burdick, *Blessed Anastacia: Women, Race, and Popular Christianity in Brazil* (New York: Routledge, 1998); and Stephen Selka, *Religion and the Politics of Ethnic Identity in Bahia, Brazil* (Gainesville: University Press of Florida, 2007).

16. See John Beverley, *Subalternity and Representation: Arguments in Cultural Theory* (Durham, NC: Duke University Press, 1999).

17. See Carolyn Dean, *Inka Bodies and the Body of Christ: Corpus Christi in Colonial Cuzco, Peru* (Durham, NC: Duke University Press, 1999); Irene Silverblatt, *Modern Inquisitions: Peru and the Colonial Origins of the Civilized World* (Durham, NC: Duke University Press, 2004); Edward L. Cleary and Timothy J. Steigenga, *Resurgent Voices in Latin America: Indigenous Peoples, Political Mobilization, and Religious Change* (New Brunswick, NJ: Rutgers University Press, 2004).

18. Eugenio Maurer, et al., *The Indian Face of God in Latin America* (Maryknoll, NY: Orbis Books, 1998).

19. See Dwight Hopkins, et al., *Religions/Globalizations: Theories and Cases* (Durham, NC: Duke University Press, 2001); Manuel A. Vásquez and Marie Friedmann Marquardt, *Globalizing the Sacred: Religion across the Americas* (New Brunswick, NJ: Rutgers University Press, 2003).

20. See Paul C. Johnson, *Diaspora Conversions: Black Carib Religion and the Recovery of Africa* (Berkeley: University of California Press, 2007); J. Lorand Matory, *Black Atlantic Religion: Tradition, Transnationalism, and Matriarchy in the Afro-Brazilian Candomblé* (Princeton, NJ: Princeton University Press, 2005); Cristina Rocha, *Zen in Brazil: The Quest for Cosmopolitan Modernity* (Honolulu: University of Hawaii Press, 2005).

CHAPTER 2

1. See Kirkpatrick Sale, *The Conquest of Paradise: Christopher Columbus and the Columbian Legacy* (New York: Knopf, 1990); and Keith Thomas, *Man and the Natural World: Changing Attitudes in England, 1500-1800* (London: Penguin, 1983).

2. *The Destruction of the Jaguar: Poems from the Books of Chilam Balam*, trans. Christopher Sawyer-Laucanno (San Francisco: City Lights Books, 1987), i.

3. Enrique Florescano, *The Myth of Quetzalcoatl*, trans. Lysa Hochroth (Baltimore, MD: Johns Hopkins University Press, 1999), 110.

4. Kay Almere Read, *Time and Sacrifice in the Aztec Cosmos* (Bloomington: Indiana University Press, 1998), 59.

5. Neil Baldwin, *Legends of the Plumed Serpent: Biography of a Mexican God* (New York: Public Affairs, 1998), 10. A rich Spanish-language source of Aztec stories and poems is Librado Silva and Natalio Hernandez, *Flor y canto de los antigos mexicanos* (Mexico City: Publicaciones Mexicanas, 1990), which includes a number of stories about Quetzalcoatl.

6. Elizabeth Hill Boone, "Introduction," *Native Traditions in the Postconquest World*, ed. Elizabeth Hill Boone and Tom Cummins (Washington, DC: Dumbarton Oaks Research Library and Collection, 1998), 5, 6.

7. David Guss, *To Weave and Sing* (Berkeley: University of California Press, 1989), 14, 52, 54.

8. Eduardo Viveiros de Castro, *From the Enemy's Point of View* (Chicago: University of Chicago Press, 1992).

9. Ibid.

10. "Yanomami in Peril: An Interview with Davi Kopenawa Yanomami." *Multinational Monitor* 13, no. 9 (September 1992).

11. See Kay B. Warren, *Indigenous Movements and Their Critics: Pan-Maya Activism in Guatemala* (Princeton, NJ: Princeton University Press, 1998).

12. See Duncan Earle, "Authority, Social Conflict, and the Rise of Protestantism: Religious Conversion in a Mayan Village." *Social Compass* 39(3): 377-88. Other scholars argue that the impact of evangelical Protestantism on indigenous populations is more ambivalent. For example, the translation of the Bible into indigenous languages has in some cases contributed to the preservation of these languages.

CHAPTER 2 DOCUMENTS

1. This document is reprinted from Thomas Ballantine Irving, ed., *The Maya's Own Words* (Culver City, CA: Labyrinthos Press, 1985), 13-15, 38-40, and 47-49. Used by kind permission of Labyrinthos Press.

2. Here and elsewhere I am omitting the names of several other deities. Notice how gods and kings tend to appear in pairs in the Mayan culture, although this couple is associated with a third being, Hurricane, the Heart of Heaven, Gucumatz is Kiché for "Feathered Snake," and is a translation of Quetzalcoatl in Aztec and of Kukulcan in Yucatecun (Yucatan Mayan). His green feathers are mentioned in the next sentence, and in the play, *Warrior of Rabinal,* the princess is distinguished by her emerald plumes, which were a symbol of deity or of royalty.

3. Compare the beginning of the Gospel of John; this may be Christian influence.

4. This was Ish-Mucanch and Ish-Piyacoc, whom we shall meet in Chap. 3. The beans, bright red in color, were from the tzite or coral tree, which also furnished the wood for the first men.

5. These sounds imitate the noise of the grindstone or metate when corn is being ground on it.

6. This indicates that the leaders of the Kiches knew Mexico before coming to Guatemala. Tula lies sixty miles north of Mexico City in the state of Hidalgo.

7. Even today in some outlying districts with poor roads the standard transportation for heavy objects is with a tumpline or *mecapal.*

8. Notice how quickly Nícahtucah is dropped; as Iki-Balam died without issue, his god was forgotten. *The Title of the Lords of Totonicapan* goes so far as to say he was a bachelor.

9. This seems to refer to the Toltec migration under Quetzalcoatl or Guku-mutz, as the Kichés called him. Some went to the "East," or Yucatan, where he was called Kukulcan while others came to Guatemala.

10. This document is reprinted from the *Florentine Codex: General History of the Things of New Spain*, by Fray Bernardino de Sahagun, *Book 3: The Origins of the Gods*, trans. Arthur J. O. Anderson and Charles E. Dibble, copyright © 1978 by the School for Advanced Research, Santa Fe, pp. 13-15, 34-35, and 65-67. The original footnotes have been removed. Used by kind permission of the School for Advanced Research Press.

11. This document is reprinted from *The Huarochiri Manuscript: A Testament of Ancient and Colonial Andean Religion*, trans. and ed. Frank Solomon and George L. Urioste, copyright © 1991, pp. 71-76. All footnotes removed from origi-nal except one. Bracketed comments are in the original. Used by kind permission of the University of Texas Press.

12. Because Corpus Christi roughly coincides with the dry season climax of the Andean ritual calendar, it has consistently become in Andean eyes the "great" festival of Catholicism and an occasion for performing nominally forbidden An-dean rites.

13. This document is reprinted from *Watunna: An Orinoco Creation Cycle*, by Marc de Civrieux, ed. and trans. David M. Guss, copyright © 1980, pp. 21-22 and 23-27. Used by kind permission of the University of Texas Press.

CHAPTER 3

1. Manuel A. Vásquez, "The Cult of the Saints in the Americas," in *Santos: Contemporary Devotional Folk Art in Puerto Rico* (Gainesville, FL: Samuel P. Harn Museum of Art, 2003), 27-42.

2. Irene Silverblatt, *Moon, Sun, Witches: Gender Ideologies and Class in Inca and Colonial Peru* (Princeton, NJ: Princeton University Press, 1987).

3. Bernal Díaz de Castillo, *The Conquest of New Spain*, trans. J. M. Cohen (New York: Penguin, 1963), 153.

4. Díaz, *Conquest of New Spain*, 32.

5. Díaz, *Conquest of New Spain*, 277.

6. Kirkpatrick Sale, *The Conquest of Paradise: Christopher Columbus and the Columbian Legacy* (New York: Knopf, 1990), 74.

7. Laura de Mello e Souza, *The Devil and the Land of the Holy Cross* (Austin: University of Texas Press, 2004), 10-13, 39-43.

8. Richard Greenleaf, "Introduction," in *The Roman Catholic Church in Latin America*, ed. Richard Greenleaf (New York: Knopf, 1971), 1.

9. Antonio Vieira, "Sermon Condemning Indian Slavery," in *A Documentary History of Brazil*, ed. E. Bradford Burns (New York: Knopf, 1966), 83, 86. It is worth noting, as a number of contemporary scholars point out, that arguments

by Las Casas, Vieira, and others opposed to the enslavement of Native Americans sometimes helped justify the importation of slaves from Africa to perform backbreaking work in mines and plantations.

10. See Silverblatt, *Moon, Sun, and Witches*, and Kathryn Burns, *Colonial Habits: Convents and the Spiritual Economy of Cuzco, Peru* (Durham, NC: Duke University Press, 1999), 88, 203.

11. Orlando Espin, "Trinitarian Monotheism and the Birth of Popular Catholicism: The Case of Sixteenth-Century Mexico," *Missiology: An International Review* 20, no. 2 (April 1992): 177-204.

12. David Tavarez, "Autonomy, Honor, and the Ancestors," in *Local Religion in Colonial Mexico*, ed. Martin Austing Nesvig (Albuquerque: University of New Mexico Press, 2006), 121.

13. Louise M. Burkhart, *Holy Wednesday: A Nahua Drama from Early Colonial Mexico* (Philadelphia: University of Pennsylvania Press, 1996), 4-5.

14. Burkhart, *Holy Wednesday*, 93-95.

15. Carolyn Dean, *Inka Bodies and the Body of Christ: Corpus Christi in Colonial Cuzco, Peru* (Durham, NC: Duke University Press, 1999), 177.

16. Dean, *Inka Bodies*, 166.

CHAPTER 3 DOCUMENTS

1. This document is reprinted from Lewis Hanke, ed., *History of Latin American Civilization*. Vol. 1, *The Colonial Experience* (Boston: Little, Brown, 1967), 149-52; originally "Ordenanzas de Su Magestad para los nuevos describimientos, conquistas y pacificaciones—Julio de 1573," *Collección de documentos inéditos relativos al descubrimiento, conquista y organización de las antiguas posesiones españolas de América y Oceanía, sacados de los archivos del reino y muy especialmente del de Indias* (Madrid, 1964-1884), 16:142-87, passim, and 16:152-54, "Title of the Encomienda Given to Julian Gutiérrez Altamirano in Chile, 1566." Used by kind permission of Joanne Hanke Schwarz.

2. This document reprinted from Bartolomé de las Casas, "Preface," to *In Defense of the Indians*, trans. and ed. Stafford Poole (De Kalb: Northern Illinois University Press, 1992, 17-22. Used by kind permission of Northern Illinois University Press.

3. This document is reprinted from James H. Carmichael, "Recurrent Idolatry and Religious Syncretism," in *The Roman Catholic Church in Latin America*, ed. Richard Greenleaf (New York: Knopf, 1971), 140-47. Orig. "Balsalobre on Idolatry in Oaxaca," *Boletín del Instituto de Estudios Oaxaquenos*, no. 13 (1959): 1-12. Interpolations in brackets are by Carmichael.

4. This document is reprinted from Nathan Wachtel, "Marrano Religiosity in Hispanic America in the Seventeenth Century," in *The Jews and the Expansion of Europe to the West, 1450-1800*, eds. Paolo Bernardini and Norman Fiering (New

York: Berghahan Books, 2001), 149-64 (plus corresponding endnotes). Used by kind permission of Berghahn Books Inc.

5. The term "Marrano" has therefore a much wider connotation than crypto-Judaism in the strict sense of the word.

6. I focus my attention on the New Christians of New Spain in the first half of the seventeenth century mainly because the series of Inquisition trials in the Mexican archives (especially those produced by the repression of the "Great Conspiracy") are extraordinarily rich in evidence. From time to time, however, to supplement the picture, I shall stray outside this main period and geographic area. . . .

7. It is true that when the accused alluded to their hesitation regarding the two "laws," this was on many occasions part of their defense strategy. Nevertheless, the terms they use and the context entitle us to give credence to their statements.

8. AGN [Archivo General de la Nación de México], *Inquisición*, Trial of Ruy Díaz Nieto, vol. 157, exp. 1 (unpaginated).

9. AGN, *Inquisición*, Trial of Antonio Fernández Cardado, vol. 378, exp. 1, fol. 176r.

10. Ibid., fol. 305v.

11. Ibid., fol. 180v.

12. AGN, *Inquisición*, Trial of Micaela Enríquez, vol. 397, fol. 266v.

13. AGN, *Inquisición*, Trial of Margarita de Rivera, vol. 394, exp. 2, fols. 370r-370v.

14. AGN, *Inquisición*, Trial of Ruy Díaz Nieto, vol. 157, exp. 1 (unpaginated).

15. AGN, *Inquisición*, Trial of Margarita de Rivera, vol. 394, exp. 2, fols. 285r-286v, 451r-452v.

16. AGN, *Inquisición*, Trial of Isabel Nuñez, vol. 401, exp. 1, fol. 17v.

17. AGN, *Inquisición*, Trial of Jorge Duarte, vol. 431, exp. 4, fols. 106r-106v.

18. Cf. Solange Alberro, *Inquisition et société au Mexique (1571-1700)* (Mexico, 1988), 213.

19. AGN, *Inquisición*, Trial of Juan Pacheco de León, vol. 400, exp. 2, fols. 705r-705v.

20. This document is reprinted from *Felipe Poma de Ayala's Appeal Concerning the Priests* [1615] in *Colonial Spanish America: A Documentary History*, ed. Kenneth Mills and William B. Taylor (Wilmington, DE: SR Books, 1998), 158-64. Used by kind permission of SR Books.

CHAPTER 4

1. On the demographics of the slave trade, see David Eltis, "The Volume and Structure of Transatlantic Slave Trade: A Reassessment," *William and Mary Quarterly* 58, no. 1 (2001): 17-31.

2. According to Murphy (1994: 83) at least sixteen nations had registered *cabildos* in Havana by the emancipation in the 1880s.

3. Palmié (2002) offers an insightful analysis of how Palo Monte was constructed as the transgressive underside of *Regla Ocha*, as the tradition concerned with witchcraft, the offensive use of spiritual forces (*bakisi*) concentrated in sacred objects (*nkisi*).

4. There is an ongoing debate on why the Yoruba came to dominate the production of religion and culture in diaspora, despite not being numerically the largest population. Arguments range from the fact that the Yoruba had the most elaborate and institutionalized religion in Africa to their relatively late arrival in great numbers to the New World to the role of European academics and transnational African elites in constructing a new identity. See Matory (2005).

5. The term "Malê," which in Bahia was not an ethnic designation but was used to refer to any African who practiced Islam, seems to have derived from the name Yorubas gave to Hausa slave traders (Reis 1993), most of whom were Muslims.

6. These groups are located in areas of Africa (i.e., the northern tier of Nigeria and the Senegambia region) that have had a long history of contact with Islam through trade networks.

7. In Venezuela, Umbanda has also interacted with the local cult of María Lionza (an indigenous queen who protects the forest. She is portrayed as an Amazon riding a *danta*).

8. As members of the same Yoruban family of African-based religions, Candomblé, Umbanda, and Santería share some of the same *orixás* and their characterizations. However, there are important differences. For example, Changó in Santería is St. Barbara, not St. Jerome, while Yemayá is La Virgen de La Regla, and Ochun is Our Lady of Charity, Cuba's patroness. See Murphy (1994) for a similar chart for Santería.

9. The other divination system is the *ifá*, which uses eight coconut rinds and is the province only of the *babalawo*, literally the "father of the mystery." See Gonzales-Wippler (1987). Interestingly, divination is much rarer in Candomblé. To the extent that it is performed, it is through the *jogo de búzios*, a "shell game" far simpler than *ifá* or *dilogún*.

10. See the text of the U.S. Supreme Court decision in *Journal of Church and State* 35, no. 3 (1993): 668-95.

11. See Motta (1998). Johnson (2002) observes a similar tendency toward textualization, bureaucratization, doctrinal systematization, and deterritorialization through television, film, and the Internet, as Candomblé goes from an ethnic religion defined by a defensive secrecy to a public religion.

CHAPTER 4 DOCUMENTS

1. Taken from Robert E. Conrad, ed., *Children of God's Fire: A Documentary History of Black Slavery in Brazil* (University Park: Pennsylvania State University Press, 1994), 154-63. Used by kind permission of Pennsylvania State University Press.

2. Editors' note: The term *"Mina"* was used to describe slaves from West Africa, particularly from the Blight of Benin.

3. Taken from Robert E. Conrad, ed., *Children of God's Fire*, 178-80. Original source: D. Domingos de Loreto Couto, *Desagravos do Brasil e glórias de Pernambuco. Discursos brasílicos, dogmáticos, bélicos, apologéticos, moraes, e históricos*, in *Annaes da Biblioteca Nacional do Rio de Janeiro*, Vol. 25 (1903), 158-59. Used by kind permission of Pennsylvania State University Press.

4. This document is reprinted from Roger Bastide, "Black Islam in Brazil," in *The African Religions of Brazil: Toward a Sociology of the Interpenetration of Civilizations* (Baltimore, MD: Johns Hopkins University Press, 1978), 143-54, copyright © Presses Universitaries de France, 1978. Used by kind permission of the Presses Universitaires de France.

5. Nina Rodrigues was the first to connect the words *"malê"* and *"malankê"* (*O Animismo Fetichista dos Negros Bahianos* [Rio de Janeiro: Civilização Brasileira, 1935], p. 30). He discusses this etymology again in *Os Africanos no Brasil* (São Paulo: Cia. Editora Nacional, 1932), pp. 109-12. . . .

6. Nina Rodrigues, *Os Africanos*, pp. 167-75; Romos [sic] *Cultural Negras*, pp. 335-41.

7. Joseph de Crozals, *Les Peuhls: Étude d'Ethnologie Africaine* (Paris: Maisonneuve, 1883); P. Henry, *Les Bambara* (Münster, 1910); H. Labouret, *Les Tribus du Rameau Lobi* (Paris: Institut d'Ethnographie, 1931), 2: 510; E. F. Gautier, *L'Afrique Noire Occidentale* (Paris: Librairie Larose, 1935); G. Cheron, "La Circonision et l'Excision chez les Malanke," *Journal de la Société des Africanistes* 3, # 2 (1933): 297-303; etc.

8. Sud Menucci, *O Precursor de Abolicionismo no Brasil, Luis Gama*, pp. 117n. My own research, as was the case in Rio, shows that no real mosque existed in São Paulo and that the black Mussulmans celebrated their cult in a private house. . . .

9. Alex J. de Mello Moraes Filho, *Festas e Tradições Populares do Brasil* [sic] (org. pub. 1888; Rio de Janeiro: F. Briguiet, 1946), p. 333; Ramos, *O Negro Brasileiro*, pp. 90-91; F. Mendes de Almeida, "O Folclore nas Ordenações do Reino," *RAM de SP* 56 (1939): 53.

10. João de Rio, *As Religôes no Rio*, p. 16.

11. João de Rio, "O Natal dos Africanos," *Kosmos*, December 1904. For the opposite view see Nina Rodrigues, *Os Africanos*, p. 108: "The *iman* tells me . . . that in Rio too there is a regularly organized Mussulman church which, unlike the one in Bahia, is not subject to the ban on high church holidays and which celebrates them with great pomp. But so far as I can make out this is actually a church of Arab Mussulmans that admits Malê Negroes."

12. Almeida, "O Folclore," p. 53. . . .

13. Ramos, *Culturas Negras*, p. 337.

14. Ibid., p. 345.

15. Manoel Querino, *Costumes Africanos no Brasil* (Rio de Janeiro: Civilização Brasileira, 1938), pp. 111-12.

16. Nina Rodrigues, *Os Africanos*, p. 101.

17. Querino, *Costumes*, p. 110. Étienne Brasil, however, says that the Mussulmans had plenty of faults. Since this is a Catholic priest speaking, he was probably thinking chiefly of polygamy.

18. This, of course, refers to free Negroes: slavery precluded the observation of these sacred times. The slaves' inability to make the rhythm of his day conform to the rules of his faith must be regarded as one of the reasons for revolts against the slave regime. This confirms our already stated thesis that the black Mussulman revolts were religious in nature.

19. Ademar Vidal, "Costumes e Praticas do Negro," in *O Negro no Brasil* (n.d.), p. 49.

20. Querino, *Costumes*, p. 111.

21. Ibid.

22. Nina Rodrigues, *Os Africanos*, pp. 89, 93, 98.

23. Raeders, *Comte de Gobineau*, p. 76.

24. Querino, *Costumes*, p. 111.

25. Ibid., 118.

26. Ibid., 111.

27. Étienne Brasil, "La Secte Musulmane de Malê du Brésil," *Anthropos* 4 (1909): 104.

28. Querino, *Costumes*, pp. 111-12.

29. Ramos, *O Negro Brasileiro*, p. 92.

30. Querino, *Costumes*, p. 120.

31. Brasil, "Le Secte Musulmane," p. 103.

32. Querino, *Costumes*, p. 113; Brasil, "Le Secte Musulman," pp. 103-5.

33. Nina Rodrigues, *Os Africanos*, p. 102.

34. Nonetheless Nina Rodrigues saw a map of Mecca hanging on the wall in the house of the *limano* Luis (*Os Africanos*, p. 102). Did the priest perhaps accomplish his pilgrimage in the fond hopes of his imagination?

35. Querino, *Costumes*, pp. 120-21.

36. Nina Rodrigues lists some of these talismans. One, for instance, is inscribed with sura 106 of the Koran and with verses 129 and 130 of the second sura. Each verse is repeated several times—in one case 36 times—since reiteration of the text enhances its magic power (*Os Africanos*, pp. 102-7).

37. Ibid., 107.

38. Querino, *Costumes*, pp. 118.

39. Arthur Ramos, *Introdução a Antropologia Brasileira* (Rio de Janeiro, 1951), 1: 248. Editors' note: In pre-Islamic mythology, djinn are supernatural creatures capable of performing (black) magic. "Genie" is an Anglicized rendition of this Arabic word.

40. João do Rio, *As Religôes*, pp. 53-60.

41. Ramos, *O Negro Brasileiro*, p. 82, n. 96.

42. Ramos, *O Negro Brasileiro*, pp. 88-89.

43. Ibid., p. 90.

44. Ibid., p. 83.

45. A. Almeida, Jr., "Sobre o Aguardentismo Colonial," *RAM de SP* 72 (1940): 155-64. This Moslem puritanism in Brazil is to be contrasted with the tolerance extended to black custums in Africa. . . .

46. This document is reprinted from Jim Wafer, *The Taste of Blood: Spirit Possession in Brazilian Candomblé* (Philadelphia: University of Pennsylvania Press, 1991), 16-20 and 55-58. Used by kind permission of the University of Pennsylvania Press.

47. Ogã Gimbereua, *Guia do Pai de Santo no Candomblé* (Rio de Janeiro: Editora Eco, 1990), 8-14, 82-84.

48. Editors' notes: We have translated *"Yaô"* to refer primarily to a female initiate, following the primary source. However, in Candomblé, the term applies to both men and women, since spiritually the initiate is considered as "the bride" of the saint.

49. Editors' note: The little mother is the second in the priestly hierarchy of a Candomblé center. She serves as a kind of mentor to the initiate, guiding the *Yaô* in daily life as well as in ritual events.

50. Editors' note: The *Deká* are the sacred artifacts (containing a high concentration of *axé*, particularly of the *Yaô*'s head *Orixá*), which are passed on to the initiate after she has completed her seven years of training and is, in effect, ready to open her own Candomblé center as a newly consecrated mother-of-the-saint.

51. Editors' note: All these terms refer to various specialized authorities in a Candomblé center's hierarchy, including drummers, singers, and ushers.

52. This excerpt reprinted from David H. Brown, *Santería Enthroned: Art, Ritual, and Innovation in an Afro-Cuban Religion* (Chicago: University of Chicago Press, 2003), 166-68. Used with kind permission of the University of Chicago Press.

53. . . . George Brandon first sought to explain the *asiento* via the throne metaphor, drawing on that same divination proverb: "As the king sits on a throne so does the newborn santero(a); as the head rules the body so is the orisha seated there in the head as the throne from which it rules the priestess" (Brandon 1983, 388).

54. Editors' note: The *ayubona* serves as second godparent of sorts, working very closely with the initiate during the *kariocha* process. In Candomblé, this person is known as the *mãe/pai pequena/o* (the little mother or father).

55. This document is reprinted from Oba Ernesto Pichardo, "Church of the Lukumí Babalu Aye," available at http://www.church-of-the-lukumi.org. Last visited October 24, 2007. Reprinted by kind permission of the Church of Lukumi.

CHAPTER 5

1. The least well known major millenarian movement in Brazil was the Con-testado rebellion, which took place in the southern state of Santa Catarina from 1912 to 1916. This movement had an explicit Sebastianist ideology. See Diacon (1991).

2. Da Cunha published *Os Sertões* in 1902 based on his experiences as a jour-nalist embedded with the Brazilian army.

3. Young Sebastian went to fight "infidels" in Morocco and never made it back. According to the mythology, he is to return from the sea with an army to restore the Portuguese crown to its former glory.

4. David O'Brien, "A Century of Catholic Social Teaching," in John Coleman, S.J., ed., *One Hundred Years of Catholic Social Thought: Celebration and Challenge* (Maryknoll, NY: Orbis Books, 1991), 14.

5. Constitution of the United States of Mexico, Articles 3 and 27, available at http://www.ilstu.edu/class/hist263/docs/ 1917const.html. Last visited October 24, 2007.

6. Clarence Senior, *Land Reform and Democracy* (Gainesville: University of Florida Press, 1958), p. 19. As quoted in Lewis Hanke, *Mexico and the Caribbean* (Princeton: D. Van Nostrand, 1967), p. 99.

7. See James W. Wilkie, "The Meaning of the Cristero Religious War," *Journal of Church and State* (1966): especially 218-25 and 229-33.

8. Juan Perón, "A Denunciation of Certain Argentine Churchmen [1954]." Re-printed in *The Conflict between Church and State in Latin America*, ed. Fredrick B. Pike (New York: Knopf, 1964), 185, 186.

CHAPTER 5 DOCUMENTS

1. Robert Cunninghame Graham, "The Guarani Missions: A Vanished Ar-cadia," in *The Expulsion of the Jesuits from Latin America*, ed. Magnus Morner (New York: Knopf, 1967), chapter 6, 72-75. We have eliminated several footnotes from the original.

2. Blas Garay, "The Guarani Missions: A Ruthless Exploitation of the Indians," in Morner, *The Expulsion of the Jesuits from Latin America*, chapter 5, 64-68.

3. "Sobre a República," in Ataliba Nogueira, *Antônio Conselheiro e Canudos: revisão* (São Paulo: Companhia Editora Nacional, 1974), 175-82. Translated by the editors.

4. Taken from *Execução do Testamento do Padre Cícero Romão Batista e Inventário do Dr. Floro Bartholomeu da Costa. Documentos em Facsímile.* (For-taleza, Ceará: Tribunal de Justiça do Estado do Ceará, 1997), 131-33. Translation by the editors with assistance from Ralph Della Cava.

5. The bishop's actual name was Antônio Luiz dos Santos.

6. Editor's note: Joazeiro is one of the spellings often used for Juazeiro do Norte in the state of Ceará, not to be confused with the eponymous city in the state of Bahia.

7. *Commendador* was an honorific title given to prominent business leaders.

8. This document is reprinted from *Ley de Patronato Ecesiástico* (Caracas, 1911), 4-25, reprinted in Lloyd Mecham, *Church and State in Latin America: A History of Politico-Ecclesiastical Relations*, rev. ed. (Chapel Hill: University of North Carolina Press, 1966), 92-94., copyright © 1966 by the University of North Carolina Press. Used by kind permission of the publisher.

CHAPTER 6

1. David Stoll, *Is Latin America Turning Protestant? The Politics of Evangelical Growth* (Berkeley: University of California Press, 1990).

2. Jean-Pierre Bastian, "The Metamorphosis of Latin American Protestant Groups: A Sociohistorical Perspective." *Latin American Research Review* 28, no. 2 (1993): 37, 38.

3. Of course, some immigration continued. For example, from the 1920s to the 1940s, large numbers of Mennonites moved from Canada to Mexico, particularly lands around Cuauhtémoc in the state of Chihuahua.

4. See "Mission and Evangelism: History," available at http://www.wcc-coe. org/wcc/what/mission/hist-e.html. Last visited October 24, 2007.

5. On the early history of Pentecostalism, see Grant Wacker, *Heaven Below: Early Pentecostals and American Culture* (Cambridge, MA: Harvard University Press, 2001).

6. Around the same time, Italian immigrant to the United States Luigi Francescon was also baptized in the spirit in Chicago and embarked on a mission to São Paulo, where, in 1911, he founded the Christian Congregation of Brazil, the country's other major classical Pentecostal church.

7. See R. Andrew Chesnut, *Born Again in Brazil: The Pentecostal Boom and the Pathogens of Poverty* (New Brunswick, NJ: Rutgers University Press, 1997).

8. See Everett Wilson, "Sanguine Saints: Pentecostalism in El Salvador," *Church History* (1983): 186-98; and Philip J. Williams, "The Sound of Tambourines: The Politics of Pentecostal Growth in El Salvador," in *Power, Politics, and Pentecostals in Latin America*, eds. Edward Cleary and Hannah Stewart-Gambino (Boulder, CO: Westview Press, 1997).

9. Virginia Garrard-Burnett, *Living in the New Jerusalem* (Austin: University of Texas Press, 1998).

10. See the joint study by the Pew Hispanic Project and the Pew Forum on Religion and Public Life: http://pewforum.org/surveys/ hispanic.

11. Deborah Huntington, "The Prophet Motive," in *NACLA Report on the Americas* (Jan./Feb. 1984): 3.

12. Enrique Domínguez, "The Great Commission," in *NACLA Report on the Americas* (Jan./Feb. 1984): 13.

13. David Martin, *Tongues of Fire: The Explosion of Protestantism in Latin America* (Cambridge: Basil Blackwell, 1990), 267-68.

14. Ibid., 284.

15. Ibid., 290. See also Stoll, Is Latin America Turning Protestant?, 312-13.

16. According to Paul Freston (2001: 23), for the Brazilian Assemblies of God, "entry into politics was an act of cultural defence: a reaction to changes in the social milieu threatening to undermine the group's capacity to maintain its culture." Further, he concludes that "pentecostal politicisation seeks to strengthen internal leaderships, protect the frontiers of sectarian reproduction, tap resources for religious expansion and dispute spaces in civil religion." See *Evangelicals and Politics in Africa, Asia, and Latin America* (Cambridge: Cambridge University Press, 2001).

17. In addition to writing *The New Revolutionary Mood in Latin America*, where he advanced a "revolutionary Christian humanism," Richard Shaull is credited with smuggling Paulo Freire's manuscript for *Pedagogy of the Oppressed* out of Brazil, following the 1964 military coup. This book has been enormously influential in progressive Christian circles. Alves, in the meantime, wrote the seminal *Theology of Hope* (1969).

18. Jose Míguez Bonino, *Toward a Christian Political Ethics* (Philadelphia: Fortress, 1983), 43.

19. Medardo Gómez, *Fire against Fire: Christian Ministry Face-to-Face with Persecution*, trans. Mary M. Solberg (Minneapolis: Augsburg Press, 1989), 52.

20. Ibid., 41.

CHAPTER 6 DOCUMENTS

1. This document reprinted from Ivar Vingren, *Gunnar Vingren, O Diario do pionero* (Rio de Janeiro: Casa Publicadora das Assembléias de Deus, 1973), 17-18, 21-22, 23-27, 33-35, 42-44, 45-47, and 65. Translation by the editors. Used by kind permission of Casa Publicadora das Assembléias de Deus.

2. This phrase is in English in the Portuguese original. A better title would be "Jesus Christ is everything to me, all that I need."

3. Christian Lalive d'Epinay, "The Pentecostal 'Conquest' of Chile: Rudiments of a Better Understanding," in *The Religious Situation 1969*, ed. Donald R. Cutler (Boston: Beacon Press, 1969), chapter 12, 179-86, 187-88. Used by kind permission of Christian Lalive d'Epinay.

4. See "La Expansión Protestante en Chile," *Cristianismo y Sociedad*, nos. 9-10, pp. 19-43. . . .

5. Editors' note: by "señorial" Lalive D'Epinay means a quasi feudal system dominated by landed elites.

6. This document is reprinted from Emilio Willems, *Followers of the New Faith: Cultural Change and the Rise of Protestantism in Brazil and Chile*

(Nashville, TN: Vanderbilt University Press, 1967), 12-15, 247-55. Used by kind permission of Vanderbilt University Press.

7. This document is reprinted from Lesley Gill, "'Like a Veil to Cover Them': Women and the Pentecostal Movement in La Paz," *American Ethnologist* 17, no. 4 (Nov. 1990); 712-15 and 719, copyright © 2004 by the American Anthropological Association. Used by kind permission of the American Anthropological Association.

8. ISAL, *Sobre la vida de las iglesias y el movimiento ecuménico en América Latina* (Montevideo: ISAL, 1969), 7-9 and 10-11.

CHAPTER 7

1. A striking example is the Juventude Universitária Católica (JUC) in Brazil, which, shut out by the conservative sectors in the church hierarchy, formed an autonomous socialist movement called Popular Action (*Ação Popular*). This movement was severely repressed by the military regime after the 1964 coup.

2. *Gaudium et Spes*, in *Documents of Vatican II*, ed. Walter Abbott (New York: American Press, 1966), no. 69.

3. This document reprinted from CELAM (Conference of Latin American Bishops), *The Church in the Present-Day Transformation of Latin America in the Light of the Council: Medellín Conclusions* (Washington, DC: National Conference of Catholic Bishops, 1979), 185, 41. Used by kind permission of United States Conference of Catholic Bishops Publishing.

4. CELAM, "Puebla Final Document," in *Puebla and Beyond*, eds. John Eagleson and Philip Scharper, trans. John Drury (Maryknoll, NY: Orbis Books, 1979) 222, 264-67.

5. See Anna Peterson, *Martyrdom and the Politics of Religion* (Albany: State University of New York Press, 1997).

6. Gustavo Gutiérrez, *Las Casas: In Search of the Poor of Jesus Christ*, trans. Robert R. Barr (Maryknoll, NY: Orbis Books, 1993).

7. Josef Cardinal Ratzinger, "Instruction on Certain Aspects of the 'Theology of Liberation'" (Washington, DC: United States Catholic Conference, 1984); available online at http://www.newadvent.org/library/docs_df84lt.htm. Last visited October 24, 2007.

8. On the links between European Catholic Action and progressive Catholicism in Latin America, see David J. Molineaux, "Gustavo Gutiérrez: Historical Origins," *The Ecumenist* 25, no. 5 (July-August 1987): 65-69. The best-known statement of Freire's pedagogy is his *Pedagogy of the Oppressed* (New York: Continuum, 1984).

9. Michael Dodson and Laura Nuzzi O'Shaughnessy, *Nicaragua's Other Revolution: Religious Faith and Political Struggle* (Chapel Hill: University of North Carolina Press, 1990), 155. See also Daniel Levine, *Popular Voices in Latin American Catholicism* (Princeton, NJ: Princeton University Press, 1992).

10. Daniel Levine, "Religion and Politics in Comparative and Historical Perspective," in *Comparative Politics* 19, no. 1 (1986): 118.

11. Camilo Torres, *Revolutionary Priest: The Complete Writings and Messages of Camilo Torres*, ed. John Gerassi (New York: Vintage Books, 1971), 325.

12. See Margaret Randall, *Christians in the Nicaraguan Revolution* (New York: New Star Books, 1984).

13. Penny Lernoux, *Cry of the People* (New York: Penguin Books, 1984), xvii; Jon Sobrino, "Espiritualidad de la persecución y del martirio," *Diakonía* (Managua) 27 (1983): 172.

14. Roger Lancaster, *Life Is Hard: Machismo, Danger, and the Intimacy of Power in Nicaragua* (Berkeley: University of California Press, 1994).

CHAPTER 7 DOCUMENTS

1. This document is reprinted from Manuel Larraín, "Latin America Looks to Catholic Action for a Program of Social Reform," in *South America: Modern Latin America: Continent in Ferment*. Vol 2, *Second Edition: Mexico and the Caribbean*, ed. Lewis Hanke (Princeton, NJ: D. Van Nostrand, 1967), 15-154. Used by kind permission of Joanne Hanke Schwarz.

2. This document is reprinted from CELAM (Conference of Latin American Bishops), *The Church in the Present-Day Transformation of Latin America in the Light of the Council: Medellín Conclusions* (Washington, DC: National Conference of Catholic Bishops, 1979), Document on Justice, Sections 3 and 20; Document on Peace, Sections 15-19. All footnotes are from original. Used by kind permission of United States Conference of Catholic Bishops Publishing.

3. Cf. Vatican Council II, pastoral constitution *Gaudium et spes*, No. 69.

4. Cf. PAUL VI, *Homily of the Mass on Development Day*, Bogotá, 23 August, 1968; Cf. PAUL VI, *Opening Address at the Second General Conference of Latin American Bishops*, Bogotá, 24 August, 1968.

5. Cf. PAUL VI, *Message of January 1st, 1968*.

6. Cf. PAUL VI, *Homily of the Mass on Development Day*, Bogotá, 23 August, 1968.

7. Cf PAUL VI, *Enc. Populorum progressio*, No. 30.

8. Cf. PAUL VI, *Homily of the Mass on Development Day*, Bogotá, 23 August, 1968.

9. Cf. PAUL VI, *Ibid.*

10. Cf. PAUL VI, *Enc. Populorum progressio*, No. 31.

11. Cf. PAUL VI, *Ibid.*

12. This document is reprinted from Gustavo Gutiérrez, "Notes for a Theology of Liberation," *Theological Studies* 31, no. 2 (June 1970): 245-48. All footnotes from original. Used by kind permission of *Theological Studies*.

13. This manner of speaking is found in the well-known work of W. W. Rostow, *The Stages of Economic Growth* (Cambridge, England: Cambridge University Press, 1966).

14. Recall how Karl Marx refers the abolition of private property to the "to be" and not to the "to have" of man. See also the "to have" of the "total man" of H. LeFebare and R. Garaudy.

15. This is the profound meaning of Hegel's dialectic Master-Slave.

16. See the inspiring three-volume work of Ernst Bloch, *Das Prinzip Hoffnung* (Frankfurt/ Main, 1959), as well as Harvey Cox's preface to the English translation of Bloch, *Man on His Own* (New York, 1970).

17. Frei Betto, *O que é comunidade eclesial de base* (Sao Paulo: Abril Cultural/ Editora Brasilense, 1985), 16-22, 29-33, 98-100, and 105-7. Translation by editors.

18. This document is reprinted from Ernesto Cardenal, *The Gospel in Solentiname*, vol. 3 (Maryknoll, NY: Orbis Books, 1979), 117-19. Used by kind permission of Orbis Books.

19. Luke 12:13-21.

20. This document is reprinted from Ernesto Cardenal, *The Gospel in Solentiname*, vol. 4 (Maryknoll, NY: Orbis Books, 1982), 1-2. Used by kind permission of Orbis Books.

21. Luke 17:20-37.

22. This document is reprinted from Oscar Romero, "The Church's Mission amid the National Crisis: Fourth Pastoral Letter," from *Voice of the Voiceless: The Four Pastoral Letters and Other Statements* (Maryknoll, NY: Orbis Books, 1985), 133-36, 143-45, and 155-56. Used by kind permission of Orbis Books.

23. Opening Address, III, 4.

24. Final Document, Section 49; see also sections 314, 547, 549, 1262.

25. Ibid., section 1262.

26. Ibid., section 49.

27. Ibid., section 547.

28. Ibid., section 549.

29. Ibid., section 314.

30. Oscar Romero, "Third Pastoral Letter," in Brockman, *Voice of the Voiceless*, 106.

31. Puebla, Final Document, 1259.

32. Romero, "Third Pastoral Letter," 108-9.

33. "Peace," section 15, quoting Paul VI, homily, Bogota, Aug. 23, 1968.

34. Final Document, sections 515-516, quoting Gal. 3:28.

CHAPTER 8

1. "World religion" is a term used in religious studies to refer to traditions that have historically spread across the globe, through both migration and conversions: Christianity, Islam, Hinduism, Buddhism, and Judaism are the usual examples. Other religions, including indigenous traditions, are often seen as more locally rooted. The term "world religion" is contested, both because it implies a value-laden distinction between "large" and "small" traditions, and because it is

increasingly inaccurate, insofar as many "local" religions, including Latin American ones such as Santería and Umbanda, have a global presence. Moreover, the category emerged as part of the colonial project of extracting knowledge and economic surplus from indigenous populations. See Tomoko Masuzawa, *The Invention of World Religions* (Chicago: University of Chicago Press, 2005).

2. Susanne Hoeber Rudolph, "Introduction: Religion, States, and Transnational Civil Society," in Susane Hoeber Rudolph and James Piscatori, eds., *Transnational Religion and Fading States* (Boulder, CO: Westview Press, 1997), 1.

3. See Manuel A. Vásquez, "The Cult of the Saints in the Americas," in *Santos: Contemporary Devotional Folk Art in Puerto Rico* (Gainesville, FL: Samuel P. Harn Museum of Art, 2003), 27-33; and Kristin Norget, *Days of Death, Days of Life: Ritual in the Popular Culture of Oaxaca* (New York: Columbia University Press, 2006).

4. In fact, the growth in immigration from Latin America in the 1980s and 1990s has been one of the key ingredients in the movement's revitalization in the United States. On the history, worldview, and practices of the CCR, see Thomas J. Csordas, *Language, Charisma, and Creativity: The Ritual Life of a Religious Movement* (Berkeley: University of California Press, 1997).

5. Alfred Hennelly, ed., *Santo Domingo and Beyond* (Maryknoll, NY: Orbis Books, 1993), 81, 82, 100.

6. This is also true of the Neocatechumenate, a lay movement with a much lower public profile than the CCR. See Anna Peterson and Manuel Vásquez, "Upwards, Never Down: The Catholic Charismatic Renewal in Transnational Perspective," in *Christianity, Social Change, and Globalization in the Americas*, ed. A. Peterson, M. Vásquez, and P. Williams (New Brunswick, NJ: Rutgers University Press, 2001), 188-209. It is important not to overstate the contrast between CEBs and the CCR, as at the grass-roots level, Catholics often move back and forth across the two movements.

7. Vicariato Apostólico de Petén, *El Grito de la Selva en el año Jubilar: Entre la Agonía y Esperanza* (Petén, Guatemala: Vicariato Apostólico de Petén, 2000), 9. Echoing this theme, Brazilian theologian Leonardo Boff argues, "The very same logic of the prevailing system of accumulation and social organization that leads to the exploitation of workers also leads to the pillaging of whole nations and ultimately the plundering of nature." In Boff, *Cry of the Earth, Cry of the Poor* (Maryknoll, NY: Orbis Books, 1997), 110-11.

8. U.S. Catholic Bishops, "Welcoming the Stranger among Us: Unity in Diversity" (Washington, DC: U.S. Conference of Catholic Bishops, 2000), 2.

9. U.S. Catholic Bishops and Conferencia del Episcopado Mexicano, "Strangers No Longer: Together on the Journey of Hope" (Washingston, DC: U.S. Conference of Catholic Bishops, 2003), paragraph 38.

10. Deborah White, "Catholic Cardinal Mahoney Slams U.S. House Bill HR 4437," available at http://usliberals.about.com/od/ immigration/a/RMahony.htm. Last visited October 24, 2007.

11. "Changing Faiths: Latinos and the Transformation of American Religion," available at http://pewforum.org/surveys/hispanic. Last visited October 27, 2007.

12. As of 2005, the percentage of Protestants in Guatemala is estimated at 40 percent. See "Religion in Latin America: Statistics," available aat http://lanic. utexas.edu/project/rla /tables/protestants.html. Last visited October 24, 2007.

13. David Stoll, unpublished lecture, University of Florida, Gainesville, 1994-1995.

14. Paul Freston, "The Transnationalisation of Brazilian Pentecostalism," in *Between Babel and Pentecost: Transnational Pentecostalism in Africa and Latin America*, eds. Andre Corten and Ruth Marshall-Fratani (Bloomington: Indiana University Press, 2001), 198.

15. On the Jehovah's Witnesses, see Patricia Fortuny Loret de Mola, "Looking for a System of Order in Life: Jehovah's Witnesses in Mexico," in *Holy Saints and Fiery Preachers: The Anthropology of Protestantism in Mexico and Central America*, eds. James W. Dow and Alan R. Sandstrom (Westport, CT: Praeger, 2001), 87-116. On Adventists, see "Fueled by membership growth in Latin America, Africa and Asia, the Seventh-day Adventist Church is reporting that its membership worldwide climbed in one year by more than 1 million to 13.6 million." *Christian Century* (Dec. 28, 2004).

16. Leonor Ayala, "Mormon Conversions Surge in Latin America," July 13, 2004, available at http://www.msnbc.msn.com/id/5378318/ #storyContinued%20 ;%20www.lds.org. Last visited October 24, 2007. 17. "Interesting Facts," available at http://www. ldschurchtemples.com/facts. Last visited October 24, 2007.

18. See Jeffrey Lesser's *Searching for Home Abroad: Japanese Brazilians and Transnationalism* (Durham, NC: Duke University Press, 2003). Brazil was not the only Latin American country to receive Japanese immigrants. There was also a significant, although smaller, flow to Peru. Immediately following World War II, there was also some immigration to Paraguay, Argentina, Bolivia, and the Dominican Republic.

19. Theosophy is an eclectic worldview, originating in the late 1800s, that incorporates a wide range of religious ideas, including reincarnation, universal consciousness, and karma.

20. In the 1980 census only 1 percent of Brazilians declared themselves not to be affiliated with any religion. This number went up to 7 percent in the 2000 census.

21. *Seicho-no-ie* (House of Infinite Growth) was founded in 1930 and established its first officially recognized society in Brazil in 1952. The movement claims to have as many as 2.5 million followers in the country, mostly among non-Japanese Brazilians. See Robert Carpenter and Wade Clark Roof, "The Transplanting of *Seicho-no-ie* from Japan to Brazil: Moving beyond the Ethnic Enclave," *Journal of Contemporary Religion* 10, no. 1 (1995): 41-54.

22. See Jeffrey Lesser, *Negotiating National Identity: Immigrants, Minorities, and the Struggle for Ethnicity in Brazil* (Durham, NC: Duke University Press, 1999), and Oswaldo Truzzi, "The Right Place at the Right Time: Syrians and

Lebanese in Brazil and the United States," *Journal of American Ethnic History* 16, no. 2 (1997): 1-34.

23. See Steven Vertovec, *Hindu Trinidad: Religion, Ethnicity, and Socioeconomic Change* (London: Macmillan Caribbean, 1992); Aisha Khan, *Callaloo Nation: Metaphors of Race and Religious Identity among South Asians in Trinidad* (Durham, NC: Duke University Press, 2004).

24. See "Communidades de Latino América," available at http://www.congresojudio. org.ar/comunidades.asp. Last visited October 24, 2007.

25. Robert Carpenter, "Esoteric Literature as a Microcosmic Mirror of Brazil's Religious Market," in *Latin American Religion in Motion*, eds. Christian Smith and Joshua Prokopy (New York: Routledge, 1999), 236.

26. Deis Siqueira and Richardo Barbosa de Lima, eds., *Sociologia das adesões: novas religiosidades e a busca místico-esotérica na capital do Brasil* (Rio de Janeiro: Garamond & Editora Vieira, 2003).

27. In fact, ayahuasca means "vine of the spirits" in Quechua.

28. Robin M. Wright, "Preface of the Book: Brazil's Ayahuasca Religions," unpublished manuscript, 7.

29. Ibid., 8.

30. Unfortunately, there is very little literature in English on Ayahuasca religions. For a good account of the evolution of the use of Ayahuasca in Brazil, see Beatriz Caiuby Labate, *A reinvenção do uso da ayahuasca nos centros urbanos* (Campinas, Brazil: Mercado de Letras Edições, 2004).

31. See Paul Christopher Johnson, *Diaspora Conversions: Black Carib Religion and the Recovery of Africa* (Berkeley: University of California Press, 2007).

CHAPTER 8 DOCUMENTS

1. This document reprinted from Eric W. Kramer, "Spectacle and the Staging of Power in Brazilian Neo-Pentecostalism," *Latin American Perspectives* 32, no. 1 (2005): 110-15. Used by kind permission of Sage Publications.

2. Yvonne Maggie glosses the term as "an act of purification during which the orixá 'discharges' evil from the client, purifying him. One is said to 'charged' or 'loaded' when suffering from an evil provoked by sorcery, by evil eye/jealousy, or by orixás" (2001: 142). "*Sessão*," according to Maggie's glossary (152), denotes a ritual dedicated to the orixás, deities of Afro-Brazilian religions.

3. The use of the term "*encosto*," since it refers to no particular Afro-Brazilian spirit, may also be favored by the church because it may lessen the likelihood that it could be charged with violating a 1989 law proibiting "religious discrimination." The state first applied this law after the Aparecida incident and made it clear that it would not tolerate attacks on religious identities in the media. Afro-Brazilian religious groups have sued the church leadership in the past, but the

use of *"encosto"* now blurs the legal definition of what could be construed as acts of religious discrimination.

4. This document is reprinted from Gary and Gordon Shepherd, *Mormon Passage: A Missionary Chronicle* (Urbana: University of Illinois Press, 1998), 69 (Language Training Mission Regulations), 290-93 (letter from Gordon), and 326-27 (journal entries). Used by kind permission of the University of Illinois Press.

5. This document is reprinted from Paulo Gabriel Hilu Da Rocha Pinto, "Ritual, etnicidade e identidade religiosa nas comunidades Musulmanas no Brasil," *Revista USP* 67 (2005): 228-50. Translated by the editors with the approval of Professor Pinto. Used by kind permission of Prof. Pinto.

6. I gathered the ethnographic data for this article during my fieldwork with Muslim communities in Rio de Janeiro, Curitiba, and São Paulo from 2003 to 2005. This research was funded by a post-doctoral fellowship from the CNPq.

7. A new mosque is being built by the SBMRJ in Tijuca neighborhood.

8. 'Alawis are an esoteric Shi'i sect that exists in Syria, Lebanon, and the south of Turkey. They do not follow the ritual pillars of Islam, such as the daily prayers at the mosque. They are considered by many Sunnis, such as the Salafis, to be heretics. The 'Alawis in Rio de Janeiro normally do not attend the SBMRJ. Some of them point to the Salafi tendencies of this institution as a factor that does not encourage them to attend its activities.

9. This number refers to the situation of the SBMRJ in 2003. The number of non-Arab Brazilian converts raised dramatically in the last three years, reaching the level of 85% of the members of the community in 2007.

10. On the connections between religious knowledge, Arab language and culture and power in the SBMRJ see the ethnography of Gisele Fonseca Chagas (2006).

11. This document is reprinted from Cristina Moreira da Rocha, "Zen Buddhism in Brazil: Japanese or Brazilian?"—available at http://www.globalbuddhism.org/1/derocha001.html, first published in *The Journal of Global Buddhism* (2006): 3-7, 10-11. Used by kind permission Cristina Moreira da Rocha.

12. For a complete list of temples, monasteries and centers see: http://sites.uol.com.br/cmrocha.

13. *Veja* magazine, "Em Busca do Zen," June 17, 1998; "Salvação para Tudo," June 24, 1998; *Elle* magazine, "Onda Zen," June 1998.

14. "Onda Zen," in *Elle* magazine, June, 1998.

15. *O Estado de São Paulo*, October 27, 1998.

16. Cristina Rocha, "Catholicism and Zen Buddhism: A Vision of the Religious Field in Brazil" (paper presented to the 25th Annual Conference of the Australian Anthropological Society, University of New South Wales, Sydney, 1999).

17. *Isto É* magazine, March 12, 1997.

18. Martin Baumann, "The Transplantation of Buddhism to Germany: Processive Modes and Strategies of Adaptation," *Method & Theory in the Study of Religion* 6,1 (1994), pp. 35-61, p. 38.

19. For a bibliography on Buddhism in Brazil and a Web directory of Brazilian Buddhist temples, monasteries and centers, and Buddhist texts translated to Portuguese, see http://sites.uol.com.br/cmrocha.

20. Baumann, 1994, p. 40.

21. Ibid., p. 41.

22. Cristina Rocha, "Catholicism and Zen Buddhism: A Vision of the Religious Field in Brazil" (paper presented to the 25th Annual Conference of the Australian Anthropological Society, University of New South Wales, Sydney, 1999).

23. Ryotan Tokuda, *Psicologia Zen Budista* (Rio de Janeiro: Instituto Vitória Régia, 1997), p. 55.

24. Ibid., p. 60.

25. Glocalization is a blend of local and global, an idea "modeled on a Japanese word (*dochaku*, 'living on one's land') and adopted in Japanese business for global localization, a global outlook adapted to local conditions. The terms 'glocal' and 'glocalization' became one of the main marketing buzzwords of the beginning of the 1990s." Roland Robertson, "Glocalization: Time-Space and Homogeneity-Heterogeneity," in *Global Modernities*, edited by M. Fetherstone, S. Lash and R. Robertson (London: Sage, 1995), pp. 27-44.

26. The word "Zen" is fashionable in the West: one sees Zen perfume, shops, beauty parlors, restaurants, magazine articles, and architecture. In Brazil, it is a common expression to say someone is "Zen," meaning very peaceful. Zen has a positive image in Brazil; it is associated with refinement, minimalism, a lack of tension and anxiety, exquisite beauty, and exoticism. One illustration of this is the fact that the word "Zen" appears almost daily in the trendy social column of *Folha de São Paulo*, one of the leading newspapers in Brazil.

27. Many books have been translated. Some of the titles are as follows: *The Zen Doctrine of No Mind* and *Introduction to Zen Buddhism* by D. T. Suzuki; *Zen Mind, Beginners' Mind* by Shunryu Suzuki; *The Three Pillars of Zen* by Phillip Kapleau; *Nothing Special, Living Zen* by Charlotte Joko Beck; and most of the books by Thich Nhat Hanh. When I accessed the Internet site of a Brazilian bookstore in December 1999, the word "Zen" was used in 39 book titles in Portuguese (http://livrariasaraiva.com/br).

28. The recent Hollywood movies "The Little Buddha,""Seven Years in Tibet," and "Kundun" were very successful in Brazil. Even though they dealt with Tibetan Buddhism, they are directly associated with Buddhism itself and not specifically Tibet. As we will see in this paper, practitioners may belong to various sects of Buddhist temples and monasteries at once.

29. Cristina Rocha, "Zen Buddhist Brazilians? Why Catholics Are Turning to Buddhism" (paper presented to the AASR [Australian Association for the Study

of Religion] Conference: The End of Religions? Religion in an Age of Globalization, Sydney, University of Sydney, 1999).

30. Cristina Rocha, "Zen Buddhism in Brazil" (paper presented to the 4th International Conference of AILASA [Association of Iberian and Latin American Studies of Australia]: Latin America, Spain and Portugal—Old and New Visions, La Trobe University, Melbourne, 1999).

31. Louis Dumont, *O Individualismo: uma perspectiva antropológica da ideologia moderna* (São Paulo: Ed. Rocco, 1985), p. 240.

32. Footnote deleted.

33. This document reprinted from Edward MacRae, *Guiado por la Luna: Shamanismo y uso ritual de la ayahuasca en el culto de Santo Daime* (Quito: Abya Yala, 1998), 108-21. Expanded translation by author. Used by kind permission of Edward MacRae.

34. See C. Monteiro da Silva, "O Palácio de Juramidam – Santo Daime: Um ritual de transcendência e despoluição." Dissertação de mestrado em Antropologia Cultural, Universidade Federal de Pernambuco, Recife, 1983, 37.

35. Although all branches of the Santo Daime Doctrine maintain great uniformity in their rituals, we are dealing here with the followers of the branch led by Padrinho Sebastião, the only one active at a nationwide level, and counting with numerous affiliated churches outside the Amazon region.

36. See A. Polari de Alverga, *Aspectos teológicos do uso religioso do Santo Daime/Vegetal*, n.d., 6.

37. Walter Dias Jr., "O império de Juramidam nas batalhas do Astral – uma cartografia do imaginário no culto de Santo Daime," Relatório de Pós-graduação em Ciências Sociais, PUC/SP, 1990.

38. C. Monteiro da Silva, "Ritual de tratamento e cura." Trabalho apresentado durante o Primeiro Simpósio de Saúde Mental. Sociedade Brasileira de Psiquiatria, Santarem, 1985.

39. Editors' note: See M. Dobkin de Rios, *Visionary Vine: Psychedelic Healing in the Peruvian Amazon* (San Francisco: Chandler Publishing, 1972), and L. E. Luna, "Vegetalismo," in *Shamanism among the Mestizo Population of the Peruvian Amazon* (Stockhlom: Almquist and Wiksell International, 1986).

Suggested Readings

INDIGENOUS RELIGIONS

Baldwin, Neil. *Legends of the Plumed Serpent: Biography of a Mexican God.* New York: Public Affairs, 1998.

Boone, Elizabeth Hill, and Tom Cummins, eds. *Native Traditions in the Postconquest World.* Washington, DC: Dumbarton Oaks Research Library and Collection, 1998.

Brown, Michael F., and Eduardo Fernandez. *War of Shadows: The Struggle for Utopia in the Peruvian Amazon.* Berkeley: University of California Press, 1993.

Carrasco, David. *Religions of Mesoamerica: Cosmovision and Ceremonial Center.* San Francisco: HarperCollins, 1990.

———. *City of Sacrifice: The Aztec Empire and the Role of Violence in Civilization.* Boston: Beacon Press, 2000.

———. *Quetzalcoatl and the Irony of Empire: Myths and Prophecies in the Aztec Tradition.* Revised ed. Boulder: University Press of Colorado, 2001.

Civrieux, Marc de. *Watunna: An Orinoco Creation Cycle.* Trans. David M. Guss. Austin: University of Texas Press, 1997.

Cleary, Edward, and Timothy Steigenga, eds. *Resurgent Voices in Latin America: Indigenous Peoples, Political Mobilization, and Religious Change.* New Brunswick, NJ: Rutgers University Press, 2004.

Florescano, Enrique. *The Myth of Quetzalcoatl.* Trans. Lysa Hochroth. Baltimore: Johns Hopkins University Press, 1999.

Guss, David M. *To Weave and Sing.* Berkeley: University of California Press, 1992.

Read, Kay Almere. *Time and Sacrifice in the Aztec Cosmos.* Bloomington: Indiana University Press, 1998.

Taussig, Michael. *The Devil and Commodity Fetishism in South America.* Chapel Hill: University of North Carolina Press, 1981.

Viveiros de Castro, Eduardo. *From the Enemy's Point of View: Humanity and Divinity in an Amazonian Society.* Chicago: University of Chicago Press, 1992.

Warren, Kay. *The Symbolism of Subordination: Indian Identity in a Guatemalan Town.* Austin: University of Texas Press, 1978.

Whitehead, Neil. *Dark Shamans: Kanaima and the Poetics of Violent Death.* Durham, NC: Duke University Press, 2002.

Wright, Robin M. *Cosmos, Self, and History in Baniwa Religion: For Those Unborn.* Austin: University of Texas Press, 1998.

RELIGION IN THE COLONIAL PERIOD

Burkhart, Louise M. *Holy Wednesday: A Nahua Drama from Early Colonial Mexico.* Philadelphia: University of Pennsylvania Press, 1996.
Burns, Kathryn. *Colonial Habits: Convents and the Spiritual Economy of Cuzco, Peru.* Durham, NC: Duke University Press, 1999.
Dean, Carolyn. *Inka Bodies and the Body of Christ: Corpus Christi in Colonial Cuzco, Peru.* Durham, NC: Duke University Press, 1999.
Gutiérrez, Gustavo. *Las Casas: In Search of the Poor of Jesus Christ.* Maryknoll, NY: Orbis Books, 1993.
de Mello e Souza, Laura. *The Devil and the Land of the Holy Cross.* Austin: University of Texas Press, 2004.
Nesvig, Martin Austin, ed. *Local Religion in Colonial Mexico.* Albuquerque: University of New Mexico Press, 2006.
Radding, Cynthia. *Wandering Peoples: Colonialism, Ethnic Spaces, and Ecological Frontiers in Northwestern Mexico, 1700-1850.* Durham, NC: Duke University Press, 1997.
———. *Landscapes of Power and Identity: Comparative Histories in the Sonoran Desert and the Forests of Amazonia from Colony to Republic.* Durham, NC: Duke University Press, 2005.
Sale, Kirkpatrick. *Christopher Columbus and the Conquest of Paradise.* 2nd ed. London: I. B. Taurus, 2006.
Silverblatt, Irene. *Moon, Sun, and Witches: Gender Ideologies and Class in Inca and Colonial Peru.* Princeton, NJ: Princeton University Press, 1987.
———. *Modern Inquisitions: Peru and the Colonial Origins of the Civilized World.* Durham, NC: Duke University Press, 2004.

RELIGIONS OF THE AFRICAN DIASPORA

Bastide, Roger. *The African Religions of Brazil: Toward a Sociology of the Interpenetration of Civilizations.* Baltimore: John Hopkins University Press, 1978.
Brown, Diana DeGroat. *Umbanda: Religion and Politics in Urban Brazil.* New York: Columbia University Press, 1994.
Burdick, John. *Blessed Anastacia: Women, Race, and Popular Christianity in Brazil.* London: Routledge, 1998.
De La Torre, Miguel. *Santería: The Beliefs and Rituals of a Growing Religion in America.* Grand Rapids, MI: Eerdmans, 2004.

Frigerio, Alejandro. "Outside the Nation, Outside the Diaspora: Accommodating Race and Religion in Argentina." *Sociology of Religion* 63, no. 3 (2002): 291-315.

Gilroy, Paul. *The Black Atlantic: Modernity and Double Consciousness.* Cambridge, MA: Harvard University Press, 1993.

González-Wippler, Migene. *Santería: African Magic in Latin America.* New York: Original Publications, 1987.

Herskovits, Melville J. *The Myth of the Negro Past.* Boston: Beacon Press, 1958.

Hess, David. *Spirits and Scientists: Ideology, Spiritism, and Brazilian Culture.* College Station: Pennsylvania State University Press, 1991.

Irving, T. B. "King Zumbi and the Malé Movement in Brazil: Research Notes." *American Journal of Islamic Social Sciences* 9, no. 3 (1992): 397-409.

Johnson, Paul Christopher. *Secrets, Gossip, and God: The Transformation of Brazilian Candomblé.* Oxford: Oxford University Press, 2002.

———. *Diaspora Conversions: Black Carib Religion and the Recovery of Africa.* Berkeley: University of California Press, 2007.

Matory, J. Lorand. *Black Atlantic Religion: Tradition, Transnationalism, and Matriarchy in the Afro-Brazilian Candomblé.* Princeton, NJ: Princeton University Press, 2005.

Motta, Roberto. "The Churchifying of Candomblé: Priests, Anthropologists, and the Canonization of the African Religious Memory in Brazil." In *New Trends and Developments in African Religions*, ed. Peter B. Clarke. Westport, CT: Greenwood Press, 1998, 47-57.

Murphy, Joseph. *Working the Spirit: Ceremonies of the African Diaspora.* Boston: Beacon Press, 1994.

Palmié, Stephan. *Wizards and Scientists: Explorations in Afro-Cuban Modernity and Tradition.* Durham, NC: Duke University Press, 2002.

Postma, Johannes. *The Atlantic Slave Trade.* Westport, CT: Greenwood Press, 2003.

Reis, João José. *Slave Rebellion in Brazil: The Muslim Uprising of 1835 in Bahia.* Baltimore: Johns Hopkins University Press, 1993.

Sansone, Livio. *Blackness without Ethnicity: Constructing Race in Brazil.* New York: Palgrave Macmillan, 2003.

Wafer, Jim. *The Taste of Blood: Spirit Possession in Brazilian Candomblé.* College Station: Pennsylvania State University, 1991.

Walker, Sheila. "Everyday and Esoteric Reality in Afro-Brazilian Candomblé." *History of Religions* 30 (1990): 103-29.

INDEPENDENCE AND MODERNITY

Becker, Marjorie. *Setting the Virgin on Fire: Lázaro Cárdenas, Michoacán Peasants, and the Redemption of the Mexican Revolution.* Berkeley: University of California Press, 1996.

Burdick, Michael. *For God and the Fatherland: Religion and Politics in Argentina*. Albany: State University of New York Press, 1995.

Da Cunha, Euclides. *Rebellion in the Backlands*. Trans. Samuel Putnam. Chicago: University of Chicago Press, 1957.

de Theije, Marjo. "'Brotherhoods Throw More Weight around Than the Pope': Catholic Traditionalism and the Lay Brotherhoods of Brazil." *Sociological Analysis* 51, no. 2 (1990): 189-204.

Della Cava, Ralph. *Miracle at Joaseiro*. New York: Columbia University Press, 1970.

Diacon, Todd. *Millenarian Vision, Capitalist Reality: Brazil's Contestado Rebellion, 1912-1916*. Durham, NC: Duke University Press, 1991.

Levine, Robert. *Vale of Tears: Revisiting the Canudos Massacre in Brazil*. Berkeley: University of California Press, 1995.

Oliveira, Pedro Ribeiro. "The Romanization of Catholicism and Agrarian Capitalism in Brazil." *Social Compass* 26, nos. 2-3 (1979): 309-29.

Serbin, Kenneth P. *Needs of the Heart: A Social and Cultural History of Brazil's Clergy and Seminaries*. Notre Dame, IN: University of Notre Dame Press, 2006.

Vargas Llosa, Mario. *War of the End of the World*. New York: Penguin, 1997.

PROTESTANTISM IN LATIN AMERICA

Brusco, Elizabeth. *The Reformation of Machismo: Evangelical Conversion and Gender in Colombia*. Austin: University of Texas Press, 1995.

Cleary, Edward, and Hannah Stewart-Gambino, eds. *Power, Politics, and Pentecostals in Latin America*. Boulder, CO: Westview, 1996.

Freston, Paul. *Evangelicals and Politics in Asia, Africa, and Latin America*. Cambridge: Cambridge University Press, 2001.

Garrard-Burnett, Virginia. *Protestantism in Guatemala: Living in the New Jerusalem*. Austin: University of Texas Press, 1998.

Goffin, Alvin M. *The Rise of Protestant Evangelism in Ecuador, 1895-1990*. Gainesville: University Press of Florida, 1994.

Gómez, Medardo. *Fire against Fire: Christian Ministry Face-to-Face with Persecution*. Trans. Mary M. Solberg. Minneapolis: Augsburg Press, 1989.

Martin, David. *Tongues of Fire: The Explosion of Protestantism in Latin America*. Oxford: Basil Blackwell, 1991.

Míguez Bonino, José. *Doing Theology in a Revolutionary Situation*. Philadelphia: Fortress Press, 1975.

Smilde, David. *Reason to Believe: Cultural Agency in Latin American Evangelicalism*. Berkeley: University of California Press, 2007.

Steigenga, Timothy. *The Politics of the Spirit: The Political Implications of Pentecostalized Religion in Costa Rica and Guatemala*. Lanham, MD: Lexington Books, 2002.

Stoll, David. *Is Latin America Turning Protestant?* Berkeley: University of California Press, 1991.

Stoll, David, and Virginia Garrard-Burnett, eds. *Rethinking Protestantism in Latin America.* Philadelphia: Temple University Press, 1993.

POSTCONCILIAR ROMAN CATHOLICISM

Berryman, Phillip. *The Religious Roots of Rebellion: Christians in Central American Revolutions.* Maryknoll, NY: Orbis Books, 1984.

———. *Stubborn Hope: Religion, Politics, and Revolution in Central America.* Maryknoll, NY: Orbis Books, 1995.

———. *Religion in the Megacity: Catholic and Protestant Portraits from Latin America.* Eugene, OR: Wipf & Stock, 2006.

Boff, Leonardo. *Ecclesiogenesis: The Base Communities Reinvent the Church.* Maryknoll, NY: Orbis Books, 1984.

———. *Church: Charism and Power.* Maryknoll, NY: Orbis Books, 1986.

Burdick, John. *Looking for God in Brazil: Progressive Catholicism in Urban Brazil's Religious Arena.* Berkeley: University of California Press, 1993.

———. *Legacies of Liberation: The Progressive Catholic Church in Brazil at the Start of a New Millennium.* Burlington, VT: Ashgate, 2004.

Castro, Fidel, Armando Hart, and Frei Betto. *Fidel and Religion: Fidel Castro in Conversation with Frei Betto on Marxism and Liberation Theology.* 2nd ed. Australia: Ocean Press, 2006.

Cleary, Edward. *Crisis and Change: The Church in Latin America Today.* Maryknoll, NY.: Orbis Books, 1985.

Dodson, Michael, and Laura Nuzzi O'Shaughnessy. *Nicaragua's Other Revolution: Religious Faith and Political Struggle.* Chapel Hill: University of North Carolina Press, 1990.

Drogus, Carol Ann. *Women, Religion, and Social Change in Brazil's Popular Church.* Notre Dame, IN: University of Notre Dame Press, 1997.

Drogus, Carol Ann, and Hannah Stewart-Gambino. *Activist Faith: Grassroots Women in Democratic Brazil and Chile.* College Station: Pennsylvania State University Press, 2005.

Gutiérrez, Gustavo. *A Theology of Liberation.* Maryknoll, NY: Orbis Books, 1973.

Lancaster, Roger. *Thanks to God and the Revolution: Popular Religion and Class Consciousness in the New Nicaragua.* New York: Columbia University Press, 1988.

Lernoux, Penny. *Cry of the People.* New York: Penguin Books, 1991.

Levine, Daniel. *Religion and Politics in Latin America: The Catholic Church in Venezuela and Colombia.* Princeton, NJ: Princeton University Press, 1981.

———. *Popular Voices in Latin American Catholicism.* Princeton, NJ: Princeton University Press, 1992.

————, ed. *Religion and Political Conflict in Latin America*. Chapel Hill: University of North Carolina Press, 1986.

Mainwaring, Scott. *The Catholic Church and Politics in Brazil, 1916-1985*. Stanford, CA: Stanford University Press, 1986.

Mainwaring, Scott, and Alex Wilde, eds. *The Progressive Church in Latin America*. South Bend, IN: University of Notre Dame Press, 1989.

Norget, Kristin. *Days of Death, Days of Life: Ritual in the Popular Culture of Oaxaca*. New York: Columbia University Press, 2006.

Peterson, Anna. *Martyrdom and the Politics of Religion: Progressive Catholicism in El Salvador's Civil War*. Albany: State University of New York Press, 1997.

Randall, Margaret. *Christians in the Nicaraguan Revolution*. Vancouver: New Star Books, 1983.

Segundo, Juan Luis. *The Liberation of Theology*. Maryknoll, NY: Orbis Books, 1976.

Smith, Brian. *The Church and Politics in* Chile. Princeton, NJ: Princeton University Press, 1982.

Sobrino, Jon. *Jesus in Latin America*. Maryknoll, NY: Orbis Books, 1987.

Sobrino, Jon, Ignacio Ellacuría, et al. *Companions of Jesus: The Jesuit Martyrs of El Salvador*. Maryknoll, NY: Orbis Books, 1990.

Vásquez, Manuel A. *The Brazilian Popular Church and the Crisis of Modernity*. Cambridge: Cambridge University press, 1998.

Williams, Philip J. *The Catholic Church and Politics in Nicaragua and Costa Rica*. Pittsburgh: University of Pittsburgh Press, 1989.

CONTEMPORARY RELIGIOUS DIVERSITY

Chesnut, R. Andrew. *Competitive Spirits: Latin America's New Religious Economy*. New York: Oxford University Press, 2007.

Corten, Andre, and Ruth Marshall-Fratani, eds. *Between Babel and Pentecost: Transnational Pentecostalism in Africa and Latin America*. Bloomington: Indiana University Press, 2001.

Gill, Anthony. *Rendering unto Caesar: The Catholic Church and the State in Latin America*. Chicago: University of Chicago Press, 1998.

Hess, David. *Spirits and Scientists: Ideology, Spiritism, and Brazilian Culture*. College Station: Pennsylvania State University Press, 1991.

Ireland, Rowan. *Kingdoms Come: Religion and Politics in Brazil*. Pittsburgh: University of Pittsburgh Press, 1992.

Mariz, Cecília. *Coping with Poverty*. Philadelphia: Temple University Press, 1993.

Peterson, Anna, Manuel A. Vásquez, and Philip J. Williams, eds. *Christianity, Social Change, and Globalization in the Americas*. New Brunswick, NJ: Rutgers University Press, 2001.

Parker, Cristian. *Popular Religion and Modernization in Latin America: A Different Logic.* Maryknoll, NY: Orbis, 1996.

Rocha, Cristina. *Zen in Brazil: The Quest for Cosmopolitan Modernity.* Honolulu: University of Hawaii Press, 2005.

Smith, Christian, and Joshua Prokopy, eds. *Latin American Religion in Motion.* New York: Routledge, 1999.

Vásquez, Manuel A., and Marie Friedmann Marquardt. *Globalizing the Sacred: Religion across the Americas.* New Brunswick, NJ: Rutgers University Press, 2003.

Index

About the Editors

ANNA L. PETERSON teaches in the Department of Religion at the University of Florida. Her writing on Latin American religion includes *Martyrdom and the Politics of Religion: Progressive Catholicism in El Salvador's Civil War*; *Seeds of the Kingdom: Utopian Communities in the Americas*; and *Christianity, Globalization, and Social Change in the Americas*, coedited with Manuel Vásquez and Philip Williams. She has also published widely in social and environmental ethics, including *Being Human: Ethics, Environment, and Our Place in the World*. Her current research explores the gap between expressed values and environmental practice.

MANUEL A. VÁSQUEZ teaches religion and Latin American/Latino studies at the University of Florida. He is the author of *The Brazilian Popular Church and the Crisis of Modernity*, coauthor of *Globalizing the Sacred: Religion across the Americas*, and coeditor of *Immigrant Faiths: Transforming Religious Life in America* and *Christianity, Social Change, and Globalization in the Americas*. He is currently codirecting a research project exploring religion, interethnic relations, and transnationalism among Brazilian, Mexican, and Guatemalan immigrants in the New South.

Made in the USA
Columbia, SC
24 August 2024

41074147R00202